Being Geniuses Together

Robert McAlmon, photographed by Berenice Abbott

Robert McAlmon

Being Geniuses Together

1920-1930

Revised, with supplementary chapters
and an afterword, by

Kay Boyle

The Johns Hopkins University Press
Baltimore and London

First edition published in 1938 by Secker & Warburg
Revised edition published in 1968 by Doubleday, New York
This edition originally published in 1984 by North Point Press, San Francisco
Reprinted by arrangement with Farrar, Straus and Giroux, Inc.
Johns Hopkins Paperbacks edition, 1997
06 05 04 03 02 01 00 99 98 97   5 4 3 2 1

The Johns Hopkins University Press
2715 North Charles Street
Baltimore, Maryland 21218-4319
The Johns Hopkins Press Ltd., London

Library of Congress Cataloging-in-Publication Data

McAlmon, Robert, 1896–1956.
  Being geniuses together, 1920–1930 / Robert McAlmon ; revised with
supplementary chapters and an afterword by Kay Boyle. — Johns Hopkins
paperbacks ed.
      p.   cm.
  "Originally published in 1984 by North Point Press, San Francisco"—
T.p. verso.
  ISBN 0-8018-5584-5 (alk. paper)
  1. McAlmon, Robert, 1896–1956—Homes and haunts—France—Paris.
2. Boyle, Kay, 1902–   —Homes and haunts—France—Paris.   3. Authors,
American—20th century—Biography.   4. Literature publishing—France—
Paris—History—20th century.   5. Americans—France—Paris—History—
20th century.   6. Paris (France)—Intellectual life—20th century.
I. Boyle, Kay, 1902–   .   II. Title.
PS3525.A1143Z464   1997
818´.5203
[B]—DC20   96-35087
                                                               CIP

A catalog record for this book is available from the British Library.

*To my five daughters
and the memory of Pegeen*

Acknowledgements

I owe a debt of gratitude to Robert McAlmon's sisters, Victoria, Grace, and Ann, for their generous assistance in the preparation of this book. Thanks are also due to Robert McAlmon's niece, Ila Wilson, and his nephew, Robert Davis, for their valued co-operation.

Warm thanks go to Florence Williams, who entrusted to me many relevant letters which had been addressed to her and William Carlos Williams through the years. Florence Williams' sustained interest and concern were of great encouragement to me throughout my work upon the book.

I wish also to express my thanks to Jack Henry for his generous assistance in contributing many of the documents and photographs which appear herein. Gratitude is likewise due to Maria Jolas for her invaluable suggestions, and to Norman Holmes Pearson for his close reading of the manuscript.

KAY BOYLE

A Note on Robert McAlmon

Robert McAlmon was born in Clifton, Kansas, on March 9, 1896. In 1934 he wrote the original BEING GENIUSES TOGETHER which dealt with that period of his life from 1920 to 1934. This was published in 1938.

In revising, shortening, and adding alternate chapters of my own to the 1938 edition, I consulted as well Robert McAlmon's typescript of this partial autobiography. In many instances, the typescript differs from the published version, and I have frequently substituted McAlmon's undeleted text rather than the edited sections which appeared in the original edition. The dates at the beginning of McAlmon's chapters apply only in a general way to the period being written about, there being a few events that occurred earlier and a few that occurred later. It is my hope that the present revision will do more than provide a deeply sympathetic portrait of a writer and publisher who deserves to be remembered for his unique qualities, but that it will as well help to accord to Robert McAlmon his rightful and outstanding place in the history of the literary revolution of the early nineteen-twenties. In the Spring 1960 issue of the *Prairie Schooner*, I wrote of him: "It was McAlmon who, in liberating himself from genteel language and thought, spoke for his generation in a voice that echoes, unacknowledged, in the prose of Hemingway and that of other writers of his time."

Although Robert McAlmon's books are long out of print, a volume published by the University of Nebraska Press in 1962, entitled *McAlmon and the Lost Generation, A Self-Portrait*, edited by Robert E. Knoll, offers a comprehensive selection of McAlmon's prose writings. In the New York *Times Book Review* for August 5,

1962, in a review of Knoll's book, I wrote that for those of us who were there McAlmon's *Being Geniuses Together* remains "the most candid and knowledgeable record of the literary argie-bargies of that time". And I noted that "in the complex role of prolific writer, generous publisher, ruthless critic, exuberant drinker and dancer, outspoken enemy of the sham, sceptical friend of Joyce, Pound, Katherine Anne Porter, and countless other writers, there was never anyone quite like McAlmon around."

Robert McAlmon died on February 2, 1956, in Desert Hot Springs, California.

But the days go on, and the tides
endlessly recoil; and one is still alone
after the passing of people,
and the turning of events, scarring
with their experience;
alone, and the winds are still blowing.
Desolation abides, and primitive fear
and watching with primitive eyes, and why—
why does one heed the fall of a leaf,
or note
the size of a raindrop in a shower,
while the covert thought runs on. . . .

—Robert McAlmon

Robert McAlmon

1920-1921

In 1920 the atmosphere of New York had been postwar despairing, but various poets were then raising passionate voices in rebellion against puritanism, shouting America's need for an indigenous culture, so that finally London, never a city bubbling with gaiety, struck me as sodden with despair. One had to admit that there were intelligences and talented beings about capable of invention and execution, nevertheless, from the first moment of leaving the train at Victoria Station, I found the smoky heaviness of the city muffling as a dull illness driving one into despairing delirium.

I had married a girl under her writing name, and when getting the licence and informed of her family name it meant little to me. However, I knew she was connected with great wealth, and was warned that her parents were difficult, as her father was a self-made man. The Audley Street house was, as Bryher warned me, "a stuffy old museum", and conversation at mealtimes was cautious and restrained so that servants would not overhear. The rooms, halls, and staircase walls were lined with French paintings of the photographically sentimental and academic kind at their most banal. I recall no picture by any painter of whom I had ever heard. Sir John, however, did have his own tastes, for which I respected him, because nothing can compete with the vulgarity of snobbist or bought correct taste. In the dining room were cow-pasture and woodland scenes; in the library was a glistening white statue of a high-bosomed young girl lifting eager lips to a cluster of grapes. There was also a painting of geese on the village downs, but of that more later.

Although then I violently disliked and was depressed by London
and its morale, it would be unjust to blame on the city the involved
and unusually complicated household in which I found myself.
Wealth, the war, and the phobias, manias, dementias, prejudices,
and terrors that come from both, were the dominant factors. Bryher's
life had been unfree throughout her childhood years. She had never
been allowed proper pets or friendships. One could not do this or
that, know so-and-so, one was being used, such-and-such a person
was trying to know one simply because of the wealth in the offing.
The family led a frighteningly anti-social and lonely life, with their
few "friends" or acquaintances, business associates or, more accurately, employees of Sir John. Her Ladyship was deaf, and Sir John
was jealous of her friendships, so that years before she had renounced
most of the friends of a more gregarious and buoyant girlhood. I
came to understand soon that she cared as little for Sir John's dismal
sisters as later I cared. If the nephews and nieces—or the aunts and
uncles for that matter—had a liveliness within them, all show of
spirit which they might possess they resolutely renounced upon
entering Audley Street, and the presence of Sir John and her Ladyship. She, when in a mood, was sure to speak her irritations and mind
without restraint.

For a man who had a monomania for planning his family's life to
the minutest detail—what plays to attend, whom to see and when,
what motor run to take on what day and hour—Sir John was
surprisingly non-interfering with me. The fact of my being a
minister's son impressed him from the first moment, and he feared
that I might disapprove of his serving wines and whisky at and after
meals. That theory of his was soon discredited, but my being an
American caused him to view me as alien, strange, one whose
reactions he could not judge. In fact after two weeks of our presence
in the household he looked a bit harried. Bryher had theories on
education which she thought advanced, and which no one but a
person of great wealth could put into practice. She was pert also
about telling Mamma and Dada her ideas, and in front of the servants. I too never did learn to be careful in front of the servants,
feeling sure that they would gossip downstairs as much if we restrained ourselves as if we didn't. In fact my first move was to let the
butler realize I was a weak mortal, so that I could have an ally in the
household when returning home late at night in a condition which
the Spanish call "joyous".

The parental attitude towards John, the twelve-year-old son, appalled me. It was impossible to think it improper for the lad to walk across Hyde Park in other than a bowler hat; there was no sane reason why he should not ride in taxis or buses and learn to pay for himself, realizing costs and the value of money in relation to various objects or pastimes. He did not then know the difference in value between a sixpence, a shilling, and a half crown; he was taken wherever he went by his parents, a governess or tutor, in either the Rolls-Royce or the Lanchester. His sister talked to him of what a disgrace it was that the parents should treat him as helpless, as they had her, a girl, and in so doing ruined her capacity for full self-expression and enjoyment of life.

It was six weeks before we moved into a service flat, and that was a great error for me, who already had a bellyful of London without that contact with the dim and stuffy Anglo-respectables. I was of nomad stock and now my unrest became more of a fever than ever. Bryher, with her fervour for education, had taken on the upbringing of Hilda Doolittle's infant. It had black hair and eyes, an utterly blithe disregarding disposition, and at the time looked a Japanese empress in miniature. Hilda, an American, understood my wails, but explained that the war had cleaned out all the best young people of the generation. She produced red-haired Brigit Patmore, and Brigit in turn endeavoured to produce some gayer young women of the town, but London had me against it. Taking a chance that Wyndham Lewis might know of me, I wrote him a note, was answered by telegram, and 'phoned him to make an appointment for that night, so quick had been the exchange of postal and telegraph messages.

At five there was no Lewis at Verrey's, nor at five-fifteen, but at about five-thirty a figure emerged from the shadows of the nearby corner. His hat shaded his eyes and a faded blue scarf was in disarray about his neck. His overcoat looked seedy. There was a pause and I spoke to ascertain that it was Lewis. He peered suspiciously at me out of distrustful brown eyes; his small mouth was tight. After the first appraising glance, however, he relaxed. Later he confessed he had expected to meet an older man, for at the time I could pass as nineteen, and my open American manner lulled his distrust. He soon became patronizing and sympathetic about my wail against the heaviness of London, atmospherically and socially.

It was not long before Lewis was doing what I came to look upon as a London pastime: informing me whom I could, or could not, properly know. Intrigue and distrusts and the talk of groups and cliques made up most of the conversation. Chelsea, Kensington, and Bloomsbury meant almost nothing to me, because my interest in the arts had always been for things Russian, Scandinavian, Italian, French, or Spanish. At the time things were very interesting as regards painting in Mexico, too, with the names of Rivera and Orozco gaining réclame. This talk of London group intrigues was vaguely irritating, because I intended to meet anybody regardless, and trust to healthy instinct and wit for self-protection. There were groups in New York, too, but why be alive if you can't like the battle of measuring your contempt or indifference or interest against that of others?

Believing that Lewis knew of my relationship with wealth, I mentioned Sir John, and when he discovered that I was Sir John's son-in-law a peculiar change came over his manner. He became—not less protective and ready to show me about London, to warn me against the people whom I should not meet—let me say, as Lewis would say, I mean to say, more interested in my personality. It seemed that there was *nobody* one could safely know in London; all of the painters were cribbing his style, or if not that they would not prove interesting to an alertly informed young American like me. I felt dismal about it all, because I have always been gregarious and used to companionship, and mainly undemanding.

Before the evening was over Lewis struck me as very sympathetic. He relaxed with a bottle or so of wine, was what we call boyish and confiding and almost lovable. I recall deciding that he was English and reserved, and that whenever I met him again I must not let him remain so but see that we quickly drank enough to relax his reticence. By midnight he was talking subtly of how much could be done with a man of wealth like Sir John by one in my situation. There was art, there were artists, and there was a tradition that rich men should patronize contemporary artists.

I agreed entirely with Lewis about the futility of money not expended, but I was sceptical about my influence with Sir John. He was by no means the first rich man with whom I had been in contact, and I had some time ago decided that the money-makers on the grand scale are monomaniacs and fanatics and self-willed. As regards finance, Sir John had that thing which need not be looked upon with awe, *genius*, but in many other aspects he was a perfect case of arrested development, suffering innumerable childish fears. It was highly improbable that he could be interested in the paintings of Lewis; for already he was trying to woo me from the pitfalls of modern literature to secure for me a position on some proper publication such as the *Tatler*, *Sketch*, or *Sphere*, all of which he at the time controlled. He presented me to Clement Shorter, a man whose presence gave me the willies. The latter no doubt had his points, but his tobacco-stained moustache, his leering interest, his aversion to modern writers, and his wounded haughtiness when I did not care to attend some old-fogey literary club, left me frozen. Having the young man's resentful belief that the war had killed off, in Europe and England, the best of my generation for moralizing hacks and elders, most worm-eaten old men with a patronizing attitude gave me the creeps in those days.

Nevertheless I did plan a campaign to help Lewis, whose drawings I liked. His paintings might have done if he had admitted they were literary or illustrative, but he would be "abstract". I might work through her Ladyship to Sir John. She and I were definitely of the same spontaneous strain, and had got together to complain that none of the rest of them were human. Once any one of them got an idea in his head never would he consider what another might be feeling.

If in those days I had known a few of the sound, hearty, humorous London types whom I came to know later on other visits I might not have had such a hate on the city. But on every side I was warned that one doesn't go here or there, and I assumed that the warners meant the places were plainly dull and boring. Certainly the secretive whispering atmosphere of one restaurant the Tour Eiffel, was that, unless it was hysterically dismaying. It was there that Lewis took me that first night, and it was there that at one time he stopped my making some harmless remark. "Shh," he cautioned, touching my arm and gesturing over his shoulder with his thumb to an empty table behind us. "They're listening."

Once when I called at his studio by appointment, he came to the door and opened it but two inches. "Wait," he whispered, and closed the door. He was gone for two minutes before admitting me. I wondered where the model or naughty rendezvous or corpse was hidden, for there was no back exit to the studio. Recalling my earlier decision, I suggested that we go to a pub and have a pale ale. After two ales he was "normal", and we went back to his studio, where he said, with dark implications, that he was doing a sketch of Lady Somebody, whose name meant nothing to me. It was about that time too that he asked me had I ever heard that he looked like Shakespeare; at other times he was looking like Shelley or Swift; and again he asked if "they" had been telling me that his teeth were false, that he wore a wig, was Jewish, and that he took five years off his age; and then he immediately added that as the war had taken five years out of all our lives we had a right to lower our ages. Probably he never believed me when I told him the truth, that I knew none of the people he accused of gossiping about him. At least he sometimes took the attitude that I was a devilishly clever deceiver.

I decided to get in touch with T. S. Eliot, although his cautious articles on criticism did not impress me, nor did his erudition, scholarship, or his lack of a sense of either life or literature. His mouldy poetry struck me as the perfect expression of a clerkly and liverish man's apprehension of life, and to me he *was* Prufrock. I prefer his then main influence, Laforgue. (Eliot never had Ezra Pound's health and vitality.) Laforgue's outlook at least has a fever and an alive wit, without the perverse intent on being a "hollow man". Much of Eliot's poetry had been written before the war, so that I knew his "spirit" had not been created by war events.

At this time the Egoist Press published a book of my poetry, *Explorations*, but as nobody paid it any attention I need not apologize, and can dare to say that much worse had been done before and is being done yet by others. In it was a poem which was rather harsh on Eliot, and in America I had written an article which caused me to think he might not receive me with pleasure.

I telephoned Eliot so that if he wished he could quickly dismiss me. It was for me a method of escaping Audley Street and that awful service flat, and to placate the family, I had promised to stay in London for at least three months. When Eliot was at the other end of the line and caught my name there was a pause, and he agreed to an appointment, but not today and not tomorrow, but would I 'phone again? I thought if he wished for an appointment he could drop me a note. He did. I was surprised to find him very likeable indeed, with a quality—to save sparring for words—of charm that few people possess. He looked tired and overworked, which was understandable as he was then employed in a bank.

Present that first evening was J. W. N. Sullivan, who at the time was religious and worshipful about Dostoevsky, mainly *The Brothers Karamazov*. We drank a quantity of whisky and the evening was amiable and entertaining. Eliot and I indulged in a bit of legpulling with Sullivan, trying to convince him that Dostoevsky was too much a soul-searcher to be an artist, but Sullivan brought in higher mathematics and a wealth of earnestness. We none of us proved a thing, but we did have a sociable time.

During the course of the evening at Eliot's I had evidently regretted my comments on him in a New York paper. At any rate he wrote me: "As for your criticism, it was so intelligent that you need not worry about my opinion of it. I like your mind and that is all that matters."

I mention this, for this matter of intelligence and Eliot comes up later, in connection with a magazine which called itself the *Criterion*.

While in Paris I heard from him again and his letter made me feel that distinctly never would he and I agree on what makes literature or life. He said of Paris that the right way to take it is as a place and a tradition, rather than as a congeries of people who are mostly futile and timewasting, except when you want to pass an evening agreeably in a café. When he was living there years ago he had only the genuine stimulus of the place, for he had not known any of the writers or painters as companions—knew them rather as spectacles, listened to, on rare occasions, but never spoken to. Joyce he admired as a person who seemed to be independent of outside stimulus (had he read Joyce's *Ulysses*?). He was sure Julien Benda was worth knowing and, possibly, Paul Valéry.[1]

---

[1] The letter from T. S. Eliot goes as follows:

9, Clarence Gate Gardens,
London N.W.1
2nd May 1921

Dear Bob:

I was glad to hear from you. I will go through your poems at leisure if I may, and write you about them in due course. I'm glad to hear that you like Paris; the right way of course is to take it as a place and a tradition, rather than as a congeries of people, who are mostly futile and timewasting, except when you want to pass an evening agreeably in a café. The chief danger about Paris is that it is such a strong stimulus, and like most stimulants incites to rushing about and produces a pleasant illusion of great mental activity rather than the solid results of hard work. When I was living there years ago I had only the genuine stimulus of the place, and not the artificial stimulus of the people, as I knew no one whatever, in the literary and artistic world, as a companion—knew them rather as spectacles, listened to, at rare occasions, but never spoken to. I am sure Julien Benda is worth knowing and

There was your snob-governess attitude. Possibly the lives of
the Elizabethans and Greeks would indicate that Eliot's attitude was
wrong, and it is hard to understand what gives validity to a tradition
if it is not the lives and conventions of living people. Is Eliot afraid
of the interchange of relationships, with their attractions and an-
tagonisms and experiences? Derain, Brancusi, Proust, Picasso,
Satie, and quantities of others of various nationalities and races were
in Paris at this period, and many of them spent much time in cafés
and bistros, drinking considerably upon occasion.

Eliot appeals to the adolescent emotions of despair and defeat. His
cerebral tearfulness, his liverish and stomach-achey wail, dominated
his poetry during his college days, long before the war, at the time he
was writing "Prufrock", and with artifice having people come and
go talking of Michelangelo, while the long-haired Pole plays Chopin.
He became then quite a butler to the arts, the "classes", and later to
the Church. If Ezra Pound spoke of tradition and discipline it could
be worth listening to, because Pound has interiorly disciplined his
craft (when he is not scolding, but is being the poet he can be). He
has at least not subjected himself to the sterile cant of a vested interest
or religion, and when reading, for example, the compact impressions
of Marianne Moore, does appear to understand what is being said,
and that Miss Moore is as definitely modelling or sculpturing as,

---

possibly Paul Valéry. But Paris is still alive. What is wonderful about French
literature is its solidarity: you don't know one part of it, even the most contemporary, unless you know the 17th and 18th centuries, and more too, in a way in which
Pound and Bell don't—Pound because he has never taken the trouble, and Bell
because he couldn't. Bell is a most agreeable person, if you don't take him seriously,
but a great waster of time if you do, or if you expect to get any profound knowledge
or original thought out of him, and his Paris is a useless one. If I came to live in
Paris the first thing to do would be to cut myself off from it, and not depend upon
it. Joyce I admire as a person who seems to be independent of outside stimulus, and
who therefore is likely to go on producing first rate work until he dies.

I should not worry at all about what Thayer says. I thought his witticisms in the
May number very tasteless and pointless. Why do our compatriots try so hard to be
clever? Furthermore, his language is so opaque, through his cleverness, that it is
unintelligible gibberish. Cummings has the same exasperating vice.

But Joyce has form—immensely careful. And as for literary—one of the last
things he sent me contains a marvellous parody of nearly every style in English
prose from 1600 to the Daily Mail. One needs a pretty considerable knowledge of
English literature to understand it. No! you can't generalize, in the end it is a
question of whether a man has genius and can do what he sets out to do. Small
formulas support small people. Aren't the arty aesthetics you mention simply the
people without brains?

Write me again soon, yours

[signed] Tom

let us say cautiously, Benvenuto Cellini. However, others have detected that Eliot, in his essays, seems unable to realize the clearly stated meaning of certain sentences, so that perhaps overcaution and gentility are inherent in him and stultify his "intelligence".

Kay Boyle

1922-1923

It was in the late twenties that I went to live and work in Paris, and
I was then still a French citizen (through my marriage). These two
facts would seem to disqualify me as a member of the lost generation
or as an expatriate. But I was there, in whatever guise, and even if a
bit late, and this memoir is part of a dialogue I have never ceased
having with Robert McAlmon. I am going to try to set it down without romanticizing and without going "Irish-twilighty", the two
things that McAlmon kept shouting out to me about my writing.
(That he also complained of Joyce's tendency to go "Irish-twilight"
on his readers, particularly in *Portrait of the Artist* and in his poetry,
was of little solace to me.)

Long before I met McAlmon, when I knew only the legend that
had grown up around him since the early twenties, I saluted him as
a man of rebellion, and I wanted him to think well of my work. I
was seventeen or eighteen when I first heard his name, and I saw him
as a poet who was coldly and bitterly sceptical of contemporary
values. When he became, with William Carlos Williams, a publisher
of *Contact* magazine, he became an element in my own rebellion
against status, fuel to my own fury for independence, and I revered
him as a man who, like Sherwood Anderson, exemplified the
mounting protest of American writers against the English literary
tradition. In those years the break from that tradition had scarcely
begun. I was proud when *Contact* published a poem of mine (in June
1923) in the same issue with Bill Williams' "New England" and
McAlmon's "Growth in the City". For a long time I murmured to
myself the lines:

Oh, let me gather myself together.
Where are the pieces
quivering and staring and muttering
that are all to be a part of me?

They spoke not only McAlmon's indecision but mine as well. In that same number of *Contact*, Williams wrote that "when man or woman climbs into the pages of a magazine it should be with the same enlargement of the intelligence accessible to the young when they climb into bed with each other; that time past—men feel lesser things; less important magazines . . .". If I was certain of anything in life then it was that everyone who wrote possessed a singular piece of knowledge from which I had been excluded. I believed that everyone—and writers in particular—had been given information of a nature quite unknown to me, which endowed them with their marvellous authority.

The present dialogue begins in 1921, when McAlmon married Winifred Bryher in New York and went to England. I came East from Cincinnati the following year, intending to make my living in New York. My sister Joan worked for *Vogue* magazine as a designer, and by grace of her close friendship with Frank Crowninshield I was given a dozen letters of introduction to editors who Crowninshield thought might employ me. Albert Jay Nock was one. I lunched with him often at the Brevoort, and he kissed my hair in the moonlight in Central Park and told me to go back West again and get a job on a small-town paper. Gilbert Seldes was another, and he advised me to get rid of the black oilcloth briefcase I carried around with my poems in it and get something more professional looking; but he gave me books to review (unsigned) for the *Dial*. Franklin P. Adams read my poems at his desk and wrote about them and my lilac-coloured suit the next day in his column in the New York *World*. William Rose Benét generously went through my poetry line by line with me. Burton Rascoe was brusque, ridiculed my use of metaphor in the book reviews I did for him, and told me not to bother coming in for more. There were others whose names and faces and advice I have forgotten, but none of the dozen had a place to offer me. One morning I took things into my own hands and I walked into the offices of the *New Masses* with my oilcloth briefcase, and I asked to see the editors. "I believe in the world they are trying to make, I believe in it very much," I said to the young girl at the desk, but she said the editors were out. Those were her words, that is, but her eyes were saying something quite different. *You are absurd, with your waved hair, and your high heels, and your purple suit. You couldn't believe in anything*, her dark and baleful eyes were saying, and I turned out into the sunlight of Fourteenth Street again, less certain than ever who or what I was.

The facts about me were that I was nineteen, and in love with a French engineer, an exchange student, who had just graduated from the University of Cincinnati. This much I knew. Also, that he was tall and dark and wore what were probably handlebar moustaches, and that his name was Richard Brault. While still very young, he had been wounded in combat in the First World War, and he sang French war songs with biting venom, and danced the cancan with remarkable spirit and agility. Indeed, he and his fellow *sous-officiers* had appeared on the musical comedy stage as Elsie Janis' guests one evening in New York. They had all sung "Madelon" together, she too wearing the rakish beret and the uniform of horizon blue that she had worn as official entertainer at the front. Richard was a rebel, a *rouspéteur*, incurably bitter about the Catholic Church, in which he had been raised, and about his father's army career, although he himself cut a fine figure in his sky-blue uniform, with his beret over one ear. Our life together was going to be a confirmation of our impatience with conventions and our commitment to something called freedom in which we believed so passionately (the terms as contemporary and familiar as that).

Through my sister's continued efforts I finally got a job as secretary to a fashion writer, Margery Welles, and Richard came on from Cincinnati and rather disgruntledly went to work for the New York electric company. He had hoped to do better than that, armed with his fine degree. But even after four years of American university he still had trouble with the sounds of the English language. He always said "for half a sock" instead of "for heaven's sake", and called his best friends "you son of a peach". This pronunciation difficulty did not help him when, as meter inspector, he rang the doorbells of apartment houses and asked to be let in.

We were married at the New York City Hall with a great group of other couples on Saturday morning, June 24, 1922, and my sister was our witness. On the first morning of our married life a special delivery letter from my father awakened us, and we sat up in bed and read it together. In this letter (which had doubtless been instigated by my grandfather, as my father was loath to take a stand on his own), I was forbidden to marry Richard until he was in a position to support me. Two weeks later Richard received a cable from his father in Brittany, saying that unless we were immediately married by a priest the family never wished to see him again. So that was done, but not in the church itself, as I was not a Catholic, but in a chapel behind the French church on West Twenty-third Street, Richard standing, as grim as if at a funeral, by my side, looking the other way.

There was little difference between our revolt and that of the young of 1968, except that it was far less desperate, in a far less critical and despairing time. We too were determined to be free, and yet that freedom did not have a specific name. Freedom from other people's money was part of it, and freedom from advice, and Richard and I intended to accept neither. We were going to work hard and save enough money to go to France and spend a few weeks with Richard's family, whom he had not seen in four years. But we had no intention of accepting them on their merits, for our judgment on them had already been irrevocably passed. We knew what we were about, and perhaps the clarity of our vision would reveal something fresh and new to them—they who had handed us the unspeakable horror of a world war and its aftermath and made no apologies about this gift. In a country that did not put its socialists in jail, as Eugene Debs was jailed in America, and did not harass its writers, as Upton Sinclair was harassed, I was going to write a novel in the quiet and peace of alien Brittany, and Richard was going to work his future out.

I had been a switchboard operator and cashier for over a year in my father's office in Cincinnati while I put myself through secretarial school at night. By then his business was going very badly, and, opposed by the men in the family, I had then become secretary to a wholesale jeweller, a Rotarian, in order to make enough money to join my sister in New York. And now, when my typing and filing and letter writing got me a job with Lola Ridge in the New York office of *Broom* magazine, I could not leave Margery Welles and the fashion column quickly enough.

Broom was probably the handsomest and arty-est of any literary publication of its time, printed as it was on very elegant paper, and published in Italy by Harold Loeb, Alfred Kreymborg, and a number of other temporarily expatriate writers. The New York office was in the basement of Marjorie Loeb's house on East Ninth Street, and even now, at this moment, when I pass that house I want to stop and draw my fingers along its steps with love. Lola was an Australian poet, born in Dublin, and she was surely not more than forty then, but I looked on her as precariously aged, and I cherished and protected her as tenderly as if she were a small, bright flame I held cupped in my hand. Her work expressed a fiery awareness of social injustice as eloquently as did Emanuel Carnevali's or Maxwell Bodenheim's, but it was always Lola's voice that spoke, a woman's savage voice, not theirs, for all her fervent response to their poetry. She was frail, small-boned as a child, and constantly in bad health, half starved, because she and her husband needed their small salaries for other things. I cooked for her (when she would allow it), answered the business letters, kept the financial records of the office (accurately but very unprofessionally), and wrote poetry that I hoped she would be able to say was good. Lola cautioned me about the inability of happiness to redeem one's life, but in spite of her counsel I was senselessly, almost speechlessly happy. I would, at that moment, have had no patience with Dostoevsky's averment that happiness is bought by man through his own suffering. In this process he saw no injustice, and had I read him then instead of a decade or more later, I would have neither understood nor accepted his belief that a knowledge of life is found only in the great chasms of man's bitterest experiences, and that happiness in all its clarity is bought, coin by blackened coin, by the currency of suffering alone.

Lola's causes became mine, and when I wrote my poems now I borrowed from her conscience and her poetic vocabulary. She gave to my rebellion a wider and, at the same time, a more indigenous setting. For a long time my heart had bled with and for the Irish insurgents, and I had carried everywhere with me a copy of Terence MacSwiney's letter to Cathal Brugha, a letter which he, the Lord Mayor of Cork, had written in Brixton Prison on September 20, 1920, after forty-six days of hunger striking. This was the way it went:

Your letter went to my heart. It consoled and comforted me. God bless you for it. But I would not have you in my place here for anything. I'm praying that you will be among the survivors to lead the Army of the Republic in the days of freedom. I feel final victory is coming in our time and pray earnestly that those who are most needed will survive to direct it. Those who have gone before will be with you in spirit to watch over the battle helping in unseen but powerful ways.

Will you give my loving remembrances to all at GHQ, and the officers and men of Dublin Brigade of whom we are all so proud and to the organization as a whole. Its work goes on splendidly. Remember me specially to Mick C., Dick McKee, Diarmuid, Rory O'Connor, Gearoid, Austin—too many names come before me. But don't forget Leo Henderson. I'm sending a line to Dick M.—too tired to go on.

Whatever I suffer here is more than repaid for by the fruit already reaped—if I die I know the fruit will exceed the cost a thousand fold. The thought makes me happy and I thank God for it.

Ah, Cathal, the pain of Easter week is properly dead at last!

I wish I could say all that's in my heart to thank you for your beautiful letters. God guard and preserve you for the future. God bless you again and again and give you and yours long years of happiness under the victorious Republic. With all a comrade's love. God bless you.

Toirdhealach

The reason for MacSwiney's death had defined for me in clearest terms the rebellion of the flesh against organized authority. The spirit of freedom given substance in that flesh had been made so palpable that it struck me like a blow. For over a year I had sought a means of getting to Ireland, to fight with the others there. Mac-Swiney's declarations and his acts were of a piece, and this was the way I wanted my own life to be. His words and his acts were as ordered as Bach's music, as resounding and as reassuring to me, and, echoing them, were the words of George Russell (AE) saying to Rudyard Kipling: "You had the ear of the world and you poisoned it with bigotry and prejudice. You had the power of song and you have always used it on the behalf of the strong against the weak." Even now when I think of the Irish Republican Army, my heart is filled with tears.

But now it was Lola who spoke the vocabulary I wanted to hear, and all I had cherished vicariously took on the shadowy dimensions of another country's history. Because I had read very little (not only because since the age of six I had written so much, but because there seemed to me no practical reason for reading), I did not know that Thoreau had said a long time before: "How does it become a man to behave toward this American government today? I answer that he cannot without disgust be associated with it. I cannot for an instant recognize that political organization as government which is the *slave's* government also." For one or another official infringement upon the rights of man (the imprisonment of Debs, the Sacco and Vanzetti case, the stoning of Oswald Garrison Villard in Cincinnati, etc.), I had acknowledged Thoreau's belief, but in my mother's gentle, meditative speech, and now I acknowledged it in Lola's passionate voice.

Richard and I lived in one room on the first floor of a brownstone house on East Fifteenth Street, and there I met my first bedbug. Richard had gone off at six o'clock to work, and I had fallen asleep again, and awoke in the dingy, furnished room with an awareness that I was being watched. There sitting on my pillow, close to my left eye, and infinitely pathetic in his indecision, was the bedbug. In the brief moment that we faced each other, his gaze spoke as eloquently to me as that of Lautréamont's shark in the excerpts that *Broom* was then publishing. I did not for an instant relish being poor, but words that Debs had spoken to the court before sentence was passed on him expressed what was true for me as well. ". . . while there is a lower class," he said, "I am in it; while there is a criminal element, I am of it; while there is a soul in prison, I am not free." I accepted the bedbug as the badge of honour of our poverty, and I wished no harm to come to him.

Richard and I cooked our meals on a hot plate in the bathroom that had no window, but at Lola's gatherings on East Ninth Street the flesh and its appetites, and the accoutrements of material poverty, were set aside. Another world took shape beneath the level of the sidewalk of that New York street. Every Thursday afternoon, and perhaps one evening in the month, Lola held open house. She and her husband were poorer than church mice, and this basement, offered by Marjorie Loeb, was their church. Where the money for the tea and cakes and lemon and milk came from every week, one did not know. Perhaps from Marjorie of the warm, shy, generous heart and the madonna face, perhaps from the donations and subscriptions sent in to *Broom*. There Lola offered tea to the known and the unknown who came, she herself hungry, and ill, and fragile enough to be blown away like a leaf whenever a gust of wind came through the door; and she offered their talents sustenance as well.

In that basement I passed cups and plates to Marianne Moore, of whom William Carlos Williams was to write: "Marianne was our saint—if we had one—in whom we all instinctively felt our purpose come together to form a stream"[1]; John Dos Passos, who uneasily toasted the revolution in tea, and to Elinor Wylie, who recited flawless line-by-line poems she had just written in her mind on the way down on the top of a Fifth Avenue bus, her short wavy auburn hair still wet with snow. I served them in silent awe: Jean Toomer, Waldo Frank, Babette Deutsch, Mary Heaton Vorse, Gorham Munson, Laura Benét, Edwin Arlington Robinson, Louis Ginsberg, Glenway Wescott, Monroe Wheeler, and countless others, listening when they read aloud their work or when they talked together, listening, listening, my critical faculties wholly numbed, believing that not one dispensable word could be spoken here. These gatherings were, in a sense, a confirmation of the meaning Mother had, in her oblique approach to truth, implied was the one meaning of value in life: the search for and affirmation of that which the hand could not touch. The function of money, I had learned a long time before, was to enable one to buy one's independence from those who did not believe this truth. But perhaps "buy" is not the right word. It was more accurately so that one need not barter for one's freedom. That was the only meaning money had.

Because of my mother, who gave me definitions, I knew what I was committed to in life; because of my father and my grandfather, who offered statements instead of revelations, I knew what I was against. I had the most satisfactory of childhoods because Mother, small, delicate-boned, witty, and articulate, turned out to be exactly my age. Owing to continuous bad health, she had had barely any education, and so her spirit had remained fervent and pure. She alone, with her modest but untroubled intuitions about books and painting, music and people, had been my education. Everything she took into her awareness she poured out again to me, gossiping, laughing, explaining, like one child talking to another—George Moore, Shaw, Dreiser, Romain Rolland, Santayana—making even the dead come to life because she knew there were really no dead, recounting to me all the great and exciting contemporary myths in which I could put my faith where it would never be betrayed. In the evenings she had read aloud *The Wind in the Willows* to my sister and me, and *Pride and Prejudice*, and *Emma*, and the stories of Selma Lagerlöf, and the

[1] *The Transatlantic Review*, Vol. II, No. 2 (Paris, 1924), pp. 216–17.

poetry of Carl Sandburg, while we sat and drew illustrations for every book she read. (My father read us Stevenson and Sir Walter Scott, and their dullness made me uneasy. My grandfather read us Conrad and Kipling, instead of the Irish poets, as was surely his duty to us, and the lack of illumination in the minds of those two authors has depressed me ever since.)

We travelled expensively, and dined expansively, in a great many different countries. But wherever we were, and at whatever age, Mother offered the milestones to measure the distance of our understanding, and these milestones have never altered. In 1913, for instance, when I was ten, she took me to the Armory Show in New York to see Duchamp's "Nude Descending a Staircase", and Brancusi's "Mlle. Pogany" and his "Bird in Space". That was the winter we lived in John Sargent's house in Bryn Mawr (when another abortive attempt was being made to educate me, this time at Miss Shipley's School, where my sister was a brilliant student). My father, a graduate of the law school of the University of Pennsylvania, was then a director of the Children's Homeopathic Hospital in Philadelphia, and on the occasions when he brought colleagues home to dinner, Mother would read aloud to them from Gertrude Stein's *Tender Buttons*.[2] She did this with her usual grace, in unassuming dedication, believing that men advanced in the study of medicine would be enthralled by such evidence of the parallel literary advances of their time.

One evening one of the doctors laughed so hard over Stein that he became ill and had to be taken upstairs to bed. He therefore missed my mother's reading of my German travel diary which followed

[2] In the appendix of Bob Brown's *Readies*, published by *the roving eye press* in Cagnes sur Mer, France, 1931, Bob Brown writes (page 161):

At the time I had written myself out I read Gertrude Stein's *Tender Buttons*. I didn't know what it was about then any more than I know what's about anything she's writing today, but I can still read it when I haven't anything more stimulating, and get a kick out of it. At the time *Tender Buttons* was published I had to read it because positively there was nothing else in America to read. No *transition* back in 1914, no Joyce, no Cummings, no Kay Boyle, just a peep of Sandburg, no tricky little playful magazines of word experiment. . . . Gertrude Stein gave me a great kick. . . . I began to see that a story might be anything. . . . I threw my typewriter into the air and huzzahed. That's the way you feel when you're tired to death finishing up the final paragraph of a three hundred page thriller and some blond angel slips in on a pink cloud with a cooling case of champagne. Sprays your scorched writing tonsils with it. Stein's book sprayed mine. It was a case of champagne to me in a time of dire need.

Tender Buttons, the diary I had kept when we crossed on the SS *Rotterdam* the summer before. I remember the doctor's face as he was led, crippled with laughter, up the stairs; and I remember the portion of my works Mother read then, dealing with the protocol of the Brandenburger Tor. I described what happened to Kaiser Wilhelm II when his horse took the bit in its teeth and raced with him, sword raised in his one good hand, the bright plumes of his helmet streaming on the wind, through one of the lesser arches of the Tor instead of the middle arch, which was reserved for royalty. The difference between Gertrude Stein's work and mine, Mother explained, was that Stein's was supposed to be true and not humorous, while mine, although equally original, was factual and not allegorical. We were equal in prominence as writers in Mother's eyes.

Mother was born and brought up on the Kansas prairies (her mother was an elementary school teacher who, at sixteen, had married the superintendent of schools); but because of the severe curvature of her spine, which made it necessary for her to wear a brace throughout her childhood, there were very few practical things that Mother could do. As a girl, when she had finally tried riding a bicycle, she was never able to get off it alone, but had to keep on going around and around the block until she met a friend who would seize the handlebars. She could not use a typewriter or a sewing machine, and she had great trouble threading a needle. Her hands were small and appeared to be quite useless, the bones in her slender, nervous fingers seemingly ready to break in two, but I know now that they could never have broken. Once as a child, when she lived on the prairie, she had picked up a lighted oil lamp to carry across the room to a table to do her homework, and the hot glass chimney of it toppled. She had caught it, and to save it from breaking had carried it in her hand. The scar it left was always in her palm, a rosy crescent moon, marking her heart line, and her head line, and her life line, with the ineffaceable signature of her bravery. She prevailed, while the men of the family were effaced, line by line, a little more every year.

During the First World War I learned to knit scarves for the *poilus* in the trenches, and to crochet bandages to Red Cross specifications, and I would spend long hours on the veranda of the Meadowside Inn in the Pocono Mountains trying to teach Mother to do these things; but she could not deal with needles. She tried, not as an adult but as a diligent child will strive in silent concentration to please, but it all ended in a mass of tangled wool and thread. I don't know how she managed to change the needles of the phonograph, but this she did very well. She played Mozart and Schubert in wartime, while my little Irish grandfather hissed his venom at the Germans from the top of the stairs. Mother would tell him gently, gently, that Mozart was Austrian, not German, and that Schubert had died at the age of thirty-one of typhoid fever (which I had had only a few years before), as if these facts would soften his judgment. One evening she even read him Romain Rolland's words, which asked: "What can speech accomplish when everything has just been said by music? After its great voice, only the deaf, those who have felt nothing, heard nothing, are eaten by the desire to speak." And day after day my little grandfather would skip downstairs and savagely bring all music to an end. He would seize up the metal arm of the phonograph, and toss the Red Seal record aside, and put on "Keep the Home Fires Burning", sung by John McCormack. Mother would then go up to her bedroom and close the door, after quite humbly inviting the ghosts of the great to join her there. After a while she didn't play these or any other records until the war was done.

When Mother was running for election to the Cincinnati Board of Education on the Farmer-Labour ticket, she did exactly what she had done in Bryn Mawr eight or nine years before. She read aloud to the labour union organizers James Joyce's *Ulysses* (which was published in part in Jane Heap's and Margaret Anderson's *Little Review*), just as she had once read Gertrude Stein to the members of the hospital board. How she came to be running on the Farmer-Labour ticket, or indeed on any ticket, is not quite clear, and she was sternly if silently opposed in this by my father and grandfather. Eagerly and earnestly she would read Joyce's pages aloud, convinced that the speech of contemporary avant-garde art could not be the speech of the contemporary labour movement as well. During these evening conferences in our house she would show reproductions of Brancusi's work to the Farmer-Labour group, untroubled in her belief that Brancusi's "Endless Column" would be recognizable to them as symbol for labour's tenacity and enduring hope.

That year she took in some of the weary little marchers of the Children's Crusade as they passed through Cincinnati on the long trek to Washington. The children were marching from cities all over the United States, converging on the White House to call public attention to the fact that their fathers, political prisoners, were still in jail although the war was through. They carried placards which read "My Father Was Imprisoned for Expressing His Opinion", or "I've Never Seen My Daddy. I Want Him to Come Home". The evening my mother took her contingent of children in, and bathed them, and washed their hair, and cut their toenails, and fed them, and put them to bed, my father and grandfather packed over-night bags and went to a hotel. Nor were they present when Lincoln Steffens had dinner with us one spring evening, although I was allowed, through their silence rather than their spoken consent, to drive him and Mother in our Model T Ford to the hall where he was lecturing.

But it was not only men, artists, political figures, who gave Mother her unassailable strength. Women were there as well. Ever since I could remember there was the vision of Mary Garden dancing her homage to God before the altar in the *Jongleur de Notre Dame*, as Mother danced her own homage to Mary Garden to the music of Mozart at night; and, later, there was her pride in Margaret Anderson's readiness to go to prison for the crime of publishing James Joyce in the *Little Review*. Mother and those she loved were a part of every decision I took; and now in New York Lola had joined that company of the great.

I could scarcely wait to get to the *Broom* office every morning, and I could not bear to leave at night. I had only two dresses and one pair of shoes, but I had a strawberry-red chiffon scarf that my sister had given me (like one of Isadora Duncan's scarves, I used to think as I knotted it around my neck). Because I could not afford to buy eye shadow or mascara, I would burn a cork in the early morning in the obscurity of our East Fifteenth Street room and smear its black on my lids before I set out for work. In the bright light of day, passers-by on the street would turn to look at me, and roar aloud, and I would laugh, too, believing we were laughing together because we shared a miraculous season that others had not yet perceived.

It was then that McAlmon as a figure began to take on shape and meaning for me. I had read his poems in Harriet Monroe's *Poetry* magazine, and Lola told me he was wild and daring and as hard as nails. She was inclined to dismiss him as a poet who drank too much, a man in his mid-twenties who at times wore in one ear a turquoise-blue earring which exactly matched the colour of his eyes. His past was obscure. It was possible that he had been a cowpuncher by trade, Lola said; and he had, according to his poetry I had read, been an aviator in the war. Lola believed that he had been working in the Washington Square Bookshop when he met Bryher, at a time when he did not know she was the daughter of Sir John Ellerman, a British shipping magnate. I gathered even then that McAlmon had had little sympathy with Lola's earnest commitment to the arts and to the working class, a commitment so dramatized that people felt the necessity of either defending or abusing her whenever her name came up. McAlmon mercilessly satirized her and the *Broom* parties in his fictionalized autobiography, *Post-Adolescence*, which was published in Paris in 1922. Yet it was at one of the *Broom* literary gatherings in 1919 or 1920 that McAlmon had met William Carlos Williams, and Bill had given him his friendship instantly.

Nearly forty years later Bill wrote that at the time of their meeting McAlmon was "posing for a living before art classes at Cooper Union for $1.00 an hour", which sometimes meant an eight- or nine-hour day. Bill described McAlmon as having "the straight, slim body, lean-bellied and not over-muscled, of a typical American college freshman". Together, McAlmon and Bill founded the magazine *Contact*, a name, Bill has pointed out, that stated quite simply what McAlmon wanted of life: "contact with a world which theretofore had eluded him". But McAlmon, in a letter written to Bill from Paris in 1921, had another interpretation of the meaning of the name.

Do an article [he wrote], and insist that both of us are back of what we mean by contact with all the force of our convictions as always. The idea of contact simply means that when one writes one writes about something, and not just to write "literature" because it is a day of publications and publishing houses. . . . When Brancusi, the sculptor here, is doing work towards the end of attaining "form" or "absolute" beauty, he demonstrates contact. But when a person like Evelyn Scott, with an analytical intelligence, writes pretty imagism, and other verses that would do for a "textbook of modern poetry" she is writing verses because that's the thing to do, and not because they show the quality of her perception, or apprehension of experience. . . . But as I said in a letter to you before departing, it isn't lack of contact that condemns most writing. . . . It's lack of an individual quality that makes the stuff worth reading, and presence of too much desire to be a "literary figure". I wish, Bill, you'd do an article and send it over to me, emphatically declaring that we've swallowed none of our propositions.

Contact continued for three years, and was supported from the beginning largely by McAlmon, for Bill was a hard-working, underpaid, small-town, general practitioner with a growing family, and he could not contribute financially as much as he would have liked. This gesture of McAlmon's—he was then living on a scow in New York Harbour, and giving the dollars he earned posing to a publishing venture dedicated largely to the work of others—was the first of the many gestures he was to make on a far grander scale once he had married a girl of great wealth.[3]

The instant recognition Bill gave to McAlmon was not an exceptional thing in his life. James Joyce, Ernest Hemingway, Katherine Anne Porter, Ezra Pound, and T. S. Eliot, among countless others, responded to his undefinable quality. Young writers, painters, composers, Paris whores, the *clochards* under the bridges of the Seine, lost girls, lost boys, the insecure, all turned to him. His quality was not charm, at least not in the sense of winningness, and it had nothing to do with affability. It was part of a determination as single as that of Peter Weiss, who said in 1967 that he is in his work opposing the building of illusions and everything else that has served as an opiate to the mind. Bill Williams described it in McAlmon when he wrote: "His narrow lips and icily cold blue eyes with their direct look left no question in the onlooker's mind that he meant what he said of any situation, and if any subterfuge was to be practiced, he would have none of it." This ruthless honesty which drew people to McAlmon demanded that those he faced with his icy stare look closely at themselves and their pretences. It was a demand that made the presumptuous turn the other way.

[3] In *That Summer in Paris* (Coward-McCann, Inc., New York, 1963), Morley Callaghan wrote of McAlmon: "My curiosity about this generous man was immense. . . . He was willing to help any writer of talent. And what did he get for it? Sneers and open hostility."

Robert McAlmon

1921-1923

In Paris I had a note from Harriet Weaver, publisher of the Egoist Press, to present to James Joyce. His *Dubliners* I much liked. The Stephen Dedalus of his *Portrait of the Artist as a Young Man* struck me as precious, full of noble attitudinizings, and not very admirable in its soulful protestations. He seemed to enjoy his agonies with a self-righteousness which would not let the reader in on his actual ascetic ecstasies. Nevertheless, the short stories made me feel that Joyce would be approachable, as indeed did passages of *Ulysses* which had already appeared in the *Little Review*.

At his place on the Boulevard Raspail I was greeted by Mrs. Joyce, and although there was a legend that Joyce's eyes were weak, it was evident that he had used eyesight in choosing his wife. She was very pretty, with a great deal of simple dignity and a reassuring manner. Joyce finally appeared, having just got up from bed. Within a few minutes it was obvious that he and I would get on. Neither of us knew anybody much in Paris, and both of us like companionship. As I was leaving he suggested that we have dinner together that night, and we met at eight for an apéritif and later went to dine.

At that time Joyce was by no means a worldly man, or the man who could later write to the Irish Academy that, living in Paris as he did, it was difficult to realize the importance of their academy. He had come but recently from Zürich, and before that Trieste, in both of which cities he had taught languages at the Berlitz school in order to support his family. He was still a Dublin-Irish provincial, as well as a Jesuit-Catholic provincial, although in revolt. He refused to understand that questions of theology did not disturb or interest me, and never had. When I assured him that instead of the usual "religious crises" in one's adolescent life I had studied logic and metaphysics and remained agnostic, he did not listen. He would talk about the fine points of religion and ethics as he had been taught by the Jesuits. His favourite authors were Cardinal Newman and St. Thomas Aquinas, and I had read neither. He told me some tale of how St. Thomas once cracked a woman—possibly a prostitute— over the head with a chair, and explained that the Jesuits were clever at logic. They could justify anything if it suited their purposes.

He was working on *Ulysses* at the time and often would make appointments to read rather lengthy extracts of what he had most recently written. Probably he read to me about a third of the book. It was impressive to observe how everything was grist to his mill. He was constantly leaping upon phrases and bits of slang which came naturally from my American lips, and one night, when he was slightly spiffed, he wept a bit while explaining his love or infatuation for words, mere words. Long before this explanation I had recognized that malady in him, as probably every writer has had that disease at some time or other, generally in his younger years. Joyce never recovered. He loved particularly words like "ineluctable", "metempsychosis"—grey, clear, abstract, fine-sounding words that are "ineluctable" a bit themselves. Had I been older and less diffident before him in those days I would have given him *Irene Iddesleigh* to read. Her author also loved words, and flung her work "upon the oases of futurity" hoping, as did Joyce of *Ulysses*, that it would not be consigned to "the false bosom of buried scorn". I don't think I ever did get around to telling Joyce that the high-minded struttings and the word prettifications and the Greek beauty part of his writings palled on me, as did Stephen Dedalus when he grew too noble and forbearing. Stephen's agonies about carnal sin seemed melodramatic, but perhaps they were not so. Several years later a son of Augustus John, Henry, who was studying to be a priest, wrote essays and letters equally intent upon carnal desire and the searing sin of weakening. Mercifully I was not brought up by the Jesuits.

Almost every night Joyce and I met for apéritifs, and although he was working steadily on *Ulysses*, at least one night a week he was ready to stay out all night, and those nights he was never ready to go home at any hour. We talked of the way the free mind can understand the possibility of all things: necrophilia and other weird rites. We agreed in disliking mysticism, particularly the fake and sugared mysticism of many poets and writers. We spoke of what a strange man Robert Burton must have been to have compiled his *Anatomy of Melancholy*, and he didn't know in the end a bit more about it than we did. Sir Thomas Browne, not to speak of Ezra Pound and Eliot and Moore and Shaw, we discussed, but sooner or later Mr. Joyce began reciting Dante in sonorous Italian. When that misty and intent look came upon his face and into his eyes I knew that friend Joyce wasn't going home till early morning.

One night he wept in his cups when telling of his forefathers. His father had parented a large family, and his grandfathers before him had been parents of families of from twelve to eighteen children. Joyce would sigh, and then pull himself together and swear that by the grace of God he was still a young man and he would have more children before the end. He didn't detect that I, the youngest of ten children of a poor minister, did not fancy his idea. He would not listen when I suggested that if one is to produce children one had better have the money to educate and care for them in the childhood years.

At the time Valery Larbaud, the French author-critic, was keen about Joyce's work and had written his article noting *Ulysses* as the first Irish book to belong to world literature. He dined with us at times and we generally went later to the Gypsy Bar off the Boul' Mich'. Wyndham Lewis arrived for a stay in Paris and he was a different man from the Lewis of London. He was free and easy and debonair. Indeed, too many Englishmen will do on the Continent what it does not do to do in London. Lewis was intent upon going to the Picasso exhibition; he must meet Picasso and Braque and Derain, although these painters of Paris were cagy and suspicious about English painters of talent. Picasso at the time was doing his pneumatic nudes, which always made me want to stick a pin in them to see if they would deflate.

Lewis was most gracious and jovial and instructed me with a constant flow of theories on abstraction and plastic values. It would not have done to let him know that I had heard most of what he was saying before, in New York, when Marsden Hartley, Alfred Stieglitz, and art critics held forth in speech or newspaper articles. Somehow there was no wonder in Lewis' discovery that the engineering demand of structures often gives them an aesthetic value. The Egyptians, Greeks, and Mayans seemed to have known that before Lewis.

It was spring, however, and for a time Lewis, Joyce, and I met nightly, and upon occasions would stay out till nearly dawn. The Gypsy Bar was usually our late night hangout. The *patron* and the "girls" knew us well, and knew that we would drink freely and surely stay till four or five in the morning. The girls of the place collected at our table and indulged in their Burgundian and Rabelaisian humours. Jeannette, a big draught horse of a girl from Dijon, pranced about like a mare in heat and restrained no remark or impulse which came to her. Alys, sweet and pretty-blonde, looked fragile and delicate, but led Jeannette to bawdier and altogether earthy vulgarities of speech and action. Joyce, watching, would be amused, but inevitably there came a time when drink so moved his spirit that he began quoting from his own work or reciting long passages of Dante in rolling sonorous Italian. I believed that Joyce might have been a priest upon hearing him recite Dante as though saying mass. Lewis sometimes came through with recitations of Verlaine, but he did not get the owl eyes and mesmerizing expression upon his face which was automatically Joyce's. Amid the clink of glasses, jazz music badly played by a French orchestra, the chatter and laughter of the whores, Joyce went on reciting Dante. I danced with Alys, and even sometimes with Jeanette, but she was six foot and buxom, and, dancing, seemed not to realize that I was there at all. In those days, and for some three years later, I didn't have hangovers. Only once, after a particularly mad assortment of drinks, I had to struggle to a lamp-post and relieve myself, and Joyce said solicitously, "I say, McAlmon, your health is rather delicate. Maybe they'll be saying I'm a bad example for you."

Frank Dobson, the English sculptor, also turned up and joined our nightly wanderings, and with him was Stephen Tomlin, student-sculptor to Dobson. In those days the English did Paris frequently; they seem not to now; but in all I think that in spite of, or possibly because of, it being postwar, people were better willed, more reckless perhaps, but gayer than now. They had not suffered peace long enough to have grown cranky and sour; and, of course, as regards these of whom I am writing, no one had become an acclaimed "great man" or "genius". There might have been slumbering envies and animosities, but Paris lulled them, and each knew that not only he but the others had to struggle for recognition of any proper sort.

Ezra Pound was in town also, and I dropped him a note. He had been a boyhood friend of William Carlos Williams and of Hilda Doolittle (H.D.), and I wrote to him as a friend of theirs and not as to an older poet. He had not written any of his cantos at the time (to my knowledge), and while I mildly liked a poem or so of his, I disliked his critical work generally. Emanuel Carnevali had, in *Poetry* of Chicago, written a review of Ezra's work, declaring the main impulse behind it was irritation. I agreed, but Bill Williams and Hilda both assured me he was—*he was*—Ezra. I could understand that he was a bit of a character and perhaps difficult, but I'm not easy myself.

We met and had lunch together. Ezra hemmed and hawed and talked of writing, being very instructorial indeed. I was merely wanting to find out about Paris and its pastimes. Over coffee he sat back from the table, hemmed and hawed, threw one leg over the other, then reversed. He had a Vandyck-ish beard and an 1890-ish artist's getup. I did detect that Ezra was shy (and, within limits, kindly), but I have that conceit also, if anybody will believe it, and know it is vanity. Having been a reporter and an advertising copy writer and salesman, and between times more or less a hobo of a not too sublime order, I may have been forced to hide shyness more than Ezra, who has been mainly and perhaps too exclusively literary and the poet, a bit troubadourish.

When editing *Contact* with Bill Williams I had written two cerebral, big-worded "poems", razzing Ezra and Eliot. At lunch I mentioned Carnevali. Ezra knew both my poem and Carnevali's criticism, I thought. At any rate there was discomfiture in the air for us both. That might have passed, but two days later somebody informed me that Ezra made the comment, "Well, well, another young one wanting me to make a poet out of him with nothing to work on."

My answer when told that is unprintable, but it said clearly that he had better discover whether these young ones liked his work and mind before being the martyred schoolmaster. I had looked him up at the behest of Williams, for comradely and not for art reasons. Perhaps remarks of mine got back to Ezra; at any rate it was about a year before we stopped avoiding each other, although often we would be in the same group with Joyce, Lewis, Rodker, Dobson, and others. Joyce and Lewis talked to each of us, persuading us that we shouldn't be antagonistic. The thing passed off; perhaps I, perhaps Ezra, became less touchy and precious about sensibility. In any case, while I still don't care for the irritated portion in his work, I thoroughly admire his poetry and much of his criticism, and would hand *How to Read* to every youngster with ordinary brightness by the time he is twelve years old. Ezra may be a bit too much the poet poetizing, but no one touches him for craft and the power of evocation when he succeeds. Where Eliot is mouldy and sogs and is everlastingly the adolescent who will perversely be an old man blubbering, Ezra is hard, and his images flash at you and awaken clear and stimulating response. Where Joyce goes Irish-twilighty and uses a word or words for their isolated beauty, without attaining much more than the beauty of the word alone as it stands in the dictionary, Ezra gives entire passages, which evoke historic and legendary memories, and satirizes coolly. His cantos don't carry on throughout. They're jumpy, often axe-grinding, pedantic, scolding, but there are other passages which compensate, and no poem of such length carries on throughout the whole. Homer's *Iliad* and *Odyssey* are narrative and epic novels; but *The Divine Comedy* of Dante and Milton's *Paradise Lost* are insufferably boring through long passages—and to me particularly because they possess the medieval or Catholic mind.

Ezra once said that advice does nobody any good, that we must learn by experience. But he will be the pedagogue, yearning for pupils to instruct, and I, whether I write well or badly, have my idea of how I want to do it. We have been friendly for ten years, and he has given me pointers which at times I have been able to use. But I wonder if he really believes that young writers put themselves in older writers' hands to be taught how. We have such different approaches and different things to say.

The influx of people who came to be called "expatriates" had begun before this, but now they hung out in Montparnasse at the Dôme and the Rotonde. At the time I was doing Lipps, the Deux Magots, various bistros, all around St. Germain or the Boulevard St. Michel. I was hardly aware of Montparnasse, even as a legend, and Sylvia Beach informed me it was ghastly, a hangout for pederasts. In the daytime I was busy writing the short stories which went into *A Hasty Bunch*, a title which Joyce suggested because he found my American use of language racy. I was at that six weeks, and just as it was finished a flock of "expatriates" descended upon the Rue Jacob, Sts. Pères, St. Germain section. They were Kate Buss, critic for some Boston paper, Djuna Barnes, the *Broom* outfit—Alfred Kreymborg, Harold Loeb, Frances Midner, late of the Washington Square Bookshop, and Kreymborg's wife, Dorothy. They all stayed in the same hotel, and Vicki Baum's *Grand Hotel* couldn't touch the drama and intrigue which occurred in that hotel, but as I didn't stay there, that is somebody else's story, but I fear the rest will be silence. At any rate, the *Broom* outfit meant to be literary at all costs. On seeing a title of Anita Loos's, *Literary at Last*, I thought of Harold Loeb of the Sunwise Bookshop, who was an editor of *Broom*. How that little group of pilgrim expatriates loved each other! As some child once noted to the remark, "little birds in their nest agree," "They do since when? That's my worm."

I had known Djuna only slightly in New York, because Djuna was a very haughty lady, quick on the uptake, and with a wise-cracking tongue that I was far too discreet to try and rival. Once I had written a letter to the *Little Review*, asking how came it that Miss Barnes was both so Russian and so Synge-Irish, a comment Jane Heap apparently used frequently to cow Djuna. Jane kept assuring her that McAlmon was not taken in by her cape-throwing gestures but understood her for the sentimentalist she was. In the end, Djuna had gathered the idea that I disliked her, and that I was a very sarcastic individual. She was wrong about the first idea at least, for Djuna is far too good-looking and fundamentally likeable for any-thing but fond admiration, if not a great deal more, even when she is rather overdoing the *grande dame* manner and talking soul and ideals. In conversation she is often great with her comedy, but in writing she appears to believe she must inject her work metaphysics, mysticism, and her own strange version of a "literary" quality. In her *Nightwood* she has a well-known character floundering in the torments of soul-probing and fake philosophies, and he just shouldn't. The actual person doubtlessly suffered enough without having added to his character this unbelievable dipping into the deeper meanings. Drawn as a wildly ribald and often broadly funny comic, he would have emerged more impressively.

Joyce had to go into retirement after a particularly hard week. And for whatever I say later or have said before about Joyce "nobly the martyr," during these days he suffered, and physical agony is distressing to watch. I realized that his eyes were weak, but I didn't know that he probably was doing heavier drinking than he had for years, or ever, and that he was worried about money, and too intensely at work on *Ulysses*, so that Miss Beach could publish it.

We went one night to the Brasserie Lutetia, and he ordered, as usual, that horrible natural champagne. I didn't know wines then and thought he did. We had but one glass when suddenly I saw a rat running down the stairs from the floor above. I exclaimed upon it. "Where, where?" he asked nervously. "That's bad luck."

Earlier in the evening he had been superstitious about the way the knife and fork were placed on the table, and about the way I poured the wine. I thought his superstitions more or less a *blague*. They weren't, however. Within a minute after my exclaiming about the rat Joyce was out, blank. I got him into the taxi and drove to the Rue du Cardinal Lemoine, where he was living in a flat lent him by Valery Larbaud. There was a huge iron gate to the courtyard, and a key which was about a foot long. I wobbled it back and forth in the lock for ten minutes and finally got the gate open. The taxi driver carried him through the courtyard and up two flights of stairs, where we deposited him, and I explained to Nora. She had started to scold him, but turned tender at once, realizing that it was fright and not drink which had put him in this condition.

The next night we were having coffee and liqueur at the Café d'Harcourt when Nora suddenly called a taxi. Joyce's face showed that he was in terrible pain. I saw them home. For the next several weeks Joyce was in bed, suffering torture with his eyes. For many days the doctor pumped cocaine into the eyes to relieve the agony. After a week when I called to see him his face was a death mask, drawn with pain, mere skin over bone. It frightened me and I decided never to drink heavily with Joyce again but that decision was useless. Like myself, when Joyce wants to drink he will drink. Furthermore, when months later I next saw him he had finished *Ulysses*, it was just about to appear, and he was feeling anxious but lively, and enough had happened to me so that I had forgotten the picture of him suffering eye torture.

One night Djuna Barnes and I were at the Gypsy Bar when Sinclair Lewis barged in, some three sheets in the wind. He had once written a story about hobohemia and evidently feared Djuna would believe he had used her as one of the characters in it. Or perhaps he merely had an admiring eye for Djuna or a respect for her undoubted talent, however uneven it may be. But Djuna was well up with drink too and was not going to get chummy. I recall that Lewis looked wistful and went away from the table, with Djuna not having introduced him.

Another night a group of us sat on the terrace of the Swedish restaurant, the Stryx, Mina Loy, Harriet Monroe, and others were at the table. Sinclair Lewis came by and said to me, "Bob, I want you to meet Gracie. People say she is difficult, but maybe you won't find her so." One had heard of Gracie, and there seemed no reason for my meeting her particularly. However, I answered, "Rot! You aren't, are you? Come into the bar and have a drink where your husband can't pick on you."

We went to the bar and ordered gin fizzes, and then suddenly she fired three questions at me: if I thought Lewis the greatest American writer, a fine artist, America's first. Her questions were too fast, and I said so, whereupon she flew out of the door, refusing to drink with me. At the time I had read neither *Main Street* nor *Babbitt,* and had read only the short stories of Lewis written in his pulp-magazine days. His hobohemia had struck me as a concession to the newspapers' ideas of Greenwich Village and Bohemia, and I conjectured that he didn't know a bit more about Main Street, or Minneapolis, or Babbitts, than did I. Our backgrounds were not unlike. I did, however, suspect that he carried Main Street about in his own mind, and that he chose to write the dullest aspects of small-town life and types, while I had memories of rather alert and lively people in those Middle Western towns. They were types who later went away, and they were as ironic about the pretentious village intellectuals of the sort Lewis depicted as Lewis could be. No, Gracie, I didn't then and don't now, after having read *Babbitt,* think Lewis even a good second-rater. He gives to the travelling salesman, the fake-superior pseudo intellectual, and to the Europeans, a picture of America which they like to believe in order to feel their superiority. He fits in with Mencken and his Americana, but before him there has been Stephen Crane, Henry James, and, at the same time, Dos Passos had drawn wholly and in a characterized way several human beings in his *Three Soldiers.* Edith Wharton's *Ethan Frome* is worth more than all Lewis has written.

Another season Lewis was silenced at the Dôme. An admirer was assuring him that he drew better characters than Flaubert, but that perhaps Flaubert had the better style. Lewis, a bit intoxicated, insisted that he depicted character better and also had a better style than Flaubert. He asserted it while standing, and someone shouted, "Sit down. You're just a best seller." Again Lewis was crushed, and old quarterites were amazed that he bothered to boast in the Quarter or the Dôme. Even if he were the world's greatest artist, some nobody would be likely to shout him down there.

It appears that at one time Lewis thought Wells great, and Wells smilingly admits himself not of the first rank. He is still more interesting to read, however, than Lewis. Lewis might better have read a bit of Trollope to learn how to depict character and situation and also to placate the mores of the larger public. As he writes his penetration is not keen, for he misses all but the hick uplifters and the boobs of American small towns and cities, and Europe also produces a great variety of sappy and pretentious morons. So far as art or writing is concerned, I recall not a paragraph written by Lewis which gives one a joy in its velocity or suggestive quality. He is too intent on types to depict character. However, the world has become accustomed to seeing the Nobel Prize given to writers of second or third rank. It is pleasing to the populace, the mediocre.

By 1922 or 1923 there were quantities of Americans who had settled in France, to stay indefinitely either in Paris or in small towns nearby. The American bars had not yet come into being, and there was a great deal more entertaining in the home than was later to occur. Man Ray was settled into his studio with Kiki, spoke French fluently and was getting a French public, in a measure due to the help of Marcel Duchamp and Tristan Tzara and other Dadaists. George Biddle, Ford Madox Ford (whom L'Intransigeant, in an interview, called "an American writer"), Sisley Huddleston, George Slocombe, Clotilde Vail, and Laurence Vail, with his then wife, Peggy Guggenheim, Jane Heap, Mina Loy, Sally and William Bird, and many others were about, and most of them entertained fairly often. Gilbert White, Jo Davidson, Paul Daugherty and Paul Manship (guarded austerely by their wives, who could tell anybody at any time just what either of the Pauls liked or didn't like).

The summer of 1923, France as a whole celebrated the three-day fourteenth of July period as usual, but in Montparnasse there were a number of people of various nationalities who extended the gala days to a three months' period. Florianne, the French queen of the Quarter, of Spanish blood, came and went in taxis, magnificently gowned and inclined to be haughty. She was being bountifully supported by a champagne manufacturer who gave her thirty thousand francs a month, it was said. She liked the Right Bank, and luxury and elegance, but deeply she preferred the casual camaraderie of the Quarter. Rita, the cleverest of the French lot, had a period of being bored with serious life. The detective who had kept her for nine years permitted her much freedom, doubtless because he realized she wasn't one to accept discipline. Unlike Florianne, she was not beautiful. She was tiny, well made, and capable of looking monkey-droll or of suddenly appearing as one of the elegant women of Paris (like Fritzi Scheff in youth). She had wit, and acting talent, and a fine sense for comedy, combined with an apache toughness. She had moments of haughtiness, too, but she was chummy with the *grues* and less successful *poules* of the Quarter, many of whom she virtually supported.

The fourteenth of July celebration started with an impetus which made its gaiety continue for weeks. Enough of afterwar recklessness and enough of dawning hopefulness were about for dissipations to have a mass velocity. This momentum, like great periods in art or history, occurs seldom, and not even in everyone's lifetime. In the Quarter, foreigners of many nationalities collected daily about the Rotonde, then in bad favour with Americans, for its *patron* was a bastard. He asked ladies not to smoke or to appear hatless on the terrace of the Rotonde, and the English-American quarterites moved at once across the street to the Dôme, which then became their favourite hangout. The Rotonde has since belonged to the French bourgeois, or to the foreigner who sits for hours over one coffee or one beer. On the thirteenth I came in from the forests of Rambouillet where I had been for two months writing on a two-decker novel. I felt entitled to a letdown for a few days before getting back to work. Kenneth Adams, with whom I'd done a number of Italian towns the year before, had written me that he was in Paris. We had done Florence, Orvieto, Arezzo, Siena, Perugia, Assisi, etc., and discovered that there is a great deal one doesn't learn in America about painters, the primitives and otherwise. Kenneth declared it did him good to realize out of what Picasso, Matisse, Cézanne, and the others sprang, as well as to learn the type of painting they revolted against.

Adams was not to be located, but it was impossible not to hear Florence Martin as soon as I entered the Quarter. She was at the

Dôme bar, electing herself Dowager of the Dôme, Queen of Montmartre and Montparnasse, Maharanee of late nights, long-distance
marathon, and Queen Bee of drinkers. With her was a dismayed-
looking Frenchman, very pretty and shy. Every time he attempted
to slip quietly away Flossie jerked him back to curse and embrace
him. He was not sure that he didn't like it, however. Flossie was a
dashing bit of colour, of the Rubens type. Her orange hair was
piled neatly above her clear, baby-smooth skin. It was easy to believe
that the Flossie of a few years back, when some pounds lighter, had
been one of the more dazzling of Ziegfeld's show girls. She was sure
to be sounding off for the next twenty-four hours, until, bedraggled
and violently protesting that she needed another drink, she would be
enticed by some friend to her room for an interval of sleep. But even
then she would be absent from the scene for only a few brief hours.
She was capable of a forty-eight-hour drinking bout, and could
keep up this routine for weeks. All our stomachs were young then,
and we put them to the test.

"Hey, Sylvia, have a drink!" Flossie shouted through the Dôme
door as she saw Sylvia Gough passing. Sylvia came in, declaring
herself depressed over newspaper publicity about her recent divorce.
She was slender and beautiful in a fawnlike way, with a fawn's
easy grace, and she was quite as eager to leap about. There was no
doubt that soon Flossie would be having a rival as regards hilarious
spirits, for Sylvia's depressions were always more "acting genteel"
moments than actual moods.

"I'm so blue," Sylvia said, delicately weary, with aristocratic
and oh, so worldly ennui. I offered her a drink, and she soon had
another, and another. Life began to stir in her. "Bob, you are the
most adorable, the most sympathetic, the most understanding, the
dearest, the most generous darling. Give me a chaste kiss. Florence,
isn't Bob the most wonderful? He's the only man who doesn't try
to come to bed with me every time we get drunk together."

"*Merde!*" Flossie exploded. Flossie never liked rivalry, and Sylvia
was as quick to make easy acquaintances as she was, and quite as
full of hot air. "Lay off your crap of being the gushing lady! We're
all bitches together!"

Buying Flossie and Sylvia both drinks was too expensive a
pastime for so early in the evening, and they'd get themselves
bought drinks by somebody anyway. So I slipped away to the Stryx
in an unobserved moment. The Stryx was the first place in the

Quarter to resemble in any way the later American-type bar. Florianne was sitting at a table with Yvonne George and Kiki, but she looked impatient. She had known Yvonne George in Brussels in the years back, when they had worked in the same cabaret, and Yvonne was now a well-known star and dominated the scene. Kiki didn't care; her style of entertainment was of a different order in any case. I stood at the bar with Rita. She always delighted me. Tonight she was dressed like a girl of the Bowery in the New York 1890s. A small hat was tilted on her head, and she wore a suit with mutton-puffed sleeves. Her waist looked wasp-corseted. Rita, as French as they come, had turned into a little Irish Bowery girl, some tough mug's darlin'. She danced and sang a naughty song. Yvonne George indicated her admiration, for she knew talent and trouping when she saw it. But Rita disliked Yvonne and nullified her praise with a cold glance.

Florianne was performing now, as the orchestra played out in the street. Mobs of people were weaving and moiling, and couples danced in the mob-encircled space. An agony of unrest was on Florianne. She was doing an Eastern dance, writhing her long-waisted hipless body. Her small, firm breasts swayed back and forth quickly as she bent backwards to the floor, her arms weaving, her sensitive mouth lovely with intensity and emotion.

"Florianne is really beautiful," Rita said with curt appreciation. "Let's have another drink. Why is she dancing? The mood is not on her. She is unhappy and jealous. She has lost her lover, and she's jealous of Yvonne, but why? I am sorry for her that she will never learn not to waste herself."

The Stryx had placed a long table across the street at which various people were collecting. Jane Heap was there with Mina Loy, Clotilde Vail, and Kathleen Cannell. Through the door I saw that Bob Coates, Malcolm Cowley, Harold Loeb, and Jim Butler were wandering about before deciding where to have the next drink. Kenneth Adams then appeared, wriggling like a puppy with self-consciousness until he was seated at the table. Then he became humorously violent about having to return to America because he lacked funds. Jane Heap and Mina Loy were both talking brilliantly: Mina, her cerebral fantasies, Jane, her breezy, travelling-salesman-of-the-world tosh which was impossible to recall later. But neither of these ladies needed to make sense. Conversation is an art with them, something entirely unrelated to sense or reality or logic;

however, I knew them both well and was more interested in dancing.

As I wandered toward the Dôme I met an excited group of Americans, headed by Peggy and Laurence Vail. It appeared that Malcolm Cowley had taken a sock at the *patron* of the Rotonde and the cops had arrested him. The lot of us flocked to the police station and swore that the *patron* had started the fight. (We knew he disliked Americans, although he had become rich through them, and that he was a sour-faced, scurvy swine). I forget whether or not Cowley spent the night in jail, but in any case the next night some fifteen of us went again to the police station, completely sober, and looking highly respectable. Kitty Cannell testified that the *patron* had caught her arm brutally and pushed her, without reason. Naturally Cowley, as a gentleman, was angry and protested. The *patron* had then shoved Cowley aside, whereupon Cowley hit. I swore that the *patron* was noted for his evil disposition and lack of manners; that, although never involved in a scandal there, I had refused since some months to enter the Rotonde. His waiters knew me. The *patron* had only his waiters as witnesses, while the rest of us were detached observers. The judge told the *patron* that he had no case, with only employees as witnesses. The waiters looked sympathetically at our crowd, and the police of the Quarter admitted that the Rotonde *patron* was known as *mauvais*.

It was thought that Cowley had been saved a six months' jail term, for they are strict in France about fisticuffing. In any case, Cowley soon went back to America and joined the staff of the *New Republic*, where he could be duly ponderous, the young intellectual fairly slow on the uptake, who startled a naïve public by daring to declare (in 1933) that war is a sell and a disillusionment, and that MacLeish, Hemingway, and all of us should say so. After that blast from Cowley's pen, I got romantic and read again *War and Peace*, and *Le Feu* and *Three Soldiers*, and other anti-war books, and recalled that Osbert Sitwell, Beverley Nichols, Storm Jameson, and a crew of English lady novelists had been declaring themselves passionately against war for some time past. Again, because of my youth and vitality, and because the Kruegers, Insulls, Staviskys had not got away with it, I took hope. But as I write this (February 8, 1934) numbers of French citizens are being mowed down in Paris by soldiers with machine guns because they did not trust the government which so trusted Stavisky.

Kay Boyle

1923

On the way to the French Line pier that morning in June 1923, Richard and I ate breakfast with a friend or two at Child's, on East Fourteenth Street, gorging ourselves on little pork sausages and wheat cakes drenched with syrup. This we had not done since Cincinnati days, and there seemed no way to explain it. Perhaps the metaphor in it was that we had so little experience of America to take with us that we were impelled by guilt to enter a wholly indigenous place on this last day and eat this indigenous meal. I was French now, having had no choice when I married but to give up my American nationality. Yet it was as an American that I cherished the words Eugene Debs had spoken, again in the courtroom, saying that the five per cent of our people who control all the sources of our wealth, all our country's industries, are the ones who declare war, who make peace, and who control our national destiny. As long as this is true, Debs said, we do not have a democratic form of government, nor are we truly a self-governing people. If this trip Richard and I were undertaking was a search for individual freedom, it was as well a humourless search for what we believed could be the true meaning of democracy.

It was not that we would be gone forever, we told ourselves. We would be away three or, at the most, four months. As soon as we got to Brittany, Richard would look for a temporary job, perhaps in Rennes, where his older brother Pierre was a prosperous gynæcologist, with his own *clinique*. I would begin my novel, and after the first few chapters were done a New York publisher would pay me an advance so that I might finish it, and this would take care of our return fare. If anyone had told me that I would never see Lola again, and not see Mother for two years, when she came to France with my sister, I would have dismissed these truths with disdain. It would have been the equivalent of saying, with Blake's simplicity and clarity, that "If the moon and sun should doubt, they would immediately go out". I did not doubt that Mother's and Lola's presence would be there, forever, nor did they. The only concern Richard and I had as we set off was that we, who had accepted poverty, had not been able in the year since our marriage to save enough money to cover the trip entirely. We had had to borrow a large sum. Marjorie Loeb had offered it to me very shyly one afternoon in the office of *Broom* after Lola had told her that we were giving up our plans to spend the summer in France. Marjorie and Harold were divorcing, and at that time a portion of Marjorie's being seemed shadowed and silenced. She was even timid about coming down to the office when people were there, but if Lola and I were alone she would come tentatively down the basement stairs, with her two young children following. I was shy with her as well, as shy as if I had come upon a tender-eyed gazelle on a forest path.

Two hundred and fifty dollars was the tremendous sum that Marjorie offered almost apologetically. It was understood that as soon as Richard had a job (electrical engineers, the family wrote, were very much in demand in France, and the salaries paid were very good), and as soon as my novel was accepted, we would begin paying the money back. (All right, this was romanticizing, McAlmon. You would have known right off that the debt was never to be repaid. Richard wasn't able to get a job that summer. The French had no use whatsoever for American university degrees, and quite possibly they were right. I was to make twelve dollars on my poetry during the next year; and my second novel, written and rewritten and then written over again, was not to be published until 1931. How could I have known that I would not return to America until 1941, after the fall of France to the Germans? "The fall of France!" What an outlandish supposition! Reality was the one totally unreasonable factor that never ceased making its demands upon our lives).

But in June 1923 the S.S. *De Grasse* came into Le Havre on an amazingly lovely morning, meandering docilely into its slip as we stood on deck, with members of Richard's family keeping pace beside it on the towpath along the quay. There were five of them walking along far below us, sauntering as the ship sauntered and bumped gently through the locks. There they were, Papa, Maman, Charlotte, Marguerite, and a little girl of three or four, Cecette, it must be, Richard decided, identifying them without enthusiasm, except when he singled Charlotte out. She was tall and strong and elegant, with hair as black as his own, and a full, cream-coloured face, with dimpled cheeks, charming under the brim of her white straw hat. She was the Ingres-fleshed beauty of the family, and later I knew she was the richer side of Richard's nature, for she was undimmed radiance and tenderness while Richard had already begun to mistrust the look of men.

"She was always the one," Richard said, leaning on the rail. "My favourite, I mean." He looked down the long flank of the ship, speaking almost with emotion, unlike himself. Charlotte was six years older than he was, which made her thirty, and there was a sister in between them, and then three younger girls, and a boy of twenty-one. Of the five sisters, Charlotte alone was married, and married well. Where in the world Jean was this morning Richard could not make out. Jean, with his town house in St. Malo, and his château on the river Rance, and his fortune from the North African *estancias* he had inherited, was perhaps still asleep in the hotel. (Charlotte had little taste for sleep, I was to learn about her. It was too similar to death. It effaced long intervals of life, and she did not have the time to spare. She, who even took heretics into her tremendous heart, in six months would be dead.)

Marguerite, a year younger than Richard, had the stride of a boy, and a boy's hoarse voice as she called up to him through the funnel of her red, square, country hands. "Did you have much rain on the way over?" she shouted as desperately as if the present and future of mankind depended on the answer he gave. "Rain?" Richard shouted. "Any rain on the voyage?" Marguerite called in true desperation to him. Richard drew back from the rail, and turned to me, and slowly shook his head. "My God, I'd forgotten. I'd forgotten how much talk there will be about the weather," he murmured, and he glanced a little wildly around the deck. But it was too late now.

Maman and Charlotte and Marguerite wore identical grey suits, but they wore them differently. Maman's shoulders were stooped in her grey jacket, weary yet cautiously alert under the weight of eternal and aggressive authority that was her lot. Her straw hat was black, and a tracery of jet beads glinted on it. A dead bird with opened, flattened wings was pressed against its crown. Charlotte wore her grey suit with good humour, as if entranced by the awareness of how well she looked in it, with a white ruffle showing at her neck, and white grosgrain ribbons fluttering from her schoolgirl hat. When she lifted her hands to wave to us, the ruffles fell back from her wrists, and the diamonds in her rings caught the light of the June sun.

What Marguerite had managed to do to her grey suit cannot be easily described. Apparent in every restless step she took, in every brusque movement she made, was the fact that she disliked the suit, and that the suit knew it, and would have liked to get away. It hung awkwardly and shapelessly around her, trapped there by secret chains of hooks and eyes, withdrawn from her although handcuffed, wrist to wrist, with her. If she could have had her way, it was certain that she would have slit the skirt up the middle and made pants of it, and hacked the sleeves off at the elbows so as to be able to row a boat, or box an opponent in the ring, or swing from a trapeze. Her soiled-looking dark hair was jerked back in a chignon that had slipped sideways on her neck with long strands escaping from it. A black beret was dragged down over her ears. Small ears she had, I noted when we finally all stood on the quay together, meaning the inability to give. All living Buddhas weight their ears at night in order to make them heavy-lobed and thus generous in spirituality.

If I had come down the gangplank wearing a grey suit, it is possible everything might have turned out differently between the family and me. During the ceremony of the customs Maman made several approaches to the subject. Perhaps I had a grey suit in one of the suitcases, *un tailleur gris*, and I had just neglected to put it on, she suggested to Richard. We would be travelling in Jean's and Charlotte's limousine, and although it was, of course, far from being a public conveyance, still it would be preferable, she said, cawing the words out like a November crow, if I had a *tailleur gris pour le voyage*. We would be eating in restaurants, and even doing a little sightseeing on the way back to Brittany, and a grey suit would make things more comfortable for everyone. Richard's annoyance had begun to throb in two separate pulses in his jaws. "So if you don't have a grey suit, then you just don't take trips?" he was asking Papa. "Is that what Maman is trying to say?" And Papa, the retired army colonel, with his military bristle of white hair and his tobacco-stained moustaches, stared in blue-eyed incredulity at this arrogant stranger whose cheeks he had embraced just five minutes before.

Charlotte was trying her slow, uncertain English on me, and laughing, laughing as if to dispel the bleakness that was already turning the soft June day to something else entirely. Her three other children at home were on her mind, and she wanted to describe them to me: Jeannot and Monique, who were older than Cecette, and Riquet, the baby, who was just two. But Richard was not finished, and his voice rose louder now. "It's like the good old dowry system," he was saying to Papa. "If a girl hasn't got a *dot*, she can forget about marriage, isn't that so? And now this farce about grey suits! I swear, the whole damned society over here—" And "Hush," said Papa, his face gone suddenly congested above the winged collar of his shirt. "I won't 'hush!' " Richard said in loud abuse, and Charlotte stopped speaking at once and gently took her father's and her brother's hands and held them close. Jean's paralysis was crippling him more and more, she began telling Richard, and tears stood in her eyes now, either for Jean or for the acrimonious climate that was on the air. That was why he had not come to the dock. He was waiting for us all, not far, on a café terrace in the sun. "We're going to make another pilgrimage to Lourdes next month," Charlotte said. "You will come with us. It is a wonderful thing to see." Beyond us, Maman and a customs official were methodically searching through our foot locker for God knows what treasures, quite overlooking the treasures that were there. Maman was seeking for something resembling a grey suit, and the *douanier* paused a moment over Richard's stamp collection. But the copy of Lola's book,[1] in which her poem about the Negro woman whose baby was tossed into the flames of a burning house never ceased to sear the pages, was of no interest whatsoever to them. And the first editions of Pound, and Eliot, and Williams, and George Moore's *The Brook Kerith*, and Morton Schamberg's photograph of Mother carried inside a catalogue from Alfred Stieglitz's "291," they cast aside like chaff.

The long black limousine was spacious enough to hold all eight of us with ease, Jean, large, placid, with the face of an enormous child, manipulated his great bulk on two canes into the front seat beside

[1] *Sun-up*, by Lola Ridge, B. W. Huebsch, New York, 1919.

the chauffeur in beaked cap and uniform. Maman and Charlotte and I, in my blue challis dress with the little red roses all over it, sat in comfort on the deeply cushioned back seat. Between Maman and Charlotte I could glimpse Cecette's golden head, and her straight tanned legs, and her black patent leather pumps. The June sunlight came through the glass and lay like a lap robe over our knees. With every kilometre that fled behind us, my French became more and more inadequate, and presently I rode in tight-throated silence, staring at the backs of Richard and Marguerite and Papa, who sat before us on the folding seats. *Un tailleur gris*, I thought; *des tailleurs gris. Il a, elle a, ils ont, elles ont, des tailleurs gris.* But hadn't Bill Williams liked this blue dress when I wore it to Rutherford? Hadn't Gorham Munson time after time admired the brilliance of the chiffon scarf I wore? "We'll have to get her a hat of some kind in Rouen," Maman mused under her breath to Charlotte as we sped along the *route nationale.* "Otherwise it's impossible for her to go inside the cathedral with us." Then, in case I had overheard and understood, Maman leaned forward across Charlotte's lovely bosom and white ruffle, and across Cecette's smooth gleaming hair, and drew her lip back from her long teeth, and smiled her chipmunk smile at me. I could only turn my face away, for the pain in my throat was almost more than I could bear.

Certainly few parallels can be drawn between McAlmon's life and mine, but both of us (he in 1921 and I in 1923) found ourselves in similar predicaments. The moments of our daily lives had been placed suddenly in the hands of families-in-law of other nationalities, into the keeping of women and men we knew almost nothing about; and they, held static within the fixed boundaries, the fixed postures, of their own nights and days, became the custodians of our existences. It can be argued that this is not an unusual situation, and that young people in every generation, in every century, find themselves imprisoned in this way without honour and against their wills. But shock and pain and grievous disappointment are always exceptional when they are one's own, always monumentally without precedent. They twist the features of the inner face into unrecognizable grimaces, and they weight the heart with a leaden sorrow. But if we were the victims of these families, they were our victims as well. Many years later one of McAlmon's three devoted sisters, Victoria, wrote to Bill and Florence Williams: "I'd like, now that I can, to go over Bryher's first long conversation with me in Paris when she supposedly told me their story. Ah, well! I've wondered if I should record this. Such unconscious selfishness and inhumanity and such satisfaction with oneself doesn't much exist. Her great grief and sorrow for herself; as I stayed on it was the Ellermans I grieved for, after my brother, who was then still motivated by an admiration for her (Bryher's) intellect, and gallantry over her troubles—though he was alive to the many deceptions he had been subjected to."

In 1958 a reviewer named Dan Pinck was to write in the *New Republic* as follows: "By 1925, in the pre-dawn of our literary renaissance, McAlmon had already—and *first*, in some instances—published Ford Madox Ford, Mina Loy, Ezra Pound, Norman Douglas, Djuna Barnes, Havelock Ellis, Edith Sitwell, William Carlos Williams, H.D., James Joyce, Gertrude Stein, Wallace Gould, Marianne Moore, Marsden Hartley, Wallace Stevens, Kenneth Burke, Glenway Wescott, and Kay Boyle." (By 1923, as a matter of fact, McAlmon had published Ernest Hemingway's first book, *Three Stories and Ten Poems*). ". . . there have been few people, not excepting Gertrude Stein and Ezra Pound," Pinck wrote further about McAlmon, "whose efforts so helped to cast significant literary reputations."

All this is true, but none of it had anything to do with the pain and outrage within McAlmon's heart because of what his life had become. In 1921 he wrote from Paris to Bill Williams in Rutherford:

Then you'd better know this, Bill. I didn't tell you in New York because I thought it wasn't mine to tell. But Bryher doesn't mind. . . . The marriage is legal only, unromantic, and strictly an agreement. Bryher could not travel, and be away from home, unmarried. It was difficult being in Greece and other wilder places without a man. She thought I understood her mind, as I do somewhat, and faced me with the proposition. Some other things I shan't mention I knew without realizing. Well, you see I took on the proposition. . . . Bryher's a complexity, and needs help, and appearance doesn't matter except in a little way that I can think above. You can use your imagination and perhaps know what I mean. I don't like pretence, unless it's necessary for other people than myself. Because if I'm a damn fool, that's what I am, and I accept it, and am not the one who created the various conditions of life, and attitudes, that are displeasing to me. So more and more I look, accept, learn to not feel morbid about things. . . . I'd like to have everything break— O to hell with that.

Of this period in Bob's life Victoria wrote in 1959 (to Bill and Florence Williams) :

[There is] another note, not to anyone, about how lied to he had been from the start, what a blow to him this was in London, and the distaste he had for Bryher's crowd there. . . . When I met her in '23, while she wished for my favourable opinion and solicited my sympathy . . . I thought her arrogant, very conceited and pontifical ; determined to have her way. . . . I found Sir John and Lady E. much humaner and really suffering from their peculiar daughter. . . . How could Bob have stayed in that situation even the short time he did? . . .

In France, in that same year, my own family drama was unfolding. The trip to St. Malo was to take two days or more. Because of Jean, it had to be taken leisurely. But it was right after lunch that first day in Rouen (perhaps because of the extravagance of the food and the headiness of the wine) that the situation was bitterly defined. We had walked to the open square to see where Jeanne d'Arc had burned, and Jean, leaning on his canes, had jerked his head toward some cigarette ashes lying between the ancient cobblestones. "*B'en*, it must have been about here!" he said, and he glanced around at us all in a parody of triumph. "Look, Lolotte," he said to Charlotte, his smile broadening under his brown moustaches. "It must have been about here that the *pucelle* burned!" Cecette asked if she could gather the ashes up in her handkerchief and take them home to Jeannot and Monique, but Maman cawed out that it was only a joke, a funny *blague*, that Papa Jean had made.

And then Papa drew Richard aside, his hands clasped under the tails of his coat as they walked down the street ahead of us, and he spoke the family's mind. They had no money at all, he made clear, but they did have standards. It was only Charlotte, through her fortunate marriage, who had wealth, he pointed out, but they would borrow the money on their house in the country, if necessary, to get me *un tailleur gris*. I was walking with Charlotte and Marguerite, slowly, slowly, because of Jean's pace behind us, as he struggled along on his canes between Maman and Cecette. We walked by the pretty façades of the hotels, with their window boxes of geraniums, and the cafés, all named for the dead peasant girl, while Papa said out of earshot these things he had to say. "Ladies don't put paint on their mouths, and they don't wear earrings as big as cartwheels," was part of what he said to Richard. "On certain occasions ladies wear small diamonds or seed pearls in their ears"; the wine perhaps giving him the courage to say it all now. "Tell her to take those white loops off, and to wipe the red paint off her mouth. God knows what people passing in the street are thinking, or what Jean's chauffeur is going to tell the other servants when he gets back!"

Maman selected a hat of white straw lace in the bazaar for me, and I wore it rather grimly perched on top of my head, for either because of my hair or the size of my skull, I can never wear hats in any other way. The family group of us walked out of the sunlight of the afternoon and into the twilight of the cathedral, and Richard stormed past the basin of holy water and stood fuming in the tall shadows of the nave. "Ladies don't put paint on their mouths. They don't wear hoops, like gipsy earrings, in their ears," he repeated Papa's words to me. "Ladies don't knot crimson scarves around their necks! I've had enough!" he said. Ah, but what if I had got off the ship with charred cork smeared on my eyelids, I thought, relieved that at least that had been spared the family. Hadn't Glenway said once that the great white hoops of my Woolworth earrings were worth coming from uptown down to East Ninth Street to cast an eye on? But perhaps, somewhere within him, he too had taken a decision and passed a judgment on me as they had.

There were to be many more times in the years ahead that I would stand in silence in the cathedral of Rouen, but because of the wine in my veins and my falling tears, this time alone the wooden St. John, with his painted beard, became a living man, with hot blood running in his veins. There he knelt with his arms outstretched to those who sinned or had not sinned, his dark eyes looking deeply, deeply, into my weakly crying eyes; and to me it seemed that Bill Williams had looked with like compassion on those who wrote or did not write, across the candlelight at Sunday night suppers in Rutherford. This time alone each separate Virgin in her hallowed place was Mother, was Lola, was Mother, was Lola again, their glass hearts flickering in their open breasts, while the small child of all credence and incorruptibility lay cradled in their arms. Marianne Moore had perhaps never spoken directly to me, but the commitment of each of us to what our mothers were made her, for this one time, my intimate. In the cool, dark church she became Ste. Thérèse, in whom every unworthy passion had been replaced by qualities as clear as light, and who leaned now across the tongues of the chapel candles and pronounced my name with love.

I feared that in a moment my sobs would tear across the soaring, awesome sanctity of this strange place, and that Richard's family, kneeling in one of the front pews, would turn their heads, shocked, grieved, outraged, each wishing, with varying intensity, that I had slipped from the top deck of the *De Grasse* while playing shuffleboard, or, having finally understood, that I would leave now and burn, burn, down to the last handful of ash left in the public square. The next morning, as tough and determined as McAlmon, I put my lipstick and earrings away, and I did not put them on again for a long time. And when Charlotte kissed my cheeks with singular emotion at breakfast on the hotel terrace that faced the square of heretics, she whispered: "Blue is your colour, you know. Blue, my little sister, not grey."

Robert McAlmon

1923

The night of July 13, 1923, was not yet over, and, without knowing how I got there, I found myself at Bricktop's in Montmartre. Flossie Martin, Sylvia Gough, a young man she called California, Nina Hamnett, Man Ray, and Kiki were there too.[1] The place

[1] On pp. 48, 49, 50, 51, of his book, *This Must Be the Place*, as told to Morrill Cody, with an introduction by Ernest Hemingway (Lee Furman, Inc., New York, 1927), James Charters (Jimmie the Barman) writes:

It is perhaps remarkable that the leaders and organizers of Montparnasse were largely women, from the famed Kiki to the inspiring Sylvia Beach, who, as far as I know, never entered a bar in her life, though, as she told me once, "we have always served the same clients, you, Jimmie, with drinks, I with books." The two who took the main spotlight, however, were Flossie Martin and Nina Hamnett.

Flossie, pretty and very jolly, certainly won in numbers of adherents, though it was whispered that Nina won in quality. . . . Flossie, a former chorus girl in New York, had been sent to Paris to develop her really fine voice. But she did little studying and finally stopped entirely. The fascination of the Dôme *terrasse* in the daytime and the Dingo at night were too much for her. But Flossie was not selfish in her pleasures. . . . Many a chap, temporarily down and out, was helped financially by Flossie, though she had no large sums at her disposal.

. . . The other stage director of the Dingo and Dôme was Nina Hamnett, English painter of note but remembered in Montparnasse largely for her singing of ballads like "Rollicking Bill the Sailor" (original version!), "She Was Poor but She Was Honest," and many others of the kind. . . . Around her she attracted a group of admirers which included some of the intellectual lights of Montparnasse, and others with resounding titles and names. In fact, it became rather a joke at the Dingo, for the telephone would ring constantly for Nina, and the waiter would announce in a loud voice that the Prince of something or the Count of something else wished to speak to Miss Hamnett. Nina had great respect for titles and famous names.

was crowded, but we didn't ask each other's names at Bricktop's necessarily. I sat for an hour at Beatrice Lillie's table, and didn't know it until Brick told me who she was, after she had gone.

Buddy, the trap drummer, came in looking cheerfully insinuating. He insinuated he wanted a gin and had it, and sat down to his drums to play and sing, "I'm in love again, and I can't rise above it". Buddy could get more music out of a drum than most orchestras do out of all their instruments. An Englishman walked over to Buddy with a half bottle of champagne. Back went Buddy's black head, his eyes glistened. The man lifted the bottle to pour champagne down Buddy's eager throat, and as he gulped he beat the drums into a madder rhythm. He gurgled down the half bottle of champagne, and his audience went wild with enthusiasm at the rhythmic beating of his drums. By seven in the morning most of the other guests had departed, but Sylvia, Nina, Flossie, and I lingered. Other Negroes came in from other orchestras about town, and two tap dancers stood at the bar drinking and arguing about their degrees of talent.

The piano player was a high-yellow boy who played classical music beautifully as well as jazz. He complained mildly to me that if he were of my race he'd be a famous concert pianist, but as he was he didn't have a chance. His name was Leon Crutcher, and presently he left the bar and I saw him outside talking to a French girl. Bricktop looked annoyed and worried. She said the French girl was ruining a good man, the best pianist she'd ever had. Brick wanted to close the place, so a throng of us went on to the Capitol for food. A crippled Englishman with an Italian woman was raising hell with the waiter, and the Englishman finally brandished a sword

---

But there was another side to Nina, the sailor side, I might call it. You see, the United States government in 1924 decided to help the tourist trade in France by sending there on protracted visits the U.S.S.S. *Pittsburgh,* U.S.S.S. *Memphis,* and U.S.S.S. *Detroit.* For days all Montparnasse was infested with sailors and petty officers moving in groups around Flossie and Nina. Nina actually wore a sailor uniform in Montparnasse and to Montmartre on one occasion. Both girls determined to do the honours for France and devoted themselves to this task with a thorough good will!

. . . Joe Zelli, the king of the night-club district, finally offered Flossie a job. She was to be in his club every night, since her reputation and gaiety would always attract a crowd. I have been told Zelli did the biggest business of his successful career during the six months Flossie stayed at his club. And poor Flossie never earned any money for her work! Not that Zelli did not pay her a salary, but because, at the end of the month, she had drawn her money and more in providing drinks for friends who were "temporarily under financial stress".

which he had in his cane. It looked dangerous, but one waiter caught his arms from the back, and they took the sword from him. At another table four Italians were singing street songs, in rivalry. A fight started there too, and they too were put out.

We had each of us finished a beefsteak and were preparing to leave when Bricktop came into the place, a grim, frightened look on her face. She was carrying a huge bouquet of flowers. "Knock on wood," she said hoarsely. "Crutcher's shot dead. The best musician in Paris."

"What? Who shot him?" voices asked.

"He was fighting with that French chippy outside my place," Bricktop said. "They went home and she threatened to shoot him if he cut up with other women. He asked her how about her with other men, and when she pointed a gun at him he dared her to shoot. She shot, and she shot straight. I got these flowers for him. There ain't going to be no sleeping for me this day. I'm getting to think Paris is hoodooed."

People exclaimed that it wasn't possible. He'd been playing the piano not more than half an hour back. We contributed money to buy Crutcher flowers, and I got out of the Capitol quickly. I didn't want to go to bed now. I couldn't have slept; nor could I stay there with the boys from Zelli's and the Palermo orchestras. All these Negro boys looked pale around the gills, and they said they were "superstitious" about French girls. Several of them had white mistresses, but now they felt cowed, and they agreed among themselves that the French girl would not be sentenced. I started to walk towards the markets, hoping to run into somebody I knew or to pick up some strangers. A gendarme, a taxi driver, or a market worker would do, or else the barman or cashier at a bistro. Fortune willed that I should encounter Hilaire Hiler and Wynn Holcomb. Wynn was wearing a flowing cape and looked very tiny. He could never decide in those days whether he was Hamlet, a toreador, or a tragic clown, so he played a bit of each. Seeing me, they stopped, and Wynn greeted me airily in what he thought was Elizabethan English. "What ho, let me unloose my dagger, and I will at thee! But, I say, theah you are, ole chappie. Boys, what we need is a drink. That's the password, and ho, if a varlet lets me I will run him through!"

"What'll it be?" I said in the bistro we entered.

"It's all venereal to me. You can make your own injection," Wynn said blithely. I was drinking gin now, having drunk myself into a second or third soberness. From now on, nothing could make me drunk.

Hiler duck-waddled girlishly to the bar and took a bow, and then pranced about making coquettish lurches as though he were going to break into a toe dance, interpreting the spirit of spring. To see Wynn and Hiler together is to think of comedy, and burlesque, and slapstick, and apparently the bistro *patron* and his customers did, for they offered us more drink. We were all drinking cognac when Kenneth Adams discovered us, and he too was intent upon going to the markets. Hiler and Wynn had other plans, so we separated.

It was a mistily glistening morning, the dazzle seeming to splinter before our befuddled eyes. We knew we were too late for the great show of meats, vegetables, and flowers, but as we walked we spoke of the wholesale market's smell and beauty, and the soundness of the market's working types. We talked of how Breughel painted fishes, game, meats, and common, low-down people. Kenneth got ecstatic about how happy his discovery of Masaccio, Piero della Francesca, Giotto, Cimabue, and other Italian painters had made him. We agreed that we didn't care for Raphael and his floating angels. If the acclaimed and ancient masters could have heard us, only some would have been pleased. We were as careless in expressing our disdains as we were in acclaiming our enthusiasms, and at every bistro we stopped to have another cognac.

Trucks, horse-drawn, and carts, man-drawn, passed us. Busy workers were cleaning up the debris and closing their stalls. A smell of horses and of human flesh, fresh with earth, was about. The day's heat was not yet sultry. "Hell, why should these people give a damn about us? Damn art. These are the real thing. Who in hell are we?" asked Adams, swaggering.

We bought flowers in quantities at one stand because the old lady was very good-natured and said she wanted to get rid of her stock and close her stand and get home. They were heavy to carry, so when we got as far as the vegetable stalls we decided to take a taxi, call on Eileen Lane, and present her with the flowers. However, as we ambled on, we encountered three women sitting near their piles of vegetables, each on a sack. One was a nice, nut-skinned and wrinkled old gal with a merry cackle and no teeth. The other two were buxom and good-natured. Bowing gallantly, Adams presented the toothless old lady with his flowers. It was a good idea. I presented mine to the other two. The women laughed heartily and compli-

mented us for being young and happy and *si beau*. They insisted that
we each accept bundles of their vegetables in return for the flowers.
So we left carrying radishes, carrots, and onions, and they also were
a problem to dispose of.

Going down the street, we were hailed by two street girls. One of
them had no middle to her nose; the other was passable-looking.
But the thin, monkey-faced girl had the quicker wit. We agreed to
buy them coffee and croissants, while we had *soupe à l'oignon*. The
girls suggested that we go home with them, and mentioned prices,
beginning at thirty francs and coming down to five, since the
gentlemen were so charming. We thanked them and suggested
another morning, as this was a gala day and we had other appointments. Instead, would they accept the vegetables? They did, for the
vegetables would make a soup. We bade them goodbye, declaring
them fine girls, and not at all mercenary.

It was past ten before we arrived at the Dôme terrace, and a few
elderly women were having their morning coffee. The livelier and
young foreigners were still certainly sleeping if they had as yet gone
to bed. Hiler and Wynn returned from wherever they had been.
Eileen Lane sat down to tell us how feeble she felt after last night.
Thelma Wood and Berenice Abbott turned up, and Adams, having
descended to the retreat, returned to report that Flossie Martin was
asleep at one of the tables inside. I became wise and grabbed a taxi,
knowing that Flossie would waken and descend upon us all, insisting
upon drink and more drink.

That night was the beginning of the season. It lasted on into the
middle of August and left me wan and weary. For once I was almost
glad to contemplate a sojourn in London, where I planned to rest,
work, retire early, drink not so much, and be alone with my thoughts.

Bryher was on the train with Hilda Doolittle and the infant. Bryher,
having educational theories, managed the "Lump's" upbringing,
and already the child, not five, could name all of the countries,
continents, and main cities of the world, so Bryher claimed. The
child also had a firm grasp on history, but she refused to show off for
me. She stared stolidly when Bryher told her to do her piece, and
finally blurted out, "You're a liar, I'm not your experiment. I'm a
wild Indian. I'll skin you alive."

As it was one of Bryher's cherished ideas that "the horde" is
dumb and should be lied to, she was delighted, but said fiercely,

"Hippo, hippo, if the Lump is naughty." She meant she would use an oft-threatened hippopotamus whip on the child, but the infant's eyes flicked amusement and she reasserted, "You're a liar." Later Bryher confided in a manner far more infantile than the child's that she and the Lump were twins. At times the Lump, who could use the typewriter, wrote me letters which were marvels of Gertrude Steinian prose, if a bit more prehistoric and bloodthirsty. She wrote when bored with Bryher's eternal instruction and thought I could save her.

Bryher, however, was persistent and, indeed, all her ideas of education seemed directed at having the child her "twin" in order to repeat her own beloved complexes, aversions, inhibitions, phobias, and manias, all of which she cherished and groomed and pampered more than either Stein or Joyce do their darling words. Whenever Bryher was particularly approving of Hilda or myself she would assert that we too were her twins or her brother monkeys. Her idea of a loving relationship was somewhat the same as her father's. The beloved was to be reduced to a state of shrieking, trembling hysteria, and then she would be conciliatory and say, "There, there, calm, calm. It's a nice kitten," or "Mother darling," in tones calculated to bring apoplexy upon the already infuriated lady, who was far too emotional and natural a human for all this involved tosh.

When Mamma darling's rages stormed through several days there was hushed silence and commiseration throughout the household. Mamma darling could not believe that they were her children or relatives. They were made of stone, and there would be no more of their maddening talk about business or education or books at her table during these periods. She would relax with me, because I was seldom about, and not without guile. When Bryher started her tactics on me and I felt helpless fury, I slipped away to the nearest pub. Bryher then would call on Hilda and, realizing that the solid Lump was too much her own emotional age to be made hysterical, she tackled Hilda, and always produced results. By merely mentioning experiences of the war years or an unhappy episode in Hilda's past, and dwelling upon it long enough, she soon had the high-strung Hilda acting much like a candidate for the straitjacket. She did this, she said, because of her own thwarted childhood. *They* hadn't let her have a carpentering set when she was a child, for fear she might cut herself. *They* hadn't let her have playmates; *they* hadn't let her stray away from a nurse or a governess. *They* hadn't; *they* were repeating the same programme on her brother. I was dismayed at my own lack of observation and intuition, that I had not at first noted what a complete child she was emotionally and as regards her capacity to meet "normal" people or experiences. Children and old ladies she encountered without becoming stony-eyed and silent. When introduced to some of my friends she was quite apt to stare past them, without response.

Nevertheless she had a capacity that then impressed me: memory. It is said that her father could remember the name of every one of his ships, their present cargoes and whereabouts, and the names of all the crews' officers. Bryher could scan a book and "photograph the page" with her eye. Months later she could synopsize the book perfectly and quote verbatim entire passages, and of a large book which she had "photographed" in perhaps half an hour's time. It took me several years to decide that she had memory rather than correlating intelligence. In conversation she did not converse; she expounded. Gradually meeting her friends, one of them Havelock Ellis, and reading books she delighted to hand me, I realized that she was an amazing example of the memory mind. There are, I suppose, compensations for whatever type of mind a person may have, but surely the mere memory mind is a great barrier to human relationships. Some people claim to be able to do without them mainly; I'm not such a person. Cities and rooms mean a great deal and have their personalities, and I quickly leave the ones of either that are depressing, but places are not enough. Some people live before they think, and when they think it is connected with an alive reality, and it is from such that the Breughels, Cervantes, Shakespeares, and Dantes, too, emerge. Their thinking is not mere cerebration whirling in space about some metaphysical point, such as Stephen Dedalus saying, "Thought is the thought of thought." Or Gertrude Stein saying, "A rose is a rose is a rose." Of course Miss Toklas says, "Miss Stein always says what she means, etc.," but it doesn't mean much and neither Miss Stein nor Miss Toklas can give these assertions a mystic significance. It is the arrested-development thought of a grown person still repeating again and again, as does a child.

Her Ladyship met Bryher and me at Victoria Station and all was sweetness and charm and love, for now I was her dear boy, one of the children. That was all right with me, because I was and am decidedly fond of her Ladyship. A nice dinner was awaiting us, for

Sir John fancied himself a connoisseur of food and wine. There was caviar served with sweet pancakes over which heavy cream was poured. There followed fresh salmon with a rich sauce, and partridge, and then apple or raspberry pie, also to be served with cream. It was a meal to dream about.

I ate that meal, but it was to me the nightmare of a delirium patient. My last night in Paris I had drunk much and was seeing green and feeling nausea. Nevertheless, I nibbled at each of the dishes. Thank fate the butler quickly removed my plate. Poor H., the butler. He did not last long after that. They had to get rid of him because of some scandal. I could hazard a guess what it was as he used tenderly to let me in at night, since Sir John never allowed the front door to be other than bolted and chained shut. Sometimes I would be a bit on with drink, but H. never uttered a word, and next day was always quick to remove my plate of scarcely touched food.

Over the weekend we went to Eastbourne, Bryher and Sir John in the Rolls-Royce, her Ladyship, John, and me in the Lanchester. The Lanchester had a roll which upset her Ladyship, and her Ladyship upset was something formidable, as I realized full blast over the weekend. I was the one member of the party who did not "have it given them" good and proper. The two, Sir John and Bryher, appeared to like punishment. John and I kept ourselves silent and scarce, except at mealtimes.

As Mamma darling went upstairs to her room, very much the pouter-pigeon dowager, she was a bit peevish, but guests were in for tea and she was then charming. At dinner Dada was solicitous about her health, but she silenced him with a haughty glare. We all understood. Mamma's deafness might be worse tonight and it might not, but if she heard she would say to stop talking nonsense. If she didn't hear she would think we were saying things we didn't want her to hear. I caught Sir John's look of appeal and talked so that she could hear, but always of what I had heard from my family or friends, and Mamma was gracious to me. She took the attitude that I was the only flesh and blood one of them all, who were in league against her and me, the only two who had impulses. She hoped I was putting some sense into Dolly at last, and when was she to have a dear little grandchild? She'd take care of it. Neither of us would have the sense to know how to take care of a child properly.

After dinner Sir John and I had cigars, coffee, and brandy together, and when we were to join the ladies Sir John discreetly pleaded tiredness and went to bed. A look between vexation and triumph crossed her Ladyship's face, but she consented to have a brandy with me and glanced disdainfully at Bryher, crouched like a monkey over a book. "Poring over print again," her Ladyship scoffed. Bryher looked much as the Lump once looked while breaking eggs over Hilda's sittingroom carpet, but she was silent. I was optimist enough to think that the storm might have subsided, but nay, nay.

As I came downstairs for breakfast next day I heard her voice in the hall. Sir John was seated at a reading table, back to the fireplace. Her Ladyship fronted him on the other side of the table. Her face was purple with fury, and she was pounding the table and Sir John looked cowed. He didn't venture a single conciliatory "Mamma darling".

"How dare you?" she raged. "I won't be chivvied! I won't have it! Do you hear me? I won't stand any more of you planning your plans and ignoring mine!"

I managed to slip through the hall unseen.

"Go back to your musty museum in London but leave the management of my little cottage to myself!" She relaxed, seeing Sir John cowed, and turned away haughtily. "There will be no grouse served at my table this day. You can throw the filthy fowl away. Give it to the servants. You will content yourself with the fare I order. And, mark me, if you dare wake me for one of your beastly runs this afternoon, I shall go for you. Go ahead with your filthy letters. Business, business, and never a thought for your family! Let those letters alone. Breakfast has been announced. You will not keep others waiting any more in my household than you permit us to in your own."

Breakfast was a very quiet affair. And that day her Ladyship did not go for a motor run to Winchelsea or Rye, and Sir John did not attempt to chivvy her. He did not insist, but looked grateful when I also did not care to go for a run. He believed I had some ability to pacify her Ladyship.

Her Ladyship came to the tearoom before the others had returned from their run. Perhaps she was refreshed by a nap. It was drizzling outside. Eastbourne depressed me violently; I was wobbly from late nights in Paris, and the whole situation had me apathetic with wonder. I am not unused to the rows and rackets of family life; they could so easily have been non-interfering in each other's lives, but each of the three seemed to think it necessary to check up on every detail and minute of the other's existence.

Her Ladyship seated herself before a table and started knitting. She looked mild, and complained that Bryher would not appreciate the dress which she was knitting once it was done. Why did she bother? Then she looked at me. "Don't look so sad, Robert. You cut me to the heart. I know how you feel. Damn those downs which stand back there as though ready to fall upon and smother us! They'll be the death of me. But if I do say it myself, I have never complained. I believe in letting people go their own ways and bother the opinions of others!"

I made some response, and her Ladyship monologued on, and the sad part of it was that by temperament, and allowed a freer life, she would have been a non-interfering person. The eternal vigilance of Sir John and her deafness had made a closed-in person out of as spontaneous and impulsive and humanly affectionate a woman as I have ever known. I recall how she struck pity into me the first night of our meeting. She had come to the bedroom to see her darlings in bed together, and leaned over to kiss my neck. Then I realized that she was starved for emotional outlet. There wasn't any doubt that Sir John was infatuated with her, but she was more companionable and affectionate and demonstrative. She was out of luck. Finance was the obsession which ruled the household.

Yet Sir John had a merry and boyish streak in him. He loved to talk of actresses who were dainty women; of adventure books he had read in childhood. His eyes grew misty when he told me of the painting of geese upon the downs. Years before he and Mamma (there was no title then and no great wealth) had stayed in a tiny village and each day Mamma fed the geese with bread crumbs. Even the geese found her charming, was his version. A painter did the scene and Sir John had bought it for her. "I must say she never cared for it," he sighed, and added, "Mamma can be so very, very charming when she feels that way. She isn't well these days."

This same man would count sixpences where most men think half-crowns. At one time he gave me a cheque for £7 10s. I was curious. Why not five pound, or ten pound, or why anything at all? Was he in some way attempting to express the extent of his approval or disapproval? He surely would have gone into a panic had he known the life I actually led; and he doubtless would have cut Bryher's income in an attempt to discipline me. As her Ladyship said, he persisted and persisted in whatever idea he had. She might escape going for a run one day, but the next and the next, for all the weeks and months and years, he would be back, insisting. Bryher had the same monomaniacal capacity to be rebuffed, screamed at, wept at, but to persist, long after one had forgotten the idea upon which she was insisting. I managed to slip away, but she got at the Lump and through her at H.D. She got at me too, but I knew someday soon I'd go away for good.

One night during a cheerful dinner some man's name was mentioned and a bright expression flashed over Sir John's face and his eyes suddenly lit up. He turned to Bryher. "Dolly, that man once did something against me. I waited fifteen years, but he had to leave England. Now I will let him return."

Bryher's face beamed also with pride. That type of emotion, the vengeful, she understood, and she understood the possessive instinct: for money and for people. The mania for management and directing she also understood, but her education had paralysed her abilities in that direction. The old biblical Father Abraham, guarding his flocks and ready to sacrifice his son because of his own megalomaniac, immortal-soul and property-desiring will, had left them his heritage.

Back in London I met Wyndham Lewis and we dined together. I told him that her Ladyship had agreed to visit his studio and see his work, and we arranged the day. Later she might ask him for tea and he could meet Sir John. During the course of the evening Lewis mentioned a man who was the son of one of Sir John's shipping-line managers. "He says that Sir John hasn't a friend in the city, he's so hard about money."

I was irritated. That wasn't right. Rend the capitalist as one might, Sir John had friends. Possibly they were more or less in his employ, but just as possibly they had come up in the world along with him, and he was loyal. I had met several at his dinners who certainly had not only respect but fondness for him, and he was often "Jack" to her Ladyship when she was feeling capricious or coquettish. He inspired more than affection in her. He gave out quantities of money, and he didn't go in for the snobbishness of public philanthropies or endowing artists or institutions. I assured Lewis that never would Sir John be persuaded to sit for a portrait, that he had better content himself with doing one, possibly, of her Ladyship. Lewis, however, would not believe that Sir John had a positive terror about being photographed. But I had tried to take a snapshot of the family group once and had seen the expression which came into his eyes.

One morning her Ladyship and I drove to Lewis' studio. He showed her his paintings, and she made little comment. When he showed his sketches, however, she indicated pleasure. Coming away, she declared they were as fine, delicate, and strong as the works of old masters which she had seen in Florence. "But of course I'm no artist, Robert. I'm just a fat old woman. I'm sorry for Mr. Lewis. I wanted to pitch in and clean his musty-smelling studio. He is too much alone, I'm sure, and he needs friends. Something has made him very bitter, but there is little I can do. Have him to tea on Sunday. I will try and prepare the way with Sir John. He will do more for you than you know, Robert. He is really fond of you. I knew that when he gave you the diamond tiepin which was a gift from his own mother."

I broke the news to Lewis and told him that her Ladyship had expressed a sympathy for him. He smiled, pleased, but scoffed, too. "She is a sentimental old woman."

Yes, yes: a sentimental woman? And decidedly no. She was capable of saying and meaning and living. "Blast my children's freedom and happiness. I had them for my own pleasure. If I had my way I'd burn every book they possess and keep them by me." The children had to fight not only Sir John but her for whatever freedom they got, but it was Sir John's regime which made the tyranny. She was a coquettish, temperamental, and capricious woman, with charm and a tremendous attraction for men; there was a maternal streak in her, but she wasn't a mother-woman. It was interesting to watch her size up Lewis and his paintings, which she disliked. "They are dry and harsh, and not real to that man. They gave me the creeps," was her judgment. Abstract they certainly were not, however Lewis yearned to have them so. He painted tyros or robots, thinking by thus doing mechanical figures he would avoid being literary or illustrative.

The Sunday on which Lewis was to come to tea arrived, and to my fury Aunts X and Y came as well, and Cousins so-and-so, all of whom were barely on speaking terms with one another. They stayed, each trying to outstay the other, and Aunt Y smelled that somebody new was to be in for tea.

Lewis did not arrive and my rage at the aunts was mounting into a fury to hurl at him. He had been told that Sir John was intent upon punctuality, and was to have come at four. It was now six. Her Ladyship said she must rest before dinner, and the aunts departed. I started downstairs. On the stairway was Lewis, looking as frightened and awkward as a schoolboy. He stroked his scant hair, which had been oiled and brushed to look more ample. He indicated his shoes, which had been polished. "Do I look all right? I'm late. Primping," he whispered.

My rage sank out of me. This, Lewis, the vitriolic satirist, the man who advocated an explosive revolution, and who was scathingly scornful of academic art, this man had been waiting outside, afraid to ring the bell! I had thought he would look at the paintings about and be discreetly ironical.

Getting her Ladyship, who was also angry that he had failed to keep the appointment, I explained why he was late. She grew charming and chuckled. "I knew I understood that man. He does need somebody to look after him."

Sir John knew that Lewis had arrived and was in the big drawing room. It is difficult to say which was more afraid of the other, Sir John of Lewis, or Lewis of Sir John. In the City Sir John had heard of Lewis as a violent modern with a trenchant wit, and Lewis knew of Sir John's financial genius, which he told me he didn't respect. Lewis, however, is not the only mythomaniac among the geniuses or the megalomaniacs.

Her Ladyship was charming and sympathetic to Lewis, who was as fidgety as a country yokel. I tried to help Sir John by talking of Paris and the Salon, informing Lewis that Sir John had always been more an admirer of French painting than of English. I don't think there were ever two men more relieved when I suggested to Lewis that we go out and have a drink, as I'd have to return soon to dress for dinner.

The next day Sir John said he would speak to some of his editors in the City, and that if Mr. Lewis was willing he might do sketches of celebrities or society people. Lewis was willing, and did some twelve drawings, I believe, only two or three of which appeared. He was disappointed not to do a portrait of Sir John, but I think one or the other would have had a nervous breakdown had he attempted the painting. Months later Lewis was bitter because more of his drawings had not appeared. He had been paid for them. Sir John gave as explanation that the editors found Lewis demanding, and also that letters had come in from all over the country from highly respectable ladies and gentleman demanding that they cease publishing the sketches. They were modern art, and subscribers would have nothing to do with such. They would cancel their subscriptions.

I can well believe that the editors found Lewis difficult. Many of his friends told me of his difficult moments. He did not turn so on me for about five years, except to hint that I was responsible for the rest of the sketches not appearing. He never would believe that I knew none of the editors, and had wangled that little consignment through her Ladyship. He wouldn't have it that I was walking very carefully to avoid having Sir John plan my life.

Kay Boyle

1923

On one side of the road that linked village to village was Charlotte's and Jean's château, with a double row of poplars beginning just inside the tall bronze carriage gate and proceeding the length of the drive. It was placed close to the water, this long and rather severely bourgeois dwelling, with no graciousness or nobility in its countenance. Between it and the river a millpond lay like a great shining shield. But the mill tower no longer served a purpose. The iron frame of the wheel it housed was flaked with rust, and the wooden spokes were pale with lichen. Beyond the sluice gates of the wall enclosing the pond was a wild chaos of boulders, cast there on the day of creation, it might have been, or massed there in turmoil when the ice floes pressed down from the north. Beyond these giant rocks lay the riverbank, half sand, half sucking mud, and finally the narrow river Rance that wound slowly through the flowering fields towards St. Malo and the sea.

But whenever the tide ran in from the Gulf of St. Malo, its waters thrust the river back upon itself, and the whole look of the landscape changed. At Mont St. Michel, Papa explained, the tide rushed in across the quicksands, and the fields where the sheep grazed, at three times the speed of a galloping horse, but here, having a longer way to go, it was more circumspect. The tide came rippling and swelling in twice in each lunar day, bearing salt water from the English Channel deeply into the French countryside, gently broadening the river to almost twice its size. "Except at the time of the equinox!" Papa shouted as we walked along the edge of it, and he gesticulated wildly so that I could picture the fury of its advance. "In March, and again in September, the sea comes right across the millpond wall and up onto the château grounds!" he cried out, as if aghast at its effrontery.

In the centre of the current of the river Rance, slightly upstream from the château, was an island dark with trees and fern, although there seemed no way for vegetation to get a foothold on its granite sides. "There're the ruins of a castle at the top," Charlotte told me as we walked together along the millpond wall. She said we would all row across in fishing dories one day soon and have a picnic, and Monique and Jeannot took hands and waltzed for joy. But Maman would not listen to talk about a trip to the island until Richard should have relinquished his copy of Anatole France's *La Révolte des Anges*. His name was on the Index, Maman cawed out, and, aside from that, he had married his cook. "His secretary," Richard said. "His cook," snapped Maman. "Secretary," Richard repeated, and Maman answered: "Cook."

But the prejudice went more deeply than that, Richard said to Charlotte one day after we had been swimming at high tide in the river Rance. After all, Papa was a retired army colonel, and *l'affaire Dreyfus* had been a living issue in his time. Don't forget that at Zola's funeral, Richard said, Anatole France had extolled Zola as the defender of a Jew. He had said of Zola: "Let us envy him, for he brought honour to his country and to the world by that one single noble act." Richard was quoting from memory Anatole France's words, and now he said: "That single act, my dearest sister, was Zola's *J'accuse*." Charlotte sat rubbing herself dry with a great, soft, white towel in the sun, and she whispered, "Yes," out of tenderness, not wanting the family to hear. "Anatole France said that Zola's genius and his heart had made the greatest of all destinies for him," Richard went on with it, but because the family had taken up residence inside us all and stubbornly refused to be evicted by any word, or sign, or the force of any imponderable authority, his voice was dark and bitter. "France said that in Zola had lived for a moment the conscience of all humanity." And with increasing bitterness Richard added: "Excepting, of course, for the conscience of our dear parents." To this Charlotte, rubbing her full, tanned arms and throat with the towel, answered in a whisper: "Yes, yes, I know."

This was reality now, this impenetrably sealed universe of the family's daily life. It was an existence strangely, almost fatally, without music. Only on the Quatorze Juillet when the martial music of the bands playing in the village squares floated over the silently dreaming countryside, increasing in volume and decreasing with the shifting breeze, did the family lift their heads and acknowledge the presence of a manifestation that they could not see. There had been nights in Atlantic City, when I was nine or ten, that I had lain in bed and listened to a record of Bach's Concerto for Two Violins that Mother played downstairs, and wept and wept that the man who had found this vocabulary of courage had had to die. "Where is his grave?" I asked my mother once, and she said people had forgotten and made a wagon road across where it had been. And there had been nights in Cincinnati when, a few years older, I heard the military bands playing with false and terrible cheer in the streets as the recruits went off to war. I had beat the bed with my fists then, and cried tears of rage that young men must march off to this artful and calculated accompaniment to places where wagon roads would be laid across their bones. The musical silence of Pleudihen, except for the trumpets and drums of that one July night and day, seemed to me metaphor for the death of the spirit in this reality that we were required to accept as if it were our own.

The family's modest house stood on the inland side of the road, its rose trees and strawberry beds and carefully raked gravel path enclosed by a high stone wall. From the road the public could not see what was taking place in the garden or on the ground floor of this rigid, straight-faced house. (That the public here consisted of a peasant passing with his horse and plough, or of workmen cycling by, or of families walking home from mass, was of no matter. The family had its privacy.) By the end of the first week I had learned to do my part in the morning ritual of flinging one's sheets and blankets into the sunshine across the window sill. This was a profoundly mystic rite, performed in order to purify linen and soul and flesh of whatever sinful memories lingered of the night before.

Every morning I carried the chamber pot down two flights of stairs, with a towel laid over it, and emptied it carefully in the one toilet in the house. Only ten years before, Papa would explain to me as I stood on the landing with the covered receptacle held perilously in my hands, the *cabinet* had dwelt in style in its own little gabled home in the back garden. At that time there had been only the well to supply the house with water, but now there was a faucet of running water in the kitchen, not as good, probably, as the plumbing in New York, Papa said, but good enough for honest people. But in Charlotte's château there were two handsome *salles de bain*, one for her and Jean, and one for the children, but that took money, said Papa, and he rubbed his thumb and forefinger together. As for the château *cabinets*, there were six toilet seats, six in a row, in the ground-floor *cour*. The openings started with one large enough for Jean and diminished seat by seat to Riquet's size. The wood the entire length of these *cabinets* was solid mahogany, Papa said with pride, and the bowls were pure porcelain. The handles, he demonstrated, also of diminishing size, which you raised in order to make contact with the cesspool below, were of pewter. "Heirlooms, antiques," Papa said through his white moustaches. The Americans might look on them with contempt, he said, for the Americans had no use for anything that lasted, and these pewter handles were just as good as the day they were made, nearly two hundred years ago.

This, and everything else I learned in the months there, was reality. In the long afternoons I learned with Annick to make darns as faultless as tapestries, for no article of clothing, no piece of bed linen, was ever cast aside. Annick was the sister who came between Charlotte and Richard, and she had not become a nun because of the grief it would have caused Papa if she were no longer in the house. With Elizabeth, the next to youngest sister, I learned how to make mayonnaise by beating oil with a fork into the yolks of eggs cracked into a deep, narrow bowl, for no article of food was ever brought home from market in a jar or can. In the billiard room of the château I learned to play pool with Jean and Richard and Marguerite, and from the family's little maid I learned to milk the goat that was kept tethered in the field beyond the back-garden wall. Every night all that summer, when Papa thought Richard and I were asleep, he would come on silent slippers into our room and close our windows against the treacherous night air of Brittany. And every night, all summer, once Papa had closed the door, Richard would leap out of bed and fling the casement windows wide again. Every Sunday morning we walked the two kilometres to high mass in the village, and every Sunday afternoon, after a furious exchange of views on religion between Richard and Papa at the dinner table, Richard would slam upstairs and pack a bag and study the timetable for trains that might be leaving for somewhere else entirely. He was going to find a job at once, in Rennes, or Paris, or Algeria even, and when he had found it he was going to send me the money to join him, wherever he was. "But you won't have to send me any money. I'll have enough to join you on my own," I'd say to him. "I'm writing my novel. I'm writing poetry." But we knew he didn't have any money to get away, and we knew, too, that we would not be separated, and until we could go off together he would not go.

But now I had entered into a sly and secretive life, and entered it alone. I lived for the letters that Mother and Lola wrote me, and for the writing of letters to them. William Carlos Williams' white chickens and red wheelbarrow, with the rain shining on it, were in every farmyard that I passed, and night after night I listened to the silences of Marianne Moore's far nightingale. "What time is it in New York now?" I'd keep asking Richard, and when he had worked it out for me, I would enter again my delitescent life. At this very moment Marianne Moore was perhaps crossing Leroy Street in the Village, on her way to her job in the Hudson Park branch of the Public Library, on St. Luke's Place. She might be looking up at Genevieve Taggard's window as she passed, or thinking unhappily about Edna St. Vincent's poem which had so distressed her, the one about the dead kitten in a shoebox, covered with fleas. Or it might be late afternoon, and Lola would be having visitors in the basement on East Ninth Street, although *Broom* was no longer being published regularly. I remembered the young poet who had not read his poems aloud there, but who had read us all the reviews of his book of poetry that had just appeared. And I remembered the strain it had always been to listen to Elinor Wylie recite her poetry, for even her beauty was possessed and marred by her intense pre-occupation with her own inner and outer self. In that peculiar absorption, no time or place had been accorded for the contempla-tion of any other thing. Or it might be night in Rutherford, and Bill Williams would be coming into his kitchen after a late night call. He would pour himself a glass of milk, and drink it, and then pick up the copper-haired dish mop in the sink, and speak softly, softly, to it, calling it the slender, tender daughter he had never had. Every morning, in the French family's closed, finite world, Duchamp's nude descended the staircase with me as I carried the *pot de chambre*, like a chalice, raised in my two hands.

"You're a fine figure of a rebel! You get on damned well with
every one of them!" Richard would rebuke me. But what was I
doing but biding my time before striking the blow that would one
day be fatal to them all? Richard had put his cards down openly,
just as he did when he won at bridge, and the family knew exactly
how strong or how weak that hand was. With me, they were fooled,
they were tricked, and they never knew until the end. I would not
admit to them, or to anyone, by either act or word, that this entrance
upon a hideously unfamiliar scene had any elements of failure in it.
And so I wrote my book about all that had happened to me as I
grew up in Philadelphia, in Atlantic City, in the Pocono Mountains,
and in Cincinnati, as if a recounting of these experiences must finally
reveal to me who I was. I wrote about the walks at night through
Eden Park, and the operas in summer at the Cincinnati Zoo, and
the wild rides to Kentucky roadhouses with young men I quickly
learned to do without. I wrote of the Conservatory of Music years,
when I became concertmeister of the young people's orchestra there;
and of the architecture courses I took at the Ohio Mechanics
Institute, and the casual, penniless lads I had loved there as if they
were my brothers, who spent every weekend in jail for stealing cars
and other justifiable offences, and who were back in class on Monday
mornings, wan, and their homework not done, but their spirits as
bright as brass.

Lewis Browne was the leading male figure in my novel. He had
been studying to be a rabbi at the Hebrew Union College in Cincinnati, and Mother was excited by his mind and felt pity for his
flesh, and hoped that I would marry him one day. But he was not the
adventure that I wanted; he was old (perhaps twenty-seven or
twenty-eight) and crippled with rheumatism, and both his mind
and flesh repelled me. I was astounded that he was troubled
because there were some among his friends and colleagues who
criticized him for taking me, a Christian, to the Sunday afternoon
synagogue dances. I had never been told by anyone at any time that
there was any difference whatsoever either in religion or social status
or race between a Christian and a Jew. Once, at the Meadowside
Inn in the Pocono Mountains where we were spending the summer,
it is true that an incomprehensible thing took place. Mother had
invited Morton Schamberg for the weekend, and other guests at the
hotel had protested to the hotel manager against his presence in the
dining room. Because Schamberg was a Jew, he had not been

permitted to stay with us. But I had accepted this as an isolated evil act perpetrated by evil people. In Mother's defence of Schamberg there was no hint that this was a tragedy of general rather than specific concern.

Lewis did not dance well, and his complexion was a disaster. These were probably the true reasons for the bitter judgments I passed on him. What was it I wanted then? There had been a labour union organizer called Duane Swift whom I would have followed to the ends of the earth, but he did not ask me to. In fact, he didn't ask anything of me at all. And there was a divorced car salesman who was twenty-six when I was sixteen, who wore a raccoon coat and drove an open Stutz car with wire-spoked wheels whom I would have married had my family permitted. But they separated us. And there was still another French officer in a horizon-blue uniform whom I had met before meeting Richard, a medical student who took me to the movies and put the tip of his tongue in my ear. There was a young writer of German descent who called me Trilby and took me to loft parties where we drank red wine; there was a cop who had suddenly turned the torch of his flashlight on Richard and me as we kissed in the Model T Ford one evening, above the Ohio River, who kept blackmailing me for a date. There were my fellow students at the Ohio Mechanics Institute, and there was the assistant architecture instructor there, an Irishman with black hair and a storm of freckles who took me roller skating. But Richard, whom I could not bring myself to write about, was my first, and, I believed, final true love affair.

I do not know on which of those summer days or nights in Brittany it was that Richard began to become a separate entity. Until that season I had thought of us as one in purpose and intent, one spirited, high will that would never know defeat. It was perhaps the day I bought Raymond Radiguet's *Le Diable au Corps* on the station platform as we took the train for St. Malo that the change began to take place. I had never heard Radiguet's name before, and I bought the book because it was small and cheap. It appeared to me to be short enough for me, with the help of a dictionary, to work my way through it line by line. And now I, who disliked to read, and who could not speak French at all well, suddenly did both because of the magic lucidity of Radiguet's prose. (Six or seven years later, long after Radiguet's early death, Caresse Crosby asked me to translate into English *Le Diable au Corps* for the Black Sun Press, not knowing that this book had led me out of the bleak silence of that summer in Brittany into the clarity of speech again.) The book presented me suddenly with a reality as translucent and untroubled as Mother's France, with the Impressionist painters in whose light and colour she brushed her long hair in the morning; with the music of Debussy, Massenet, Charpentier, to which she danced; with a France as moving as the voice of Mary Garden singing Mélisande, Louise, Thaïs, Camille, or the Juggler of Notre Dame; a France I had not touched the actual substance of until Radiguet's book said: "It is still here."

And so I wrote and wrote, and wept at times when I was alone, but there was not much time for weeping. My new, separate life made even reality bearable, until the week in August that we spent in the family's winter quarters in the walled town of St. Malo. We went swimming every day in the strong, clear sea, blue even in its crystal depths, except where the shadows of the enormous rocks stood emerald and opaque as stone. As we rested on the coarse-grained sand we could see Chateaubriand's island in the windy channel, deceptively close and always rimmed with light, unlike the dramatically gloomy engraving of it that hung in the salon of the family's house. Chateaubriand had loved his sister, Richard told me, and even slept with her, for she had returned his love. There she lay in the engraving, her body swept up by the wild waves on the beach where we now stretched out in the sun, and Chateaubriand, lace at his young throat and wrists, and his wig in disarray, was madly kissing her dead mouth. She had drowned herself, Richard said, on discovering that she was bearing her brother's child. He recounted the story at dinner one night, and Papa cried out there was not a word of truth in it. "I must ask you not to bring up things of this nature in the presence of your sisters," Papa said. "The unfortunate girl died one afternoon while bathing." Richard jumped up from the table, hastened into the salon, and took the framed engraving down from the wall. "So she went bathing in her nightgown?" he said, setting the engraving upright against the carafe of wine. "With the moon shining on the water? And a thunderstorm, black as hell, breaking over the island where the family had incarcerated him because of his incestuous ways? Come, come, *mon cher* Papa!"

Every day I would leave my clothes and my straw hat in a public bathing cabin, and there it came about that lice moved into my hat and made themselves at home, and eventually settled in my hair. Only at the end of the week did the reason for my continuous scratching become apparent. "American lice," Maman said in a hoarse whisper, identifying them without hesitation as she examined my scalp. "Impossible!" shouted Richard. "Neither her mother, nor her grandmother, nor her great-grandmother, nor her aunts, nor her uncles or cousins, nor her sister, nor her father, or her grandfather, have ever had lice in their hair!" We were to fight them in absolute silence, Maman cautioned, and Annick was sent out to buy a fine-toothed comb and a bottle of turpentine. It might take weeks, Maman warned, but not a word must be said about them, for Papa would move out of the house and the summer would be ruined if ever he learned that his daughter-in-law had lice in her hair.

Robert McAlmon

1923

Miss Harriet Weaver of the Egoist Press had subsidized Joyce so that he was able to complete *Ulysses*. She had at the time given up the publication, the *Egoist*, and the publishing business. Before and during the war she edited the paper, first as a feminist sheet and later as sponsor for the new poetry movement. In the *Egoist* appeared the works of Ezra Pound, William Carlos Williams, H.D., Richard Aldington, Wyndham Lewis, Marianne Moore, Storm Jameson, Joyce, and others, many for the first time in any publication.

There had been an episode when I was last in Paris. Miss Weaver had got word that Joyce drank, even to intoxication. She was frightened of drunken people, and pained to hear the report, and she wrote to Joyce expressing her fear. Since Eliot believes Joyce capable of working without "outward stimulus", it is not surprising, considering Miss Weaver's background, that she should have read *Ulysses* without noting that he knew a bit about bars and brothels. Perhaps she did not even know what particular passages in the book meant, or thought it all "pure" imagination.

Miss Weaver told me a little of her background. She had grown up as a Quaker and her family were most orthodox and severe. When she was nineteen she was caught reading George Eliot's *Mill on the Floss* and was publicly reprimanded from the pulpit by the village minister. Later she had freed herself intellectually, but still she disliked hurting people, mainly her family; so that she feared she was a bit of a coward about "facing reality". She published the works of Dora Marsden, who was writing an apparently endless book dealing with metaphysics from the feminine aspect. It was for Miss Marsden's work that Miss Weaver had begun publishing a paper.

Joyce in Paris worried because of her anxiety about his drinking. I wrote her a letter explaining that he drank, but in moderation, and my letter assured her that so gentle a type as Joyce became merely released with drink, but never did he fail to hold his drink properly and as a gentleman. His courtesy was unfailing. In London I called upon her. She is . . . reticent or shy? Difficult to get at in any case. She would let me talk and answer with a short-gasped "yes" or "no", and looked into space. Whether she heard or was bored stiff, I couldn't say. I feared that she believed I led Joyce astray, and his income then was dependent upon her. At last she came through with a confession: she feared she had never faced life with sufficient courage to accept things as they were. She had been afraid from her childhood days of people who drank, but she agreed with my point. Joyce was working and well, and it was by that she was to judge him; but she hoped to be spared seeing him intoxicated, and she did hope someday to meet him. Yes, she would consider visiting Paris if she would not be in the way; she would cross over with Bryher and H.D. and me when we left in a few days' time.

It is some kind of commentary on the period that Joyce's work and acclaim should have been fostered mainly by high-minded ladies, rather than by men. Ezra first brought him to Miss Weaver's attention, but it was she who then supported him. The *Little Review*, Sylvia Beach, and Harriet Weaver brought Joyce into print.

There was a charming old man for dinner at Audley Street one night, asked in by her Ladyship because Sir John's associates always talked business over their after-dinner cigars. His name was, I believe, Smedley, and he had a valuable Shakespearean library. (It went later to a museum in America.) Mr. Smedley was intent upon proving Shakespeare was Bacon, and he gave me a book telling of Shakespeare's life as a draper's assistant. His proofs sounded perfect and he was far too sweet for me not to agree with him that Shakespeare was whoever he yearned to have him. After dinner, however, Mr. Smedley, nearing eighty, became very sad about my generation and there having been a war, and he was depressed about life. There were tears in his aged eyes, so thinking to buck him up by proving that my generation was not licked yet, and that there had been the spirit of futility in the world before, I mentioned St. Augustine, Job, and quoted Hamlet's soliloquy, suggesting that even Bacon had felt despair. The old man broke into tears. Sir John and I looked helplessly at each other, and each reached for the bottle of brandy to fill first Mr. Smedley's glass and then the other two. The old man was a staunch soul, and not gone in senility. He had lost a son in the war, and his tears were doubtless for more than merely a sentimental notion about the young. During the spell of his weeping there was a true bond of sympathy between Sir John and myself, and little as I could ever understand his financial and other obsessions, there were small moments that revealed delicacy and sensibility in his nature.

Her Ladyship had a spell of the grippe and we prolonged our visit. Frank Dobson suggested modelling my head and, to pass the time, I submitted, thinking that perhaps her Ladyship might buy it. Dobson at least understood that had I the say-so I'd have had several artists, good, bad, and indifferent, subsidized by Sir John. The other man's art is not my affair and so long as I saw that he was a serious worker my attitude was to give him a chance.

At one sitting for Dobson a man named Lawrence came and watched for well over an hour and talked of excavating near Sumer. He brought a small statuette, which he gave to Mrs. Dobson. It was not until after he had left that I was aware he was Colonel Lawrence of Arabia. I would have been more curious, for there were varying reports as to his achievements and his personal magnetism. At that time he was feeling let down and disillusioned because of his treatment by the government; at any rate, the impression he left on my memory was not a strong one. It is difficult to conceive of him as a bold leader of desert Bedouins.

Dobson finished his head of me, and it looked like a gaping fish. Perhaps Dobson has spiritual insight. But her Ladyship looked at the head, made little comment, did not buy, and there the matter was dropped. Perhaps it would not have fitted so well into the library interior. There the high-bosomed girl eating grapes bespoke herself the star.

As her Ladyship kept to her room while ill, I took my chance to eat out every night, and generally at the Tour Eiffel, which was the rendezvous for what people I knew, mainly those I had met in Paris: Tommy Earp, Nina Hamnett, Nancy Cunard, Curtis Moffat, Iris Tree, Dobson, and others. Augustus John drifted in frequently to hold court. The place was small enough and the habitués well enough known to one another, so that usually we got together, and often went upstairs in the private dining room if strangers arrived in any great numbers.

Tommy Earp and I were sitting together when Ronald Firbank came through the door. I knew of him by name only. He was introduced, tittered nervously, covered his face with his long hands, and would not stay to talk. "I'm nervous," he giggled. It was possible for me, as I looked Ronald over, to believe that this was not affectation. He was tall and thin, with a high nose and cheekbones and colour. He belonged to the Aubrey Beardsley tradition, or more properly to the court entourage of one of the more decadent Cæsars, such as Heliogabalus.

He wouldn't stay and he wouldn't go. Finally I said, "Sit down, Ronald. I'm just a cowboy from the Wild West, too dumb to cause your nerves."

He tittered and sat down, delighted to meet an American, and at once began to show me letters from Carl Van Vechten, who certainly threw adjectives out of joint in expressing his admiration for Ronald's writing. Ronald was so pleased at the praise that I didn't answer when he asked about Van Vechten's writing, which he hadn't read. Later he talked of the book he was then doing, *The Flower beneath the Foot*, and he was brightly malicious of an Oxford man against whom he had a grudge. Wyndham Lewis came in that night, and Firbank, with some ten cocktails in him, was mildly at ease and consented to sit for Lewis the next day, for a sketch. He did, and the sketch was a fine one, although Lewis claims he couldn't get Ronald to stop fidgeting for ten seconds. However, he gave the sketch to Ronald, who promptly gave it to his publisher, Grant Richards, to use as a frontispiece in *The Flower beneath the Foot*. Upon hearing of this, Lewis was angry and insisted that either Ronald or the publisher pay him. Ronald, however, for all his butterfly flutterings, was strictly a businessman. He was difficult to find, and the publisher said the affair was not his.

The night before we were to leave for Paris, I was with Lewis and he said that he would drink quietly and have a good talk, but the Tour Eiffel, which he wanted to avoid, was where I wanted to go. Lewis had been telling me that I must read a book by a Frenchman, Georges Sorel, on the necessity of revolution. He was on the verge of bursting forth into an endless book, an endless series of books, and he told of Bogoraz, a Russian anthropologist of a past generation, who wrote that on the peninsula of Kamchatka there were shamans given to homosexuality. I gathered that Mr. Lewis had been spending a great deal of time at the British Museum, doing research work, and never would he deign to look at anybody contemporary who was more or less respected by specialists in whatever particular line. Lewis these days was being very much a man of many ideas, but most of them were other men's.

In London at the time it was being said by painters that Lewis was a good writer but couldn't paint, and by writers that he was a good painter but couldn't write. I added mentally that he was naïve if he thought that spending his days at the British Museum, in what he called research, was going to make him know what it was he wanted to prove. Reading books he has turned out by the volume since, I wonder if he ever will know what he wants to tell the world, for the facts and statements in one of his paragraphs are destroyed by those in the following ones; just as he piles up adjectives to be horrifically satirical, only to have one adjective ruin the force of the other. In *The Apes of God* he is supposed to have been cruel to several people, whom I also know, but I could feel no force in the strained narration.

I submitted to a Bass at a quiet pub, but was restless; we had Bass at another pub, but still I felt restless. With every pub we got nearer to the Tour Eiffel. I was going there whether he came or not, but he came. He generally relaxed his intense aversions and became easy after a few drinks.

We were seated over a bottle of moselle when Tommy Earp entered and stood, rather pelicanish, looking dumbfounded with shyness as only Tommy can look. His arms dangled woodenly. It was a safe bet he'd had an absinthe or so and felt lonely. He seemed pinned to the floor. I got up and asked him to join us.

"Really, Bob," he squeaked in his strange, semifalsetto, or shattered, voice. "I rather fancy Lewis doesn't fancy me."

Earp came to the table, slowly, his beady brown eyes glistening in a face that gave the effect of rosiness. At the suggestion of Lewis we went to the small dining room upstairs as it looked as though there might be a heavy after-theatre crowd this night. We were all jovial now. The waiter soon informed us that Mary Beerbohm was downstairs and had asked if anyone she knew was there.

"Poor Mary. She is so hating London. She wants company," Tommy Earp quavered.

Mary was hating London; so was I, and the others generally declared that they were too. Some of them were because, depressing as London can be normally, in those soon-after-the-war days it shrieked ennui and despair, and no form of activity seemed worth the effort. Naturally, Mary joined us.

Mary was authentically whimsical by nature. None of the Peter Pan or Milne tosh. Mary's whimsey had a sense of reality and irony within it, but her manner suggested a continual state of wonder that she should be alive. She isn't now, and not because of that, but because Mary was what she was, every memory that remains of her to me is sweet.

She never was strong. Her face was a child's on a tall, slender body, and her legs looked breakable. A slight rash on her face gave it the appearance of a child's who has been at the jam jar. "Do give me some champagne," she wailed, as she came into the room. "I'm so glad somebody is here. It's been too awful the last two days. Do you think we're going to have a thunderstorm? I woke up last night and thought I was going to faint in bed. I'm sure there's going to be a thunderstorm. They terrify me, and my heart beats so faintly." She looked around, her weak eyes bothered by the light, and then smiled a wistful, understanding, and sympathy-asking smile.

Mary was always thinking there was going to be a thunderstorm. It was her way of explaining that she had never recovered from air raids over London in the war. Her brother, of whom everybody had expected great things, had been killed in the war. Mary had no defences. Some of the others had recklessness, hardness, rebellion, hatred, or somebody to fight or to take care of. Mary had an elderly mother, but she was well provided for, and she was not made for defiances.

Tommy was sympathetic, as always. "Mary darling, I understand how you feel, but I assure you it isn't going to thunder. You mustn't really stress the horrible things we can feel. It becomes too much to bear."

The atmosphere in those days was most terrifyingly afterwar, or was it only that I was young and did not know London?

"I'm sure if one were a scientist this would be an interesting age to live in, but one isn't a scientist and it isn't amusing," Mary said.

Lewis was feeling merry, but felt called upon to be sardonic. "War," he said prophetically. "An internal war that blasts the bourgeois aristocratic idea. Must happen every second generation."

He was at it again, spouting his old Frenchman, Sorel.

"I should die, simply die," Mary wailed.

Lewis explained how machines would fight the war, and talked of how ultimately we could have machines live our lives, and I added, have machines be our egos for us, too. In the end Lewis flowered into tremendous fantasy and simultaneously Tommy Earp and I accused him of being a frustrated writer of tales for children. It did not haunt him. This was one of the nights when he forgot his idea of himself as a ruthless intellect.

The waiter, bringing more drink, told us that Ronald Firbank was downstairs, and Mary Beerbohm at once wanted poor dear Ronald to join us. I went to collect him. Downstairs Ronald hid his face in his hands when I spoke to him. "I couldn't come up. I'd bore you all," he tittered.

Rudolph, the *patron*, chest pompous and protruding stomach, came up. "Ach, dis man," he said of Ronald. "Vot vill ve do vit him? Alvays he drinks de cocktails, and eats de caviarre and pairheps de strawberries, but nefer he eats a meal. Und such good food ve haf. He vill be ill."

It was true. Of all the people who knew Ronald, few ever saw him eat really solid food, and he frequently put twenty cocktails down in the course of an evening. He refused still more to come when he understood that Lewis was with us. "He is angry at me."

"Not if you'd give him a cheque for the sketch he did of you."

"I'm afraid," Ronald tittered. "He might tear up the cheque and throw it in my face."

"No chance. Let me hand it to him."

To my surprise Ronald made out a cheque and did come up-stairs, and all was peace between him and Lewis. Once there, Ronald ordered more champagne but would not sit at the table. Instead he sat on the floor in the corner. As he drank he fumbled his coat buttons with long nervous fingers. Soon he was completely intoxicated and talked constantly, as though to himself. As he had the habit of going off to lonely villages in France and Italy and living entirely alone for months, it is probable that he did so talk to himself. One could not judge Ronald by that rather silly standard of "normal". He never was, never had a chance to be, and as Mary Beerbohm commented, no greater cruelty ever happened than his being sent to Eton and made to indulge in "games".

"I love my hands," Ronald crooned, holding them out before

him. "They are too beautiful. Don't you love my hands?" He minced and draped them one way and then another. "When I am alone I am never lonely, because my hands are beautiful."

"They are really," Mary encouraged.

They were; long, beautifully manicured and cared for. They were a dream of Aubrey Beardsley's. Ronald's head was beautifully formed too, but his neck was a stork's.

Ronald was struck by the word "really", and recalled that I had spoken in praise of one of his books. "Don't ever say the word 'reality' to me. Where should I be if I admitted reality? You needn't laugh. It is so. But I do love my hands and my lovely books that are beautifully obscene, but the censors don't understand and never bother me. But reality is too awful." He turned his head birdlike to the side, tormentedly registering tragedy. He was being Duse or Sarah Bernhardt, or no, he was being Ronald, and what he was saying was too true if one was serious. "Life is too awful, too tragic. How do I bear it? I have only my beautiful hands. I love to sit before a mirror and watch their gestures. See, how beautiful!"

Ronald's idea of grim realism in literature was George Meredith. He revealed this one night in Paris, when, with Curtis Moffat and me, he swallowed twelve cocktails, having, he said, eaten nothing since the day before. That night he was intent upon taking a taxi to Maxim's, for what reason I don't know. I would not go with him, and neither would Moffat. He was repeating his "Life is too, too awful" wail steadily, and we realized that it was, for him, but there was nothing we could do. His last remark before getting into a taxi was, "Save me. Save me." It was grimly, hysterically funny, for Ronald was being a tragic actress while being distressingly real at the same time.

Rudolph, knowing Ronald, now came into the room. He realized it was time for Ronald to be put into a taxi and sent to his hotel, but Ronald must believe that the rest of us were being turned out too. "Ladies und chentlemen, ve close," Rudolph said with pompous austerity, but there was a twinkle in his eyes. "Fritz, you ged de taxi vor Meester Firbank. He is a goot man und a goot gustomer, put he is trunk."

Every night Rudolph went through his category of invitations, asking us to leave so that he could go to bed. It was "Ladies und chentlemen, ve close." After that he would become fraternal and plead with us as a brother. "Brudders and sisters, go to ped. I vant to sleep." He would finally let his head fall on his chest, and snooze. After another bottle of champagne had been drunk by the rest of us, Rudolph would awake with a start. "De sooner you go de bedder I ligk you. Ged oud, blease," he would declare decisively.

That particular night I recall as one of the less grim London nights in those years. Too many nights there was no talk except of how bored we all were. It was doubtless my fault that I didn't discover another London, but that point will come up later.

Kay Boyle

1923

In early September we set off by train for Paris, sitting up all night on the varnished wood of a third-class carriage, counting every centime that we spent. For Charlotte, with her seemingly naïve and innocent gaze, had looked into the despair of our situation with a courage that had failed us and seen the one way of escape. "In Paris you will be able to find a job. That is certain," she had said to Richard one afternoon on the beach at St. Malo, and she had given him three thousand francs. Like all miracles, the childlike miracle of Charlotte's understanding, not performed because of our adherence, or lack of it, to the precepts of the Church, cannot be given a simple name. "I am not thinking of me when I ask you to go," were the last words she said to us, turning her head away. "Without the two of you, what will become of everything that speaks only inside my heart?" Her, and Jean's, limousine had taken us to the station, their money lying heavy with promise in Richard's pocket and lying with the heaviness of actual gold on our consciences. "We will go away and be ourselves again," I said in some kind of solace to our guilt, but Richard cried out impatiently: "Ourselves? Who are we? Who in the name of God *are* we? Answer me that!"

When the train stopped at a station in the twilight of early morning, Richard got out to buy coffee and cold croissants at the platform *buvette*, and grimly ate and drank. But I had taken a vow in silence to eat only one meal a day until we had money of our own to live on, and, although ravenous with hunger on that first morning, I told Richard I was train-sick and could not eat. "Go to Notre Dame and to the St. Sulpice and light candles," Charlotte had said to me at the end, whispering it so that Richard would not hear; "then everything will turn out well". So while Richard made his appointments and went to be interviewed, I walked uneasily from Paris church to Paris church, lighting tapers within every chapel where the placid eyes of lady saints looked uncomprehendingly down at me as I prayed in desperation for a job for Richard and also for diligence for me to finish my first book. Then I would get up from my knees and drop the big, dark, copper sous that I begrudged for food into the alms boxes in payment for those pale stalks of wax that would light the obscurity ahead.

It was not easy to kneel in the churches or to climb onto buses, for I wore a very tight black silk dress that reached nearly to my ankles. It had been made for me by a friend before we left New York, and she had miscalculated on the amount of material required to walk with ease. But I had saved this dress for Paris, and now, with the red chiffon scarf knotted around my shoulders, it was what I wore day after day. I had put on my white hoop earrings again, and once more smeared lip rouge on my mouth. (What my shoes were like I cannot remember, and this troubles me, for shoes divide the rich and the poor. They are always a statement of one's greatest weakness, and I do not even know if my heels were high or low.) Guilt about money had become almost an obsession with me, humiliating me so that I could not bring myself to raise my head to look into the faces of the people who passed. I walked up and down the lavish blocks of the Faubourg St. Honoré and studied the elegant shopwindows in which were displayed objects contrived of shining beads and golden threads and variously coloured silks—purses, vanity bags, ballet slippers—my mind scheming and scheming, seeking a way that I might copy them and sell them to humbler shops in other quarters, and make a living for both of us that way.

On the third or fourth day I crossed the Seine to the Left Bank for the first time since I was a child, and walked through the Luxembourg Gardens, up the same paths where I had once rolled a yellow hoop; and finally up the Rue de l'Odéon towards Sylvia Beach's bookshop, to number 12, thinking that if I came here every day and watched I might catch a sight of James Joyce or George Moore either going in or coming out. But once I actually saw the sign, Shakespeare and Company, I did not have the courage to approach the door. I stayed on the other side of the street, my back half turned, glancing at the bookshop from the corners of my eyes. Before Richard came back to our hotel room behind the Opéra that evening (a room that was barely wide enough to hold the double bed and night table, and whose one narrow, dirt-darkened window opened onto a light shaft that held neither light nor air) I scrubbed the rouge from my lips and brushed my hair straight back and wrenched it into a knot. This was the guise in which I would present myself to Sylvia Beach, I thought, staring at myself in the armoire glass. When Richard had a job in Paris, I would ask Miss Beach to let me sell books for her, and then the inner resolve and the exterior action would at last be of a piece. But this temporary and sensible mask I exchanged the next morning for one with mascara-weighted eyes under a broad-brimmed black hat that Annick had found for me in the attic of the family's house.

It was in this outfit that I arrived one morning at Harold Loeb's Paris flat, around ten o'clock, it must have been, the hour seeming to me to be quite late in the day. I had walked through the Tuileries gardens, where I had so often walked hand in hand with Mother, and as I would have walked now with her if I could, to the benches of the Guignol show, still feeling on my forehead the pressure of the stiff black patent leather hat that I had worn twelve years before. This month, the leaves were turning frail and golden in the trees by the Jeu de Paume, and the children were sailing white-winged boats on the smooth waters of the fountains. The benches before the Guignol theatre were empty, and the wooden curtain was lowered at this hour, but I remembered how the children had crowded on certainly these same green benches, crying out in excitement in voices that I had never quite ceased to hear. Harold had been still asleep with his current lady when I rang the doorbell, and he stood there in the partly opened door in a silk dressing gown, a bit put out, but suggested that we meet on the terrace of the Café de la Paix that afternoon at four.

I looked up the café in the telephone directory, arrived a half hour early, and walked around the block until I saw Harold arrive in a taxi and make his way across the crowded terrace to one of the small, round-topped tables whére a young man in a grey suit had already begun his apéritif. Before I could bring myself to join them I had to walk twice around the block again, berating my own reflection in the shopwindows, saying to it, *Oh overweening ego! Who cares that you are thin as a rail and smeared with make-up like a whore? Yes, the earrings*

are uproarious, and the hat is a scream, and the skirt may split up the sides
at any minute, but these men and I have died the same deaths for the same
poets, and they will hear me saying all the things I have not said yet and
cannot say, and all the things I have not yet written they will know I will one
day write. They move on the same sad, troubled waters with me. They are not
the same as the family in St. Malo. But I was numb with shyness as I
reached the table and murmured Harold's name.

Until I had taken two swallows of the pernod Harold ordered for
me I was stricken blind and deaf, and only gradually was I able to
see that the American at the table with us, whose name I did not
know, was probably in his late twenties, that he had a profile not
unlike John Barrymore's, and that he appeared to be totally without
conceit. His lips were thin, and there was a half-humorous, half-
mordacious twist to them as he talked, and he talked quite steadily
and wittily, his steel-blue eyes unchanging even when he jerked his
acrimonious laughter out. Whoever or whatever he was, in his
presence Harold Loeb had no more personality than a clean,
expensive blanket lying folded across the café chair. And sentence
by sentence I began to understand that the young man was talking
about Gurdjieff, who had opened a school of philosophy at Fontainebleau, and who was now sitting a few tables from us on the terrace,
with a cream-coloured turban on his head.

"The cult has been spreading among people I thought were more
or less sensible," the young man was telling Harold. "Jane Heap
got involved out there, and Margaret Anderson, and Georgette
Leblanc, and Isadora Duncan was also ready to join the bandwagon,
I suppose out of her despair with life." I remembered, then, that it
was there that Katherine Mansfield had died. "It's a mass hypnotism of some kind," the young man went on, speaking directly to me
now. "Gurdjieff started years back in the East as a hypnotist, they
tell me, but nobody knows very much about his background.
Anyway, out there in Fontainebleau he gets people of various
nationalities—Dutch, French, Spanish, Chinese, Hebrew—to
repeat numbers and words in their own language, to repeat them
over and over, and after ten minutes he asks other pupils to repeat
the sounds they have heard, and I'm told that they do it without
error. Then a pianist plays music which the pupils, sitting in a
circle, speak in time with, repeating 'twilight', or 'dawn', or 'tragedy',
or 'labour', or 'love', over and over, in their different languages.
This in itself hypnotizes, of course, and they all sway as they speak;

but in the middle of the circle are placed bottles of armagnac, and the master is disturbed if these bottles are not emptied, and this adds to the hypnotism. It sounds pretty much like what we do every night in Montparnasse."

The young man was laughing now, and he called the waiter for another drink. I sat sipping nervously at my milky pernod and looking across the tables at Gurdjieff.

"Who pays for the armagnac in Fontainebleau?" Harold asked.

"Oh, Harold, Harold, be not so sordid!" the young man said. "The spirit provides! Each bottle is purchased by devoted service. You build houses in the forest, and you chop wood, and you subsist on bread and soup, and you live in fear that you will be turned away. There is one boy," he said, "a kid in blue jeans, who has been two years there. He says when he has stayed fifteen years he'll be admitted to the inner fold. But by that time, I tell him, he'll be dead, or mad, or uncaring, for in their state of half starvation and overwork, they don't care to think or feel on their own. They live on their hallucinations." He began the new drink that the waiter had set down. "This kid," he said, "he told a friend of mine that he's miserably unhappy but that he is at peace, for he is one with the mysticism of the master. And it could be that Gurdjieff's régime is no more rigid and bleak than the routine of many a monastery or nunnery. They are all serving some master for a future that is nebulous. As for me, I'll take my future now."

I had half finished the pernod, and although I had not eaten since breakfast, I did not feel any drunkenness, but I knew without putting the words of it together that this man was not really talking about a mystic named Gurdjieff, or about a boy in blue jeans, but about something else entirely. His eyes had scarcely left my face, and their icy blueness had not altered as he asked (as he must have asked everyone he met), using quite other words, exactly what and who I was, and I did not know what answers to give. He was saying that if a man and his situation are difficult to explain by tactile argument, then the definition by other means must be as solid as a statue, maybe bigger than life size, but anyway something you can acknowledge with your hand.

"God's got to be a good poet or a good composer before I'll genuflect," he said.

"McAlmon," Harold said without warning, "I'm going to have another drink. What about you?"

McAlmon said he would, but when Harold turned to me I got up quickly. I said Richard was waiting, and I had to go. Harold said he would call me at the hotel and arrange a dinner, but I knew he would not call. I could not bring myself to look at McAlmon when I said goodbye.

Robert McAlmon

1922-1923

Before leaving London Harriet Weaver had gone with several of us to a music hall to hear Nora Bayes sing, and declared herself highly entertained, particularly with Nora's rowdy, "No one ever loved like Samson and Delilah." So my idea was that, as Miss Weaver generously helped artists, she might learn to be not afraid of their less high-minded pastimes. We persuaded her to do a Paris cabaret, namely Bricktop's where she would hear snappy songs and see, close to, dancing that clicked. Djuna Barnes, H.D., Bryher, Thelma Wood, Harriet Weaver, William and Sally Bird, and a number of others made up the party, and Ezra was to come in after dinner for coffee. Throughout the meal everything went charmingly. Several were newly acquainted with one another and Miss Weaver's obvious dignity and reserve dominated the affair. Hilda Doolittle, who had known Miss Weaver for years, joined me in urging her to have at least one glass of wine. The rest drank more generously. By the time dinner was over Miss Weaver may have sipped half a glass of wine, and then Ezra Pound arrived.

Ezra had left England some years before and not seen Miss Weaver since, but surely he recalled that she was reticent. Ezra doesn't drink, but seemed gay as he entered, so that he may have had an extra cognac or so. In any case he greeted us all jubilantly, and suddenly turned to Miss Weaver, saying, "Why, Harriet, this is the first time I've ever seen you drunk," his eagle eye having spotted her half-filled wineglass.

Hilda gasped and her eyes caught mine, and we both turned

scarlet upon seeing Miss Weaver. She sat back as though struck. Later Hilda and I agreed that Harriet concluded she did look drunk because of that thimbleful of wine. The party was dumb with consternation. Ezra realized that his comedy had not gone over and he sat down, self-conscious and fidgety, looking at Djuna and at H.D., at Bill Bird and at me, hoping that some one of us would rescue the situation.

Djuna did best. She saw that Miss Weaver wasn't going to recover through a wittily made remark or even a short and earnest explanation that it was a joke. She asked her quietly if she wished to leave. It was well past ten, and Miss Weaver did want to leave. Hilda saw her to her hotel, across the square, and returned, explaining that Harriet thought her very brave to venture again into that scene. When H.D. said broadly, "I haven't seen dear old Ezra for ages. I'll walk home with him," Miss Weaver had been overcome with admiration at her dauntless courage. Ezra sat cowed and self-conscious, doubtless reflecting that once more he'd been awkward, and perhaps this time more awkward than usual.

The next morning I called on Miss Weaver and we went for a long walk, across the Seine into the Place de la Concorde down the Champs Elysées with a stop at Fouquet's, where we had coffee. It was discouraging for me as I talked, for not a sign of believing me did Miss Weaver show. I argued that Ezra was to a great extent a thwarted comedian; he hadn't been intoxicated; he was a self-conscious and shy individual and had made an awkward remark to cover his late entry into the party. As I was leaving her at the hotel she said, "I am sure you are right. If you will give me Ezra's address I will call on him at teatime. I have always admired his work and must not let my prejudices get the better of me."

I guess Ezra gathered the amount of persuasion Djuna, Hilda, Bryher, and myself put up to bring Miss Weaver round, and I suspect to this day that she nurses a fear that she, once a good Quaker, was actually intoxicated that night. Fortunately it did not seem necessary for me to be present at the Ezra-Weaver tea because surely one's heart would have had to bleed for Ezra; his self-consciousness is enough to put one ill at ease even in normal circumstances.

Miss Weaver never went to Bricktop's; never saw a Paris cabaret. She went back to England and was soon worrying about Joyce's *Work in Progress*, which she could scarcely believe the work of a rational being. Because of this, Sylvia Beach invited Miss Weaver to Paris a year later, and somehow the Paris atmosphere helped to persuade her that when a man has proved his genius it is not for others to ask explanations about his new and unfinished efforts. As Miss Beach has said of Miss Weaver, "She is an authentic saint," but saints can be difficult.

By this time William Bird and I were publishing books in Paris, and most of them books that I am still glad to have published, but, so far as getting distribution was concerned, silence is better. The mere fact that the books were printed in English on the Continent made them suspect by both the English and the American customs officers. One shipment of *A Hurried Man*, a distinguished but certainly clean book by Emanuel Carnevali, was rejected and never returned. One shipment of Gertrude Stein's *The Making of Americans* was refused entry at New York. It was a shipment of five copies, and already one hundred copies of the book had been sold to a publisher in America. John Herrmann's boyish and, for the present day, naïvely innocent book, *What Happens*, was steadily refused entry, even after Herrmann protested with a pamphlet signed by several noted people. As we printed only 300 to 500 copies of each book, of works for which America was the logical market, the venture was not a cheering affair. It was not only the customs; reviewers in America were ruthless about them. They would not comment on them as books; they were always mentioned as expatriate and Paris publications even when the authors had never seen Paris. Since, some of the books have been republished in England or America and have been greeted with praise, among them Robert Coates's *Eater of Darkness*; Mary Butts's *Ashe of Rings*; Hemingway's *In Our Time*.

Later in America, wanting to get a copy of Gertrude Beasley's *My First Thirty Years*, I was asked forty dollars for a book for which we had charged two-fifty. Some three hundred copies of that were lost in America. The author, not having registered her residence in London, got into trouble with the authorities at the time proof was being sent her. The ensuing newspaper publicity made it impossible to attempt distribution of her book in England. In the publishing of some twenty books only two authors got "temperamental" and they were both Gertrudes, Stein and Beasley, and, may it be said, both megalomaniacs with an idea that to know them was to serve them without question in all their demands.

Events were lively in Paris and I kept putting off a trip to Berlin. Hilaire Hiler opened the Jockey, on the Rue Campagne Première, the first Paris cabaret which he decorated, and, in this case, conducted. Innumerable people, English and American and French, congregated there nightly. Les Copeland, an ex-cowboy, who had a great assortment of songs, cowboy, jazz-blues, and comic, was at the piano. Les, a Christian Scientist, had an unexpected streak of purity in him for a cabaret singer. He would not sing bawdy ditties, and for that reason should doubtless be thanked, since every shipment of eternal collegiates arriving insisted upon their "Christopho Colombe", "Bollocky Bill", "The Bastard King of England", on through the list of "naughty" ballads. One bar then rang with the voices of young souls declaring their release by tunelessly shouting songs which long ago deserved respectable burial because of old age and decrepit wit.

Hiler's Jockey, however, was, so long as he had it, an amusing and sociable hangout. Dramas and comedies and fights did occur there, but generally comedy and good will prevailed. Hiler looks a comedian-clown. Had he willed he surely could have been famous as a stage comedian; as it is he has great talent as a burlesque comic, and at that time painted bistro and barroom and cabaret scenes and types with much gusto. His spirit was of the elder Breughel lineage. Of later years he had himself psychoanalysed, and went in for being "abstract". His paintings now are mathematical, orderly, clean, and exact, but I hope he gets back to being "literary". There he had genius, and there is nothing against Goyas, Hogarths, and Breughels.

Jane Heap, Mina Loy, Clotilde and Laurence Vail, Mary Reynolds, Man Ray, Harold Van Dorn—among the French, Cocteau, Jacques Rigaut, Radiguet, Louis Aragon, René Crevel, Marcel Duchamp, Kiki—almost anybody of the writing, painting, musical, gigoloing, whoring, pimping or drinking world was apt to turn up at the Jockey. Don't think I'm confusing my world. The so-called "bohemian" or art world has so few intolerances about morals, or the way people make their living, that people of the last three named categories prefer mingling with the artists' world in their non-working moments, because these bohemians don't bother to disapprove of them.

Mary Reynolds, Mina Loy and her daughter Gioella, Katherine Murphy, Djuna Barnes stand out in my memory as the more elegant, witty, or beautiful of the girls or women about at the time, and at that period a Ziegfeld or a Cochrane, had he been looking for outstanding women, would not have done badly at all to have picked them for their poise and their beauty. Many of the famous stage beauties in revues would have come off decidedly second, not only for wit but also for looks and style.

Mary Reynolds was handsome and Mary Butts called her "the world's most charming woman". She was, indeed, too charming, and that is dangerous when accompanied by a striking head set magnificently on a fine neck above as fine a pair of shoulders and as beautiful a back as Aphrodite. She drank with, and was friends with, all of the better people of each type, artist, gigolo, drunk, scrubwoman, *poule*, or parasite, and generally she paid the bills of them all. Her friends of longer standing tried to prevent her from stranding herself by giving away her money to everyone.

Somewhere I met André Germain, who at the time was much excited by the vitality of young Americans; and he used occasionally to appear to look us all over. Generally we saw to it that he paid all bills, as Monsieur Germain was a man of great wealth, though very careful with his money.

Like Ronald Firbank, André was different. His voice was thin and high; his hands showed age, but they were delicately scrawny, like a small blue-blooded old lady's. "*Tiens, tiens,*" he used to say to me. "Come, come, Monsieur Mackaylmon, you are a type. You know people of all the classes. The high, the low, so very low, and the in-between too. But what a type you are!"

One night at the Boeuf sur le Toit with Djuna Barnes and Sarah Kelly, Monsieur Germain was made very unhappy. He dearly loved beautiful and elegant people, particularly women, and both Sarah and Djuna were looking so that night. Djuna had on a gown with a ruff about the neck and looked very elegantly Victorian. Sarah was elegant with a smartness that I shall not try to describe. Thelma Wood came in with Margot Van Schuyler, both looking neatly tailored and handsome boyish girls. The party grew. We ordered food, starting with caviar, on to roast duck. Afterwards there was fine old brandy with coffee, and André paid the bill without demur. He was looking admiringly at Djuna who, handsome to look upon, was also being very much the lady.

André showed her a collapsible diamond ring, of platinum. Djuna took it to admire and then, turning naughty-girl, shook her finger at

Monsieur Germain and said, "André, where did you get that ring?"

Monsieur Germain looked thunderstruck, and answered, "Honourably, Miss Barnes." I doubt that he ever forgave her. At the time I was hopeful about getting Monsieur Germain to have some of Djuna's stories translated into French and published in a magazine or by a publishing house which he virtually controlled. Instead, Monsieur Germain shortly fled into the night. He remained romantic about high-spirited Americans for some time, however.

One Sunday morning he called at my hotel with Philippe Soupault. We drove into the country, where we dined with a typical provincial French family, and I was not at all comfortable, for the wine was far down the table and nobody appeared to want to touch it but me. I comforted myself a little by looking at a marvellously beautiful Persian boy who was staying with the family to learn French, but that wasn't enough to stop me from swearing at myself for having come on the motor trip. We left the family, however, and drove to Princess Violet Murat's country place. I knew her, and felt relieved.

No sooner had we arrived than Violet commanded me in an austere tone to go at once to the keg in the corner and have a glass of *marc* (French applejack). Naturally I didn't disobey, and was even overobedient perhaps.

Violet knew that André Germain thought that I drank too much, and she seemed a bit impatient as she talked to him. Finally she said that dinner was to be served. André and Soupault were to go and wash their hands. I started to go with them, but was again ordered by Violet to remain with her. Her command was given in a low voice, but still I again obeyed.

"Quick, while they are gone," the Princess said. "I don't want André talking about me." She grabbed the whisky bottle and filled almost to the top our two tumblers. There wasn't an inch of space into which one could squirt soda water. Up went her glass and mine, and down went the whisky. Never before or since have I ever drunk so large a quantity of whisky, virtually straight, in so short a period of time.

"There's time for another quick one before they get here," Violet said, but this time I poured, and did not fill our glasses by more than a third. When Germain and Soupault arrived we went to dinner. My head was spinning and reeling but I felt magnificent, and, watching Violet, knew that she did also. Both of us were sure that we carried on, aggressively, a sparkling conversation, leading Monsieur Germain and Soupault into areas of wit heretofore unbeknownst to them. We were both sure that we showed no sign of intoxication. Only Germain or Soupault could know and now it is too late for them to prove us wrong.

Germain did have some of my stories translated and later published, but when I was in Berlin he sent me an article which he had written about me and wanted me to wire my permission to have it printed. I was about to do so when I showed it to somebody who read French better than I did, and immediately wired "No". Not in Paris could even an inebriate permit so adulatory an essay as that one, and I wasn't the hardy, buccaneering cowboy he thought. Monsieur Germain never quite forgave me that refusal, because he thought the article beautiful and full of poetry. It was, much too much so. Poor André did not have much of a chance among the cynical young men of those days. There were several of the Frenchmen, one, Jacques Rigaut, now dead, and several others, who had much the same ironic attitude toward him as we Americans had. There was competition among some of the French lot as to who could advance himself most through Germain's wealth and position. It was quite a game, because Monsieur Germain was most careful with his money, and, being lonely, he wanted the companionship of those he aided. That was a demand, because talking to André was rather like talking to an elderly maiden aunt who has a taste for the risqué but whose lack of experience makes her humour "extenuating" after a time.

Migration season struck the Quarter as the first wintry chill began to drive habitués into the smoky and thick interiors of the customary hangouts. I went to Berlin, and there, or soon to be there, were Thelma Wood (sculptor), Marsden Hartley (painter), Djuna Barnes (writer), Berenice Abbott (photographer), Harriet Marsden (dancer), two musicians whose names I have forgotten, Isadora Duncan, and quantities of others, and everybody ready to step out. No one knew from one day to the next what the dollar would bring in marks, but everybody knew that, whatever happened, the dollar bought in Berlin as much as ten or twenty dollars would buy elsewhere. It made for wildness. In spite of the poverty-stricken situation of the people there were several smart cabarets and one futuristic dance place for tea dancing as well as for night encounters. Otherwise there were joints and dives of every order, and there was no telling whom one might encounter, anywhere. From Russia, Poland, the Balkan States, from Scandinavia, England, France, and South and North America, visitors flocked into Berlin, and even hardened Berlin night-lifers could not tell with certainty how the tone or quality of any night club might change from week to week.

Fern Andra and Pola Negri were rival cinema queens and when one arrived at a cabaret and found the other present one of them was sure to leave. Charles Chaplin passed through and Djuna Barnes interviewed him, to report that every bit of scenery or landscape which Chaplin saw in those days looked to him like some Corot painting. Perhaps he had but recently heard of Corot.

Hirschfeld was conducting his psychoanalytic school and a number of souls unsure of their sexes or of their inhibitions competed with each other in looking or acting freakishly, several Germans declared themselves authentic hermaphrodites, and one elderly variant loved to arrive at the smart cabarets each time as a different type of woman: elegant, or as a washwoman, or a street vendor, or as a modest mother of a family. He was very comical and his presence always made for hilarity, as did the presence of a chorus boy from New York. The chorus boy was on in years, but he fancied himself Bert Savoy and was ribaldry outright and extremely weird.

Dopes, mainly cocaine, were to be had in profusion at most night places. A deck of "snow", enough cocaine for quite too much excitement, cost the equal of ten cents. Poverty-stricken boys and girls of good German families sold it, and took it, as they congregated in the dreary night clubs for the warmth not available on the streets or in their homes, if they had homes. I had a huge room at In den Zelten 18. Djuna Barnes had a room in the next house, but Djuna those days was working and did not, as did most of the others, do night life. After several weeks she went to Freiburg to gather material for an article on twilight sleep.

Marsden Hartley was beamingly merry these days, because for the first time in years, on account of the exchange, he could live as he liked to live. One night at a night club, a gala night, he appeared in evening dress, with a huge orchid pinned to his coat lapel. Next to the Adlon Hotel was one of the finest flower shops in the world, and marvellous flowers could be had for little in American money. Because of this Marsden could this night cease to think about the beefsteak realities of existence, and he certainly did luxuriate in orchidean emotions for a time. Not once, but daily, several times, Marsden renounced art and the serious, boring aspect of life. He was weary of reality and intended enjoying the divine trivialities. He liked young people and there were a quantity of them about, and particularly the young German boys and girls were glad to sit with him, telling of their troubles. Marsden was benign and sometimes munificent. He could give away marks, which, meaning but a few pennies to him, meant a day or more of living for the Germans.

It couldn't last, however. Marsden eventually had to return to Paris and to America. He was still giving up art and denouncing grim reality last time I saw him, but he was still painting. It is a horrible admission, but some of us are driven to work at times to forget about living life. That creative urge, if you will, or is it that something remembered or contemplated is more entertaining than the actual scene and event being experienced? Somebody else spoke of Marsden as an "eagle without a cliff", but aren't we all? That somebody else was one of those hard-boiled wisecracking girls, whom I have learned to suspect to be the softest and greatest sentimentalists and liars-to-themselves of any.

Several times I did the night in Berlin then, to arrive at my huge room at eight in the morning accompanied by a retinue of various sexes. The dives having closed, they had no place to go, and my room was large. The first time I sent out for beer and drank on till noon with them and then cleared them out. If any there wanted to steal anything, he or she could, but there was not much chance, as I had not collected them all at any one place and some were unknown to each other. In any case nothing ever was stolen, to my knowledge, unless it was money, and in marks. An American in Berlin then had a right to expect this from virtually starving natives. For about three weeks one girl, Fritzi, stayed around with me and doubtless saved me from various perils. She certainly was of good family, well educated, intelligent, and well dressed; but she was taking cocaine recklessly. Years later I saw her on Unter den Linden, with a man who looked a comfortable and well-off businessman. I wondered if she had married. In any case, while she looked at me I did not show any more sign of recognition than did she. If she had come through to some kind of settled comfort she surely did not care to remember those crazy, despairing days, when there was no gaiety or joy, only recklessness.

Marsden Hartley had been in Berlin before the war and had a

number of friends among the theatrical and artistic people there. Ronnebeck, a sculptor, was about, and Robert Bell, who admired Oscar Wilde's work and painted erotic things far too Beardsleyish to be interesting. In fact too many Germans were Wilde-Beardsley fans in those days. Archipenko was there too, and working. There was an occasional exhibit at the art galleries, but there could hardly have been much incentive to work then, because nobody had money with which to buy, and "Auslanders" passing through were not looking for art.

Lett Haines and Cedric Morris, two English painters, stayed on for a time, and it is possible that Cedric sketched a fawn or two, being the new Gaudier-Brzeska, or perhaps used oils to make painting which looked like water colours in the great English manner of parlour and plush gentility. Thelma Wood, who shows considerable talent both as a sculptor and in her silverpoints, talked of working, but I do not think she got beyond talk, or perhaps a sketch of a camel, flower, giraffe, jungle of monkeys, or under-sea species. She, Lett, and Cedric were about much together, and not one of them but preferred a café to painting in those days, as did all of us.

Mr. and Mrs. Mills (Heyworth and Mariette) arrived from Paris and I met them. Knowing nobody, they asked me to dinner and the theatre frequently during their stay in Berlin and I led a quiet life for a time. But Berlin was making me restive. Heyworth talked of Russia, which I did not want to see then; but he talked of other cities and I began to know that Berlin was getting under my skin and depressing me. The innumerable beggars, paralytics, shell-shocked soldiers, and starving people of good family became at last too violent a depressant. At nights along the Unter den Linden it was never possible to know whether it was a woman or a man in woman's clothes who accosted one. That didn't matter, but it was sad to know that innumerable young and normal Germans were doing anything, from dope selling to every form of prostitution, to have money for themselves and their families, their widowed mothers and younger brothers and sisters.

I went to Munich when the Millses returned to Paris. The Bavarians hated foreigners, particularly Americans, it seemed. I continued on towards Italy, but got sent back from the frontier because I had no *Ausreise* pass. In Munich it was refused me and the American Consulate could do nothing. I returned to Berlin, and by bribing the woman at the passport bureau got an *Ausreise* pass and scurried on into Italy, cursing bureaucracy and damning the Bavarians to deepest hells.

There was no peace anywhere those days. I arrived in Rome unknowingly the day that the Fascists were marching upon the city. I took a room in a *pension* above a garage, and for the next several nights had no sleep. Truckloads of roaring, rowdy boys from the hill towns were in and out of that garage constantly. In Rome were Harold Van Dorn, phlegmatic and sentimental about the glory of old Rome and mad for culture; Eugene McCown, flippant, facile, catty; and later John Mosher, who was a good feeder for McCown and generally bested him as a wit. Mosher was bright and nagging, but barmy enough to be comic when he was at his most serious and, unlike some who look comic, he was keen enough to sense when he had gained a laugh without intention. It was beautiful hearing him tell McCown what he thought of him. None of us liked one another, but for the time being we were around together as Americans in a Fascist-mad Rome. Mosher found his proper occupation on *The New Yorker* later; Van Dorn became head man in a small city museum, and McCown still paints like whoever may be the chic painter of the moment. Then he was out-Picassoing Picasso, with just what is needed lacking.

We heard rumours about Americans having been forcibly fed on castor oil for not having saluted a Fascist parade, or for not knowing the Fascist song. One night at the theatre we failed to rise when the song was being sung, but we got up all right when shouts were directed at us. Another time my hat was brushed violently from my head as I stood on a street corner watching a parade go by. I yearned for a handful of bombs, and took a hate on Italy from which I have never recovered. Still, I did a bit of sight-seeing with Van Dorn, who was more hot on the trail of cathedrals and paintings than I. I prefer other towns in Italy for paintings. Rome never could be a city for me, for the city Italians generally fancy themselves as irresistible, without any basis so far as I can see, though there were quantities of exclamatory American women around finding them "too beautiful".

There can be no more dramatic hill line anywhere than that of Capri, on the road mounting from the piazza to the Hotel Paradiso. I had a room which looked down upon the sea, seven hundred feet below, and the hill line was as subtly carved as Brancusi's golden bird. If there were any of the usual mad foreigners on the island

I did not know them, but the island was rather deserted of foreigners that season. Axel Munthe was there, and Peter Johnson, an English boy, introduced me and we were to go to tea. Upon our arrival for tea, two savage police dogs came at us with murderous intent. Nobody called them back and I, knowing nothing then of Munthe, said, "To hell with that Swede. He must have a nasty disposition to keep savage hounds like that. Let's go to the wineshop and drink." Upon reading Munthe's *San Michele*, I don't regret my attitude. He does seem to fancy himself as an oracle and soothsayer and medicine-healer, and I'm agnostic and sceptical. I may wrong Munthe as a social being, however, but those dogs were savage, and it is a master who influences the disposition of a dog.

Besides Peter Johnson and me there were two other people staying at the hotel, and they kept much to themselves. It was not before the third night that we got into conversation. Peter was telling of Proust's death, and the man spoke. He was plump, black-haired, rosy-cheeked, and eager-looking. He spoke with a strange Irish accent which I could not place.

It was Ludvig Nordström and his wife, also a writer, Maryka Stjernstedt. They both had had considerable reputations in Sweden, and before the war Nordström had been translated and was well known in Germany. As his mother was Irish, his father Swedish, that accounted for his Irish-Swedish English accent. Having been pro-Ally, he was at that time no longer accepted in Germany.

After that, nightly, we sat over a bottle of wine, talking of innumerable things; one of them being the way each of us, Maryka, Ludvig, and myself, found Dostoevsky a disappointment upon rereading. Nordström was at the time working, as he probably still is, on an endless book, tracing the sociologic-psychologic development of mankind. He was to call the innumerable volumes *The World City*, and he had many theories about "totalism", and about how the world would improve only as population increased. Nordström had any amount of imagination and wit, and a lovable personality. It was not necessary to believe in his theories, but as both he and his wife were working, that infected me. We were a hard-working quartet on the hill in Anacapri those six weeks, for Peter Johnson was doing a translation of *Daphnis and Chloe*, which he intended to show George Moore, who "might" do a foreword. I think instead Mr. Moore gave Peter a long talk on "pure poetry", and republished his own translation of *Daphnis and Chloe*, but I am not sure. I doubt the wisdom of young men who consult the aged master, who tells the world of his own beautiful prose style. Young or old, those who have anything to say will have their own way of saying it, and it would be too bad for letters to have an epidemic of Moores breaking loose on the world.

Kay Boyle

1923

In Paris that year I wanted so much to *know* what was taking place inside me ("to know," which D. H. Lawrence saw as a total evil) so that I could put what I was to some kind of use. It was homage, service, to the spirit, perhaps, that I wanted to give, but what good was it if I could not find for it a concrete gesture and name? Bill Williams complained that there are no American servitors, that Americans fear to serve one another, or any man, because of the possible loss of face, the awesome danger of diminishing one's self-esteem, and this seemed true to me. For Americans to serve with a high, clear devotion is nearly impossible, Bill said; and it was perhaps this conviction that had moved him to serve as poet and doctor and friend with such simplicity. Americans look on the ability and willingness to serve as "a trick for foreigners", he wrote; and as a result America got what it deserved: maid service, room service, two-hour dry-cleaning service, while the devout soul went on its lonely humble way.

I wanted to find work in a bookshop (Sylvia Beach's), or with a publishing company (Robert McAlmon's), and give my daily allegiance to the words that others were able to set down, or to the musical notes that others were able to put on paper, or the brush strokes with which others would transform a canvas into history. I was entirely without wisdom or learning, and it seemed to me the fires that burned in me were strong and furious enough in themselves to burn ego and false pride away. But how do I know that I am telling the truth now about what I believed and wanted then?

Then it was 1923, but time was passing, and although I had sat down at a café table with McAlmon, I had been unable to speak to him. Katherine Mansfield had already written that "the stories in *A Hasty Bunch* are extraordinarily good. All of them interested me intensely. There is something fresh and unspoiled about the writer, even when he is self-conscious, in a youthful way. But he has real talent and I think he will do awfully good work. I'd like to help him in some way, but I expect he'd scorn the idea."[1] And Ezra Pound had said of his own review, the *Exile*, that McAlmon was one of his reasons "for starting the thing". Soon it would be 1926, and the young Irish-American editor of *This Quarter*, Ernest Walsh, would write of McAlmon that he was "a great white father" contemplating all humanity, and in his books, as in his life, shutting the door on no one, no matter how grotesque those he encountered seemed. Soon after that it would be 1932, and Katherine Anne Porter would be writing in one of her many affectionate letters to McAlmon that she could line up a dozen points of opposition between his work and Hemingway's, but that she would not for one very good reason, "I consider Hemingway a fraud," she wrote, "and not eligible for any serious comment." And she would go on saying: "I cannot imagine where anyone could find a common starting place for the two of you." (Apparently some critic had.) "As for the point of view, I think Hemingway's is as false and incomplete and superficial as any memoirs of an ex-wife. . . . I remember, not by name but by personality, dozens of your characters, persons who really exist so clearly by themselves I can almost forget that you made them. Hemingway never created one plausible human being, not even that handsome hero of light literature, Mr. Ernest Hemingway."

Almost immediately after that it would be 1934, and Katherine Anne Porter would be writing to McAlmon that in the manuscript of his *Being Geniuses Together*,

> . . . you bring one over to your side very completely; that is to say, you bring me over; merely in the matter of belief. I have read or heard several versions of several events you have told again—Ford, Hemingway, Beach, *et al.*, versions of things—and I swear I take your version always as the true one. . . . I can't begin to write you in detail about the memoirs. I have only

[1] Katherine Mansfield's *Letters*, Vol. II, p. 497.

read them once, but I can say straight off I think the whole
tone is right and good . . . and all kinds of qualities in your
mind—a nice sour humour and sharpness of eye and the ability
to size up people and situations—show up better here than they
ever have when you worked in fiction based on fact. After all,
your book is a history, a very original and first-hand one; it is
better to publish now as much of it as you can get accepted,
and leave the full first complete version to be done later. Meantime, our concern is with the present.

That was exactly it. My concern was so desperately with the
present that when I got back to the hotel room after that first meeting with McAlmon I was consumed by a rage of impatience for the
immediate past and the wasted months in St. Malo. What difference
did it make that I had written over a hundred pages of a book, and
countless poems, if I had not found a way to bring that brooding,
inner life into the field of action? The pernod was still winging in
my blood as I sat down on the shiny, chrome-yellow bedspread
(glossy artificial silk, it was, interwoven with the coarsest cotton into
the horror of a spurious brocade). Tonight, great decisions must be
taken, I told my rather drunken reflection in the armoire glass as I
waited for Richard to return. For the moment, cease to write,
I ordered myself; fling introspection out of the window until you
can give your professed intentions the substance of granite, marble,
unassailable stone. At last Richard came in, hungry and depressed,
after his all-day round of interviews. "French businessmen," he said
bitterly. "I've seen six of them since I started out this morning:
La Compagnie Générale de l'Electricité du Sud et des Basses Alpes,
and La Compagnie de l'Electricité des Eaux et du Gaz de l'Ouest et
du Nord-Ouest, and La Compagnie Anonyme de l'Electricité
Algérienne et des Pays Lointains, and—"
    I interrupted this in virtuously drunken accents to tell him that
in this instant of the present we must find our people and commit
ourselves to them; that we must cast aside all others; that we must
do this without delay, for time was short and the years were passing;
that it behooved us now to *know*. "Know *what?*" Richard asked with
a good deal of sense; but sense at this moment affronted me, and I
picked up my big black hat from the bed, and jerked the eternal red
scarf into place around my shoulders, and I went out of the hotel
room and down the narrow, cheaply carpeted stairs, and out into

the street. Only now do I recognize that the costume I wore and the tumult of my spirit were a moment in the same history of protest that is being acted out by the tormented young today. Three young men bumped into me as I walked under the corner street light, and one cried out in ridicule: "*Mon Dieu*, I didn't know it was *mardi gras* already!" So there I was, just one more preposterous figure in the endless masquerade ball of the generations, one of the infinitude of outlandishly attired girls harassed by agonies and doubts, crying out the repeated and forever unanswered questions—there I was running half drunk down a cobbled Paris street. It was not carnival time, or anything like it. I was decked out merely to conform with the total absurdity of my particular despair. And now, almost half a century later, girls wearing their grandmothers' clothes wander the city streets of the world barefooted, their hair to their waists under the floppy brims of velvet hats. Hand in hand with them go bearded, questing young men in the piecemeal uniforms of Confederate soldiers or of shepherds in ponchos, leather-thonged sandals laced to their knees. But listen, world, it is not carnival time. It is not *mardi gras*. The hearts are not light. There is absolutely no confetti to throw.

I do not know how I got to the Bois de Boulogne that gentle September night, or even why I went there. It was perhaps by bus, but more likely by walking street after street, avenue after avenue. I do not know how late it was when I at last sat down on the dark wet grass beside a lake which appeared to be as far-reaching as the sea. I sat there seeing, or else believing that I saw, the shadowy forms of swans drift past; believing that I heard them seeking for food beyond in the tall reeds to the musical rippling of the tide. There may have been a moon, or perhaps only a great many stars, but I know there was light that glimmered and died and glimmered again in long silver lances on the mist-veiled water as the swans moved by. After a little (or after hours, perhaps) I got up and found a bench under the soft boughs of the trees. I took off my wild hat, and I lay down on the wood of the bench, and unknotted my scarf and folded it, and placed it for a pillow under my head. Neither despairing nor lamenting, and not in gratification, but quite immune to all emotion, I fell asleep; and I dreamed that the swans came dripping from the water and spread their wings in strong, metallic shields across my long, thin dress.

I awoke in the morning to the voices of birds in the branches over me, and I got up from the bench and went to the lake, or pond, or pool, or inland sea, and kneeled down and washed my face. My mouth was parched, but I was afraid to drink this captive water. I was hungry, too, but I knew the few francs I had in my purse must be saved for other things. I walked past the little Bagatelle palace-farm, where Marie Antoinette had played with her ladies in waiting at being a milkmaid, following the direction of what I now intended to do. I would go to Sylvia Beach's shop and ask her for Robert McAlmon's address, and once I had found him, I would ask him to give me a job. I could type, I could take dictation, I could read proof. I would tell him that I wanted to give a shape to life that would be solid and symmetrical and illuminated by the clearest flood of active light. Its logic and its aura would be such that Richard would suddenly be enabled to see the way to build his own career. "The scales will fall from his eyes," I kept thinking, and the image this evoked filled me with wonder. I could see the ebony scales fall like the shells of beetles from Richard's lids, and the imagined radiance of his gaze, released now from the cave in which it had always lurked in darkness, abruptly filled me with joy.

But even if I could not explain to McAlmon my need to serve, he would somehow hear the words I could not say. I caught a bus at the Avenue Henri Martin, and I rode standing on the back platform, holding to the railing in the early light of the sun. I would get a cup of coffee and a croissant on the quais, I thought, and then saunter idly across the bridge to the Rue de l'Odéon, and present myself to Sylvia Beach almost casually; intensity, nervousness, uncertainty, set aside for the moment, as the white earrings and the lip rouge had once been set aside. It was perhaps an essential part of the heedlessness of my protest that I did not wonder at all about the state of mind that Richard must be in over my absence since the night before. I would hurry back to him when I had triumphed, and the scales on his eyes would wither and fall. But for some reason Shakespeare and Company was closed, and I could not understand it. It was not a Sunday, the *Quatorze Juillet* was past, and the *Jour des Morts* lay almost two months ahead. And then I saw the face of a clock down the street, the hands of it marking seven-fifteen. I would not believe this until I had walked four blocks on the Boulevard St. Germain, and confirmed it by a clock seen through the plate glass of a pharmacy as an employee rolled the corrugated metal curtain up, and by the clock in the church tower of St. Germain des Prés.

So I crossed the Seine again, and the quayside stalls were beginning to open, one here, one there, and the prints and etchings and books were laid out in the sun. The bird shops, too, were opening, and I stopped to talk to nightingales and mourning doves in their separate cages, and to acquire a new boldness from the royal blue and scarlet tail feathers of a parrot with his scaled ivory foot chained to his perch. And then, with no warning whatsoever, no bending down of the trees in salutation, no rising of the river's waters in exultation, no halting in reverence of the buses, the taxis, or the people who were beginning to fill the street, I found in one of the bookstalls a Tauchnitz edition paperback copy of George Moore's *The Lake*. It was worn, and the cover ragged, and gone brown around the edges. There was a thin little string around it to hold its pages together. It cost twenty-five centimes, and I held it tenderly, rejoicing that I had not eaten a croissant after all. I carried it back to the Tuileries gardens, and climbed to the terrace overlooking the Place de la Concorde, and sat down and began to read.

I read on into the afternoon, thinking of nothing beyond the miracle of these pages, Sylvia Beach forgotten, and McAlmon, Richard, Paris, forgotten, forgotten. There was only Ireland speaking to me now. When I came to the final page it seemed to me that life itself was coming to an end; but then in the last paragraph, as the priest lays his cassock aside and prepares to swim the waters of the lake, the words that I have since loved like music came swelling to the brink. "There is a lake in every man's life," they went, "and he must ungird his loins for the crossing." I jumped up, so filled with emotion that I could scarcely breathe, and I ran down the stone steps to the gravel path, and crossed the gardens quickly to the Rue de Rivoli. As I walked, the words kept changing in my mind from "life" to "heart", from "heart" back to "life" again. "There is a lake in every man's heart", I would recall it at one moment, and in the next it would be: "There is a lake in every man's life." I ran across the Avenue de l'Opéra and finally reached the small back street where the hotel was. In the narrow passageway Richard was standing at the desk, and he turned and saw me, and we rushed into each other's arms.

He said: "Thank God," and I saw the scales fall from his eyes. There they lay on the cracked marble squares of the entrance hall, and now the tears could fall through. "I have a job," he said almost in apology. "I have a job. We'll have dinner in a restaurant tonight, and a bottle of wine. We're going to live in Le Havre. We'll get a place to live near the big docks where we can see the ships coming and going. Normandy's closer to America than Brittany. It will have different kinds of things to say."

So we had pernod before dinner, and we didn't eat pickled pig's feet or tripe out of a cardboard container, sitting together on the side of the hotel bed, as we had every night before. We ate on the Boulevard des Capucines, talking with assurance of all that lay ahead. We would be poor as the French were poor, and the mere fact of this would define our meaning and our geographical place. But with the vision washed clear by wine it is strange I did not see then that the lake I had slept beside in the Bois and George Moore's lake in Ireland were the same, and I had failed to make my way across.

Robert McAlmon
1923-1924

In Paris I lingered over the Christmas-New Year period. The Rotonde and the Dôme were then both small cafés, crowded and smoke-filled. To enter either was to encounter a mass of dark and gloomy faces: Russian, Polish, and other despondent nationalities. The gayer souls had all flown to Italy, the south of France, and various sunnier places. Mariette Mills, however, gave frequent dinner parties, and I dined with her or other friends and kept away from cafés. Mariette had studied sculpturing with Bourdelle, and she now had her beautiful studio in the Rue Boissonnade in which hung paintings by Oleg Skrypiscin and Picabia, and where Heyworth Mills either manufactured wholly or repaired model ships. At that time Picabia, Blaise Cendrars, Léger, Satie, Brancusi, and innumerable others frequented her place. Mariette Mills has a handsome head, a refined Caesar Borgian type, with iron-grey locks, slightly protruding Egyptian-wolf eyes, and a quick apprehensive wit and sensibility. She could have been a hostess in the grand manner, but she sculpted, liked her country home, and preferred permanent friendships rather than acquaintances who were entertaining for the moment. When Picabia, Léger, Brancusi, Mina Loy, Marcel Duchamp were there to dinner, there was brighter and more intelligent conversation than one was apt to get elsewhere in Paris.

Blaise Cendrars had been in Africa and South America, and had recently translated a book of primitive Negro songs and poems. He brought with him to Mariette's parties explorers, scientists, and anthropologists. The ambition of the moment seemed to be to become as African-Negroid as possible, and after dinner, when guests congregated in the studio, a great deal of stamping and shouting, and primitive dancing and singing, took place. Brancusi, a Rumanian peasant with a patriarchal beard and mild kind eyes, had lately procured a phonograph and a few records. Brancusi loved Americans and things American, and pranced about as the spirit of the jazz age, although at times wearing his wooden sabots. Léger and Heyworth and Cendrars stamped and hooted and catcalled until Mariette quieted them down so that Suzanne Penoit could sing selections from Satie in her thin, high, clear voice.

Brancusi too liked to give dinners, which he cooked himself. The Mills had given him one of their white Samoyeds, a bitch, with a lovely bush of a tail. Brancusi kept her faultlessly clean, and her white fur made her a wraith-dog as she moved quietly about in the studio filled with great chunks of white stone and marble. The dining table was a huge round slab, and the stove had been made by Brancusi himself of stones piled one on the other. The meals started with a kirsch, Rumanian hors d'œuvres, and then steak or roast chicken, salad and fruit, and, of course, quantities of wine. Brancusi delighted in cooking, and he and I managed to exchange conversation with a certain amount of fluency in spite of the fact that my French was slight and Brancusi's accent difficult. One night after dinner we did Montmartre, and naturally did the non-de-luxe places where we could express ourselves freely. At three in the morning Brancusi was leading a parade of cabaret habitués over tables, downstairs and up again, and back over the tables to where we sat, and there everybody had champagne. He was singing a Rumanian song and the *poules* were singing the current song hit of Mistinguette. Brancusi, who looked dignified and patriarchal, always retained the folk ability to celebrate as though it were a fête day, or some event dear to the heart of the singing-dancing pastoral Balkans.

Pascin too liked to give parties, and the more various the types present the better pleased he was, so long as good will prevailed. Pascin and I did not like each other at first, for no reason that either of us could explain, except that each was a type new to the other. Having spent some time in the East Indies, Pascin managed to inject a good deal of sultry colour into his parties. There were generally two or three Negro models—one beautiful girl child—and the atmosphere could not have been more informal. Pascin himself was usually quiet, perhaps even morbid, but he obviously liked to entertain and to let people be themselves. It occurs to me as I write of him that there were rarely French painters or writers in our group. Léger, yes, but the others, Brancusi, Pascin, Nils de Dardel, Picabia, were not French, however long they may have been in France. A few French writers—such as Jacques Baron, René Crevel, Cocteau, and Soupault—had gone in for cultivating Americans. I have had several passing friendships with French-Frenchmen, but always there's a drifting apart. It is possible within a few months to know a Spaniard better than it is to know a Frenchman, ever.

The Boeuf sur le Toit[1] was then the popular tea-dance and cabaret place. Cocteau had a hand in starting it, and Les Six, composers headed by Erik Satie, frequented the Boeuf. Mary Butts came there frequently. Her hair, which looked as though it had been soaked in red ink, framed her full white face and her thin-skinned liquid lips. Mary breathed in an exalted ecstasy of being. "My lamb," she would sigh. "You clean, pure, young American. You are a gentleman, one of us, but you don't know the depths, the depravity of Europe. There are sinister forces, there is a black cloud gathering to overwhelm us all, and we must combat it with the good, the pure, the sweet, the true."

I had published her *Ashe of Rings*, and she was most effusive. After a time I got squirmy when Mary started her "My lamb, you are a gentleman, one of us" line, and I wondered how much Mary, who at these times was being very much the aristocrat, wanted to nick me for. But she may have been right. Perhaps we pure, we clean, we healthy young Americans didn't then know anything about the depths of Europe, or that grim darkness which was about to descend on us. Possibly we have learned a little, and are still learning more, but Mary, Mary, to be one of you? I ask myself, do I want that?

Now, after a month of Paris, I felt I must get away. I had no love, merely an infatuation for the place. Upon arriving there after an

---

[1] The Boeuf sur le Toit, located at 28 Rue Boissy d'Anglas, is described as follows in a Paris guide book published in 1925:

> This pleasant restaurant symbolizes very well the work of Jean Cocteau its god-father: the wildest fantasy within the finest of established traditions. At the Boeuf one encounters the artistic trend of the moment, the literary trend of the moment, and, briefly, *the* trend of the moment, whatever it may be. If one hears here the most astounding declarations that are being made in Paris, one is at the same time certain to eat exceedingly well. There are Alsatian specialities, such as *foies gras* in pastry; and there are excellent Rhine wines, not to mention quetsche and mirabel, to transport you far away from Paris. Average price of a meal: 25 francs.

absence, I was always in a fever of excitement, and couldn't do quickly enough the bars of Montparnasse and the cabarets of Montmartre, and the Champs Elysées district. Like Fanny Hill, however, my fever for curiosities abated as the blood stream flowed more coolly and the arteries hardened. Crossing the Seine into the Place de le Concorde on a misty spring morning, or seeing Notre Dame des Champs from river level at dawn, when well on with drink, still brought a foaming ecstasy into me, a stroke of lightning to the heart or mind about the wonder of it. But I knew all too well that Paris is a bitch, and that one shouldn't become infatuated with bitches, particularly when they have wit, imagination, experience, and tradition behind their ruthlessness.

About this time there appeared on the terrace of the Dôme two girls who looked like walking wax models. Call them Sari and Toni. The younger of them, then sixteen, was feeling her oats and endeavouring to attract attention. She was slight, and beautifully formed, and full of an adolescent, sullen vitality. Very soon she and Toni were at my table having coffee and a sandwich, and Sari explained that she was bored with posing for inferior artists. "It is no fun to be sixteen and to know too much about life," she said.

Sari wanted a gin fizz, her first, she claimed. And she had it. She was eager to dance. I, having danced weekly my ten to twenty miles during the great days of Irene and Vernon Castle, was still a dancing fool, so we headed toward the Boeuf sur le Toit, and that day, as always, Toni came along. In after days Sari complained with melancholy bitterness that Toni always stayed with her because Toni herself did not attract people. Toni was pretty, with finely delineated eyebrows, and a skin as smooth as wax, but she lacked *élan vital* and was not magnetic. Almost daily we Quarterites went to the Boeuf: Nina Hamnett, Florence Martin, onetime Follies girl, Mary Reynolds, and others. The French frequented these tea dances too. By the third day Sari and Raymond Radiguet had become acquainted. She loved to dance and was always ready for a whirl about the floor with me, but she returned to the bar to talk to Radiguet. I was left to talk with Toni or Nina Hamnett, and generally chose Nina, who had a ready wit and an experience of the Paris-London bohemian world dating back before the war. She had been friendly with Apollinaire, Modigliani, Gaudier-Brzeska, and, indeed, knew everybody and everything, and never let facts ruin a story she wanted to tell.

And now love's complicated dream was having its way with young Sari and Raymond Radiguet. At whatever time I might turn up in the Quarter, Sari was sure to be there. She swore that she was not in love with Radiguet. She was young, but she insisted she knew love was a myth; but she wanted to dance. Would I take her to the Boeuf? No, no, she couldn't go alone. She didn't want to go because of Radiguet. He probably wouldn't be there. But she *must* dance. Of course I took her to the Boeuf, and there Radiguet was. The days when he came late, she was in a fever of torment until he arrived. Cocteau, sensing danger regarding his "baby" Radiguet, took to turning up nightly, and the four of them, Toni and Cocteau, Radiguet and Sari, went to dinner together. Finally Sari admitted that she and Radiguet did like each other very much. Being Polish, she was afraid that Cocteau in his jealousy was trying to have her deported so that he might have Radiguet to himself. She swore that he followed them, and many the trick she and Radiguet played to evade his surveillance.

At one time Cocteau declared that Wilde's *Dorian Gray* had ruined his life, as he had remained an incomplete narcissist. He had Berenice Abbott and others photograph his hands and his face as he slept, and the hands and the face emerged in these photographs as waxen masks, almost death masks. His obsession with his own "beauty", however, did not prevent his being devoted to Radiguet.

It all ended when Radiguet died.[2] He caught a cold, and it developed into pneumonia. It is said that when he was dying Cocteau let him have all the drink he wanted so that he might die as he was born, unconscious. At all events two people, Sari and Cocteau, were heartbroken at his death. I think Cocteau was generous to Sari then. I had never cared for him, but three times I saw Cocteau come through with sympathy and understanding and competence in tragic circumstances. He had wit, if it was a bit on the malicious side. There's the belief that witty people are cruel, but they are perhaps less dangerous than the adulators who insist upon finding qualities in us which we have no desire to possess.

Radiguet was surely older than his acclaimed seventeen when he wrote *Le Diable au corps*, but he remained till the end a sweetly sullen child, burning with the pubescent heat which tormented him. He had got involved in "lavender" circles, but in various other

[2] Djuna Barnes's short story, "The Little Girl Continues" (*This Quarter*, Vol. I, No. II, 1925), describes Radiguet's death.

groups he was just another precocious and energetic youth who wanted amusement. On one occasion, after a dinner party, he and Brancusi, in dinner jackets, boarded a train for Nice and then took a boat to Corsica, and there they fitted themselves out in fishermen's clothes for their return to Paris. Radiguet also was too prone to like girls for the contentment of the group that had elected him a genius.

Later the Sari child got involved with another French artist, bore his baby, and told him to go to hell when he offered to adopt the child and pay for its education. Perhaps she calculated and knew her man, but I think she was authentically impulsive. In the end, however, the child's father married her, and he might have done far worse.

Ford Madox Ford (né Hueffer) made his appearance and intended to publish the first of the English-French periodicals, the *Transatlantic Review*. I had never read his works but was prepared to believe Ezra Pound that he was "one of us". He was stout and blond, with a walruslike moustache. He wheezed and talked in an adenoids-clogged voice, often in a secretive manner, so that I had difficulty understanding him, and did not necessarily believe him when I did. It was quite impossible to talk of a place or a person without Ford topping your story. Various people had informed me that before the war he claimed to be German, and a friend of the Kaiser's. But as soon as the war was declared he became most British and had his name legally changed to Ford. At the time I met him he was being, and telling the world that he was, the master of prose style in the English language. Later I found his books (except for *The Good Soldier*) meandering and fuzzy and impossible to struggle through. He is another of those writers who make the character, drawn from himself, compensate for the frustrations which occurred in his actual life. Without hesitation, I can categorize Ford as a mythomaniac.

On one occasion Ford assured me that he was a genius, that he was born of a family of geniuses and in the tradition of genius. Another time he assured William Bird, Harriet Weaver, and me that his works had more readers than those of H. G. Wells, but that his readers were willing to wait to get his books from the libraries. Mr. Ford was one of the "masters" who likes to believe that all of the young come to sit at his feet. Miss Stein was another. I am not, and was not, one of the adorers of or listeners to either Stein or Ford. But from now on I'll be tender about Ford, who had many likeable and admirable traits. He gave some very amusing parties, having the sense to give them in a bistro, and leave them wide open, with no one taking too much responsibility.

A very sad and funny episode occurred about this time with Joyce. *Ulysses* was out, and he had not, to my knowledge, started his new work. His eyes had been operated on and he was feeling high-spirited, when an old friend of the Zürich days, an Englishman named Frank Budgen, arrived in Paris. Joyce was feeling "right proper" and was, because of Miss Weaver's subsidy, no longer poverty-stricken. Budgen, however, was very poor and much impressed by the réclame with which *Ulysses* had been received. The staid English papers were fully horrified and righteous, while patronizingly admitting a talent. The London *Pink 'Un* was less intellectual. It merely stated that "the main contents are enough to make a Hottentot sick . . . not alone sordidly pornographic, but it is intensely dull." The book *is* dull. It takes a person highly curious about life and letters, one of those supermorons, an intellectual, to read it through. Still, it is sad that the *Police Gazette* of America did not also comment on *Ulysses*.

Joyce, Budgen, and I were at the Gypsy Bar, for old time's sake, and Djuna Barnes and Mina Loy joined us. The girls were very adoring toward Joyce, the master. Joyce and Budgen were a few drinks ahead of me, but I, having the zeal of youth, quickly caught up. The girls were not slow at drinking, either, but while tolerating me they didn't fancy Mr. Budgen. He kept the conversation from becoming profound or brilliant, and soon developed a drunken man's feeling of having been cut down and thought inferior. Finally he rushed out into the night, and Joyce believed that Budgen had thought him lacking in loyalty and bigheaded over his success. Joyce then enjoyed a thoroughly Irish period of despair and melancholy. The women tried to comfort him, but he preferred drink. Finally they departed, slightly huffy.

Joyce and I lingered until five in the morning, when the *patron* told us to get out. Out we got, and ensconced ourselves in a small bistro on the Boulevard St. Germain. We bought cigars, and we drank. As we had decided to drink through the list of French drinks, Joyce began dropping his cigars. At first I leaned to pick them up and return them to him. When I could no longer lean without falling on my face I took to lighting the cigars and handing them to him. He almost immediately dropped them, and I lighted cigar after cigar until they were all gone, and then we took to cigarettes. At ten in the morning we sat alone in the small bistro, the floor covered with some twenty cigars, innumerable cigarettes, and the table with the forty glasses which had held our various drinks. The *patron*, whom I saw later, could not believe that such animals as we were had ever lived. He thinks he dreamed that early morning, but he helped Joyce into a taxi, and Joyce and I drove to his hotel. The taxi driver would not carry him upstairs, and I praise my own youth and ability to hold drink then. I carried him up. We got into the big room that he shared with Nora, and she looked at him and began.

"Jim, you've been doin' this for twenty years, and I'm tellin' you it's the end. Do you understand? You've been bringin' your drunken companions to me too long, and now you've started McAlmon in the same way."

I flopped Joyce on his bed and told Nora that Joyce had received a great blow this night, Budgen having rushed out into the night, laying the curse upon him.

Nora turned tender. "I always told him that man would do him no good."

I stripped Joyce of a few of his clothes and went back to my own hotel to sleep, to die, to know agony, to curse Joyce, life, myself. My head was vertiginously in torment; my eyes revolved in red-hot sockets; my stomach quivered with nausea. Just as I had got to sleep, at three in the afternoon, a boy arrived with a telegram from Joyce saying that I must not fail him. I must be in for tea at four-thirty. Although it took me three months to get my health mildly into order after that night, I did struggle into my clothes and go to Joyce's hotel. He sat looking owl-like and earnest as I entered the room. "And, McAlmon, what have you been hearing today about the apartment the man said we were to have?"

In a second, which was a million years, my mind received the idea that Joyce had been telling Nora a cover-up story. "Oh, he's seeing about it now. I'm to meet him at six o'clock," I answered. For a long time Nora had been intent on moving into an apartment and living a non-hotel life, and Joyce now, who was given to expecting that things would be done for him, hoped not only that would I cover his tales to Nora but that I would locate an apartment for him. If he'd been bright, he would have secured a promise from me when I was drunk and I might have made an effort, as I had kept my word about typing the last fifty pages of *Ulysses*, the Molly Bloom interior monologue.

At that time the husband of the English typist who was typing his work had destroyed some forty pages of the original script of *Ulysses*, because it was obscene. Joyce was naturally scared about handing out his work to typists, and most typists would insist on putting in punctuation which he did not desire. He knew that I typed not well but quickly and had suggested it one night as we were drinking. I thought then, "Fifty pages, that's nothing, sure I'll type it for him."

The next day he gave me the handwritten script, and his hand-writing is minute and hen-scrawly; very difficult to decipher. With the script he gave me four notebooks, and throughout the script were marks in red, yellow, blue, purple, and green, referring to phrases which must be inserted from one of the notebooks. For about three pages I was painstaking, and actually retyped one page to get the insertions in the right place. After that I thought, "Molly might just as well think this or that a page or two later, or not at all," and made the insertions wherever I happened to be typing. Years later I asked Joyce if he had noticed that I'd altered the mystic arrangement of Molly's thought, and he said that he had, but agreed with my viewpoint. Molly's thoughts were irregular in several ways at best.

During all this period I had a room at the Foyot, and through the months innumerable acquaintances stayed there. There was much visiting back and forth between rooms, and much ordering of drinks, but it was comradely, and we had moments of enjoying the sodden destruction of time in a weary world. The moral and righteous will accuse us of lacking standards and intelligence, but it was neither intelligence nor standards which any of us lacked. It was belief. Curtis Moffat, for one, made an art of boredom, and advocated a tornado of it. Though American, he expressed boredom in an accent more English than any educated Englishman's I have ever known. Curtis let me in for one of those typing sessions too. Perhaps I was foolish to let people know that I typed quickly.

I was having coffee at the Dôme bar one day when Curtis approached and informed me that Michael Strange (then Mrs. John Barrymore) was in his taxi. "She has a short play she wants typed by tomorrow night, and I thought you might do it, Bob. Only half an hour's work."

I wasn't pleased, but had heard that Michael Strange was beautiful and entertaining. I told Curtis to bring her in. The next day Michael Strange came to my room at the Foyot. She wore a tailored suit, with pockets, and after a little chitchat we got down to the typing of the script. It was a play about Antony and Cleopatra, and in it Caesar's son played a part. Oh, glamour, and draperies, and poetry pouring voluptuous colour and rhythms upon our prose-worn minds! Miss Strange put her hands in her pockets and strode back and forth across the room, from time to time brushing back her hair with an inspiration-fevered hand. I sat stolidly at the typewriter and wrote as she dictated, only now and then halting her as her inspiration sprang to flower too quickly for my not too nimble fingers. I was far too busy catching her fervid words to laugh, and also too riled at Curtis for having suggested that I do this typing. Miss Strange failed to strike me as beautiful, clever, or attractive, and the play was the most awful tosh I have ever allowed myself to sit through. She should have paid some poverty-stricken typist the highest commercial rates rather than impose on the unknown acquaintance of a friend. Miss Strange had wealth then, and I didn't forgive the imposition.

Kay Boyle

1923-1924

So we journeyed to Le Havre, and there, as if it were the most natural thing in the world, we became members of the proletariat. Richard's salary was three hundred and fifty francs a month, which meant, he said, that we could pay fifty francs a month for rent, and every other expense must be kept within ten francs a day. With what remained of Charlotte's gift to us, Richard bought a secondhand bicycle, so there would at least be no daily bus fare to pay out, and he also paid a month's rent on a two-room furnished apartment. It was on the Rue du Jardin, within walking distance of the English Channel, *la Manche*, the grey sleeve of water that lay between England and France. That tattered sleeve was blown night and day against the jetty—the jetty past which all the great ocean liners, and all the cargo boats, and the tramp steamers, must manœuvre when they came into the harbour—and blown so wildly that it seemed like the wide-open sea. The rent of the apartment was seventy-five francs a month, which was more than we could afford, but it was only a temporary stopping place. While Richard worked all day at the electric company, I would walk through the poorer sections of the city, looking and looking until I would find a cheaper place. In the meantime we read *L'Humanité* every morning, and the voices of the family in Brittany, and the sight of their faces, were wiped away as if they had never been.

The apartment was on the ground floor, which was convenient, for water for every purpose had to be carried to it from a street pump half a block up the hill. The toilet, which took up a corner of our slimy-stoned court, was shared with two other families. There was no light in the court, but the toilet could be found quite easily even in the dark by the enormity of its odour. In the kitchen, which had seen so much of life, there was one modern appliance: a gas ring on which to heat the morning *café au lait*; but this was not at all in keeping with the rigorous spirit of the place. The main business of cooking must be done on an inscrutable coal-burning stove which took up the entire back wall of the sad and menacing kitchen. It had a broken grate and a clogged flue, this stove, and from every hinge and screw seeped wraiths of smoke. Also it lacked understanding of what its functions were, for it sought to snuff out any flame that contrived to tremble for an instant in its iron depths. It was asked of it to heat the rooms, as well as the water consigned to it, but it had no intention of complying; nor did it have any interest in cooking anything at all. On bad days it took me from six in the morning until nearly noon to get a fire started, and even when I had apparently succeeded, still the food I placed in the vast oven was merely insulated from draughts, and emerged two or three hours later in exactly the same condition as when I had put it in.

Once during those dreary autumn weeks Jean's chauffeur in his handsome leather puttees knocked unexpectedly at the door. He had been sent by the family with a limousine full of apples and pears from the château orchard, and cabbages from Papa's garden, and there he stood in peasant amazement, holding his cap in his gloved hand. Richard was still at work, and although it was nearly dusk I had not turned the light on, in order to save electricity. I had done the week's wash in the stone sink that day, and Richard's shirts and underwear and our sheets and pillowcases now hung dripping from the lines strung from chandelier to armoire, to window jamb, and back to the chandelier again. This great silent company of clothes completely filled the room. Pools of water had collected on the ancient linoleum, and Jean's chauffeur ducked under the hanging sheets and stepped cautiously around the spreading water as he carried basket after basket in. This was one kind of apple, and this was another, he explained, and the pears were green enough still to keep all winter if put on shelves in the cellar, or even in the attic; and after he had said this we did not look at each other any more because we suddenly knew that neither cellar nor attic was permitted to the working class.

When the limousine was empty he straightened up to go, but at the moment that I reached for the string of the chandelier to light his way, the clothesline slipped from its moorings and down on top of us came the washing in a great sagging, sodden mess. He fought his way free of the wet winding sheets, and shook off the clinging white arms of Richard's shirts, and left; and I began picking up out of the lakes of water and coal dust on the floor the filthy sheets and pillowcases, and the long-legged, grotesque underwear that Papa had given Richard when we left Brittany. And now I began crying for everything in the world, crying for Charlotte's death, and for the unborn child that had died within her, and for the great hopes we had had for our life in France that had come to nothing in the end. I cried like the weakest woman in the world for the shirts and the underwear and the bed linen that would never be entirely white again; and then I flung a bucketful of *boulets* into the black and evil stove, and I watched smoke as opaque and green as phlegm ooze from every fissure of its rusty armour. After a while the hideousness of my own face and of everything around me made me stop crying, and I went out into the autumn dark to the pump for water, and began all over again, working fast so as to get as much cleaned up as I could before Richard would come cycling home.

It was then that I recognized the truth about tears : that, whatever the circumstances, they are always shed in self-pity. From then on, this stunning realization kept me dry-eyed for the greater part of my life. The next day I avoided the stove, and although it was damp and cold in the apartment I started writing again, taking up where I had left off with a long poem called "The Book of Cincinnati", and beginning one about Le Havre which was finally called "Harbour Song". And that day too I began writing to an Italian poet who had gone to America at the age of sixteen, so as to avoid the war in Europe, and worked as a dishwasher and a waiter in New York, and eventually became an editor of *Poetry* magazine. His name was Emanuel Carnevali, and it was Lola who had first spoken of him to me, and showed me his poems, and every time she had said the syllables of his name it was like a song beginning. He had fallen ill with sleeping sickness, and for a long time he had been taken care of by Harriet Monroe and the poets of America, but then in 1922, just before I arrived in New York, they had had to send him back to Italy.[1]

[1] See *The Autobiography of Emanuel Carnevali*, compiled and edited by Kay Boyle. Horizon Press, New York, 1967.

Once Lola had read me his poem "The Return", a long poem which closes with these lines:

> I have come back and have found you
> All new and friendly, O Fatherland!
> I have come back with a great burden,
> With the experience of America in my head—
> My head which now no longer beats the stars.
> O Italy, O great shoe, do not
> Kick me away again!

Despite the love the poets of America bore him, Carnevali had written in fierce denunciation of Lola, and of Bill Williams, and Alfred Kreymborg, and Maxwell Bodenheim, saying: "If you are poets, as they say, then I don't want to be a poet. I say you discovered yourselves and you're disgusted with the find and you are hiding behind a thick-woven, ragged curtain of image-words, stunts, tricks, of verse that lacks even the one-two-three-dip of rhymes which would at least make them decisively comic. . . . Like the rest, you have forgotten your youth. You have been defeated by the world. If you say that you never fought, that will only place you as cowards. If you say nothing, then I'll shout into your ears that the world expects a formal surrender from you!"[2]

I sent my letter to Carnevali to the address Lola had given me, to the public hospital in Bazzano, and every day that I looked for his answer to come I thought of the poem he had written as he lay ill and despairing on the shore of Lake Michigan. He had lain on the sand, and every night he had said to the sweltering city: "Tomorrow will be beautiful, for tomorrow comes out of the lake."

And now, as a member of the proletariat of the world, I began to lie and steal. The lie concerned the gas and electric bill which we did not have the money to pay when we left the apartment in the Rue du Jardin. It amounted to twelve francs, and I told the landlady to send the bill on to us at a fictitious address. So shy and modest and well bred I must have seemed to her that she allowed me to move our few possessions out. Many months later we came face to face at a bus stop, and I turned and ran. She pursued me for two blocks, a thin, dark, birdlike little woman in a long rust-coloured coat, and when

2 Ibid.

I reached the old, shabby building that housed the post office, I fled in one door, and past the barred wickets, and out another door. For a long time after that I kept off the main avenues, and I turned my face in another direction whenever a bus went by. The theft I committed was the stealing of a cat as it sat contentedly on a garden wall watching the activity of sparrows in the wintry branches of the city trees.

I was coming home from the fish market, and this handsome, well-fed cat spoke to me in greeting as I went by. I do not know why I retraced my steps, after I had gone a block or so, and stole it; or why, having carried it, struggling, the mile back to our room, I did not return it under cover of darkness that evening to the house and garden which were its rightful home. It was an exceptionally beautiful cat, with eyes of transparent jade, a grey and ebony striped coat, and the mindless face of a chorus girl. Perhaps it was the cat's very opulence, its slothfulness, and its unperturbed well-being, that made me wish to transfer it to our poor and colourless room, as one transfers a bright decalcomania to the faded paper on a wall. That room without a window, without a rug, without a comfortable chair, was marvellously embellished by the cat's presence. Whenever the live crabs I brought home from *les halles* escaped from my *filet*, the cat would drive them out from under the bed and help me to round them up and subdue them, Once, when I tried to boil a sea spider in a saucepan that was too small to contain its long, armoured legs, only the cat's untroubled and quite merciless translucent gaze saved me from losing my senses as the spider legs did a tap dance to the death on the top of the stove.

But there were moments when my guilt as liar and thief made it impossible for me to work, that is, to continue with my obsession of setting words down on a page. A long time afterward when I read Gandhi's *Story of My Experiments with Truth*, I discovered it was at the exact period of my stealing the cat that he was writing in jail of how he, when young, had stolen "coppers from the servant's pocket money in order to purchase Indian cigarettes". And there was as well the more serious theft he had committed, he wrote, when he had removed a bit of gold from his brother's armlet.

These revelations of Gandhi's would perhaps have been of consolation to me, but there remained the fact that Gandhi had confessed to his father, writing a letter to him about what he had done, in the belief that "there could not be a cleansing without a clean confession". Richard, who had lived through so many years of confession, smiled rather cynically when I spoke of writing of my lie and my theft to my grandfather, who had as a young man studied in England for the priesthood. *"Tu es folle,"* Richard said. "You aren't even on speaking terms with him; and anyway you've already confessed to me." But it might bring us together again, me and my brilliant little Grandfather Boyle, I argued; for after all wasn't it he who had taught me neatness and order, who had dictated letters to me when I was ten years old, and shown me how to space them on the page; and who had, when my sister and I were children, financed for years our little magazine? But in the end there was only one person I could write to about it, and that was Carnevali, because he knew so well how poverty can twist the features of the face and turn the heart black in the breast. And so I wrote him a second letter, although there had been no answer to the first. But even while I wrote I was thinking of my slyness in dragging in poverty as an excuse for what I had become.

The little room in which we lived that winter was separated by a comfortably warm wall from the kitchen of a restaurant that faced on the esplanade. The water spigot (swathed in potato sacking to protect it from the cold) was in the alleyway just outside our door; and the toilet, which had no seat, but two grooved porcelain rests on which one placed one's feet and squatted, was situated not in an open court but in the shelter of the café hall. The Café-Restaurant de l'Univers just missed commanding a view of the jetty and the English Channel, for the corner of another building had contrived to edge out in its way. So there it stood, squeezed between the city and the sea, narrow and humble, with its eight long marble-topped tables standing on heavy iron legs beneath the mirrors that ran the length of the two walls. The leather of the banquettes was split with use and age, and here and there the coils of springs and stuffing had broken through. But still this place seemed extraordinarily luxurious to us. The rent of our one room was so low (and electricity to light its perpetual darkness included in the forty francs a month we paid) that every week we could afford to eat Saturday night dinner at one of the marble-topped tables, and drink a bottle of Algerian red wine. On Saturday nights all that winter I did not cook dinner on our potbellied stove, and even if the wind and the icy rain were beating against the plate-glass window and the café door, still it was always a night of celebration. Richard could gripe with the *patron* and his wife, and with the working men who came in for a *coup de rouge,* about the high cost of living, and about the shame of French wages, and the French military and French taxes. It was certainly only the Communist platform, they all said, that offered any hope of change.

Not far from the Café-Restaurant de l'Univers was a public bathing establishment, and once a week I would go there for a hot bath. I walked with a certain difficulty, particularly coming back, for I would wear the week's supply of underpants and slips under my coat in order to wash them in the steaming water after I had bathed. It was on my return from the bathhouse one late November afternoon that Carnevali's first letter came. It was typed on very thin paper, entirely on the red part of the ribbon, and the address was not the same as the one Lola had given me. "Your letters came to me after a long delay," he wrote, "for I am no longer in the public hospital. A great man, Robert McAlmon, came to see me here some weeks ago, and when he saw the conditions in which I was living, he paid a year in advance for me in a private sanatorium. Besides this, this unbelievable man whose smile is like a scar from the many wounds he has borne took all my writings with him, and he will perhaps make a book out of them!"

I quickly took off all the wet clean clothes I was wearing, and put them one by one over the backs of our two chairs to dry before the little stove. Then I sat down to read again the many silky pages of Carnevali's letter. Here he spoke quite differently of Lola, saying she was one of the most beautiful signs we have of woman's emancipation, and that her rebellion was sanctified by beauty, whatever revolutionary name she might seek to give it. Even if she called it socialism, he said, still it had nothing to do with politics. It was a matter of burning, human blood. "It's a matter of such damning hatred and love as would turn a modern city to ashes," he wrote. "I have said all this in print about her, and that she is a woman suffering, but suffering with the snarl of a lioness and not with any self-pity. Her poetry is intensely vivid, and she herself, both in her poems and in her life, is a lioness flinging herself madly against the walls of the ugly city."

In this first letter he asked me many questions about myself: what I was proud of in my ancestors, and whether or not I was beautiful. As for himself, he said that "the dear sufferer, Lola

Ridge, had spoken of a wind in such a way that I saw the hand of God bringing clean stillness to man, and I was ashamed, I, the restlessness that has no direction". He added in a postscript that even if he were to write me a letter a day he would never be able to describe all the abject loneliness that was in his heart. The next day his second letter came, and here he referred to my confession about lying, but he did not speak directly of the lie I had told. He said that life is composed of two movements, which may be called the ebb and the flow. The artistic movement is the flow, and all that is opposed to the artist, and to his creation, his creativity, that is the ebb. All that is evil, such as cynicism, bitterness, and lying, belongs to the ebbing of the power of life, while the flowing is concerned with man's vision and his faith and his acknowledgment of the truth. Every lie, every denial, he wrote, makes a man a little less than he was, or what he was intended to be, so, finally, lie by lie, he is diminished until in the end he lies to his own will.

Carnevali did not mention my stealing the cat, or even stealing, and it was only years later, when McAlmon referred to Carnevali removing books from other men's library shelves and pawning them, with the excuse that they were stupid books, that I understood why he had not bothered to speak to me of my particular theft. But he said in another letter that he had stolen from his love for Bill Williams the emotion demanded for the writing of great poetry, and then recognized that the poems he had written were not great, and so he had thrown them away. "But listen to this," he wrote me in excitement in still another letter; "I have put everything down in a book[3] that McAlmon, that prince of men, is going to print! I have said in this book—and this is maybe the whole reason for the book—that there was once a great Balzac and a great Dostoevsky, but today an artist is nothing but an awful scream from the dry musty throat of the earth. Today is a time of death and ending and hurry, and Bill Williams dances better than Romain Rolland the dance, macabre and splendid, of today." The trouble was, he said, that America, the most powerful country in the world, did not want the truth—America, a land without a physiognomy, he said, a land of enemy aliens and moving pictures. America gathers the rebels, the miserable, the very poor, the hungry people of the world, he wrote, and gives them new hungers for the old ones. "In America a man must yell if he wants to be heard," he cried out. "He must yell

[3] *A Hurried Man*, Contact Editions, Three Mountains Press, Paris, 1925.

as poor Bill Williams did in *Others*."[4] In his letters Carnevali said many other things, among them that it was the destiny of Italians to be driven from pillar to post, and that even Dante in his time had been chased like a stray cat from one town to another.

I wrote him that I knew very little about Dante, perhaps nothing more than that when Dante walked through the streets of Verona mothers would draw their children close and whisper to them: "Don't let his garments touch you! That is the man who has been to hell!" Because Carnevali had asked me, I told him I was not beautiful, that I was thin as a rake and had a broken nose. I said it was difficult to set down the names of my ancestors and what they had accomplished, the reason being that I disliked the look pride gave to the features of a man's or woman's face.

Of his own appearance, Carnevali wrote: "I look a little like a poet, by way of wistfulness and dreaminess, but my face is often fierce, especially when I get up in the morning. My face is hopelessly romantic, and I have noticed that my eyes have a Chinese slant which is not pretty. Once I fell in love with my hair: so smooth, unwavy, straight in a not unpleasant way. I always had a funny way of walking which is now accentuated by my sickness. I bend my right leg at the knee and swing my feet as though I wanted to throw them away. Since I fell ill my reservoir of tears dried up and I can no longer cry. This is a terrible thing."

The room behind the restaurant, where we lived all that winter, became notable to me because the correspondence with Carnevali began there; and because it was the room which Flossie and Bill Williams did not come to when they passed through Le Havre on their way to Paris; and because the cat had kittens in bed with us one February night; and because I finished my first novel there.[5]

[4] A magazine founded by Alfred Kreymborg in 1915, of which Williams was associate editor for six months during 1916. The final number of *Others* (July 1919) was "compiled and edited" by Williams.

[5] The only copy of this book was given in 1928 to Robert Sage, then an associate editor of *transition*. Sage, in all good faith, sent it to a friend, a Chicago publisher, and after a number of letters concerning the possibility of publishing it, the friend mislaid the manuscript and it has never been heard of since.

Robert McAlmon

1924

The autumn in Venice. *Venezia bellissima!* Those nights in gondolas which poured with glamour and romance and champagne amidst the laughter of beautiful women.

In short, I have vague memories of how, why, or when I got to Venice, but I poured off the train somehow into a gondola and was checked in at a hotel with my baggage. Whoever managed this for me had to tell me the name of the hotel next day, because there was a party that night which lasted till morning, and, knowing no Italian, I had refused to bother about the name or the location of the hotel. During the course of the party some Englishwoman talked to me about us healthy, eager-eyed, expectant young Americans. We were not effete. We didn't know ennui. An even younger and more eager American swore that he could turn handsprings. The ballroom was large; there was the liqueur table and a few statues about, and he attempted to prove his boast. He couldn't turn handsprings that met with my approval. I showed him how. The hostess was worried about the statuary being knocked over, but she would have another glass or so of champagne. In the end quite a few of the guests, men and women, French, American, English, and Italians, were trying to turn handsprings; but I was the one and only, and said so, and turned more handsprings. Perfect, clean-cut, straight, hands down, and a quick neat turnover, and then landing whole on my feet. Will Gertrude Stein try that and then say that she is the one and only of her generation, lost or wandering?

For two weeks all days were gala. The sun poured upon the city, and many enjoyed it, seated at Florian's on the Piazza San Marco, if they were not sleeping, or at a cocktail party, or dead drunk at Danieli's, or somewhere else. Those days of passion, and love, and intoxication! I recall sitting one day with a Lady Colebrook, Nancy Cunard, and the better-looking of the Di Robilant boys, Conte Mundano. Next to us was an obviously American woman, certainly an ex-actress, Nancy believed. I glanced at her and listened to her, not wisecracking, but being bravely witty, really witty. She didn't look happy, however. She looked to be an ageing woman who'd been about a bit and knew it wouldn't get her anywhere to let down. A darn fine type. Suddenly my memory operated. It was Marie Dressler.

Years before she had played with Charlie Chaplin and Mabel Norman in *Tillie's Punctured Romance*. In a flash I was back in those innocent days when slapstick and a laugh came from the belly. I had seen the film after a sizeable Thanksgiving dinner, and laughter at Marie Dressler had caused pain to every portion of my anatomy, and sent thrills of stuffed laughter-pain into every ounce of turkey, cranberry sauce, plum pudding, nuts, raisins, and fruitcake that dwelt within me. A pang of sorrow shot through me now. Of course Miss Dressler had not saved money, and the producers would be telling her her day was past. It was for me the moment to make one of those unkept resolutions to be sensible and practical and prepare for old age and the inevitable rainy day.

Wyndham Lewis arrived in Venice, and with him and others I did wedge in a bit of cathedral- and picture-seeing, although I have never been hot on the trail of cathedrals. However beautiful their exteriors, their interiors are apt to depress me with the smell of incense, the chanting of priestly voices, the singing of eunuchs, and the general determination to put awe into one's spirit. Nevertheless, in order to see many magnificent paintings it is at times necessary to visit some cathedrals. Lewis was intent upon seeing the paintings of Tiepolo, and frequently. I, personally, preferred Carpaccio and a quantity of others. But it appeared that Tiepolo had painted even the shadows in the draperies with an absolute verity to life. Lewis and other painters had informed me on other occasions that painting should do more than copy nature, that it should "create" a composition and have a geometric being of its own. Therefore the shadows in the draperies of Tiepolo did not impress me. It was those days in

Venice that decided me that one had better like what one likes in painting, and to hell with what any painter or critic may become impassioned about. I had always followed this practice, but now I decided to be outspoken about my feelings.

Osbert and Sacheverell Sitwell, and Willie Walton, a composer, were in Venice at the time, but they appeared only to disappear around corners like frightened deer who have sniffed a hunter in the wind. After one party at Nancy Cunard's they almost relaxed, and as the party headed across the Piazza San Marco toward Danieli's Sacheverell walked ahead, prim and sedate, with that wooden-man-on-stilts walk which the English do achieve. There was a slight slithering to his gait, however; possibly he had taken a cocktail or so more than usual. I galloped after Sacheverell and caught him by the arm to make him run. "Hell, Sachy, don't you ever feel abandoned?" I asked him. Osbert has a touch more of the wild within his nature, perhaps, but he is *Captain* Sitwell, and a bit too pompously constructed for galloping gaieties. He had not yet begun to register horror about the oncoming war, but he was even then sick of the hypocrisies of England.

Lewis started to do a sketch of me, but it didn't congeal. It struck me that he was afraid my vanity would be hurt if he did me "justice" in a portrait. And so the Venice days came to an end. It is no fun going home, alone, in the early morning in a gondola, and whenever I started home on foot I found I was merely doing circles around the city, and I would find myself five times farther from the hotel after an hour's walk than at the beginning. This gave me claustrophobia, and I decided that Florence would do as a period of cure from Venetian glamour, and from drinking and the re-realization of the emptiness of having "too many pals". Kenneth Adams was there, studying the primitives to be seen at the Uffizi and Pitti galleries, and he would be good to wander about with, and see paintings and towns. He had his enthusiasms, but he did not insist upon one's response.

Norman Douglas was also in Florence, and as he was a friend of Bryher's I dropped him a note, although aware that he had been "shocked" by my book, *Post-Adolescence*. It was too full of anarchic spirit and of irreverence for tradition, old age, and conventions, as such, for "Uncle Norman". Because of this, my first dinner with him was not what I had expected. Conversation was formal and courteous, almost stiff. After wine we talked of later Roman history, and he eventually explained that he had become an author only because he needed money. He had been paid a very small sum outright for *South Wind*, he said, a book for which he had had small hopes while he was writing it. So, in spite of the continued sale of the book, by now a minor classic to many, he had received no further payment.

Later I would have been curious to know what Norman thought of my *Distinguished Air (Grim Fairy Tales)*, one tale of which appeared translated into French in the French-Italian quarterly, 900. The translation was done at Joyce's suggestion, and various French people thought the story "Miss Knight", a stark and sharp presentation of a type new to literature but not to life. All of the stories in the book deal with variant types with complete objectivity, not intent on their "souls", and not distressed by their "morals". On another occasion, when Kenneth Adams and I had dinner with Douglas, he again overlooked the opportunity to be the older and more worldly man, and showed no inclination to twist us for our uncouthness.

Before arriving at the restaurant Kenneth had had an encounter with a young Fascist who wanted him to remove his hat because the "Giovinezza" was being sung. Adams and I had both been in the army, and he had done quite a stretch of kitchen police. In short, both he and I had learned a good deal of our language in the army, and when rage was upon us our vocabularies were free and expletive. We sat down with Norman Douglas and began to express our opinions of Mussolini and Fascism. I had been in Rome in 1922 and heard Mussolini speak. He had come to the second-storey balcony, stood silent for a minute, hand on chest, being Napoleon. A friend interpreted for me as he spoke, Mussolini reached out a hand and appeared to crush something within his mighty grip, and his masterful voice said slowly: "I hold Rome in the hollow of my hand."

Norman Douglas watched us drinking absinthe, and wondered at our language, and was later reported as saying that he guessed he wasn't keeping up with the younger generation—at least, the American. The dinner was very nice, however, for Douglas soon began to deplore things also. We all deplored Italy and its state. We started mildly enough, at least while food was before us. Adams and I deplored New England and the New Englanders with their "conscience" and something they call "morality" of "ethics". Douglas deplored England and her public school types and her editors, publishers, newspapers, book reviewers, and hypocrisies; and he also deplored the military, the middle class, and the aristocratic class of England. We deplored Germany, and the Prussians particularly; France, and her police, her provincials, and her virtual lack of imagination; and Fascism.

Douglas snorted. Lack of imagination! He *excoriated* the ingrown, island-warped, and underground viciousness of England, and specified the limitations of each class, with particularizations. By this time we were drinking red wine. I began to deplore the taste of Italian red wine, which tastes the way mice smell. By the time our deploring session was over we felt rather wrung out and needed coffee and liqueurs, whereupon we sauntered out into the night to see what Florence had to offer. Both Adams and I had forgotten that we intended to get Douglas to talk about the Roman Empire in its decay, for he was known to be an authority on that subject.

At this time Douglas was writing his pamphlet in response to D. H. Lawrence's introduction to Monsieur Magnus' book on the Foreign Legion. Magnus, the Foreign Legionnaire, was dead, and Douglas took the attitude that he didn't give a sizzling damn about what Lawrence wrote of him, but he did resent his picking on a dead man. His pamphlet was being set up, but he was still revising and adding more to it. At times he would read a short passage of it aloud, but he would never, as does Joyce, read entire long passages. He always gave the impression that he was reading for himself, in order to judge how he might change and make more forceful the particular passage.

Leo Stein was in town, and we met now and then, and Leo would explain his sensibility and his creative strain as compared to Gertrude Stein's. I went to see Loeser's collection of Cézannes, but Loeser *would* tell one the history of each, why Cézanne painted it that way, and how he had discovered Cézanne, and it made me think of Alfred Stieglitz explaining the mystical origin of Georgia O'Keeffe as manifested in each of her paintings. How do these men acquire such complete insight into the inspirational sources of the production of other people? Kenneth Burke, too, at about that time was doing a series of essays on various poets, explaining their methods. He wrote essays on Marianne Moore, William Carlos Williams, and T. S. Eliot, I believe. I recall hearing the poets he explained saying that they didn't understand the explanations in Burke's articles any better than I did.

During the two months in Florence, Douglas and I saw a great deal of each other, a great deal, certainly, for two people who didn't quite click. I had no particular admiration for his books, although *South Wind* was amusing enough for a reading, but won't, for me, stand rereading. There were few people in Florence then who were ready to sit over the wine bottle and converse into the late hours of the night, so Douglas and I were often together. One night C. K. Scott-Moncrieff turned up from Pisa. He was taking a needed rest from the translating of Proust and Pirandello. Later I heard that he had never recovered from the loss of a friend in the war, and that he was virtually a shell-shock case. He certainly gave no such impression this night. He drank along with Douglas and me and was most genial and ready for humour. When Douglas left us, well past two in the morning, Scott-Moncrieff surprised me by showing me the script of some poetry which he had recently written. It was an uncomfortable moment. I didn't know he wrote; thought of him only as a first-rate translator, and even if the poetry had been good there was little to say. It made me feel that I was very afterwar, very calloused, and non-literary (if to be literary means showing back and forth one's efforts at inopportune moments). Long before, in New York, I had got more than a stomachful of poetry gatherings and readings and sighings.

Word came to me that Emanuel Carnevali was in a sanatorium in a small town near Bologna, so I boarded a train and went to see him. Years before this, Carnevali and I had exchanged letters over a period of a year, while I was at college and when he was on the staff of *Poetry* magazine in Chicago. We had met but once and then he was ill, but Carnevali's critical articles and short stories in those days were about the best, so far as intellectual content and "sensibility" (however hysterical) were concerned. Their violence was the violence of adolescence, but he had wit and irony of the Latin order which one finds in Italians and Spaniards. Had he remained in good health he might have developed into a fine satirist; his idols were Rimbaud, Dostoevsky, and the generally prophetic. In America he took on idols which I refused to be sold, but in my college days I concluded that it was because he was a foreigner that he so passionately loved Whitman, and, later Sherwood Anderson and Carl Sandburg. Neither Anderson nor Sandburg rang true to me. The former liked to daydream and be an actor for both himself and the world, in order to prove his soul and his sensibility; the latter mixed Whitman humanitarianism with advertising and newspaper-headline imagism. With his banjo and the chanting of his own poetry, Sandburg was certainly not so near "the soul of poetry" as many a backwoods philosopher or cowboy narrating a yarn.

Carnevali was to me more interesting than his American heroes. He was purely Italian, with the Italian lack of cant about "morals" and "soul" and "conscience". If he was broke, and stole valuable books from a friend to sell for food and drink, he did so without remorse. He didn't take the attitude that the world owed him a living and fame without some effort on his part, but if a soft lady or man gave him money and talked of subsidizing him, he was willing, as a favour to them, to accept their offers. That didn't mean he liked or respected them. He was perhaps more apt to admire and respect someone who refused him loans, someone who was unafraid of his diatribe attacks and his wit, and who would "talk him down".

Carnevali's condition was a shock. When I called in the morning he was asleep, like a doped animal, having just been given an injection of scopolamine. The nurse told me he longed for gramophone records, as someone had given him a rickety gramophone. He also wanted books. In the afternoon, on my return, he was awake. He sat up in bed, black eyes peering out of a thin, oval face covered with parchment-yellow skin. His arms, his legs, his whole body twitched and jerked. It was only when doped with scopolamine that he got any rest. He had encephalitis lethargica, a form of sleeping sickness which, at the time, the doctors did not know how to treat. The gramophone records and books and cigarettes I brought pleased him, and he started talking at once. The nurse said that he could leave the hospital, and he came hobbling across the street, as though his right leg were shorter than his left. In the simple peasant trattoria we had dinner—chicken, salad, pasta, and two bottles of a vile, sparkling red wine, sweetish and yet with a vinegar taste. Carnevali thought it more marvellous than champagne, however, and so we had it. He asked about Jane Heap, Harriet Monroe, Mitchell Dawson—all the people, in short, whom he had known in the New York and Chicago literary sets. His mind was quick and alert, and he shot a question at me which he had asked me years before: "What kind of a man are you?" Then he proceeded to tell me, and immediately apologized, thinking I would be offended.

When it was time for him to go back to the sanatorium he seemed to walk almost erect and he was not trembling. He gave me a pile of manuscript which he had written on his rickety typewriter. It was badly typed, naturally, his hands constantly trembling as they did, but it was fresh and interesting, this account or history of the types in the sanatorium and in the little hill town where he lived. The village barber, the *sagefemme*, the priests, the nuns, the male nurse, the town whores, workers, housewives, were all described. As I read and remembered how alive and stimulating his conversation had been that day, I knew there were other writers (had it been left to me) that I would have wished his disease on, if someone had to have it. As it was, how could he be an "artist", a finished or polished "writer", a man of letters dutiful about his "craft", "technique", etc.? He didn't have enough conscious hours a day or enough control over his muscles to discipline himself. But Carnevali's will to live and his capacity for joy and hate were seeing him through. He did get a kick out of mere living; and in some of his letters to me later he expressed a terror of death more intense than one could imagine. Yet neither his childhood in Florence nor his days in New York and Chicago had been happy days.

Kay Boyle

1924-1926

That was a winter of tremendous and determined walking. In the twelve hours of every weekday that I was alone, I wrote or I walked, and there was not an avenue or alley, a dock or jetty, of Le Havre that I did not know. I collected stones and driftwood from the beach, that harsh, ungiving beach where shells could not survive an hour but were ground to sand by the beating of the surf. I walked, and I wrote poetry, and I began my second novel, the story of the family in Brittany[1]; and every day I wrote so many letters that often I did not have the price of the postage to send them off, and must wait for the first of the month and Richard's payday to come around again.

On Sundays, no matter how violent the weather, Richard and I would pack a lunch and start off early for the cliffs or for the farthest reaches of the shingled beach. If it was mild, and the tide low, we would take off our shoes, and roll our clothing above our thighs, and wade out over the evil, water-worn knobs of gravel to the jutting rocks. There we would spend hours picking the blue-shelled mussels from the high stone turrets to which they clung, for they were food, and they would save us the cost of a dinner or two in the week ahead. The mussels were fixed as close as sequins to the rock, and the rocks themselves were riddled porous with salt and decked with strands of algæ. But in the end the mussel shells, or else

---

[1] *Plagued by the Nightingale*, Harrison Smith and Robert Haas, Inc., New York, 1931. Republished 1966 by the Southern Illinois University Press, Carbondale, Illinois.

the substance of the rock, tore our fingertips to shreds and we had to stop. They could be poison, these handsome, healthy *moules* in their dark blue armour, Richard said, but that was only if they had clung to the copper cables of a buoy or ship. After a meal of them, steamed open in butter and parsley and chopped onion and no more than a single glass of white wine, it was just as well to have milk in the house, to drink in quantities if the pains began.

Other times we went inland on a Sunday, and came back carrying fresh eggs from a farm, for eggs were high in the market at that time of year. One wet cold afternoon we forgot about money, and we went into a country bistro near the wide mouth of the Seine and sat down close to the iron-bellied stove. Suddenly Richard flung all caution to the dripping winter winds, and he ordered a bottle of *cidre bouché*. I can still see the dark brown of the bottle glass, and the shape of the cork, and hear the delicate explosion when the *patron* opened the bottle in the scarcely lighted room. The cork hit the ceiling as recklessly as if it were champagne the bottle contained, and the sour golden foam ran into our glasses and across the table top. That time we couldn't walk home because we were laughing too hard, shrieking with laughter at everything we saw. Even when Richard found the streetcar line for Le Havre in the dusk, there seemed no reason to stop laughing, and we rode on the back platform of the trolley car in our muddy clothes, with our drenched shoes squeaking aloud, laughing until our sides were sore and tears ran down our faces. That was one of the best days of the winter, although we had squandered a fortune on cider and carfare. "Do you know what romanticism is?" Richard asked me suddenly. "Maybe the opposite of realism, classicism, naturalism," I tried to say, but I couldn't stop laughing; and Richard went on saying: "It's what we appear to build our lives on, and it's probably no good to anyone. Maybe we ought to try something else for a change." When we got back to the little room where the cat was complaining about the cold, Richard looked the word up in the old dictionary I had carried everywhere since Cincinnati days. " 'Characterized by a romantic spirit, outlook, or tendency,' " Richard read, swaying a little in his wet shoes; " 'that is, fanciful, fictitious, visionary; not practical, having no basis in fact.' " After that we didn't laugh quite so hard.

Because we never seemed to stop walking, it was nothing to walk to the dock that January morning when Flossie's and Bill Williams' steamer came in past the jetty and through the harbour's ice. Richard took the day off from work, and we ordered lunch for four in the Café-Restaurant de l'Univers. The meal we planned would begin with pernod and have two courses in between, and end with *mousse au chocolat* and coffee. We made an arrangement with the *patronne* to pay so much a week for the next month to take care of this celebration. It was clearly some kind of stubborn and quite meaningless romanticism which had persuaded me that Floss and Bill would not take the boat train to Paris, but that they would send their baggage on ahead, and after lunch we would put them on a later train. All this was obviously an impossibility, and yet even after Bill had written me from Rutherford that they would not be able to stop over, I persisted in the senseless plan. Their fare was paid straight through to Paris, Bill wrote. Friends would be picking them up there, but in the meantime we would have at least an hour's visit on the dock. I paid no attention whatsoever to these pronouncements of reality or to the manifest ponderability of facts. I kept on writing to Carnevali that the thing which concerned me most about Flossie's and Bill's visit was that we didn't have a window in our room.

Carnevali had once written of Bill: "With his mobility, Williams reaches almost every part of the truth at the same time—the synthesis of it being a mere exclamation, a magic single word." And now he answered me quickly: "You will have to paint a window before they get there. This is what we do in Italy. But we do it not because of love for a man who is a poet and a doctor of all the world's ills, but because of our hate for the tax collector. In my country, there is a tax on windows that dare to look down on the street. Here, if you don't want the front of your house to look as if it had lost an eye, you paint a window where one is missing. The tax collector has not been told to count any window that is a work of art. Sometimes we paint a girl standing in the window, holding back the strings of different-coloured beads that keep the flies out. And listen: even if a deluge of rain is pouring down the glass of the real windows, the sun is always shining in the others. Paint it on the inside of your room, and put such a burst of meridional light in it that the snow outside will run down to the beach and take the next boat for Iceland, and Bill will feel all his meridional blood rushing to life."

And Bill had once written of Carnevali: "Emanuel Carnevali, the black poet, the empty man, the New York that does not exist . . .

I celebrate your arrival. It is for you we went out, old man in the dark. It is for you that the rubbish stirred and a rat crawled from the garbage, alive! . . . What else was *Others* at that time: a rat in the garbage heap of New York. . . . *Others* has come to an end. I object to bringing out another issue after this one. *Others* is not enough. It has grown inevitably to be a lie, like everything else that has been a truth at one time. . . . The reason for our having been alive is here! What do I care if Carnevali has not written three poems I can thoroughly admire? Who can write a poem complete in every part surrounded by this mess we live in? . . . He is wide open! . . . He is wide, Wide, WIDE open. He is out of doors. He does not look through a window. . . . Jesus, Jesus, save Carnevali for me. He is only beginning to disintegrate. . . . But he is slipping into the afternoon at twenty-one. . . . I believe he will go crazy or quit rather than write in a small way. . . . Rimbaud, Laforgue, Corbière, they offer him solace. They prove to him that he is foredoomed. . . . Carnevali, perhaps you will do as they did. . . . We salute you."[2]

Because I had studied to be an architect at the Ohio Mechanics Institute in Cincinnati, and for another year at the Parsons School in New York, I was able to draw the frame of a window with accuracy and symmetry. But it had meant first peeling the ancient maroon-coloured paper from that section of the wall where the tall window was to be, and I lived in trepidation of the *patronne* coming in and seeing what was taking place. The oblong of exposed plaster gave a new light to the room at once but there the undertaking halted. To simulate the sun and vegetation of a meridional world, I needed a great deal of brilliant paint, and that we could not afford. For over a week the frame of the empty window faced our bed, a window that allowed no weather of any kind to penetrate, and permitted us no view of anything beyond it, although I had left one casement slightly ajar. And then one evening we suddenly began glueing pieces of bottle glass onto the plaster, glass that did not look like what it was any longer, it having been worn to opaque jewellery by the constant milling and moiling of the sea. I had carried them in handfuls from the beach all winter, these bits and pieces of delicately turned sculpture. Three shades of green, they came in, and a dark and a light turquoise, and also a dark and light gold; and now, set in our window frame, it was like a forest of foliage pressing in from the bleak and leafless world outside.

[2] *Others*, July 1919, under the title "Gloria!"

It took us four or five nights to finish it, and during the day I searched the beach up and down and back and forth, clawing among the debris of single rope-soled shoes, and the remnants of drowned cats, and the tangled nests of seaweed with glaucous pods that exploded under one's foot, seeking mile after mile for bottle glass of the shapes and colours needed to complete the illusion of—what? It was crazy, the whole affair. But as we worked on it, the smoothed amber bits of glass became like the leaves I had laid, wet and alive, against my mouth in September after the first frost in the Poconos; and the jet-green pieces were like the pine needles that carpeted the aisles of Pocono Manor's "Cathedral Woods" when I walked there with my mother; and the turquoise ones were the gems set in the Indian bracelets my mother's mother used to wear. In the act of our constructing this phony window, a strange thing happened: I was able to answer Carnevali's question about pride. I did not write him that I was proud (although these things were in my mind) that my mother had once lunched with Mary Garden, or that my great-great-grandfather had served on George Washington's staff, but that I was proud of my mother carrying the glass of the chimney lamp across the room when she was a little girl on the prairie, carrying it and not crying out when it burned through the palm of her left hand. And I wrote I was proud of my grandmother, Eva S. Evans, the first woman to work in a government office in Washington. It was in the land-grant office, where land claims were established for those who had set out to open up the West. Sometimes their claims would be written out on a piece of birchbark and sent to Washington rolled up like a scroll, tied around with a bit of string, she had told me; and sometimes they drew maps showing the tree, the creek, or the curve or incline of that section of the logging road which marked the boundaries of the land they were staking out.

That Tuesday morning in January, as Floss's and Bill's luggage went through customs in the draughty hangar of the dock, there was only one mention of the room we wanted them to come to and of the lunch we had ordered at the Café-Restaurant de l'Univers. And then Bill in his grey tweed tourist cap, which seemed to have nothing to do with what he was, looked sadly, sadly at our faces. He said McAlmon was meeting them in Paris, that he was expecting them on that train, and they could not disappoint him. (Almost forty years later I was to write that Bill Williams was a soil, a core, a homeland to which McAlmon always returned, and to which he gave a total loyalty.[3] There was no way then that I could have known this, no way at all, but the bond of their commitment was present that day in Le Havre, and it made the fact that Bill could not stay, and the winter ahead, less difficult to bear).

I remember only the uneasiness on the air and nothing of what we must have talked of as we waited in the cold. But it was a great and good experience, and while it was taking place (or perhaps later that night, or perhaps in the days that followed) I learned this simple thing: that people of dignity are not to be dragged by the hair of their heads into the precincts of one's life, and that to attempt this is to violate their probity. That threshold lying at the entrance to each man's and woman's life, I knew without equivocation now, must be recognized and genuflected before. Neither strangers nor friends could be urged to cross it, not even as onlookers were they to be invited in to view the spectacle of one's avidity for love and one's inexcusable despair.

It turned out to be quite an intellectual winter, as if life were offering me compensation for what had taken place. Mother sent me a copy of D. H. Lawrence's *Studies in Classic American Literature*, and these essays, read and reread, gave me a singular courage as they signalled to me a new and quite ruthless way of thought. And on the outdoor, dusty stall of a second-hand bookshop I found two books I wanted, and I stopped to look at them on my way to market every day. Both were in English: one a novel by a woman named Rebecca West, whom I had not heard of before; the other Norman Angell's *The Political Conditions of Allied Success*.[4] Mother owned all of Norman Angell's books (he being one of her inner circle which included, among perhaps a dozen others, Max Beerbohm, Clive Bell, George Santayana, Romain Rolland, Bernard Shaw, and John Cowper Powys). Together we had heard Angell lecture one night in New York, but it was not only because of her that I desperately wanted his book. There was another and equally urgent reason. I believed that if I could ever get my mind to functioning I would one day be able to acquire some kind of specific knowledge. It was perhaps in this hope that I had studied the violin and counterpoint year after year, and not done very well with either, and turned to architecture, and, aside from the seraphim and the cherubim I placed on cornices, not done well at all.

[3] "Brighter Than Most," *Prairie Schooner*, Vol. XXXLV, No. 1 (Spring 1960).
[4] G. P. Putnam's Sons, New York, 1918.

And then Richard came home one Saturday night with a raise of thirty francs a month, and this was the beginning of our affluence. On Sunday afternoon we went to a *café-concert* and we each had a glass of vermouth, drinking slowly, parsimoniously, as we listened to the singers imitate Mistinguette and Chevalier. On Monday morning I ran like a crazy woman to the second-hand bookstore, arriving there an hour before it opened, and waited to pay out the fifty centimes they were asking for both books. Rebecca West's novel I read and reread all winter, not beginning work in the morning until I had read a paragraph or two, or even an entire page of it. I read it as a textbook, studying the shape of the sentences, looking up in the ragged dictionary the words I was not sure of, coming to know her characters as well as if they were people who had moved into our room with us, people I did not like, but by this time there was no way of asking them to leave. All that mattered to me was that she was a woman, and that she had written a novel, a very long novel, which was what I was seeking to do. This novel was entitled *The Judge*, and years later when I mentioned it to H. G. Wells he said: "It was her way of beginning life again. It took courage, but women have so much of that. It was her way of going on."

The Angell book was something else again. In my attempt to understand it I turned great portions of it into blank verse, for once things were put into poetry they rang with unexpected clarity in my mind. It may very well be that his thoughts, his words, became an uneffaceable part of my awareness, or of my unawareness, and shaped my predilections, which were, indeed, hope for the democratic process and despair for national particularism. Week by week I would send sections of Norman Angell's long poem to Mother, some of the paraphrased lines reading like prophecy.

> If we are to use power successfully
> During this war and at the settlement
> And afterwards, we must achieve a consolidation
> Not based on the material predominance of
>   one member
> But on a moral factor; the voluntary
> Co-operation of equals—
> Achieved by a democratic internationalism
> Based necessarily on a unity of moral aim.

The parties which among the enemy favour
Aggression will realize that, however finally
Their purpose may appear to be defeated,
The greater material unity of their alliance
Will enable them sooner or later
To overcome those states which have shown
    themselves
Superior in the sum of their power, but
Have shown themselves inferior in their capacity
To combine it for a common purpose.

The truth is of greater importance to us
    than to the enemy.
He can in some measure ignore it. We cannot.
His unity is based on the old nationalist
    conceptions.
Our unity depends upon a revision of them,
Upon an enlargement of them into internationalism.

In the spring we moved inland. We moved to a little town we
had come across in our long winter wanderings. It was named
Harfleur, and in the Baedeker Richard read of it that "under
Richelieu and Colbert the prosperity of the town rapidly increased".
But that was three centuries ago, and by this time there was no
sign of prosperity anywhere around. We rented a third-floor
apartment, spacious and quite bare of furniture, in a strong, stone
building that had been a monastery once. Its garden was surrounded
by a massive ivy-covered wall, and the garden and the remnant of
orchard were divided into three parts, marked off by paths, each
part belonging to one of three *ménages* who now occupied the former
lodgings of the Carthusian monks. There were also three chicken
sheds, with enclosed runways, three sets of rabbit hutches, and three
separate outdoor *cabinets*, with wooden seats, clean cement paving
underfoot, and brass locks on the doors. It was our responsibility to
put furniture in the top-floor rooms, and chickens and rabbits in the
places allotted to them and us. This we did little by little, and in
time acquired a vacant piece of land not far down the lane, where
we could set out long rows of winter cabbage and turnips and potatoes.

There we lived for two years, and so totally French did I become that I scarcely recognized the look of my own features when I happened to catch sight of them in the glass. I surrendered totally to those whose lives I had entered, to these men and women who may have been chosen to enact within my nights and days the entire spectrum of drama of a France I did not know. The cast of characters went like this: Monsieur and Madame Sweet-as-Hay, and their two children, who lived on the ground floor, he a railway labourer in dark corduroys with a bright red flannel band wound twenty times around his waist, who slept in the dog's wooden kennel with the silver-haired sheepdog on nights when humanity had seemed to him to have betrayed him (which it had), and who wept when the caterpillars came in the autumn and ate the leaves from the orchard trees; Monsieur and Madame Far-Better-Than-Thou, who lived on the second floor (without children), he a train conductor between Le Havre and Paris, wearing blue serge and a gold watch chain, whose soul would have poisoned even running water, and who could be heard making love to his firm-fleshed, odorous wife every Saturday night at exactly a quarter to ten.

These were our intimates, and outside, beyond our walls, were the farmers: the rich one, Farmer Falstaff, white-maned and enormous of belly, who drove his truck into *les halles* twice a week at night, and knocked his ailing wife downstairs when he came home drunk the next day; and the poor one, across the lane, Farmer Black-of-Ear-and-Eye, who moved, with a nicotine drenched cigarette butt hanging from his lip, across the mess and rubble of his fields, and in and out of his greenhouses (of a kind), who boasted of the power of his horse (which was half dead), and of the high quality of his produce (which was scarcely good enough to feed the pigs he didn't have). These people were so close a part of my life that how I had previously existed without them, or how I would live without them at some future time, I did not know. It was not for an instant by love that we were plighted, but by the unalterable confines of daily living which held us so fast that none of us could look the other way.

To complete the cast, there were Monsieur and Madame Bien-Talonés our landlord and landlady. Their house, just outside the town, was quite a little château, and the evil that dwelt within its highly polished salons, that reclined on its lace-covered beds, and was coiled deep in the stuffing of its exquisitely upholstered chairs and sofas, was enough to make the blood turn icy in the veins. They were perhaps in their mid-thirties, but they were older than the dying, the drowning, as they clutched at all that was fixed and ponderable to bind their flesh to life. They had been married ten years, and they were childless, she told me one afternoon over the silver tea service in her garden in which twelve different varieties of roses bloomed. She had brought the money to the marriage, and the château, as well as the ancient monastery where we lived. He travelled for a horticultural firm, although they had quite enough without his salary. But he travelled for another reason, she whispered to me: he had his infidelities. She confessed this in hard, bright tears when he was off on a business trip to Italy. She had made up her mind to go with him and frustrate his plans, and when he learned this, he had emptied the contents of her suitcase out the château window, and jumped up and down on the new straw hat she had been going to wear. But it was for the hat she wept so bitterly that day, and in compensation she had locked the *bonne* in her attic room so that she could not take the afternoon off. It was *jeudi*, and the girl had the right to go out, Madame Bien-Talonés said, but she had burned a casserole the night before. "It's a kindness to them to teach them young what is good and what is bad," she said, seeking to dry her tears. "She won't be bored up there. She's got the ironing to do." And without any warning, Flaubert came slowly across the garden grass in the sun, with Madame Bovary on one arm, and Félicité of the simple heart on the other; but Madame Bien-Talonés was pouring me a second cup of tea, and she did not see him linger for a moment, with the two women he had created, or who had created him, stop and look at the dying roses by the château gate.

Every Tuesday and Friday afternoon, rain or shine, I loaded my vegetables with those of Farmer Black-of-Ear-and-Eye onto his cart, and towards dusk we would set out for *les halles*. In the dark months lighted lanterns hung on either side of the dashboard, and they swung gently with the slow pace of the horse, who made the long trip walking, nodding, stumbling, as if he moved in sleep. Two hours, or even three in bad weather, it took us to reach Le Havre, and there in the open market square we set up our licensed stall. A good percentage of what I made on my produce went to the farmer in payment for the sharing of his cart and his location. More often than not I would be the one to hold the horse's reins as we returned to Harfleur in the early light of the next day, for Farmer Black-of-Ear-and-Eye, Prince des Petits Verres de Cognac et des

Couennes de Camembert, Marquis des Ongles Sales, with his foul beaked cap on the side of his head, spent as much time in the bistros of the wholesale market as under the sagging canvas awning of the stall. On the homeward ride he would lie down on the cabbage and turnip leaves and the mouldy potato sacking in the back of the cart and sleep as deeply as the plodding horse, its long-lashed eyes closed behind the blinkers, its long bony head nodding, nodding, its hoofs striking like metal on the cobbles, knowing, even in sleep, which way to go.

I had stopped writing the book about the family in Brittany, although it was half finished, and I began a third novel,[5] simply because all the details of Le Havre and the sea, and Harfleur and the land, were clamouring in my mind. I did not want to have wiped from my memory the things I had borne witness to, and the things I had learned in this unhappy town. For instance, Madame Far-Better-Than-Thou, on the second floor, had taught me how to remove with my thumbnail the scab on the underside of an ailing chicken's tongue, so that it need not die of the pip; and every week I had watched her hold the heads of squabs, one by one, in a glass of water, drowning them for dinner that night while she told me stories of the young viscount, for whose family she had worked on their grand Normandy estate, who had tumbled her in the stable loft while she was looking for eggs, and taken her virginity away.

From Madame Sweet-as-Hay, on the ground floor, I had learned to buy country butter in the summer months when the price was low, and salt it away to use throughout the grimmer months ahead; and from her I learned that newly picked, slender green beans, fresh from our garden, should be cooked for exactly one minute and a half, and then laid out to dry on cheesecloth in the sun. The wide-mouthed earthen crocks would be standing ready, with a layer of rock salt at the bottom, and we would fill them with a layer of beans and then a layer of rock salt and then another layer of beans, until the crocks were full. There they stood in the cool vault of the monastery cellar, each covered with a cap of tightly stretched linen, enough to keep her family and mine in green beans for the autumn and winter and spring. And I bore witness to Madame Sweet-as-Hay kneeling night after Saturday night, once the children were asleep in bed, beside her husband's legs in their dark, impervious corduroys,

[5] *Gentlemen, I Address You Privately*, Harrison Smith and Robert Haas, Inc., New York, 1933.

and his workman's heavy boots as they emerged from the door of
the slope-roofed kennel, urgently, gently, modestly, speaking the
syllables of his many names. The better part of his Saturday pay
cheque would be gone, and, as if summoning every franc and
centime and sou of it out of the cash drawers of the bars where he
had passed, he would lie singing the valiant, stirring verses of the
"Internationale" to the sheepdog on his straw, or croon lullabies,
rocked in the crazy, off-key cradle of red wine, into the sheepdog's
feathered, silvery ears. If only she could get him up on his feet and
into the house before dawn broke, Madame Sweet-as-Hay must have
murmured to herself as she knelt, as she prayed to his broad red
flannel sash, and his corduroys, and his mud-clogged shoes:
Valentin Octavius Raoul, *mon doux amour!*

Sometime in 1924 or 1925, Lola sent me Evelyn Scott's novel,
Escapade, and this, like Rebecca West's book in the months before,
became a textbook from which I learned enduring truths. Among
them was to mistrust a woman's analysis of her own motives, and
another was concerned with the remarkable word "imponderable."
Imponderable, meaning "that which cannot be weighed or measured", was the word I used now in rebuttal of the ponderability of
the France of which I had become an inextricable part. I used it in
the endless letters I wrote, and in my poetry, in opposition to all
that could be weighed, evaluated, measured; in defiance of the
farmers on both sides of the road, and of Monsieur and Madame
Far-Better-Than-Thou and Monsieur and Madame Bien-Talonés.
In Le Havre, I had seen fishermen stand on the sea wall, while
waiting for the tide to change, and shoot the flying sea gulls down.
The birds would die in a small explosion of feathers, and fall, and
their bodies would drift away in the warring currents of the sea,
and I could find no rhyme or reason to the wantonness of this thing
that was taking place. The almost incredible imponderability of
their airy lives, of their sculptured wings, opposed to the ponderable
substance of the guns, the rocks, the fishermen's flesh, were a recur-
ring and obsessive dream. In *Gentlemen, I Address You Privately*, the
young renegade priest calls on the editor of the Harfleur newspaper
and asks him to start a campaign against the slaughtering of the
gulls. And the old man replies:

"It is of no importance. In this village . . . there is no sewer
system, no way to drain the marshes. . . . These things are of

importance. . . . Time enough for birds twenty years from now.
Fifty years. Five hundred years. . . . There's a munitions factory
out there on the marshes. . . . And practically every worker in
it a Chinaman. Imported cheap labour, while in this town
hundreds of Frenchmen are unemployed. Filling orders for
dissident tribes in Morocco, in order to destroy Frenchmen!
And you come to me talking about *gulls!*"

And further, the old newspaper editor says:

"The church is cold as the tomb. And the people come there
for services, for the weekly funerals all winter, and quake to
the bone with the cold, coughing and spitting in one another's
faces. There's the foul water stagnating in the marshes under
and around us. . . . Birds . . . birds! If you came out once
through this town with me, that would be the end of it."

The old man says of the people of Harfleur that they want to go
back to what they had before the war, not knowing that things
cannot be like that any more.

"There has never been any talk," whispered the old man,
"of a sewer system." For the unseen world he was withering
and perishing in the cold. . . . "They have to be given a new
idea of life, a new dream," he whispered.

It was that "unseen world" that I wanted to write of, and in
Evelyn's book I could find no vision of that world. Hers, I kept
thinking as I studied her pages, was a gaze as constricted as
Katherine Mansfield's, and her helplessness in that narrow world
was a thing with which I had no patience. At least Rebecca West did
not whimper (although this may have been due to her English blood
and bone). I had come to demand a great deal of women, and more
of women writers than I was able to express. It was an actual pain
in the heart when they failed to be what they themselves had given
their word that they would seek to be. I think I never forgave
Evelyn for this.

Lola wrote me that Evelyn was living in the south of France,
or perhaps it was Spain at that moment, and she sent me her address.
And so a correspondence began between us, and a rather hostile if
dedicated friendship that lasted, with some lapses, for the next

forty years. It ended the week of Evelyn's death. I had shown my
first novel to no one, and now I gave it the title of *The Imponderables*,
and I sent it to Evelyn to read. The brilliance and the ruthlessness of
her criticism so excited me that I began the book again at the beginning, and I wrote it entirely over. She had said that a veil hung
between my work and the reader, and that I would have to tear
that veil away before my writing could have value. Night and day,
week in, week out, I worked at the tearing away of that veil, not only
in the hopelessly laboured *Imponderables* (as I remember it) but in the
new books and the poetry as well.

Once, when Evelyn was passing through Paris, she—who had so
little herself—sent me the money to join her and her entourage for a
few days there. But it was not an easy visit. One was aware at every
instant of the nervous complexities of Evelyn's marital, and sexual,
and professional lives, and in the smoke-filled, crowded hotel room
I found it impossible even to hear what was being said. Perhaps I
had lived too long in an almost unbroken inner silence, and now in
my own confusion and insecurity I trembled for Evelyn's shattered
depths. Was she wife, lover, mother, or none of these things, or all
of them? It was difficult for me to determine, although all the elements and all the protagonists were there. Each meal we had, in
modest restaurants, was taken over by her young son's loud and
steady hiccoughing. Evelyn would accuse him of doing this in order
to disrupt all conversation, and perhaps it was true, but it seemed
to me a quite normal retaliation for having been given the name of
Jigaroo.

The reality of our friendship resided in our letters, and this may
have been because each of us was writing not to a stranger but to
another facet of herself. In Paris we were abruptly two separate
human beings, women with actual faces, voices, and we must look
into each other's eyes and decide whether or not we believed in what
we found there, whether we were comforted or discomfited. Evelyn
in the flesh before me (was she ten or fifteen years older than I, or
more, or less?) had neither the delicacy of bone nor the subtlety of
wit of Marianne Moore. She had neither the saintlike head nor the
burning presence of Lola Ridge, nor Lola's shining aura of belief.
She seemed to me desperately intellectual, as these women I loved
were not, and I decided this was because of her more formal education. She had been a college student at the time she eloped with a
married professor, Cyril Scott. This I had learned from *Escapade*. But

now, in which direction could she possibly go, I asked myself, in the intellectual uproar of her life? She had exchanged her dreams, her unseen world, for something I could not name. The first day she told me she had seen McAlmon the night before, and that she had known him in New York before his marriage, but that he was always alien and cold. Remote, like a homosexual, she said. No, I said; that I don't believe. She said she didn't believe it either, but she could find no explanation of why no fire was ever struck between them, as it had been between her and Bill Williams, for instance. She wanted McAlmon to respond, she said; she wanted him to be seduced in the mind at least. She was asking surrender of him, as she asked it insidiously, with a terrible, terrible hunger, of everyone she met. But I was asking a great deal of women too that year. I didn't want them to use "little" adjectives, such as Katherine Mansfield used, so that the universe itself was diminished; and I didn't want women sashaying around to the right and the left, with an eye for what flicker of response the flesh of all and sundry gentlemen might give.

In that crowded hotel room I met Louise Theis, over from London to visit Evelyn, whom she adored. She was American, Louise, but she worked on the editorial board of an English weekly, and her husband, Otto, in a publishing house. Some months after we met Louise wrote urging me to come with Richard to London and spend a week with them. Evelyn had told her of my writing, and she thought I should meet the kind of people who might one day be useful to me and my work. So one fine night in the spring, thanks to a twenty-five-dollar cheque my sister had sent me, Richard and I took the midnight Channel boat for Dover, travelling third class, which was segregated; that is, the women could not share the same sleeping quarters with the men.

My joy was great when I found that Louise and Otto had rented for a year Norman Angell's chambers at 10, Old Square, Lincoln's Inn, just inside the City of London Boundary, which is known as Temple Bar. I do not remember meeting anyone who might have been useful to me, but the time in London was memorable for two things: every morning in Norman Angell's bathtub I sang aloud to the hot-water spigot and the cold-water spigot, and to the rubber halo of the shower, the blank verse of his political treatises; and one evening about half past ten, at a party given by friends of Louise's, I met a young man named Vyvyan Holland. When he saw me barefoot (having lost the sole of one slipper on the way), dressed in the golden silk of an old portière Mother had sent me from home, and which I had stitched together to make an evening gown, he asked me to dance. He was blond, and ruddy of complexion, and he danced very well. Then he said good night, and he took his young lady home, and he came back alone and asked me to go out for a walk.

Richard was dancing with Louise, Otto was drinking champagne, and a group of people were singing the Eton boating song. Outside it was raining very gently, and Vyvyan took off his shoes to keep me company, and then carried them carefully in one hand. He had the key to the gate of the private garden square in his pocket, and he opened the gate, and we went in. We began by picking all the flowers in the flower beds, and then we climbed trees, and sang arias from Mozart and Puccini, and tossed the flowers to each other from tree to tree and branch to branch. It was three o'clock in the morning now, and we sat on the wet grass and talked for a long time in the gently falling rain. When the sky began to go light, we walked hand in hand back to the house together, and Richard was angry that I had been gone so long. "He is Oscar Wilde's son," Louise said to Richard the next day; "he is very unhappy"; but Richard's heart was not touched. For a year we wrote to each other, Vyvyan and I, and sent each other pressed flowers in our letters, but we never met again.

I do not remember at what time of year Ernest Walsh's first letter came. I believe it was written from Paris, although I am not sure even of that. He wrote that he had got my address from Carnevali, and that he was starting a literary quarterly co-editing it with a Scottish lady named Ethel Moorhead. They had read my poems in *Poetry* and in *Broom*, and they would like some of my work for their first issue, which would be out in a few months' time. The review was to be called *This Quarter*, and they already had as contributors Robert McAlmon, Gertrude Stein, Carnevali, Yvor Winters, William Carlos Williams, Ernest Hemingway, James Joyce, Bryher, and numerous others. This first number would be dedicated to Ezra Pound. I sent Ethel Moorhead and Ernest Walsh excerpts from my novels, and a few new poems, and in this way another steady correspondence, such as I had with Mother, Lola, and Evelyn, unexpectedly began.

In the winter of 1926 I had bronchitis for so long and I grew so thin that Madame Bien-Talonés took me to her doctor in Le Havre, who concluded I had tuberculosis. That January Monsieur Far-Better-Than-Thou, in his conductor's blue serge suit, annoyed by the crying of our cat at mating time, had lifted the top of the cesspool we shared and thrown her in. For a month, or an entire season, or for the long century of that winter, I almost lost my mind in anguish, thinking of the slow horror of her suffocating death. She became symbol and sign for me of all we had forgotten to defend, of all we had allowed to perish, to vanish, from our lives; but the exact name of our loss I could not find. I was obsessed by the search for it, and I grew too tired to eat, too sick of coughing and drenching sweats to sleep, too excited by fever and the vision of the struggling cat to set down any words of sense. The family in Brittany sent us all the money they could spare and wrote that the climate was obviously too harsh for me, that I must somehow get to the sun. Evelyn asked me to join them in Perpignan, but into the intellectual and sexual turmoil of her life I would not go; and six days a week, month after month, Richard cycled through the rain and snow to work, and back from work, and cooked the food, and cleaned the house and the rabbit hutches and the chicken coops, and put glass jars with flaming cotton in them on my chest.

I had hated Brittany, and now I hated what Normandy had become, and Richard, so sick of it all himself, at night would say to me: "Is there any place you think it would be good for you to go?" And yes, yes, I would cry out in silence; I knew exactly where I wanted to go. I wanted to go back in time, not forward. I wanted to go back, perhaps to a field in Pocono, and start everything all over, and do it better this time, do it completely differently. I wanted to go back ten years and play cops and robbers on horseback, and eat and sleep in the Meadowside Inn, under the same roof with Mother, and dance the polka the length of the Meadowside ballroom, and listen in bed at night for the long wail of the train as it came to the cut in the mountain pass before the train station of Pocono. "Is there any place you think would help you to get well?" Richard would ask, and I would cry out:

"I don't want to go ahead, I want to go back to where I was a long time ago!" God knows how he had the patience to bother with me at all.

And then Ernest Walsh sent a telegram from the south of France, saying: "Insist you see my lung specialist in Paris. I will take care of everything. *La vie est belle*. We want you to join us here. Come quickly." Richard and I worked it out very carefully. With the family's gift of money, and with what little I had saved from the weekly sale of vegetables, and with what Richard could manage to send me from his salary, it could be done. (By this time I had stopped saying that I would make money from my writing.) I would go to the south of France for a month or six weeks, not longer. At the end of February, I left Harfleur, so blinded by my tears that I could scarcely see Richard standing on the station platform. In an orgy of self-pity, I cried halfway to Paris, as if knowing exactly what was going to take place.

Robert McAlmon

1923-1924

Intending to return to Paris, I stopped en route at Rapallo, which was then Ezra Pound's permanent residence. Ezra was not there at the time, but the night I checked in at the hotel I encountered Ernest Hemingway and his wife, Hadley, and also Henry (Mike) Strater, a painter, and his wife. I had never heard of any of them before. Hemingway was a Middle Western American who worked for a Canadian newspaper, and he was a type outside my experience. At times he was deliberately hard-boiled, case-hardened, and old; at other times he was the hurt, sensitive boy, deliberately young and naïve, wanting to be brave, and somehow on the defensive, suspicions lurking in his peering analytic glances at the person with whom he was talking. He approached a café with a small-boy, tough-guy swagger, and before strangers of whom he was uncertain a potential snarl of scorn played on his large-lipped, rather loose mouth. Mike Strater was a far simpler and direct young American, a Southerner, not only unpretentious but actually modest. He later did the illustrations for the Three Mountains Press edition of Ezra's *A Draft of XVI. Cantos.*

We all worked. There was a French painter about with an American wife who was a stage designer and interior decorator, and one of the other wives was inclined to think she was designing in other ways. Nevertheless, we worked: Strater painted portraits of his wife and infant son; the Frenchman painted; Hemingway and I wrote; and at night we all drank moderately. Rapallo is situated in a bay, which I find imprisoning, although along that coast are hotels beautifully situated. However, they are generally occupied by the elderly English, and although the Sitwell trio seemed happy in that environment, Rapallo after the sun goes down struck me as dismal and depressing.

Hemingway had just suffered a minor tragedy. His wife had lost a briefcase containing the script of writing he had done over the period of nearly a year. However, he had three short stories and a few poems on hand. He knew Sherwood Anderson and Ezra Pound, and perhaps Ford, and he talked of Ring Lardner's work. As I was publishing books in Paris, I decided to do his three stories and ten poems. One story, "My Old Man," was distinctly in the tone of Sherwood Anderson's "I'm a Fool" and some other race-track story of Anderson's, but the other two stories, or, rather, sketches, were fresh and without derivation so far as I could detect. It's difficult to say who started the attitude in writing which one finds in "My Old Man" and most present American work. It isn't so much a style or an approach as an emot'onal attitude: that of an older person who in-sists upon trying to think and write like a child; and children in my experience are much colder and more ruthless in their observations than the child characters in this type of writing.

Ring Lardner wrote about boob baseball players for boobs to read, but he knew it, and therefore his work took on a satirical value amusing to adults. Anita Loos, a sophisticated woman, did the same thing in *Gentlemen Prefer Blondes*. Whether these two took the manner from Sherwood Anderson and added adult wit, or whether Sherwood Anderson took their ironic attitude seriously and became childishly soulful about this naïve outlook, one cannot know. Since then, however, Hemingway, Morley Callaghan, and a number of others have written in that, to me, falsely naïve manner. They may write of gangsters, prize fighters, bullfighters, or children, but the hurt-child-being-brave tone is there, and all conversation is reduced to lone words or staccato phrases. Possibly I forget my own childhood. I have a theory that quite a gang of us in South Dakota—a wild and dreary plains' state—talked whole sentences and paragraphs, and calculated and often outwitted our elders as very astute intriguers. I grew up with football and baseball players and track stars, and roughnecks from the roundhouse gang. We used to hop freight cars, and bum about doing the harvest seasons, and mingle with the hoboes in the jungle. My sceptical nature tells me that in war books, and in this false-naïve type of writing, there is altogether too much attitudinized insistence upon the starry-eyed innocence and idealism and sentimentality of not only the child but the "sensitive roughneck". Possibly South Dakota's hot summers and freezing winters and its pioneer qualities of that not so far back period made us different, however. As it is, I read with incredulous eye the reviewers' comments about this or that writer's ability to capture the "inflection" and "intonation" of American types and of the American language.

This incredulity is not present when I read the work of Dos Passos, from *Three Soldiers* on through his trilogy. He has set down types I know and have been intimate with. Some are college-educated or good family types; others are wanderers, restless and grousing and young. They, however, all talk in paragraphs and sentences, and they have opinions rather than emitting grunts expressing bewilderment and the thwarted emotions of arrested development. For a time Whit Burnett and Martha Foley, editing *Story* magazine, appeared to think no story "sensitive" and good unless it was about children or somebody childminded. Collecting statistics at Camp Zachary Taylor after the armistice, I found that out of two hundred and fifty men from Kentucky and Tennessee, ninety were complete illiterates, several were actual imbeciles, two had syphilitic rheumatism; and any number had married at child-hood ages, from twelve—the youngest—to seventeen. They had married girls from nine—the youngest—to fourteen. So I am ready to believe that the Faulkner and Caldwell depictions of ingrown sections of the country are based on actual conditions; but don't they concentrate on the feeble to the extent of seeing nobody but?

Dos Passos manages to convey horror enough without picking complete mental deficients or prize fighters, or gangsters, or hurt children of whatever age. Possibly the old Spanish writers of picaresque novels got their tough lads better. Certainly now in Barcelona, Berlin, Paris, it's possible to talk to children of the streets and find no hurt-baby wail in their conversation. They're tough and they're knowing. The fake child-mentality was not there in Hawthorne, or Henry James, or O. Henry, or Dreiser; it is not there in a quantity of present-day writers, but reviewers seem to look on it as truly American. Surely America produces many adults and types who are as alertly aware and sophisticated as any in the world.

A year or so later the lot of us were in Paris at the same time, and after a trip to London I talked of going to Spain, Hemingway wanted much to see a bullfight, and after a week of talking about it, we headed towards Spain. Hemingway and Hadley had a fondness for pet names. Beery-poppa (Hemingway) said a loving goodbye to Feather-kitty (Hadley), Bumby (their baby), and Waxen-puppy (their dog), and he and I, well lubricated with whisky, got on the train.

The next day, on the way to Madrid, our train stopped at a wayside station for a time. On the track beside us was a flatcar, upon which lay the maggot-eaten corpse of a dog. I, feeling none too hale and hearty, looked away, but Hemingway gave a dissertation on facing reality. It seemed that he had seen in the war the stacked corpses of men, maggot-eaten in a similar way. He advised a detached and scientific attitude toward the corpse of the dog. He tenderly explained that we of our generation must inure ourselves to the sight of grim reality. I recalled that Ezra Pound had talked once of Hemingway's "self-hardening process". At last he said, "Hell, Mac, you write like a realist. Are you going to go romantic on us?"

I spurted forth some oath and went to the dining car to order whisky. Not only was the sight of the dog before my eyes, its stench was in my nostrils, and I have seen many dead dogs, cats, and corpses of men borne in on the tide of New York Harbour while working on a lumber barge. Several years later Paul Rosenfeld told me that Hemingway had told this story to prove his assertion that I was a romanticist. However, Hemingway was realist enough himself to join me in the dining car and have a whisky, but he certainly had duly analysed all of his sensations "on seeing the maggot-eaten corpse of a dog on a flatcar in Spain while wondering what it is that makes a guy shudder who has seen so much of life as McAlmon has".

The day that we were to see our first bullfight we agreed that the horse part of it might bother us, so we had a few drinks before taking our seats. We took a bottle of whisky with us, with the understanding that, if shocked, we would gulp down a quantity to calm ourselves. My reactions to the bullfight were not at all what I had anticipated. At first it seemed totally unreal, like something happening on the screen. The first bull charged into the ring with tremendous violence. When the horses were brought in, it charged head on and lifted the first horse over its head. But the horns did not penetrate.

Instead of a shock of disgust, I rose in my seat and let out a yell.

Things were happening too quickly for my mind to consider the horse's suffering. Later, however, when one of the horses was galloping in hysteria around the ring, treading on its own entrails, I decidedly didn't like it. I have since discovered that many hardened Spanish *aficionados*, and in one case I knew of, the brother of a bullfighter, had to look the other way on such occasions. Hemingway became at once an *aficionado*, that is, a passionate bullfight fan or enthusiast, intent upon learning all about the art. If I suspect that his need to love the art of bullfighting came from Gertrude Stein's praise of it, as well as from his belief in the value of "self-hardening", it is only because his bullfight book (*Death in the Afternoon*) adopts such a belligerent attitude in the defence of bullfighting. There are countless English and Americans who were bullfight enthusiasts many years before that summer of 1924 when Hemingway and I both saw our first, but he made it into a literary or artistic experience.

By the end of that day my temper about everything connected with the bullfight was much what it is now. I resented the crowd's brutality and the way people threw mats and articles of clothing into the ring at moments in which the matadors were in danger. The crowd itself was taking no chances. The bull was—when he was— a magnificent animal, a snorting engine of black velocity and force. The matadors did their dance well, moved beautifully, and played seriously with death. The role of the horses I decided to overlook as confirmation of Spanish brutality, which was probably no worse than many French and Anglo-Saxon cruelties.

Bill Bird, who was by then associated with me in the publishing of books, joined Hemingway and me in Madrid, and we did a tour, seeing Granada, Seville, Ronda, and more and more bullfights. Bird also liked bullfights, but neither he nor I were putting ourselves through a "hardening process". After the first bullfight, Bill and I took them as matter-of-factly as if we'd been seeing them all our lives, and our criticism of the matador was as ruthless as any Spaniard's.

Before leaving Paris, Hemingway had been much of a shadow-boxer. As he approached a café he would prance about, sparring at shadows, his lips moving, calling his imaginary opponent's bluff. Upon returning from Spain, he substituted shadow-bull-fighting for shadow-boxing. The amount of imaginary cape work and sword thrusts he made in those days was formidable. Later he went to Key West and went in for barracuda fishing, and I wonder if he took then to shadow-barracuda-fishing, or coming back from Africa he would shadow-lion-hunt. He has a boy's need to be a tough guy, a swell boxer, a strong man.

All of this shadow-boxing was to keep himself fit, naturally, and several years later when Morley Callaghan, also a bit of a boxer, arrived in Paris, he and Hemingway staged bouts. *The* famous Callaghan-Hemingway bout that took place in 1929 was reported to me several ways: by Hemingway, by Callaghan, and by Scott Fitzgerald. Callaghan's report was that Scott was to referee, and they were to have three or four two-minute rounds. Hemingway was the taller and heavier man. Callaghan, actually, was short, and inclined to a look of flabbiness and rotundity. Scott was sure that Hemingway only needed to play with Callaghan, and let him down easily, without showing him up in a mortifying way. The first round did not turn out that way, however, and so Scott forgot to tell time. Callaghan had Hemingway backing away and getting winded, but the fight went on and on. Neither of the boxers wanted to suggest that the round-time was up, but after a long delay Scott did call time. Callaghan was sure that Hemingway thought Scott forgot to call time purposely.

Hemingway's story was that he had been drinking the night before and was boxing on three pick-me-up whiskies, and that his wind gave out. The decision results were, however, that neither Hemingway nor Callaghan could decide what the bout proved. Was one a better boxer but not so good a writer as the other, or was the other a better writer *and* boxer, or had Scott framed one or the other of them? At this time Hemingway felt that Callaghan was imitating his style, and it is true that Callaghan was writing about prize fighters, gangsters, and inarticulate roughnecks. But Ring Lardner had done this a bit before either of them. Gertrude Stein had already been the repeating child, and Sherwood Anderson had injected "soul" and highfalutin sensibility into the hearts of childish boobs. Possibly, then, their writing bout was a draw, and the final bell has not yet rung.[1]

Callaghan, admittedly a pedestrian writer and perhaps even dull (although it is the fashion in some quarters to court the dull), seems interested in wider and more normal phases of life. At least, much less of his writing is a defence and explanation of himself and of the reactions and emotions he feels he ought to have. Hemingway is always

[1] For Morley Callaghan's version of this bout, see *That Summer in Paris.*

protesting and explaining his emotions, so much so that one is inclined to wonder if he has not invented some convention for himself as to how one should feel in particular circumstances: to be professionally brave here, tough there, gentle and inarticulate with tenderness somewhere else, the rough man, so reticent but oh so full of sensibility.

In the year 1924 articles were appearing in American magazines and newspapers about the life of the deracinated, exiled, and expatriated who lived mainly in Paris, leading, the articles implied, non-working and dissolute lives. An American journalist, long a resident of Paris, was riled and asked me to compile a list of the foreign artists who had been in the Quarter throughout the last year or so. He suggested that I make a note as well of what work they had accomplished, and what their dissipations were, if any. One night, with several others who had been in Paris for some time, we drew up a list of two hundred and fifty names, English and American (and some were the names of those responsible for the American articles against the so-called exiles in Paris!). We listed none but working writers or painters; one of the writers has since been awarded the Nobel Prize; several others have been Book-of-the-Month Club selections, or best-sellers, or merely acclaimed as great writers.

There need be no apology for talking about the work which the Paris exiles produced. Mina Loy, while painting and writing, and decorating her own small and gloomy apartment to make it liveable, decided to open a shop off the Champs Elysées. Mina was known for her beauty and wit, slightly overcerebral, but she had a distinct talent for inventing fantasies. She made abstract paintings or designs by pasting coloured papers of different shapes one upon the other; she transferred archaic pictures and maps upon glass globes and bottles, and inserted lights inside them, and marketed these as table lamps. She invented calla-lily lights, searched antique shops for medieval paintings and etchings, and, having done all the work of painting and decorating the interior of her shop, she went into business. Fortunately she had a degree of commercial success.

Laurence Vail had an exhibition of paintings in Mina's shop, and Isadora Duncan attended it. She drank copiously of the punch that was furnished, and went across the street to drink more at a bistro bar, and returned to talk grandly of what paintings she would purchase. As she was then living more or less on charity, nobody took poor Isadora seriously. But the shop prospered. Orders came in from

England and America, Mina was given contracts on the Continent, and she patented many of her designs. At one time she employed a dozen French girls, and she worked along with them daily. A few years later Djuna Barnes worked with equal zeal when writing *Ryder* and *The Ladies' Almanack*, which she illustrated. Djuna coloured by hand the drawings in forty of the books.

William Bird was also a hard-working man, for besides doing his work as a journalist he had his hand press and his own publishing business. Although he and I had joined forces, many of the books which I picked were long and we had them printed by Darantière in Dijon. Bird was interested in fine printing, book-binding, and hand-set type, and he had a press on the Quai d'Anjou, next to Ford Madox Ford's offices of the *Transatlantic Review*. Nearby was the restaurant which Sherwood Anderson and Dos Passos discovered shortly after the war as a simple bistro, where one could procure very good food. Ford worked steadily, but he delighted in giving tea and other parties. Since the days of his editorship of the *English Review*, Ford has had yearnings to be "a grand old man of letters", to whom the young would come to submit manuscripts and ask advice. Ford's teas were not highly interesting, but as Bird and I were often in the shop we dropped in.

Shortly after Conrad's death that year, Ford sent wires to a number of writers asking them to do an article on Conrad's place in English letters. Among the ones with whom I later spoke were Mary Butts and Hemingway. Each of us thought that his article was to be the sole article, and, if I remember rightly, not any of us had ever been Conrad enthusiasts. But Ford edited that issue of the *Transatlantic* so that the glory which was Conrad's appeared but a reflection of Ford's glory, for Ford had been Conrad's instructor in great English prose, and his collaborator in his better novels.

William Carlos Williams and his wife, Florence, came for a sabbatical year on the Continent, the first lengthy vacation from doctoring that Bill had had in fifteen years. He had not been in Paris long, however, before he was worrying about his "practice". He was a child specialist, but as he practised medicine in the same town in which he had been born, he was easy prey for numerous old ladies, Negro and Italian working people, and poor families who wanted no other doctor. He was not only modest in the fees he charged, but he wasn't much good at collecting accounts, and as a consequence he had always had to do a great deal of general practitioner work.

Possibly it was his generation, or else his early association with Ezra Pound and Hilda Doolittle, but however it was Bill was inclined to go literary and nostalgic about things Greek. It is not unreasonable to ask if the Greek and classic tradition is not needlessly restrictive, because much fine literature has come to life entirely outside that tradition, as we are even now discovering. Arthur Waley having translated Lady Murasaki, and Pearl Buck having done likewise with *All Men are Brothers*, literatures are revealed to us which indicate an ongoing panorama and do not inflict an arbitrary pattern upon life for all eternity. That pattern does well for small nations and races whose conventions have hardened into a mould, England, Denmark, and possibly provincial France, but it is not suitable for a polyglot America any more than it is, or ever was, for Russia. It's quite possible that Russia, with her *Dead Souls* and various lengthy novels of family life in the process of decay due to a social order, has more to say to Americans than the so-called classic tradition, derived from Greece by way of English literature. In our time Proust, Joyce, Dorothy Richardson, Dos Passos, Jules Romain, and others have departed from the "classic" formula (as, indeed, did Cervantes long ago). Joyce has retained a precious and literary nostalgia for the Greek poetizing, word-prettifying (qualities also dear to Pound's heart), such as *melopoeia, logopoeia, phanopoeia*. He has persisted in his interest in words as words, for their evocative and suggestive potentialities, to the point of indifference to content-concept and the whole compositional realization of relationships rooted in a social order.

That "I am a poet, a bard, a singer" attitude has disposed many people to view poets as flighty creatures incapable of observing reality or of coping with actual experience. It is an attitude that has bred a spirit in the universities which makes very precious lads and lassies indeed of young people who, if they must be poets, would be much better off making use of the idioms and symbols of their own time. We simply don't happen to live on a Mediterranean island, where the sun flashes on the sea's wine-dark waves, like the reflection of light on shining helmets. Greek gods and mythological figures mean nothing more to most than Hans Christian Andersen or Grimm characters. Today one gathers there are as many children interested in primitive Mayan or Toltec civilization as in the Greek.

Williams can tell amazing stories about his experiences during his years of doctoring. On the outskirts of Rutherford is a colony of settlers which has remained intact throughout a two-hundred-year period, ingrowing and interrelated, preserving the customs of centuries ago. Because Bill is kindly and understanding, he has always had quantities of patients from amongst those Italian settlers, and some of his stories are weirdly amusing or tragic, but always deeply based in life. Now and then he wrote poems about these characters, or short stories, but these stories he did not rate so highly as some precious poem inoculated with Greek names or qualities or Greek mythology. Bill, actually, as an organism, is one of the most interesting "sensibilities" America has produced. He is overimpressionable, to the extent that the quiverings of his sensibility are so constant he hasn't the time to clarify his observations, but instead is lost in a species of life-wonder, bewilderment, and torment. He has written many fine poems and short stories, but he is apt to think his best not worth publishing because it has come straight from a direct and stark impulse, because it doesn't perplex and irritate him and make him restless. In New York I had kept him from destroying one such poem, one of the most beautiful in any language. It was the "Portrait of an Author," which appeared first in *Contact* and later in his book *Sour Grapes*. Marianne Moore later said of it: "It preserves the atmosphere of a moment into which the impertinence of life cannot intrude."

But Williams thought it too intimate, or not art, or not Greek, or whatever. Miss Moore persuaded him at other times to spare other poems of his which he rejected. I cannot go deeply into the reasons for this blind spot in him. Joyce and Pound and H.D. and many others strike me as being "bards" in the worded and traditional sense. This is undoubtedly literary, but it doesn't make literature in a sound sense. An obsession with the qualities in words is, I suspect, a preoccupation for the younger and still developing years. The first and autobiographical novel of almost every writer who has proved himself first rate in the last few years is filled with passages of ecstasy and rhapsody concerning words and their lovely flavours. That isn't nearly enough.

There was a good deal of party giving in Paris for Bill and Flossie, Sylvia Beach and Adrienne Monnier had them to dinner with Valery Larbaud, and both the American and the French poet came away feeling powerfully stimulated, for both had quick responsive minds and broad sympathies. They also shared what can only be described as a tremendous expectancy, which made me, as I watched and listened, feel a jaded and worn-out cynic, not less than ten million years old and serving his last incarnational sentence before joining the infinite.

Bill was intent on meeting young French writers, the Dadaists, Tristan Tzara, and the surrealists, to get to the root of what they were driving at. I suppose he felt I let him down. I never was romantic about French groups, and I knew many of the Dadaists who enjoyed being Dadaists because Dada is nothing, so they could do nothing and feel fine about it. It was impossible to know them, and to glance at their work, and to come away impressed. They were frequently likeable and bright and good conversationalists, but Bill would have it that they were profound and moved by a significant impetus. At first, at least, he would not be convinced that this one was a calculating opportunist and publicist, or that this other one was no more than a likeable young man bent on becoming a man of affairs, with status in the bourgeois world; or that a number of others had very definite ideas about establishing themselves in order to enjoy leisure.

Before Bill and Floss headed for the south of France there was a party at the Trianon, which was then the restaurant at which Joyce always dined. Mina Loy, Sylvia Beach, Adrienne Monnier, Kitty Cannell, Laurence Vail and his wife, Peggy Guggenheim, and his sister, Clotilde Vail, were in the party of twenty or more. Bill had perhaps expected Joyce to be more staidly the great man of letters, but Joyce had been having apéritifs before the dinner began, and he dearly loves a party. He wanted there to be singing, preferably of Irish songs and in an Irish tenor voice. He wanted there to be dancing and general hilarity. Bill wanted these, too, but one gathered he also wanted there to be profound discussion. Someone at the table asked Nora Joyce if she read her husband's work.

She answered: "Sure, why would I bother? It's enough he talks about that book and he's at it all the time. I'd like a bit of life of my own." She later admitted that she had read the last pages of *Ulysses*, in which Molly Bloom's thoughts are portrayed. Her comment was short but to the point. "I guess the man's a genius, but what a dirty mind he has, hasn't he?"

I assured Nora that, had it not been for her keeping him down to earth, Joyce would have remained the word-prettifying bard, the martyred sensibility, Stephen Dedalus. But Nora would not have it that he had learned about women from her. "Go along with you! People say I have helped him to be a genius!" she scoffed. "What they'll be saying next is that if it hadn't been for that ignoramus of a woman what a man he would have been! But never you mind, I could tell them a thing or two about him after twenty years of putting up with him, and the devil take him when he's off on one of his rampages!"

The party became joyous, as Joyce wished. He sang Irish "come-all-ye's," and all of us got together on a few like "Love's Old Sweet Song" and "Carry Me Back to Ole Virginny". Clotilde Vail knew a few "blues" songs, and I recalled some spirituals and cowboy songs. The Trianon stayed open late that night, and it all ended when Nora decided that Jim was going too far and there would be no handling him if she did not get him home. "It's you who see him in a jolly state," she said, "but it's me who has to bear the brunt of it if his eyes get ailing, and what a martyr that man can be, you've no idea!"

Williams revealed one day that he was annoyed by a written comment of Mencken's which, with yokel wit, mentioned one of Bill's books and stated that he was a village horse doctor, or some such remark. Here the difference in generation unexpectedly became a barrier between Bill and me. It had never occurred to me that Bill would look on Mencken as anything but a Babbitt iconoclast exclusively for Babbitts. It simply was not in the minds of our generation (the younger generation then) to look on Mencken as a person with a feeling for literature. Axe-grinding articles, pieces with purported sociologic or documentary contents, and attitudes showing up the boobs for other boobs to chuckle at, this he could and did do, but his mediocre mind was dated pre-war and never sensitive.

Even his insistence on American booberies was an indication of Babbitt provincialism; for to bring our own booberies into perspective he might have turned occasionally to a symposium of English, French, German, Italian, and other national booberies. Mencken, however, is "a case". There is hardly a travelling salesman, or a store clerk, or an insurance or real estate salesman, who is a "great hand at reading something that makes you think", who doesn't view Mencken with awe. Gertrude Stein believes she belongs to a great and common public; and perhaps Williams has a germ of that same feeling in him about himself. Mencken's public is not simple and honest, and when the yokels and hicks and mediocrities take on what they think is intellectual and brilliantly ironic, it's time to worry about their pretensions getting control of the book clubs, etc.

Williams' concern over Mencken's lumbering comment on his manner of making a living only proves the need for Bill to get away from a suburban town full of residents whose reading fare consists of the *Saturday Evening Post*, the *American Mercury*, and other publications of this kind. That Larbaud, Valéry, Gide, and a quantity of other continental and English writers find Bill's work unique among that of American writers in its appeal to a highly organized mentality is more interesting to me than anything Mencken could have to say. It's hard to select one out of Bill's many books to comment on, because he is a force, an influence, a direction, and a sensibility in American literature rather than the mere author of "books".

Williams has often said that I have "a genius for life", while in the same breath he bemoans his own New England soul and the fact that he has not ventured far or long from the town of his birth, where he practises medicine. He may be right about me. If absolute despair, a capacity for reckless abandon and drink, long and heavy spells of ennui which require bottles of strong drink to cure, and a gregarious but not altogether loving nature is "a genius for life", then I have it. But with Bill I always feel more or less gay, and he is one of the few who can talk of his soul problems and probe the deeper darknesses of life without irritating or boring me.

Presently Bill, Floss, and I headed for the south of France for a period, and I remained there when they went on to Italy.

Kay Boyle

1926-1928

Ernest Walsh and Robert McAlmon were enormously generous not only in response to other writers but in their judgment of them as well. Bill Williams' way of living his life, and his poetry and prose, were the counsel he never ceased giving all of us. (There was no venom, no imbalance in the man. When Alfred Kreymborg lost the only script in existence of Bill's play, *The Old Apple Tree*, all Bill said in reproach was that he was "sick over it".) McAlmon and Walsh were about the same age—ten or twelve years younger than Bill— and although they were both too proud and jaunty to be any man's disciples, still they had a particular deference for Bill's genius as writer and as man. They learned from his example to listen for the sound of the poet's voice speaking out in the climate and setting of every day; but they listened with less patience and temperance. The Irish-American aviator named Walsh, and McAlmon, the Presbyterian minister's son of Scottish descent, despite the debonairness of their stance, nursed an uneasy anger in their hearts that was never a portion of Bill's passionate forbearance. "My furious wish," Bill has written in his autobiography, "was to be normal, undrunk, balanced in everything. . . . I would not court disease, live in the slums for the sake of art, give lice a holiday. I would not 'die for art,' but live for it, grimly! and work, work, work . . . and be free . . . to write, write, as I alone should write, for the sheer drunkenness of it. . . ."[1] Walsh and McAlmon had in them a violent dissatisfaction with themselves, with what they were,

[1] *The Autobiography of William Carlos Williams*, New Directions, New York, 1967.

and they sought, in their different ways, to rock this impatience to sleep with drink, but it would not sleep. Drink was the most fearsome of deceivers, as Bill knew, for it promised one thing and came through with quite another. Yet these three men had one enduring thing in common, and that was their commitment, as selfless as a woman's, to the work of other men.

McAlmon could not be bothered writing criticism in any sustained way, but whatever criticism he wrote was exceptionally astute. First Carnevali and then Ernest Walsh responded to Bill's urgent and explicit voice as critic, that voice which said: "The thinkers, the scholars, thereupon propound questions upon the nature of verse, answering themselves or at least creating tension between thoughts. They think, and to think, they believe, is to be profound. . . . But who, if he chose, could not touch the bottom of thought?" Carnevali and Walsh added to such predications their own fiery defiance, and it is probably quite true that then, at that moment, there was no way except through the anger of a few men's minds and hearts to clear the air, the ground, the sea, and the literary periodicals of the time of all that defiled them, that there was no other means of restoring to the entire writing scene its lost purity.

In his book *A Hurried Man*, Carnevali cried out that a poem nowadays cannot be a poem unless it is violent.

> Either I die uselessly as so many other fools have, or I go crazy as so many other fools have, or something must be done [he wrote]. A coalition of the artists, a new religion, a universal prohibition forbidding . . . everything that is now being sold, or something. . . . Criticism is hellfire, death and destruction, war and revolution, and all the fun there is in rockets and gas bombs and smoke-screens and camouflage, butchery and a dance macabre of ghosts, of murdered kings and princes gone mad withal, that's what criticism is. William Blake stuttered and stuttered until he went insane, went insane for the sake of showing you how he could stick to it . . . and you ask whether rhymed poems are better than free verse, and how I like Sara Teasdale! Rimbaud threw it all out in cataracts of gold and emerald and ruby and it was done for at twenty, and you ask what symbolism is. Symbolism is the sinister will to get out of the filth you live in, that's what it is!

McAlmon had published Carnevali's book in 1925, and the first issue of *This Quarter*, dedicated in homage to Ezra Pound, came out the same year. In the exuberance of this revival of letters, Carnevali's attack on Pound (in *A Hurried Man*) was looked on as less a personal attack than an assault on intellectual and academic authority. (Pound's "profession of faith in art", Carnevali complained, consisted of a few "don'ts" shouted at some imaginary followers. Dostoevsky was sorrow, wrote Carnevali; Walt Whitman was joy; while Pound was irritation. "Irritation inspires him and he inspires irritation in his readers.") In a letter Bill Williams was to write me in 1932, he said that Pound "is too 'like' the classics. He is a classicist, almost a pedant, according to some. His actuality is what has been forced on him by his disposition and the mode of life he affects. He writes in America as far as he writes in any language, but his metre is the purifications of older orders used with modern words. He has brought back the modern language to the water of excellent poetic usage, then what the hell? He is teaching it classic dancing. A dash of grotesquerie thrown in with a great sense of time. Pound is one of the few moderns worth reading. One can differ with him so easily and excel him with the greatest difficulty. He is still a worthwhile beginning for any poet writing in our language. I don't think he has solved anything for us. His line is classic adaptation, no more."

Bill saw all the little magazines, from *Others* to *This Quarter*, and before and after them, as one single magazine, "a continuous magazine . . . with an absolute freedom of editorial policy and a succession of proprietorships that follows a democratic rule". Take the little magazine away, he wrote, and a prominent support is cut from under the poet, and for years he may get nothing into print; "loose ends are left dangling, men are lost", he wrote in true sorrow, "promises that needed culture, needed protection and wit and courage to back them simply die". And now here were Ernest Walsh and Ethel Moorhead undertaking that proprietorship as a handful of others through the years had undertaken it before them, taking it on in a special time of need for the poet (although for poets all times are times of need), seizing that proprietorship with an enthusiasm and a generosity that surely the little magazine world had never seen the like of before.

When Ethel Moorhead and Ernest Walsh met me at the railway station in Grasse that morning in late February, Ernest Walsh had a copy of *A Hurried Man* in his overcoat pocket. The overcoat itself was a soft, light-coloured wool and he wore it like a supple cloak across his shoulders. He was tall and slender and ivory-skinned, with bold, dark, long-lashed eyes, and his black eyebrows met savagely above his nose. As the three of us walked down the platform, he had to speak of Carnevali's book. He couldn't keep quiet about it. He was writing a review of it for the next number of *This Quarter*, he said, and he was ready to take the book out of his pocket and start reading it aloud as we walked. "For heaven's sake, wait until the poor girl has caught her breath!" Ethel Moorhead chided him.

She was then between forty and fifty, I suppose, dressed in a sensible but very expensive-looking suit of the plaid of her clan, and she had a Scottish clang to her voice which suited her very well. She had short bobbed hair, with only a little grey in it, and the pince-nez she wore gave her an air of authority; but there was at the same time something like shyness, or wariness, in her small uneasy brown eyes and her tense mouth. She and Ernest Walsh had found a modest room for me in a low-priced *pension*, which I had enough money to pay for for six weeks anyway. The *pension* was within walking distance of their villa, and I was to walk over and dine with them every night, they said. The report from the Paris lung man had not yet come through, and when it did, if the news was bad, we would look into the matter of sanatoriums, Ethel said. Ernest Walsh himself had been in Saranac, after the air force plane he was piloting had crashed in Texas. "I'm fine," he said to me sometime in that first evening, when we had drunk a good deal of wine. "I've got another five years to live."

Before the war Ethel Moorhead had been active in the women's suffrage movement in England. She had smashed plate-glass windows with a hammer, trembling with nervousness as she struck; she had set fire to churches, been arrested, and been forcibly fed. But quite apart from this, she was a painter and she was writing a book about her experiences as a feminist, and of breaking not only windows but the ties with her wealthy Scottish family, and the conventions into which she had been born. She had inherited a good share of that Scottish money now, and because she painted well and wrote well, she had come over to Paris, in loneliness and discontent with England, to settle for a while. And there, at the elegant Claridge's hotel, she had noticed this young American in the long hall, or strolling through the lobby, or sometimes sitting at the bar. He was striking enough in appearance to catch anybody's eye, but she also noticed that he was alone, that he looked ill fed, and that his cheeks were flushed at night; and in the end, after he had given her Ezra Pound's poetry to read, and shown her some poetry of his own, she got up her courage to show him the oil paintings she was doing in her room. "We were birds of a feather in one way or another," she said at dinner that first night, very pleased that they had found each other. She had learned from the hotel manager that the young American's belongings were being held because he wasn't able to pay his bill. The army pension cheques had gone out to California, Ernest Walsh said, and no one had thought to forward them to Paris, where he was.

So Ethel Moorhead had paid his bill, and without quite knowing how it came about they began making plans for a magazine, a literary quarterly, that they would edit together. Ernest Walsh had known Harriet Monroe in Chicago, and some of his poems had appeared in *Poetry*, side by side with those of McAlmon; and in the back of his mind, he said, there had always been the idea of bringing out a magazine of his own. Ethel had her Scottish income, limited though it was, to put into it, and he had his pension from the government to help out with, and they would print all the writers in whom he believed so fiercely, so defensively, and the work of painters, sculptors, composers as well. They had called on Brancusi, and come away with reproductions of his sculptures for the first number; and they had looked up Hemingway and written to Joyce; McAlmon was in England, but he sent them parts of a novel from there; and they had journeyed to Italy to see Carnevali and Ezra Pound. It did not seem strange to us then, in those years (and perhaps there was nothing strange about it), how the scattered bits and pieces of the lives and hopes of writers kept falling into place, finally making a mural, a frieze, of such continuity that people would look on it for a long time to come as literary history.

The villa Ethel Moorhead and Ernest Walsh had rented for the winter was on the side of a steep hill that rode out of this town of many perfumes. It had belonged to a retired French shoe manufacturer, and it stood above endless terraces crowded with flowers that were cultivated for the perfume manufacturing trade. In my novel written in 1930 (and dedicated to Emanuel Carnevali)[2] I wrote of this place:

[2] *Year Before Last*, Harrison Smith, Inc.. New York, 1932. Reprinted by Southern Illinois University Press, Carbondale, 1968.

In the hallway stood Monsieur Simon's own likeness, life-size, in bronze, with one of Ezra's overcoats over his shoulders, and a beret. When they came into the house it was the first thing Hannah saw in the candlelight: the French shoeman's bronze wart on his cheek and the hair water-waved over his head. The bastard, said Martin. We found his papers put away in a drawer, and you know they were after him because he made nothing but paper soles to shoe the French army. You great big patriot you, he said. Martin held his nose. Do you know what he does now? The ghost of him flushes the cabinay-wish-box at any hour of night or day.

And this was true. Even sitting downstairs, with the fire of sycamore wood and pine cones burning in the chimney, you could hear the toilet on the second floor flushing every ten minutes or so. After a glass or two of wine, Ethel looked at me rather shyly and laughed about this, and Ernest Walsh laughed, and he stood up in his grey flannel pants and his brown suède shoes to do a little dance to the music of it, and I sat laughing in some kind of inexpressible relief at everything that was taking place. If I was going to die of tuberculosis, it would be easy to die in the white blaze of the plaster and stone of the walls that lined the precipitous road outside, and in the white and blue blaze of the houses, with drifting curtains of wisteria hanging at their doors. It would not be difficult to die, I thought, with these two people speaking of poetry to you, and holding your hand in their hands as you turned towards darkness from the fire of meridional light. I suddenly knew, without any preparation for this knowledge, that to be gay is one of the postures of courage, and that the loss of heart is an indulgent name for cowardice, and I wanted to be courageous more than anything else in life.

Ethel talked in her clanging Scottish voice of the places they would go: perhaps a brief visit to Ireland, when the weather would be good there, but not for long, as the climate would not be a good thing for Michael. Michael was the name Ernest Walsh preferred to his own, and I described to them the figure of *mon chevalier*, St. Michel, who stands on the spire of the abbey of Mont St. Michel, and who had been struck thirteen times by lightning through the centuries. "That's me," Michael said, dancing. When they had travelled to Scotland, Ethel said, he had not only started hæmorrhaging, but he had quarrelled with all her suffragette friends, and she chuckled at the memory of it. "I fell in love with the nurse you got for me," Michael said; and at the sound of this a look of acrimony came over Ethel's face. "It's bad for your health to be falling in love," she said. "The doctor warned you." "She was a damned pretty girl," Michael said, "which is more than can be said about your feminist friends. And what did Ethel do," Michael said, and he stopped dancing and turned towards me and spread his long-fingered, narrow hands; "what did she do but pack up and go away!" "It was the only way to bring you to whatever senses you have," Ethel said.

That first night Michael read for a long time to us, reading a poem of McAlmon's which goes:

> To have as heritage
>   Space!
> and nothing less.
> More,
> an immensity of snows,
> forests,
> lakes and cities.
> nothing within but time,
> butterfly intervals
> between
>   day's platinum
>   night's ebony
>   pillars
> pouring all entity and events
> into constricting tubes.

And he read a poem of Carnevali's, which ended:

> Oh, then the old accustomed, impudent
>   ghost came in:
> He wore my bagged, ragged pants, and was
>   unshaven;
> And his face was the one I had seen in the
>   mirror
> Too many times.

One of the last he read was Joyce's love poem, which I hear forever outside my window on April nights:

> Rain on Rahoon falls softly, softly falling
> Where my dark lover lies.
> Sad is his voice that calls me, sadly calling
> At grey moon-rise.
> Love, hear thou
> How desolate the heart is, ever calling,
> Ever unanswered—and the dark rain falling
> Then as now.
>
> Dark too our hearts, O love, shall lie, and cold
> As his sad heart has lain
> Under the moon-grey nettles, the black mould
> And muttering rain.

In that first week there were letters from Hemingway, Pound, Carnevali, and half a dozen other writers, and as we sat by the fire in the evening Michael would read all or parts of them aloud. Every morning the mailbox at the gate was stuffed with manuscripts, Michael said, and after a glass or two of wine he would begin to sing his pleasure out. He sang in an Irish tenor voice such as Joyce would have liked to listen to, and such as Joyce would have liked to sing aloud with. But Michael sang not for the music and not for the sentiment, but because he knew now that *This Quarter* was a door swung suddenly open to all those who had been writing in hermetically sealed rooms, without so much as a skylight of hope above their heads in promise that the words they were wringing out of their hearts would ever be read. Hemingway wrote to Michael that he was feeling a good deal better about writing since *This Quarter* was there, and Ezra Pound, among other directives as to how Michael was to lead his life and run his magazine, sent a post card saying: "DEEnye Boyle evr. publ. Shat Revyou or Lavatory Broom. Yur discov. sech as is. Yipe loudr. than Benet clique."

During those first days Michael told me he had been born in Cuba, of Irish parents, his father having owned a coffee plantation there. On the mantelpiece in his bedroom he had a photograph of his parents, and he took me in to look at their faces; but they did not seem to me to be the true authors of his grace and vehemence. His mother wore a handmade lace collar that came up high under the lobes of her ears, and a smooth little wreath of blond hair, like a halo, was set above her swollen brow. His father had long silky black moustaches, and his black hair fell two ways on his forehead. Beneath his father's small, set mouth hung a strongly hinged, determined jaw. One night, out of the verity of wine, Michael said that something becomes of a man's fidelity when he gives it to a number of women. "Had I kept mine to myself, there might be more of it left to offer now," he said. Some of it he had given to an American poetess who had no use for it; and some more of it had been given to a Russian girl who played the violin. "Fidelity!" snorted Ethel. "That's one thing you never knew anything about!"

If there are words to describe the beauty of the hills reaching beyond Grasse, I cannot find them. In the drives with Ethel and Michael recklessly behind the wheel of the rattling old French car, the bitter cold of all I had left behind me was tempered, transformed, as startlingly as if the Gulf Stream had decided to alter its course and come along the coast of Normandy. The ice-roofed marshes of Harfleur thawed, and the memory of the munitions factories was turned to palm trees and to cacti standing as tall as men. I saw for the first time layer upon winding layer of rock strata, terra cotta, and mauve, and bronze, rising and breaking over the hills in a violent sea of stone. "There is the earth's entire history, as complete as a poem, as explicit as music," Michael said; and Ethel smiled sardonically and said if you had any sense at all in your head you could see that rocks and hills were far and away better than any music or any poetry.

In a while, word came from Michael's doctor in Paris that there was nothing wrong with my lungs except scars—perhaps from whooping cough—from some infection of years before. Good food and rest, and cod-liver oil, he said, and a great deal of sun, would take care of everything. I had begun typing in my *pension* room, wanting to finish *Plagued by the Nightingale* in the few weeks that I would be there. And then, quite early one morning there was a knock on my door, and Michael came in with his light-coloured overcoat worn across his shoulders like an opera cloak. I was typing, sitting up in bed, with the *café au lait* not quite finished beside me, and he said: "Ethel's moved out. She saw what was happening to me, and perhaps to you. She packed all her things and went away. I don't know how you'd feel about taking me on." And I, who had preached fidelity and denounced betrayal, accepted faithlessness as if it were the one thing I had been waiting for. At that moment I gave not a thought to what would become of Richard or whom Ethel would turn to now, for nothing mattered to me except Michael's beauty and his courage, and I wanted to pay homage to what he was for all my life.

We lived in the villa in Grasse until April, when the lease would come to an end, and I took dictation on the typewriter, and answered letters, and returned rejected manuscripts; I shopped and cooked, and sang the songs Michael liked to hear as I hung the laundry out to dry. Once Mary Butts came, bringing her manuscripts and her sad, sad effusiveness with her; and once Joan, my sister, came down from Paris with a friend who also worked with *Vogue*. She was small-boned and lively as a partridge, this young woman called Pauline Pfeiffer, with dark bangs on her forehead and long, emerald-jewelled earrings hanging from the neat lobes of her ears. I remember so clearly how the muscles were knotted, firm as tennis balls, in the high calves of her rather short but shapely legs, and I remember the dicta she spoke on marriage, and literature, and the Catholic Church.

For a week before their arrival, a letter a day had come for Pauline from Ernest Hemingway. My sister explained to me in confidence that Pauline was one of Hadley Hemingway's closest friends, and that Ernest was writing to her about a certain kind of perfume that was bottled in Grasse, and a certain kind of lingerie that could only be found in Cannes. He wanted Pauline to buy these things for him to give as a surprise to Hadley, whom he deeply loved. Pauline talked to us brightly and efficiently about Hemingway, speaking with authority, and even a trace of condescension, of the difficulty he had getting words down on paper; and she said she was in the process of converting him to Catholicism. "The outlet of confession would be very good for him," she said. She took her religion very pragmatically, and she would sit for hours arguing with Michael, about the Church with unshaken moral certainty. Michael, too, had been brought up a Catholic, a fact he resented with the greatest bitterness, and he had no patience with anything she said.

After dinner on the first evening, his cheeks flushed and his voice eloquent with wine, Michael read aloud some of the poems he had just written. He read one he had written to Ethel Moorhead (although he did not speak her name), which goes in part:

What is there to be done with a woman
    who must be alone to
Feel and who being left alone is
    pleased with herself past
Gentlemen, I address you privately and
    no woman is within hearing
You may confess yourselves as never before
    I am too old to
Remember too young to gossip satisfy your
    taste for speech at
The point where satisfaction ends. . . .

And he read two of his early English sonnets, written in the
language he was experimenting with:

I

How coulde I call thee wife no thou
    art notte
For the quicke violent steps of a
    husbande
In thy chamber nor the lawful claiminge
Hands of a husbande atte thy brests nor
    marriage
Speeches or the vulgar nameplate mistress
Thou ladye thou dame thou girlbrested thou
    art
Thighplumed-white sweeteyed thou loitering
    assent
Sylkwrapped flesh of flowers thou vase of
    lite thou
My handes my handes alonne these shalle
    telle thee
These shalle close the dore andde without
    werds these
Shalle seal the dore against springge andde
    somer
Autum andde winnter and daye
    andde nyghte putte
Away all butte neded then still notte idle
My handes as thou wen thou lovest werdsnonne

II

There is joyelove and saddelove mine was
    joye
Andde she wentte alonge the streete
    dreamminge she
Was Quaker and slending and her haire
    was
A boy's blacke and blacke eyes she had
    too smyled
Seriously and weppt cheerfully timid
    brave
Coward knave virgin strumpet woman girl
Miser spendthrifte poet wenche gold tin
    pearle
Pure obscene dirty cleane princess witche
    childe

She wenttee alonge the siddewalke like the
    milde
Newe sunboye aheade of her and I creppte
In backe of her wilde newe shadowe brande
    newe
And I remember her in Egypt I
Remembered her in Alexandria andde
Quaker girls China quakerlove yes yes

That night he read some paragraphs of the editorial he was
writing for the next number of *This Quarter:*

Outside of *This Quarter,* the Three Mountains Press of
William Bird in Paris, and the Contact Publishing Company of
Robert McAlmon, there is at present no place in the English-
speaking world to which an artist may bring his work.

Robert McAlmon has published at his own expense the work
of the most important of his contemporaries, who otherwise
would not have been published. Gertrude Stein wrote *The
Making of Americans* nine years ago but lacked the spirit and
faith in her own work to publish it at her own expense. She
waited for Robert McAlmon to come along with his rare faith
and to invest his money . . . in publishing this book. This con-

tempt, this arrogant fine scorn for people who play safe, for people who have social vanity without social conscience, for critic and publishers who stand between creator and reader, as between producer and consumer, like a middleman retailing grocer wearing the soiled apron of his trade . . . this contempt which McAlmon possesses as a publisher is also one of the distinctions of his prose. . . . His prose is long, hard, loose-legged stuff and it strides along like a tall man with flapping unpressed trousers. It does not move with mean precise mincing steps. . . . It has the stride of a man walking over prairies where there are few houses. It is lazy. It knows how to sit down cross-legged. It knows how to pause before a jump. It knows how to kick. It knows how to run. It knows how to dig its heels in when it climbs. It knows how to stand still before something it respects.

Pauline seemed impatient as Michael read these sentences from his editorial, and when he was finished she said she didn't want to hear anything about McAlmon. He had been spreading outrageous stories about Hemingway, and she said Hemingway was going to knock him down the next time he ran into him.[3]

"Christ!" Michael shouted, and he slammed his hand down hard on the kitchen table. "McAlmon was the first to publish Hemingway!"

"Ernest owes him nothing!" Pauline cried out. "He paid that debt back—if it was a debt—by getting McAlmon a New York publisher, his own publisher! But when McAlmon repeated to the publisher these stories about Ernest, that was the end of the whole thing!"

"You're talking through your hat!" Michael shouted in his rage. "You with your foul insinuations—you've been trained by the Jesuits all right! Ernest is as close to me as a brother, and he's never had anything but good to say of McAlmon and his work!"[4]

[3] In *McAlmon and the Lost Generation*, p. 234, edited and with commentary by Robert E. Knoll, University of Nebraska Press, 1962, Bill Bird writes that on one occasion when he "met Bob in a Montparnasse bar—his upper lip was covered with surgeon's plaster. He could speak only very indistinctly, but made me understand that Hem had socked him. It was during that same period when Hem was assaulting Dreiser, Max Eastman, etc. . . . it seemed to me that he felt flattered to be in such good company."

[4] In *That Summer in Paris*, pp. 76–77, Dell Publishing Co., Inc., New York, 1964, Morley Callaghan writes: "In his letters to me, he [McAlmon] had shown himself arrogant and contemptuous, but I didn't hold it against him; it had given his

However it was, once Pauline had returned to Paris, Hemingway's long weekly letters to Michael ceased; and Michael himself had a bad taste in his mouth by then because of Hemingway's betrayal of Sherwood Anderson in *The Torrents of Spring*. But in the next few months the look of everything would be different: Michael would be dead, and Hadley would have been put aside, and in her place Pauline Pfeiffer would be Mrs. Hemingway; for the letters that he had written her to Grasse had nothing to do with a particular kind of perfume or a particular kind of lingerie. And in those next few months, Michael and I, like the young men of the Irish Republican Army, would be on the run. We set off to a little hill town called Mougins, to be near Picabia, for Michael was getting together reproductions of Picabia's paintings for the next number of *This Quarter*, and from there we journeyed from mountain village to mountain village, seeking a place where we might stay. Since February, Ethel and Michael had had a number of stormy meetings in Monte Carlo, where she had decided to live. *This Quarter* was to continue, financed by Ethel as before, but, as before she needed Michael's critical flair, and his exuberance, and his poetry and editorials, in order to go on.

Michael and I talked a great deal of McAlmon, whom he had never laid eyes on, and whom I had only seen once. It would have been a good thing for us then, a kind of balm to our hearts, could we have known, word for word, what Jimmie Charters, the barman of the Dingo and the Falstaff, would one day write of him. We wanted to know exactly what the man was like, and in defiance of all those who would diminish him, Jimmie the barman knew. He said:

> Bob McAlmon was one of my best friends among the writers.
> . . . I don't know much about Bob as a writer, because I have
> little time for reading, but I know he's a good fighter. Perhaps
> our friendship sprang up because we are both small, both have

letters an edge, a tang. And I felt the secret envy of him in some of my friends in New York for marrying Bryher, the writer, who was the daughter of Sir John Ellerman, the shipping magnate. . . . After bumming his way across America, doing everything from dishwashing to modelling for painters and sculptors in New York, it had been a very nice thing for him to marry a rich girl and get a handsome divorce settlement, but I had always believed his story that he hadn't been aware it was to be a marriage in name only; he had insisted he was willing to be interested in women. And with the money, what did he do? Spend it all on himself? No, he became a publisher, he spent the money on the other people he believed in."

an independent attitude towards others. Bob has a winning smile and they tell me I have that, too, though I'm sure it cannot be compared with his.

Bob's smile has an effect of magic that I have never seen equalled. One night a tough-looking, hard-boiled American by the name of T———— was giving a party in my bar, and during the course of the evening entertaining his friends with various popular songs which he sang in a loud voice. Bob, who was at the bar with several pernods in him, thought he could do better and launched into an aria from one of the operas. Bob, incidentally, is a good amateur singer.

But T———— did not appreciate opera, it seems. He became quite annoyed, and when Bob did not stop he started towards him with teeth clenched and fists closed. I thought there was going to be murder. "Be careful!" I whispered to Bob. But when they came face to face Bob simply smiled, while T———— stared at him blankly. I saw T————'s fists slowly unclench; then I saw a slight smile come over his face; and once again Bob had charmed someone who was prepared to punch his face.

"Have a drink," said T————. "Make it a whisky and a pernod, Jimmie." They drank and they talked, and T———— was so interested in Bob he forgot all about his friends at the table until they became decidedly annoyed and threatened to leave.

But Bob had other weapons than his smile. I have seen him in the ring, and I know he's a good fighter. We were in Bricktop's, a coloured night club in Montmartre, one night when Bricktop said to him jokingly, "Give me a kiss." Bob replied, also jokingly with a gesture, "I'll give you a punch instead!" A Negro waiter, seeing the gesture, came over to hit him, but Bob was quicker and sent him sprawling. Soon the whole place was in turmoil, Bob and myself against half a dozen coloured men. Bob and I spent the night in jail, but we thought it was well worth it.[5]

We did not have a fixed abiding place, for once a hotel-keeper had heard Michael clear his throat or cough there would be no room available; or if a mistake were made and we were given a room for

[5] *This Must Be the Place*, pp. 59, 60, 61.

the night, there would be complaints from other guests, and we would be asked to move on the next day. It was difficult, for a fixed address he had to have not only for the manuscripts that poured in from would-be contributors to *This Quarter*, but also because of his government pension cheques without which we had no money at all. By the end of June, not admitting to each other our despair, we reached a mountain village called Annot which seemed far and high and lovely enough to stand above and beyond the judgment and condemnation of man.

It was almost evening as Michael stopped the car under the eucalyptus trees in the dust of the wide square. Arm in arm we strolled to the *terrasse* of the one hotel and sat down to drink a glass of wine in the bluish mountain air; and Michael tried not to clear his throat, tried not to cough. We could not go on; the cheques had not caught up with us; there was nowhere else to go. How good it would be if we could stay a day or two in the quiet of this place, his gentle eyes and his weariness were saying, but no force on earth could have brought him to speak these words aloud. We looked away from each other and watched a young man, modishly dressed in linen of various pastel shades, stop suddenly short beside the car parked in the square. He peered through the windows at the bundles of manuscripts, at the copies of *This Quarter* stacked on the back seat, and then he hastened through the dust on his elaborate sandals to the table where we sat. "I cannot believe it is you, that you have really come here," he said to Michael, speaking barely above a whisper. "I have the first number of *This Quarter* up in my room. I know every word of it by heart. I recognize you from your photograph."

At Michael's insistence, he sat down with us diffidently, almost incoherent in his excitement and astonishment. And, as if this was a celebration of great moment, Michael ordered three pernods in tall glasses packed with ice, the colour of it as fresh as spring and vibrant as the mountain dusk. After a sip of the strong drink he told us he was a Scot, and that his name was Archibald Craig, this young man whose face had a weak and vulnerable beauty, and whose lightish cap of hair was fitted, like that of a Greek statue's, to his classically modelled head. All his features bespoke nobility, and yet he appeared, in his shyness, to fear the demands that nobility would make on him. So, for the moment at least, he had set the thought of it aside. He had a bad lung, he told us, and had been a year at the

Passy sanatorium of Thomas Mann's *Magic Mountain:* but his flesh, his voice, were so ethereal that one did not know if what he said had once been true, or if it was a dimly remembered portion of a dream he had dreamed sometime, somewhere, and perhaps was dreaming still. Not that first evening, or not that first month, did he mention the unsubstantiality of his own being, a fact of which he was miserably aware. He murmured to me of this handicap with which he lived only long after, in the years ahead, when he had become my gentle brother, saying: "When I speak the truth, everyone concludes I am lying; whereas when you make a statement, even if it is not completely accurate, nobody ever doubts for a moment that it is true."

Archie Craig was in Annot with his English cousin, the Dayang Muda of Sarawak. She had married the brother of the white Rajah of Sarawak, and after the birth of their six children they had divorced. And now she had rented a villa just across the stream, on the mountainside of tall pine trees, and she was keeping house for a retinue of friends as well as for her young cousin, and he was writing there.

"You must stay here a little while. You must get a room in the hotel," Archie kept urging Michael. "My cousin will speak to the *patron*, and everything will be all right," he said, exactly as if he knew all the grief that we had had.

The Dayang Muda spoke immediately to the manager, and he gave us a room at the back of the hotel, where, he confided to Archie, the coughing would not be heard. He was a good man, a kind man, and he and his sister stood that summer between us and those who did not like the look of Michael and wanted him to go. The manager valued the transient English visitors whose bills the Dayang Muda paid, and valued the fine weekly dinner parties she gave in the hotel. And she, born Gladys Palmer, of Huntley and Palmer biscuit fame, became our most eloquent defender. Archie had given her a taste for the arts, and because her mother had been an intimate of Oscar Wilde and George Meredith and other English writers of her time, the Dayang Muda was conditioned to all that Michael was.

It might have seemed reasonable now for Michael and Ethel Moorhead to have taken life up together again as literary discoverers, and for me to have journeyed back to Harfleur. But logic and reason were excluded from our deliberations. Michael believed that in a little while Ethel and I would live harmoniously under one roof, they editing *This Quarter*, and I taking care of the business correspondence and the accounts, as I liked very much to do. Logic, reason, disease, and the menace of death, these things meant nothing at all to us. We were committed to other values by which the poet had always lived in defiance of all that society demanded of him. We were quite simply, and without pretensions, Marlowe, and Villon, and Rimbaud, and Carnevali. We were thin as rakes, white-skinned, hollow-eyed, as poets had always been. Our clothes were so shabby that not even the art I had learned from Annick, the elaborate weaving in and out of darning needles through the cotton and silk and linen and wool that remained to us, could give us a look of respectability.

Michael wrote letters like one possessed to Joyce, McAlmon, Bill Williams, Picabia, Carnevali, Pound. (Once he asked Pound to send him some *avant-garde* magazines from Italy, and Pound answered on a typed post card that he was not the errand boy of Ernest Walsh. Once Michael wrote Pound that he was in love, and Pound answered, again on a typed post card, his favourite and perhaps most successful means of communication: "Corresponse suspended herwith until without'er of ((pssbl.?)) yu cummup fer air.") Archie had sent to a Nice newspaper an announcement concerning the arrival in Annot of the famous American editor, Ernest Walsh, and Michael was now deluged with pleas for money from destitute Frenchmen and women, their quavering handwriting imploring the rich American editor to help them in their daily plight.

Michael wrote poems, essays, book reviews, and long letters to Ethel Moorhead, and there were days when his face was dark with brooding, and other days when it was radiant with hope. Among the last poems he wrote were these:

I

Iffe I cud have a sonne I wude want his
    mother to
Be a beutiful happye ladye andde she to shayke
    her hed atte me
Lyke a marygolde O the wynde has notte anye nose
    to mayke
Its chekes thyne butte a brest itte has to crushe

The flowers offe springe agenst inne yonge
    wulde wulde tormente
Iffe I cude have a sonne I wude wishe him
    a fool withe the
Voyce of a miror that forever singes the
    songe offe its luvers
Andde the fayce offe a wyse man the wunde
    the wunde to crunche
Unlocked wyndos andde to clymbe tres lyke
    anger throughe
A colde madde irish brane a furye ther lyke
    beutye onne the
Hilsyde stons lyke flowers inne manye colours
    flowers that
Beginne withe thum owne footes andde ende atte
    sonsette inne a shadowe
Andde the beutiful ladye wude tayke him frum
    me his father
Andde I wude finde him agane as winde findes
    the ende offe a storme

II

It has come to this:
I would be alone
For people are too much in my veins
For their love to flatter me
I would be noticed in some new way
That is neither love nor hate nor fear
They sit about little
They who go into the hills to be alone
Because they dare not be alone in public places
They sit about too much with sharp eyes
For greatness not for what is great
And they are all a fever in my blood
My flesh is in for a great cooling
My eyes to be black death
In the face like polished stone.

Archie Craig paid such emotional homage to the tradition of
poetic defiance and poetic tragedy Michael represented that not

only the Dayang Muda and her changing retinue defended us, but half the village of Annot appeared to wish us well. There was first the doctor whom I had been to see (for now we were going to have a child), who was also the village veterinarian; and when I walked across the square for fruit or milk in the early morning, the villagers would stop to say *bon jour* to me, and to ask me how my husband was; or they would say *bon soir* to us in the evening, when Michael and I walked up the road in the dusk. Michael had been a professional magician once, and he could make lumps of sugar disappear from the palm of his hand and reappear instantly in one of the sheepdog's ears. He would do this trick for the children in the evening, or he would draw a green silk handkerchief, with the gold harp of Erin on it, from the inside pocket of one of the little boys' short jackets, or draw a cigarette, as if with the greatest difficulty, out of the novice priest's white collar, and the priest himself would laugh aloud. Michael laughed as hard as anyone else at his own tricks, but even if the laughter started him coughing, still none of the children or their parents drew away.

In July Richard wrote me that he had got a very good job with the Michelin tyre people in Clermont-Ferrand. There he would be given a company house, and all kinds of benefits, he wrote, and he sent me the money to meet him somewhere for the day, somewhere not too far from Annot, to decide what we were going to do with our lives. Michael put me on the train in the early morning, and as the train went careening down the alpine hills I saw him driving like a madman along the narrow, winding road, racing the train for fifteen minutes or more—and making it—to the unguarded crossing ahead. And when I returned in the evening Michael was there at the same crossing, with the Dayang Muda, and Archie, and their current guests, waiting with him. When he saw me through the window he jumped onto the steps of the perpendicularly inclined car in which I rode, and dragged me to the open door. The conductor pulled the alarm switch, and the engineer brought the laboriously climbing train to a halt, its whistle wailing through the steeply descending pine forests and the lonely hills. Once we stood on the cinder track, Michael asked the conductor and the engineer to have a quick *pastis* with us and our friends in celebration at the bistro at the crossing, and this they did. But the talk with Richard had got nowhere at all. He said he could not give me a divorce because of Maman and Papa and the sisters. He had told them nothing as yet.

"Maybe one day everything will change," he said, and so it had ended there.

By the end of August the next number of *This Quarter* was ready for the printer, and Ethel wrote to Michael that she would be dropping in on him to settle the final details. We decided that I would spend the time she was there in the Dayang Muda's villa across the steeply running mountain stream. Ethel's visit was a disaster, for she announced as soon as she arrived that she had come to collect the contributions for *This Quarter*, and that she was removing Michael's name from the masthead. She had taken the decision to bring out the magazine alone. McAlmon had written her that he was planning to drop in on Ernest Walsh in Annot, she said, and she replied that, as publisher and sole editor of *This Quarter*, she was the one on whom he should call. That bitter day, Michael had refused to hand over the collected material to her, and she had refused to show him the contributions she had brought along. She and McAlmon might be bringing out the next number together, she said, and Michael had thrown a carafe of water at her. The pieces of it were on the floor still when I came back late to the room.

In the middle of September the terrible process of dying by hæmorrhaging began for Michael. Ethel came up from Nice at once with an ambulance and a doctor, and Michael, with an oxygen tube in his mouth, undertook the long descent towards death. He died on October 16, 1926, at the age of thirty-one, with Ethel's renewed promises for the magazine in his ears, and fresh confidence in his heart. At four o'clock in the morning, a few minutes after his quiet death, I walked out on the terrace of the villa overlooking the city of Monte Carlo, and watched the dawn beginning to come, and the lights of the city slowly going out. And then Ethel stood beside me. "And what will you do now, you poor forlorn girl?" she asked me, with the Scottish clang in her voice. I said I would go back to America, back to my mother and sister, back to Lola, to the women I loved. "Stay here," Ethel whispered. "Stay here. I had only him, and now I have only you and the baby that's coming. We must try to work it out together. We owe that much to him and his child." When I put my arms around her, all strength seemed to leave her, to drain from some fatal wound that could never be staunched and that she wanted no hand to touch, no eye to see. She slipped to her knees, and I knelt with her, holding her in my arms still, rocking and cradling her now as if she were my little child.

This is the woman, the moment, I have tried to remember without confusion through the years, but the other Ethel in her Scotch plaids strides into the room, and with one impatient gesture of her hand she sweeps the rest away. The woman who once kneeled with me on the flagstones, while the dawn drifted up from Monaco and moved in a white mist through the mimosa and palm and orange trees, became lighthearted as a girl at the Casino when she taught me to play *trente et quarante* and roulette. With our winnings we would start a trust fund for the baby, she said, and some nights we did come home with our handbags bursting with five-hundred and one-thousand-franc notes; but in the end we lost a great deal of Ethel's money. That too made her laugh, our recklessness, our daring, and she had a queer little hornpipe she liked to dance after a drink or two of wine in the evening, with a cigarette in the corner of her mouth. (But there was another, sadder dance she did sometimes, and she called it with high scorn the Dance of Pregnancy. She would lean back from the hips, as if doing the cakewalk, and strut to the music of her own whistling, her stomach thrust forward as far as it would go. When she had danced and whistled herself breathless, she would stop before me—this was a part of the ritual—and tear the knitting from my hands. "You don't have to walk down the street the way you do. D'ye hear me?" she'd cry out. "There's absolutely no necessity, none, for you to stick your stomach out so everyone can see!")

In the beginning we had been "lively as crickets, and Scotch crickets at that", as she described us with great delight to her English friends (all former suffragettes) who came to visit. We had fixed up the Monte Carlo apartment on the Boulevard de France with bits and pieces of Richard's and my furniture shipped down from Harfleur, and the Persian rugs and family silver Mother had sent from Cincinnati. She was entirely fearless, Ethel, and she perjured herself before the American consul in Nice in an attempt to get me a pension from the government, swearing I was a veteran's widow, that she had been present when Ernest Walsh and I were married in Edinburgh, in her family home.

Once we were settled, Richard came down at Christmas time from Clermont-Ferrand and slept on the divan in the sitting room; and on Christmas Eve he brought champagne, and he and I talked all night together. When he went back he started sending money every week for me and the baby who was not yet born. And in March Ethel perjured herself again, out of the greatness of her heart and in her contempt for all official authority, when she registered Sharon at the Mairie de Nice as Michael's legitimate child.

Robert McAlmon

1924-1925

It developed that Ezra Pound was writing an opera, namely the setting to music of several of Villon's poems. People who had known Ezra for some time did not take his composition abilities with great seriousness as, so they claimed, Ezra was virtually tone deaf. He was not a trained musician, and it was said that he plunked away at a mandolin or banjo and jotted down notes, seeking a return to the establishing of musical values which the older world had known and which sentimentalized tradition had destroyed. At this time Ezra had elected himself sponsor of George Antheil, or so Antheil claimed. At one point, not being a musician, when her ladyship found Antheil "boyish" and "needing to be taken care of", I managed to get him subsidized for a two-year period. I must confess that George struck me a bit too deliberately boyish, naïve, and ingenuous, for the lad never neglected to cultivate, in his naïve-est manner, whoever might serve his ends.

William Carlos Williams was back in Paris, and he sat one day with Hemingway, and me, and two other writers, and confided to us that George Antheil had appointed him to write the libretto for his American opera. He, Williams, Antheil had said, was the one writer most certain to get into it the spirit of America. Hemingway and I exchanged knowing glances, and I noticed that the two other writers also looked "so that's the way it is". For George had talked warmly and with much enthusiasm about how I was the logical writer to do this libretto. His innocent and childlike ardency about the quality of my work was heart-appealing. The others had thought his fervour about their work most pleasing too. I wonder if he had read anything any of us had written.

By now life was striking Ezra as far too complicated, for after years of marriage his wife suddenly gave birth to a son whom they named Omar Shakespeare Pound. Ezra got himself a piece of marble and started to sculpt in *taille directe*, but perhaps the chisels were difficult to guide. So Ezra made notes on his bassoon, and sorrowed over a romantic, hophead poet whom he had tried to save from dope—but that is a long and very involved story. The night of the production of Ezra's opera was approaching, with much ado among the Anglo-American members of the Paris world. In those days we all delighted in attending such affairs; people moved *en masse* from performance to performance, but this did not mean that they dearly loved art. In fact most of those who attended Cocteau's show at the Cigalle—*Romeo and Juliet*—did so because there was a bar at the far end of the main theatre room. (Also, Yvonne George was playing the role of the nurse in his production, and she was one of the livelier steppers of Paris at this time.) There was always the question as to which end of the auditorium attracted the most attention. Surrealists and other enemies of Cocteau would be shouting down the actors and the play from all parts of the house, and the drinkers at the bar retaliated by shouting at the surrealists to pipe down. The Anglo-American lot were strangely unimpressed by the obstreperous violence of the French *avant-garde*. Louis Aragon, "the wild duck," as he was known, could become very savage in protesting against Cocteau and his productions, but he somehow failed to strike terror in the American breast. At the time that Aragon was much about with Nancy Cunard, his nickname was changed to "le Cunard sauvage", and it was generally agreed that she was the most impressive of the two.

Ezra's opera was given in a small hall, and it was not as well attended as the French affairs or the Swedish and Russian ballets, but still a sizeable audience arrived on time and waited patiently for the performance to begin. I was with Jane Heap, Djuna Barnes, Mina Loy, and Kitty Cannell, and all around us were people we knew well. As the opera got under way I saw T. S. Eliot slip into a seat in the back row. Mina Loy and Jane Heap said that they would like to meet him, and I thought surely he would remain to go behind and greet Ezra, but before the performance was ended he slipped away as he had come. Perhaps he was living up to his belief that to know people is mainly futile, or perhaps he did not approve of Ezra's music or the Paris congeries, which were certainly very unlike those of London.

The singers held our attention far more than most of us had anticipated. Perhaps Ezra *had* caught the right sort of music to suit Villon's poems. Afterwards, several groups from the audience headed for Le Boeuf sur le Toit, and later went on to Montmartre, and the night was a hilarious one. Ezra's delight in having held an audience as a composer was, for the time being, flawless. He was, however, no jealous composer, and he arranged various musical affairs at which George Antheil's music was played. The first was at Mrs. Christian Gross's apartment, and it was well attended by both French and Americans of the art and diplomatic worlds. Later, Natalie Barney gave an afternoon at which a new symphony of Antheil's was played.

Virgil Thomson tells of showing up at Antheil's concert at Mrs. Gross's, and having Ezra point at him and shout: "There's the enemy!" Ezra claims not to remember the incident, and refuses to take Thomson's work seriously, but now that Florine Stettheimer's stage designs and a chorus of Harlem Negroes have brought a New York success to Thomson's and Gertrude Stein's opera, it would not seem the moment to question the force and the originality of either Thomson or Stein. However, Thomson might have done better had he set Mary Butts and Villefranche to music. There were more than four saints there, with Cocteau the "master". Later, at the Champs Elysées Theatre, an afternoon concert of Antheil's music was played. I believe it was his *Ballet Mécanique*. In any case a great variety of trick instruments was used, one of them being a huge electric fan which caused such a draught that it disarrayed the coiffures of the ladies and blew programmes out of people's laps. Mariette and Heyworth Mills sat in one of the boxes, and as the great fan whirled, Heyworth opened an umbrella for protection. This delighted Antheil, who was convinced he was creating as much of a furore in Paris as had Stravinsky in years past.

About a year later Sylvia Beach told me in hushed tones that Antheil had tuberculosis and must get away to a sanatorium. Several among us rallied to collect money to help the invalid. William Bullitt was dubious and wished to have George examined by his doctor. George finally submitted, and it appeared that his lungs were sound. By then, various sums of money had been delivered to George for the purpose of his cure. Perhaps coincidentally and perhaps not, a number of old friends seemed to find that their interest in Antheil and his music had gone lukewarm. I'm afraid the paternal or protective impulse in me doesn't stand too much strain, and he was constantly the naïve boy who needed to be taken care of much more than other equally hard-up people about Paris.

Within this year or so—and this tale is certainly not chronological —Satie's death occurred. It was about a week before his death that he was at Brancusi's, for the two were old friends. For the past year Satie had often appeared in the Quarter, generally seated at the bar of the Stryx. He looked unwell and brooded, appearing not to like people. But that last evening at Brancusi's, he relaxed. He liked Nina Hamnett, who had come with me, and he knew I was a friend of Brancusi's, and he drank and was half-way gay. There was a remarkable procession at his funeral. All or most of the *poules* of the Quarter turned up, as well as quantities of people from the French art world. I think only in Paris could such a procession have followed an artist to his grave. The half-worlds or low-life worlds of other countries seem completely unaware of the artist's existence. But the *poules*, and the gigolos, and the *maquereaux* of that section not only knew of Satie and his music, but they knew him, had been bought drinks by him, and had been pleased that he was ready to frequent their places of rendezvous.

There was a quiet three weeks in London then, although the telling of it may make it appear as an active period. I read a great many travel books, biographies, autobiographies, and books of scientific adventure. Too many writers were doing books about people whom one also knew, and about circumstances which one had observed. It was not startling, it was pathetic rather, to note how differently from their conversation most authors presented themselves in writing. They based their novels on fact, but it was more pleasing to read historical, or documentary, or biographical things. With a novel, one has to grant altogether too much to the author's "sensibility, delicacy, power of insight, and capacity to create a work which is in itself a unique and distinguished organism".

There were occasional parties. Bryher had become friends with Dorothy Richardson, whose endless autobiographical novel appealed to her as a book which ought to be a best-seller amongst schoolgirls. Miss Richardson's approach and technique are her own, and her book was certainly no duller than long passages of Joyce, Stein, Proust, James, Dreiser—and certainly not so gruellingly mystic as Thomas Mann's *Magic Mountain*. Her work had moments of vitality and even brilliance, and while she, like many others, depicted life as more monotonous and dull than had Flaubert in *The Sentimental Education*, at least she did not go in for Walpurgis Nights and *tour de force* passages intended to dazzle and dismay and awe us with their brilliance and erudition. (Flaubert, incidentally, did that before all of them in his *Temptation of St. Anthony*; a more metaphysically, religiously, and pretentiously erudite book than this would be hard to achieve.)

Dorothy Richardson talked much as she wrote, so whether her protagonist, Miriam, was Dorothy, or Dorothy, in writing about Miriam, had made herself think as Miriam in order to protect her particular flow-of-the-conscious technique need not be decided here. Decidedly Miss Richardson was a monologist, and by no means a stammering, repetitive, and somehow inarticulate person, such as Gertrude Stein. She used words to confound one, but she knew their meanings; and when confronted with an idea new to her, her mind worked flashingly, and whether or not she convinced her opponent in an argument, at least she brought pyrotechnic imagination into the discussion.

Miss Richardson had a rose velvet evening gown which she wore to all parties. Her rust-coloured hair, slightly streaked with grey, was drawn back from her round, merry, and dimpled face, and rested bun-fashion on her neck. Her eyes were keen and observing, the only restless part of her. Once seated, she would sit as calmly as a Buddha, saying: "Alan, a cigarette," or "Alan, my glass. I'm comfortable, and having placed it on the floor I don't wish to move." Alan Odle, her husband, served her wishes, while Dorothy herself oracled on, but beamingly kind, a seer, an authority, an instructor, who uttered her messages without austerity. He was a black-and-white artist, an etcher, and a very 1890-ish and Aubrey Beardsley-ish figure. His long, ink-stained fingernails were uncut, and he used them, he said, to sketch with. His hair as well appeared to have been uncut for years, and was piled scraggily on top of his head and held there by hairpins. Nina Hamnett informed me that, upon first leaving school in the years past, he had been "too beautiful for words". He had good features, a febrile and attenuated quality, and he was emaciated. But one could without much difficulty visualize him as he must have been in other years, and so believe Nina's remark.

Havelock Ellis, long a friend of Bryher's, came to the apartment now and then. Before knowing him I suspected that his case reports had been given him by neurasthenics who dramatized their subconscious moments and thought up dreams in the hope of interesting someone—and Dr. Ellis turned out to be the most sympathetically ready-to-be-interested person around. When I met some of his patients, my suspicions tended to be confirmed. He himself was very noble in appearance, quite patriarchal, and certainly intent on helping out individual cases of human frustration. He spoke slowly, in a laboured manner, and in discussing literature it was clear that he responded to works of a past epoch, to writers such as Verlaine, Huysmans, the romantics, and the decadents. I don't question Dr. Ellis' contributions to the science of psychology and to human knowledge, however, since he made few pretences beyond that of compiling the findings of others; but it is probable that he and I were simply not each other's kind.

Louise and Otto Theis came to these parties also. Otto had, with Donald Evans, been the first to publish in America a book of Gertrude Stein's, *Tender Buttons*. Otto was at this time literary editor of the *Outlook*. Louise did book reviewing and profiles of various English writers. Their presence at any party was always a relief to me, for when some of the megalomaniac geniuses, seers, or high priestesses held forth at too great a length one could exchange understanding glances with them. There was always the nearby table with its whisky, brandy, and gin bottles, and certainly Otto seldom refused a drink. Dorothy Richardson did not need alcohol to intoxicate her. She could throw herself into a trance and talk on, utterly inebriated with the joy of her own illumined thought. She was delightful to watch at such moments, beaming and sweetly patronizing, her dimples coming and going, her eyes bright with the joy of how quickly her subconscious supplied her conscious with a flow of continually novel but authentic ideas. Occasionally Osbert Sitwell ventured in to tea with Bryher. He believed that he and Bryher were the same kind of person and shared each other's aversions to many English institutions, conventions, and snobbisms. It was conveyed to me that he was never so glad that he was not an American as when he observed me.

Chaplin's *The Kid* was playing in London, and Bryher's kid

brother John wanted to see it. Sir John would not allow this. Without ever having seen Chaplin—or any moving picture, in fact— he believed Chaplin was vulgar. One night her Ladyship said jokingly to her son: "Ask Robert to take you to see the film. You can slip away after dinner without your Dada knowing." What took place then was sheer old-time melodrama. A fanatical light came into Sir John's eyes, and he said sternly: "No son of mine leaves this house tonight."

John's upbringing was certainly none of my affair, and I dislike interference in other people's lives. Still, a parent's prejudiced denials to a son of accepted pastimes is certainly human interference. Next day I gave John money enough to see the film, said that he might say at lunch he was having tea with me, and do as he wished. He went to the film and turned up at the apartment to ask what he should tell his father. He did not like to lie. "Don't lie. Just keep quiet. Here's tea. You can say you enjoyed your tea with us."

Generally Sir John appeared a courteous and genial host, a travelled and liberal man of the world, and one who did not judge people too harshly. Strange emotional moments came upon him, however. One evening after dinner he came into her Ladyship's sitting room and, hemming and hawing, produced a letter. "Mother darling, this letter," Sir John hedged. "It is from that man you and Lady Andrews met in Droitwich." (Her Ladyship had recently taken a cure there.) "And a charming man he was!" Her Ladyship was arch. "He asks us to dinner," Sir John went on. "Now, Mother darling, you know how to be charmingly tactful. You answer the note, and I should say that we seldom dine out. You will know how to phrase it." "Indeed," coquetted her Ladyship, "I will say we shall be delighted to dine with him and his charming wife. She must be that to have so charming a husband!" "Mother darling, you know how so many try to get at me!" "But no, it's me that he wishes to see again! He is a wealthy man, and hang your conceit! He has no need of aid from you!"

Sir John snatched the letter from her. His eyes had gone dark. "I will answer the letter myself," he gasped, and hastened out of the room. Her Ladyship laughed, delighted. "You see, Robert, he doesn't permit me that much freedom!" She snapped her fingers. It was obvious Sir John was still irrationally jealous of anyone's attention to her Ladyship, and while that imprisoned her, it also pleased her. I was amazed, but concluded that people do to a large extent buy what they fundamentally want of other people; but is there some charity that will aid the offspring (or others) caught in the coils of such a relationship as that between Sir John and her Ladyship?

Louise and Otto Theis too had nights at their apartment off Fleet Street. At that time Evelyn Scott was staying with them, and various literary workers came to their evening affairs. Miss Scott, vibrant-voiced, intense, would be significant about a book she was writing. *The Wave*, which I read in part in manuscript, I found to be probably the world's dullest book, with its horrible "spiritual" messages beneath its hack pretences. Probably she believed it recreated history, but her intensities and significances always made me feel squirmy. She'd be more restful if she would just admit her mediocrity. Also there was Compton Mackenzie, who had taken up Catholicism, and who insisted on talking about religion and the disciplinary beauties of Christianity, particularly Catholic. I stood it for as long as I could until memory rose up and smote me into wrath. I am a Presbyterian minister's son, and the Protestants certainly have their hypocrisies, disciplines, and trickeries quite as much as the Catholics. The institutions surrounding religion have had some thousand years to prove themselves, and have preached of things spiritual while delving in intrigue and politics, accumulating capital, and, by means of fear, drugging the masses into stupidity, ignorance, and superstition. When Mackenzie tried to prove that the Christian Era gave birth to the world's greatest art, I started talking, aided by the heat of several whiskies and some knowledge of history. With many contemporary painters going bear-age or African primitive, others going Sumerian, archaic Egyptian, Greek, or Mayan, how do these newly converted Catholics get thus about that new religion, Christianity?

To put it mildly, Mr. Mackenzie concluded that he was not talking to a potential convert. When some religious spirits will prove historically that formal religion has ever disciplined a people towards a higher spiritual life, has ever established conventions and traditions purer and finer than the pagan or the agnostic, they will be worth listening to. They will have to consider what Catholicism has done to the masses in Mexico, Spain, and also Ireland. The Indian stock in Mexico, the peasants anywhere, in their handcraft and in their capacity to respond to fine sculpturing and painting, will develop of themselves if allowed their natural outlook, untyrannized by fear or needless poverty. Several of the best artists of today are of peon stock: Orozco, Guerrera, Brancusi.

On the channel boat, as I returned to Paris, were Mary Butts and Zelda and Scott Fitzgerald. The Fitzgeralds dearly loved Mary's short stories, particularly one which was another version of the Christ and Virgin Mary legend. As Anatole France, Thomas Hardy, and (later) Ernest Hemingway, among many others, have all tried to be startling with a viewpoint concerning the characters in that tale, I insisted that Mary Butts's story was a stunt, and not worthy of her. When Scott discovered that I didn't dote on Eliot's poems, he sorrowingly gave me up as a hopeless case. Perhaps my Scots blood gives me a different outlook from Scott's Irish blood. When they had gone on deck, leaving Mary and me to our second cognacs, Mary sighed. "The precious lambs," she said. "Just babies, Bob, my pet. Of course you are right about that story. I did it as a space filler. The publisher thought the book too short. You want your qualities pure. We understand, don't we? But you don't know the depths of Europe. What will become of us all?"

I'm sure I didn't know then, and I don't know now, but that "ole debbil" despondency isn't going to get me down. If the world's going to hell, I'm going there with it, and not in the back ranks either. So much suspicion assails the mind about the spiritual, and the reverent, and the religious. My mind is not scientific, and it *is* tainted with much bias but, such as it is, it roots for giving materialism and science their day.

Before I had come to Europe, it had entered my mind that Amy Lowell and Gertrude Stein were much the same type. Amy certainly preferred second or third-raters, who talked of her art and genius, to people of understanding who occasionally found this or that poem of hers not quite a success. This was not an experience I had had personally with her, but the source is authentic. So also is the source for the story of Amy Lowell being caught in London in 1914 when war was declared. She was late for an appointment because of the crowds massed in the streets, and she was indignant that the police had done nothing to help her make her way to the hotel. "Don't they know I'm Amy Lowell?" she shouted, and she lit herself a long cigar and strode up and down the hotel room. "And it was this month that my book of poems was coming out here! What attention will it get with this going on? What has happened to England? Why doesn't she simply stop the war?" But one thing was certain: Amy did weigh a good deal more than Gertrude.

In consequence of this suspicion of mine about Miss Stein, I had not met her in the several years I had been in Paris, although my admiration for "Melanctha" was great. Gertrude Stein's name was one that newspaper columnists used to twit, and there were innumerable legends about her since either she or her brother Leo "discovered" Picasso, Braque, Matisse, and so on. Her *Tender Buttons* I found amusing enough, but by this time she had written only one sound book, and that was *Three Lives*. The second life was that of Melanctha, a Negress, and her romance with an idealistic, intellectual, and dumb Negro doctor, and I considered it a masterpiece. It reiterated, stammered, but moved with a pure force to the conclusion: Melanctha's annoyance at the lack of sensual understanding in the doctor, and her wanderings, and her end. In this story, all of Gertrude Stein's sluggish, but virile, feeling for life emerges.

Miss Stein constantly appeared on the streets in her "uniform", wearing sandals with toes like a prow of a gondola, and she could be seen driving around Paris on the high seat of her antiquated Ford. There could be no doubt that she knew how to stage-set herself as an eccentric, and thus to become, aside from her writing, an exotic character and celebrity. She had sufficient money to conduct a salon, and many people who later became famous attended her gatherings. Some went because her teas were bountiful, and they were hard up and hungry; others went, as people do in the bohemian world both then and now, in order to regard the menagerie. Gertrude, with a child's vanity and love of praise, believed all the soft-soaping and flatteries, and, one gathers, still believes them. In a recent book of hers in which she becomes her close friend Alice Toklas, and Alice Toklas becomes Gertrude, they merge into one individual who sings the praises of Gertrude, and Alice-Gertrude frequently tells what people think of her and how much they love her.

Miss Stein is a pronounced example of the rich and pampered and protected child who has never been allowed to face actual hardship. Her brother Leo discovered painting for her. She had inherited an income, and with Leo she purchased a good many of the pictures by painters who came to be called "cubists" or "moderns". She ensconced herself securely in a fine studio on the Rue de Fleurus, and let herself be known as a patron of the art of painting. The word spread. Painters naturally desire to sell their pictures, and it came to be that shortly it meant réclame to have Gertrude Stein possess one's work. Not only would hangers-on see the picture hanging in her home, but they would believe they must think it great merely because Miss Stein owned it. Some of the paintings she owns, particularly of more recent years, are horrible trash—above all those of Sir Francis Rose, who paints everybody's pictures but has no manner of his own.

During the early years of Paris and Florence—long before there was any talk of "abstraction"—Miss Stein was protected from "reality" and vulgar contacts by her hangers-on, who sat, looked and listened to her as to an oracle. Aside from them, she knew an occasional person like herself: wealthy, secure, and protected, and capable of assuming a "great personality" quality because he or she could afford to entertain freely, and be kind to the flatterers and curt to the independent if they intruded and dared to insert a contrary opinion. Such a one also was Mabel Dodge. It is interesting to surmise what these women would have been without inherited security.

One night, however, I did finally go with Mina Loy to see Gertrude Stein. Surprisingly enough, she struck me as almost shy. She did seat herself in a large, higher chair in the middle of the studio, and she did monologue, and pontificate, and reiterate, and stammer. But she was much more human, indeed a much better specimen, than Amy Lowell, though they were a species of the same family; doubting and spoiled rich children, hurt only when they discover they can't have the moon if they want it. Perhaps Gertrude was extra shy with me. I can't say. Perhaps my manner is critical or analytical, and I may have said a doubting "Yes?" to some of her pronouncements, but in the main we got on well.

We discovered a mutual passion for Trollope's novels, for documentary, autobiographic and biographic writing. I added travel books, but she wasn't so sure of them, although she would read anything. She had read every book of Edgar Wallace's, and I'd read those which I felt weren't rewrites of the others. She recommended Queen Victoria's letters, and I recommended those of Cardinal Manning. I left thinking that one could become fond of Gertrude Stein if she would quit being the oracle and pontificating, and if she would descend from the throne chair and not grow panicky any time someone doubted her statements or bluffly disagreed. Our rapport never resulted in friendship, however. Miss Stein is apparently interested only in people who sit before her and listen. That does not mean she will not strike a blow at their solar plexuses at some future time, however, for she is shrewd enough to recognize the craven, hanging-on spirit in those who are out to succeed and believe they can do so by praising all the qualities, even the worst ones, indiscriminately.

Let us now add Gertrude Stein to our list of megalomaniacs, and add that on occasion she could be much of a mythomaniac as well. In her recent autobiography extolling herself, she says that McAlmon wanted to publish her *The Making of Americans*, and she graciously allowed this. The fact is that she wrote to that individual asking him to tea, and suggested that he publish the book in a series of four to six volumes over a two-year period. Thinking it over, McAlmon decided: "All or not at all. It's a unity." As Miss Stein assured him that she was sure of about fifty people who would buy the book, he took it on.

Months later, when the book was in the process of being bound, he again had tea with Miss Stein and he assured her that he would not allow the edition to be shipped to a New York publisher for distribution without a definite contract, or the payment outright by those publishers of the printing costs. That interview took place in Paris. That night he went to London. The next day he received a wire from the printer in Dijon, Monsieur Darantière, asking if it was indeed his wish that the lot of books be delivered at once to a Paris shipping agency for shipment to America. After numerous wires and letters, it evolved that Miss Stein had telephoned Darantière that it was on McAlmon's instructions this shipment should be made. As it was in direct contradiction to what he had said, McAlmon was very angry. Miss Stein explained in a letter that Jane Heap had assured her McAlmon would not object. McAlmon's anger did not cool when Miss Stein involved Miss Heap in the matter. Miss Heap had never been McAlmon's agent, she had no connection with his business, and he had not seen her while he was in Paris. Since Miss Stein so believed in her own genius, it occurred to McAlmon that she might sell a painting from her collection for fifty times what she had paid for it and pay her own printing bill. She sold not more than ten of the fifty copies she had counted on selling, and the remaining forty she gave out as review copies, or to friends, who were at that time her only substantial public. What happened to the rest of the edition is another and quite as sordid a story.

The book got few and mainly unfair reviews. I wrote a review of it myself, "The Legend of Gertrude Stein," which appeared in the *Outlook*, and I quote it here in part.

> Gertrude Stein is a writer of quality in that she uses words in a new way. She handles them repetitiously, darkly, sluggishly-understood, slowly-utilized, in vast quantities like mud and plenty of mud, and mud can with difficulty be made to take on a suggested sculpturesque effect. Unfortunately, a naïve, fairly childish person has had thrust upon her a legend as a leader of modern literature. Those who elected her are generally too insistently "modern" and "stylish-minded". She is sounder than they if only in her lethargic vitality and heaviness. Her manner of writing may upset people; what little she has to say cannot. She has a deep, aged-child kindness and resignation to certain inevitabilities. In her later years she has perhaps lost her stride trying to live up to the "innovator" legend which has been imposed upon her.
>
> One feels that Miss Stein triumphs within herself to think that she can put words together, and, having done so, feels charmed enough to repeat them again and again, as a three-year-old child who is playing with clay might say to a nurse, "Shall I make a man? Shall I make a man?" Her characters have not the distinguished qualities of the baby's clay man. They go on being. She is obsessed with being.
>
> She might object to what is high praise. In Hebraic, Sumerian, and primitive literatures, in the realm of incantations, and in the way children think and write when they are allowed to do so on their own, a sensitive reader might find the "secret" of such style as Miss Stein possesses.

Incidentally, *The Making of Americans* is a beautiful bit of printing and make-up and binding, and Miss Stein complimented Monsieur Darantière on the job. Monsieur Darantière did do a very fine job, but the publisher chose the paper, the print, the binding, and designed the jacket and make-up of the book. Nevertheless, Miss Stein has qualities which command admiration: she has vitality and a deep belief in the healthiness of life, too great a belief for these rocky days.

1. Kay Boyle and rolling chair, Atlantic City, New Jersey, 1907.

2. Kay Boyle and maternal grandmother, Eva S. Evans, Germantown, Pennsylvania, 1907.

3. Jesse Peyton Boyle, paternal grandfather, Pocono Mountains, 1912.

4. Kay Boyle, Pocono Mountains, 1912.

5. Howard P. Boyle, Kay Boyle's father, Beach Haven, New Jersey, 1909.

6. Joan Boyle and Kay Boyle, Cincinnati, Ohio, 1919.

7. Kay Boyle, Cincinnati, Ohio, 1918.

8. Robert McAlmon and his wife, Bryher.

9. From left to right: Unidentified friend, Nancy Cunard, Robert McAlmon, Venice, 1924.

10. Photostat of the passport of Kay Boyle and Richard Brault, 1923.

11. Robert McAlmon.

12. Florence Martin and unidentified friend, Montparnasse.

13. From left to right: Laurence Vail, Kay Boyle, Alfred Kreymborg, Clotilde Vail, and Dorothy Kreymborg, on the terrace of the Monte Carlo Casino Café.

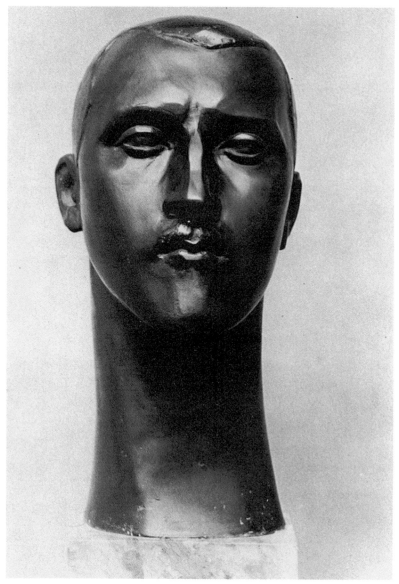

14. Black marble sculpture of Robert McAlmon which was on exhibition at the Louvre in 1923. Sculpted by Mariette Mills.

15. Ernest Walsh, 1925.

16. Kay Boyle, photographed by Man Ray, 1930.

17. Robert McAlmon and James Joyce, as sketched by Paul-Emile Bécat.

18. Gertrude Stein.

19. Sylvia Beach in front of her bookshop, Shakespeare and Company, Paris.

20. Ezra Pound, photographed by Sylvia Beach at her bookshop.

21. William Bird, editor of Three Mountains Press, and the colophon of Three Mountains Press.

22. Ernest Hemingway and Sylvia Beach in front of Shakespeare and Company, Paris. Below is an envelope addressed to Sylvia Beach from Ernest Hemingway, on which he calls her Madame Shakespeare.

23. William Carlos Williams.

24. Portrait of James Joyce and abstraction of James Joyce, both by Constantin Brancusi.

25. George Antheil climbing to his quarters above Sylvia Beach's Shakespeare and Company Bookstore.

26. Harriet Monroe.

27. Standing, the third man from the left is James Charters, the famous "Jimmy the Barman." The woman seated on the left is Lady Duff Twysden, whom Hemingway used as a prototype for Lady Brett Ashley in THE SUN ALSO RISES. The woman seated on the right is Kiki, the famous model who was married to Man Ray. The photograph was taken in 1925.

28. Drawing by Ethel Moorhead of Emanuel Carnevali which appeared in *This Quarter* in 1926.

29. Harry and Caresse Crosby, Le Moulin, 1928.

30. Sharon Walsh at Raymond Duncan's colony, held by Raymond Duncan's daughter, 1928.

31. Robert McAlmon, John Glassco and Graeme Taylor, Nice, 1928.

32. Laurence Vail and one of his screens, 1929.

33. Robert McAlmon and John Glassco (known as Buffy) on the beach at Nice, 1928.

34. From left to right: Countess of Polignac, Laurence Vail, Kay Boyle (with her arm around Hart Crane), and Caresse Crosby on top of Le Moulin, 1929.

35. Kay Boyle and Caresse Crosby, St. Aulde, France, 1929.

36. Caresse and Harry Crosby, 1927.

37. Laurence Vail and Kay Boyle, Le Moulin, 1929.

38. James Joyce and Augustus John, Paris, 1930.

39. Katherine E. Boyle.

40. Eugene Jolas and James Joyce.

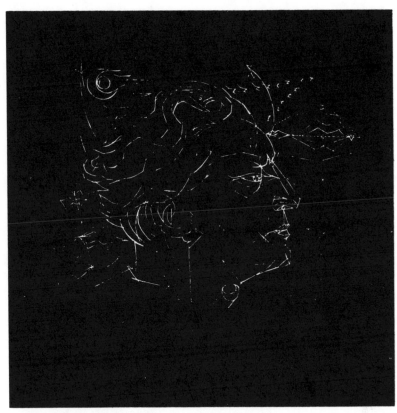

41. Portrait of Eugene Jolas by André Masson.

42. Lucia Joyce.

43. Emanuel Carnevali.
Photograph appeared
in *This Quarter*, no. 4,
1929.

44. Photograph of the model Kiki taken by herself at Villefranche.

45. Kiki as sketched by Foujita. Notice especially at the top the inscription from Foujita to Flossie Martin who owned the copy of the book in which this sketch appeared.

46. Kay Boyle, photographed in the south of France in 1930 by
Laurence Vail.

47. Kay Boyle, Nice, 1930.

Kay Boyle
1927-1928

But Ethel was at least two women. She was all the other things I have written of her, and she was as well the woman who had shouted with rage the day of Michael's funeral in Monaco because a man named Eugene Jolas, whom I did not know, sent me a telegram from Paris saying that he was going to go on with what Ernest Walsh had not been able to finish. He was going to start a magazine, he said; it would be called *transition*, and would I send him my stories and poems as quickly as possible for the first number. The telegram should have been sent to her as Michael's co-editor, Ethel cried out, and not to a fly-by-night who had sought to usurp her place. And this same Ethel was one whose anger was a bitter thing to see in the hospital room in Nice. Picabia had brought a blue lace dress and bonnet for his goddaughter, Sharon, and he was trying the bonnet on her as she slept in her basket by my bed, laughing out loud at himself as he did it, when Ethel came in and I introduced her to him as Miss instead of Mrs. "In Europe, every woman over twenty is a madame, not a mademoiselle!" Ethel roared at me once Picabia had gone, and she was probably quite justified in this rebuke. But I felt such pity for myself as the fury of the scene increased that I cried as loud or louder than the baby cried when Ethel had gone home. Quite another Ethel was the one who said to McAlmon, as we sat at dinner one night in April in the Monte Carlo flat, that Richard was paying for Sharon's keep. "So that," she said, laughing as if no funnier after-dinner story had ever been told across a festive board, "that should give you a hint of whose baby it is!" And she added that I had once left Michael alone for an entire day in Annot, oblivious to the state of his health, while I went gallivanting off to join Richard in another town.

McAlmon came more or less unannounced and stayed three days with us, and during that time he and I exchanged not more than a dozen sentences. There was so much to ask him about Bill Williams, about Carnevali, and to tell him about Ernest Walsh; so much to inquire about Paris, and what Eugene Jolas and Elliot Paul, the editors of *transition*, were like, but I found it impossible to ask him anything. I think it was because he had written so much: type-scripts over a thousand pages long he had with him; and because he had published so many writers; and because he spoke so cynically of the great with whom he was intimate. However it was, I quailed before his icy gaze.

"She has no ideas at all on any subject," Ethel Moorhead told him the last evening, when the three of us had come back from an after-noon in La Turbie, where Bob had entertained the idea of buying a house. "Ask her opinion on anything, and she simply doesn't know. Ask her what she as an American thinks of Negroes, for instance."

"I'm not interested in what she thinks of Negroes," McAlmon said, looking down into his glass.

"Very well. I'll ask her what she thinks of Negroes," Ethel said, her fixed, bright smile freezing my heart.

"I don't know—I don't know what I think of them!" I cried out, and I could feel the tears of true self-commiseration filling my eyes. "I only know I like them! I've always liked them!"

"You see? said Ethel in delight. "She likes Negroes! Isn't that kind of her? Isn't that really wonderful?"

"Yes," McAlmon said, abruptly looking up. "It is wonderful. It is a thing very few Americans would say."

Another night, in a gale of mirth at dinner, after a glass or two of Château d'Yquem, Ethel had advised him to go before I ruined a third man's life. "Hell's bells, my life was born ruined!" McAlmon said, jerking his laughter out. But God knows it shouldn't be these small, evil things I remember of Ethel but rather the generous and fearless things she did for me. But there had been nights during the past winter when I thought I could not bear to see again the elegant little iced glasses of martini she fixed for herself before dinner every evening and carried in separately on a silver tray. And there were days when I so hated the jade and diamond rings on her fingers that I had to bring my knitting into the room in order not to see them. It was not the rings I disliked but the value she put on them, merely because they were hers. It was like the lavishly embroidered Boxer coats she wore to the casino at night, or to the ballet, that she would allow no one else to lay a finger on. She must have known personally the silkworms who made them, or so it seemed to me. But most obsessive of all were the visits she paid me in the bathroom when I'd be lying in the deep greenish water in the tub. She would study my breasts, my thighs, my swelling belly, and sadly, sadly, shake her head. "I'll never understand it," she would murmur then. "You're really not that beautiful, you're really not. How in the world, or why in the world—no, it's really a mystery to me," she would murmur, and she would go out and close the door again. But then the next night, or the night after that, she would come back and try to work it out, the reasons for Michael's love.

McAlmon and I had only one means of communication that April when he came, and that was the baby. She was a month old then, and she was ill, and when I went out to do the shopping he would sit by her cradle and rock her and sing to her, the frozen blue of his eyes not melting for an instant, his cowboy voice yodelling the hillbilly songs louder and more melodious as she cried. The day after he left, he wrote me from St. Tropez, saying: "I don't want to butt into anybody's life, and you've certainly been around enough to know what you're doing. But you don't belong there. You haven't asked me, but I would say get out. Write me to Paris, c/o Sylvia Beach. If you need money, which I would think to be the case, Williams and I between us will get it to you, and quickly."

These were undoubtedly the words I had been waiting to hear, but no one else had said them loudly and clearly enough. I wrote to McAlmon in Paris, asking for fifty dollars to get to England. When the money came I cabled Richard in Stoke-on-Trent, where the Michelin Tyre Company had transferred him, knowing even as I came to this decision that it was an immoral, self-seeking, and humiliating thing to do. My sister, too, had been sent to England, to the London office of *Vogue*, and Mother was keeping house for her there. "Tell the baby's father that its resemblance to him is *striking*," once Ethel said as she put us on the train in Monaco; and the train began to move, and she walked along beside it for a few steps, with the smile of another Ethel twisting her mouth like acid, and tears running down her stricken face.

To compound the evil and perfidy of my return to Richard, Marguerite was sent by the family from Brittany to take the baby and me to a Paris hotel, and care for us overnight. There she was at the station, her beret still seeking to hold the pinned-up strands of her hair in place, and not succeeding, her grey suit for travelling as distraught as on the day—now four years ago—when she had come with the others to meet us at Le Havre. And I, I was still travelling from one place to another without a *tailleur gris*. In London it was Mother and Joan who met us, and never before in my life had I felt a greater humility. I, who had always talked so madly, so foolishly, of the things in which I believed and the things I was certain I would do, stood in failure and defeat before them. It was my sister, not I, who had accomplished the miracle of independence. She had done it entirely alone, through the hardest kind of work, and now she needed no one's help and no one's advice on how to live. It was she, not I, who was taking care of Mother, a dream I had always cherished, and that would take me so long, so long, to realize. In my shame I could not bring myself to say to them that there was not a promise to myself I had not broken, not a vow to others I had not betrayed.

Sharon and I stayed three or four days in their little house, and I did not want to go on to anything else. This was the return, the retrogression, that I wanted; it was like turning the years back to Atlantic City or to Pocono. But Sharon and I travelled on to Stoke-on-Trent, one of Arnold Bennett's Five Towns, and there we were to stay a year. The first number of *transition* had come out in April of that year, and all that it spoke of so clearly was a continuation of the exchange between artist and audience that had come to an end, at least for the experimental artist, with Michael's death. In that first issue appeared the "Opening Pages of a Work in Progress" by Joyce, and—among twenty-odd contributors—a long poem by Gide, "An Elucidation" by Gertrude Stein, a poem of Hart Crane's, and one by Archibald MacLeish entitled "Signature Anonyme", the words of which I used to sing to Sharon as I pushed her pram along the hedgerows, and which ends:

> You that pity
> Labour done in pain at night and in bitterness
> Think if you read these words in a better time
> Of the shape of my mouth forming the difficult letters.

The editors' introduction to this number stated that *transition*
wished to offer American writers "an opportunity to express
themselves freely, to experiment . . . and to avail themselves of a
ready, alert, and critical audience". To the writers of other countries,
who spoke another tongue, the editors extended an invitation to
appear side by side with American writers, in a language Americans
could understand. Here, for the first time, I read Philippe Soupault,
and also Robert Desnos, whose two poems, "The Dove of the Ark"
and "I've Dreamed So Much About You", immediately became part
of my singing repertoire for the baby falling asleep in her rocking,
rolling pram. Some of the lines of Desnos' last poem go:

> I've dreamed so much about you
>
> that my arms grown used to lie crossed
> on my breast from clasping your shadow
> might be unable to enfold the contours
> of your body
>
> I've dreamed so much about you
>
> I've walked, talked, and slept so much
> with your phantom that perhaps nothing
> remains for me
>
> but to be a phantom among phantoms and
> a hundred-fold more shadowy than the
> shadow that walks lightly and will
> continue to walk on the sundial of your
> life

In that first issue I reviewed Bill Williams' *In the American Grain*,
and I also had a short story published; but having my work appear
in *transition* was for me only a part of what its existence meant. Jolas
and I wrote to each other almost every week, and his belief in my
work and in the work of countless unknown others gave a new
meaning not only to my own life but to the international writing
scene. "The fact that an author's name is unknown will assure his
manuscript a more favourable examination," Jolas and Elliot had
declared. And later Jolas was to write that *transition* was "a proving

ground for the new literature, a laboratory for poetic experiment",
that he hoped would express his "almost mystic concept of an ideal
America". But the vocabulary of that ideal America could not be
formed, he said, without "new words, new abstractions, new
hieroglyphics, new symbols, new myths. . . ." I remembered
Michael saying to me that my rôle was that of homage-giver to the
great, and this seemed to me increasingly true.

It may appear to have been a time without much humour in the
avant-garde literary movement, but it must be remembered that it was
a time of the gravest crisis in letters, of furious schism and revolution
in the arts, and it is not the way of revolutionaries in any uprising
to go lightly to the block to lose their heads. And, it being a time of
peril, gravity was demanded of writers who fought against the
sentence of death, of oblivion, passed on their work by critics and
publishers, and on the life term offered as alternative, to be served in
the ancient strongholds of the established conventional forms.
Joyce, Jolas, Williams, Walsh (in his brief moment), and the
troubled vision of the Surrealists prepared the way for the anti-novel
the anti-hero, for the type of poetry that Cummings was writing,
and the quite new type of novel of Céline. And out of oblivion the
revolution retrieved the work of Kafka, and Rimbaud, and Lautréamont. This was a serious business, and if one laughed a good deal
over café tables, one did not laugh very loudly on the printed page.
(Had not an admirer of my sister's in Cincinnati once told her that
I could not expect to be popular if I talked of Betelgeuse when out
on dates, and attempted to find its actual body in the heavens; or
discussed the meaning to poetry in Einstein's theory of relativity?
Had I not always been ready to take on the grave responsibility of
creating an entirely new system of astronomy?)

In the endless letters I wrote from Stoke-on-Trent to Jolas, and
Lola, and to McAlmon (who rarely answered), and to Evelyn
Scott, and to Mother, and Carnevali, I was doing no more than
submitting a full and doubtless inaccurate account of who I thought
I was, or seeking to be. Letters became the means of relating with
familiar, living people the mystery of the dreams and realizations of
the night, a way of marking my return to a native coast after the
long voyage of drifting in seemingly interminable loneliness. It was
necessary to write these letters at once, soon after awaking, and not
relegate the writing of them to the evening, or to one day set aside in
the week, while I got on with the daily concerns of life. They must be

written quickly; I must reach out quickly to these spokesmen who were my bond and contact with humanity before the dark, lonely tide of dreams had ebbed entirely away. As for the daily life itself, I became involved in the chattering, voluble reality of the French enclave in which we lived. I cooked, and I shopped, and I gave dinner parties for Richard's colleagues and their wives. I had a little maid called Appleby, who wore a white lace cap and apron, and I finished writing *Plagued by the Nightingale* and returned to the writing of *Gentlemen, I Address You Privately*.

And here a hymn of recognition, a paean of the tenderest homage, must be sung aloud to the memories of Germaine Garrigou. She was the wife of one of the Michelin Tyre Company engineers, a woman a year or two older than I, born in Marseilles, black-haired, black-eyed, who knew only a few words of English. But she did not need to know any language at all, for when she laughed the fogs of the Five Towns managed to take on the colour of the sun. I have always been in awe of women whose flesh is as hard and bleached as bone. Germaine's throat was made of this kind of flesh, and her breasts and thighs of the same untrembling substance. But if her flesh hurt the knuckles when one knocked for entry to her heart, there was within her a core of uncertainty as soft as the petals of a rose. Because of Sharon, our friendship was instantaneous. Germaine had always wanted a child, but none had come, and this was perhaps because her marble body could never have given sufficiently to relinquish the life of the other that it held.

There was nothing I could not and did not tell her. She would study Michael's photograph (which I kept at the bottom of a suitcase), and seek to learn his poems by heart, agreeing with me in a passionate whisper that I should never embrace another man and that I should wear black for the rest of my life. But when summer dresses appeared in the shopwindows (difficult though it was to distinguish them through the Five Towns' eternal gloom) she urged me with equal passion to be like all other *jolies femmes* and, if only for the baby's sake, begin to wear mauve and pink and blue (except on the Jour des Morts, when obviously I would have to put on black again). Germaine divided all women into two categories: those she knew without question that we ourselves were, animated, exciting to be with, and definitely *jolies*; and the vast legions of others who fell under the heading of *les femmes laides*. No English-woman, she insisted, could possibly be of the former group; didn't their feet look like pieces of their legs bent under to look like feet, and fail in this intention? On weekdays we drank white wine together before lunch, and danced apache dances wildly up and down the living room until we were weak with laughter and fell gasping on the sofa; and for long hours she took care of the baby while I typed my pages out.

Germaine, *amie fidèle, confidente adorée, ma chère vieille,* for nearly twenty years we were to meet, and dance, and drink white wine, and laugh like fools, in so many cities of England and France that I can no longer count them. You were there, always on the threshold of my life, until the war came in 1939; and even then for a little while we exchanged ration tickets for bread and sugar and soap in the hard days of the German occupation, and stood in line together for the weekly ration of meat. But you were not there when I looked for you in 1945, for during the course of the war you had died in the city where you were born. When I was twenty-four and filled with grief, Germaine, you transformed the look of every day for me. You made me buy green kid slippers with straps across the instep, and others of black patent leather with heels so high that I stamped like a flamenco dancer as I walked. You taught me to do my eyes with variously tinted pencils, and to wear a white mantilla over my hair.

With what suppressed annoyance our husbands must have endured us all that year with our secret jokes and our sudden, inexplicable bursts of laughter. It was perhaps our rapture for cooking which we rejoiced in as though performing the rites of a religion, as well as our obsession with waxed and polished surfaces, and with the gleam of copper utensils, and the scrubbing clean every morning of the front and back steps of the Five Towns' soot, which made us at least bearable to the two men we had ceased to love. Moreover, Germaine had shown me how to draw the threads from the seams of trousers and jackets in order to mend invisibly the burns or tears in our husbands' suits, and this we did with the same dedication as the knitters of the French Revolution executing their articulate work. To clean a room *à fond* was another facet of this meticulousness, not unlike the cleansing of one's soul, just as the scrupulous scrubbing of a floor equated the expunging of one's conscience. It seemed to me then that the French—and I myself one of them by this time—who scoured *à grand' eau* doorsteps and sidewalks before seven in the morning were at the same time seeking to efface, and not succeeding in effacing, the blood of the Revolution that still stained the cobbles of their streets.

In August of that year Sacco and Vanzetti were to be executed. After their sentencing by Judge Thayer in April, Lola Ridge had been knocked down in one of the mass demonstrations of protest, and been trampled under the hoofs of a policeman's horse. Mother had taken part in the manifestations in London, and I had decided to burn the American flag before the American Consulate in Stoke. On August 22, Germaine managed to find an American flag for me in a secondhand store, and she brought it back to the French enclave folded up small in her handbag. "You *must* burn it," she kept saying to me. "You are absolutely right. The Americans are always after France to pay some kind of war debts, and now they go out of their way to kill these two poor Italians." The next day the two Italians were to die in the electric chair.

I set off early in the morning, pushing Sharon in her baby coach, for I wanted her to take part in this with me. As always, lines of poetry kept pace with the rhythm of my walking, and I sang the words of them to Sharon, as I did every day. At other times it might have been Vachel Lindsay's "Congo" I drummed out, or Rupert Brooke's "If I Should Die", jazzed up a little, or even Eliot's "Prufrock", or a poem that Sharon's father wrote for a Negro voice, or else his "Fielde Songge", beginning:

> Then was ther a field offe flowers
> kwipped I stoode
> As the winde blewe withe tail hucked uppe
> my eares
> Hupped the flowers yo-inggee Thou Thou Thou
> Thou
> Andde the winde yiddered and skiddered thum
> byne

But on this day, and without my choosing them, it was lines of my own poetry that came to me, poems I had written for Michael both before and after his death, and the poem to Bill Williams I had just finished, entitled "The United States". One poem to Michael was called "To America", and the other "To an American", and as I sang the words of them to Sharon, England went away, and the English people who passed us in the street were suddenly not there.

"How shall I come to you with this to say to you," I asked America, "with soft steps saying hush in the leaves or with anger, to say that a wind dies down in an old country, that a storm makes rain grow like white wheat on the sand." As I pushed the baby carriage up one street and down another, Michael's and Bill Williams' country and mine, and its speech, and its people, formed a great wide avenue before me, so that I did not walk the streets of England any more, and I did not walk alone. America, the only America that would endure, I believed now with a conviction as sharp as a knife turning in my breast, did not belong to Judge Thayer, or to Governor Fuller of Massachusetts, or to the President of the United States, who had refused a shoemaker and a fish peddler his word of clemency. The American that lent me its direction forever now was Lola's, and it was Bill Williams', and Mother's, and Michael's, and mine; and I knew, with a terrible humility in the presence of their innocence, that it was Sacco's and Vanzetti's as well. My other poem had said to an American that the miracle was to keep this alive between us,

> laid like a thin hand between us;
> a clear small sea between us in which
>   anemone, sea-plants and petals move
>   and ripple and stir murmuring:
> There is this between us. Through the pale
>   fans of the fish and the weaving weed
> Breath ascends the tide and stirs the
>   smooth brows of foam saying:
>
> Only this one could turn from you with me:
>   one who had known the glacial
>   bone curved to the body:
> Could move softly through the clear water,
>   lifting it like silk in the fingers,
> Smiling softly, smiling like sly soft tears
>   down the face. . . .

I walked the long way back to the French enclave, with the flag spread, untouched, under the baby's blanket in the pram. "I could not burn it," I said to Germaine, and I put it in the suitcase with Michael's photograph. "*Tu as raison, ma chérie,*" she whispered "I could have told you if you had asked my opinion. It would not have made the Americans understand what it is to be a foreigner and poor."

Archie Craig had kept close to me in letters, and the announcement of a yearbook of poetry that we planned to edit together had appeared in the second number of *This Quarter*, which had just come out as I left Monte Carlo. "The first volume of *Living Poetry* will appear in January 1928," we informed the public, "under the editorship of Archibald Craig and Kay Boyle, who deny that romance went out to the slow music of sewing-machines and motor-cycles, and who affirm that poetry is going on with a hot foot and a true stride. . . . The editors believe that it is not only the perfect poem which deserves to be reprinted, but even more the personal adventure, the contemporary escapade. . . . This Yearbook will be not only the best anthology of poetry ever published," we stated without a moment's hesitation, "but the most read, sought-after, and renowned". It is perhaps unnecessary to add that the yearbook never appeared.

But in the spring of 1928 Archie wrote me that the Dayang Muda wanted me to come to Paris and work with her on a book. They had rented a fine apartment in the Rue Louis David, and she would take care of all my expenses while Sharon and I lived there with them. We would collect poems for our anthology, Archie wrote, while I helped the Princess with her writing, and it would be the beginning of the kind of life he believed I should have. So at the end of April Sharon and I set off again. Richard and I told each other again that it would be only for a little while. It would be just until I had helped the Dayang Muda to do her book; but we must have known then, because of all the pain I had caused him, and the sorrow we had lived through, that what we had been to each other once had come finally to an end.

Robert McAlmon

1925-1926

Nina Hamnett and Ford Madox Ford got together and observed that there were a quantity of talented foreigners—English-speaking —about. Would it not be advisable to have fortnightly gatherings and discussions? Ford now disclaims being author of the idea, but my memory is clear. I was at the table when he and Nina discussed the idea. As there were the intimate bistros and the café terraces, and as Paris is casual, it struck me that such people as found each other sympathetic generally got together anyway, and two or three who had naturally drifted into one another's company could have more profound discussions than a large group collected expressly for an intellectual evening. However, Nina was hopeful, and Ford, always eager to head a coterie of followers, made arrangements for a gathering at L'Avenue, across from the Gare Montparnasse. It would be on a Saturday night, a fortnight hence.

Joyce, unbeknown to himself, and not having been informed that that there was to be such a gathering, was supposed to be the guest of honour on that first Saturday. Bill Bird arrived to find Ford Madox Ford and his wife and a few disciples. But where was Joyce? Bird went to get him, and Joyce, protesting that he hadn't known, came with Nora. Soon Miss Hamnett arrived, primed for gaiety, and then Miss Florence Martin, orange-haired and of ample avoirdupois and a high-larking spirit. But, miracle of miracles, Miss Martin was cold sober, and very much the dignified and gracious lady going to do honour to the masters, and not getting oiled for one night in her life.

Time passed, and it may seem from this account that Mr. Joyce and Mr. Ford did not extremely care for each other. But they are both courteous gentlemen. Nora was heard to comment in fresh-toned but acrid Irish, "Jim, what is it all ye find to jabber about the nights you're brought home drunk for me to look after? You're dumb as an oyster now, so God help me."

Miss Martin did her best to make the conversation general, Miss Hamnett, feeling the party had dropped, was having a drink, and Mr. Ford looked as usual like Lord Plushbottom of the Moon Mullins cartoon. Presently Miss Hamnett disappeared discreetly, having spotted the beautiful red hair of Bob Coates, whom she adored. Then James and Nora Joyce decided that they must retire, Sally and Bill Bird got into a taxi, and the intellectual gathering of the epoch was over. It was well past midnight, however, and we hardier souls headed towards the Sélect.

Harold Stearns had his plump stomach glued to the bar as usual, while he sipped at a glass of port wine. Before long he had his customary wrangle with Madame Sélect. She was the *patronne* and cashier for whom evenings were not complete without innumerable rows and arguments. She loved battle and was never known to give a drink to anybody who did not give her a snappy argument. At the bar as well were Sophie Victor, Steve Green, and Evan Shipman, all of whom believed at the time that Harold Stearns, because he was the sports writer, Peter Pickem, of the Paris edition of the Chicago *Tribune*, had the inside dope on sure winners at the races. Evan Shipman told me he had been helping Hemingway get his belongings together to move to a new apartment, and had discovered that Hemingway possessed a dozen or more paintings or drawings by Utrillo. It was always very interesting in those days at the Sélect. You mentally tossed a coin in your mind and decided, I believe, or I don't believe.

Augustus John was there with Adrian Daintry, a young English painter, who was not unwilling to accept a little aid in the way of patronage. Caridad, a Cuban girl with ashen skin and bright mahogany hair, gave Madame Sélect one of the better battles of the evening, and as both of them loved "the Vaudeville" they thoroughly enjoyed themselves. George Moore was also in town, and Ford Madox Ford remarked on one occasion that he was supposed to look like Mr. Moore. (And Wyndham Lewis looking like Shelley-Shakespeare-Swift!) Ford was very holy about Moore and his beautiful prose style, but I believed that Moore had been a better writer before he went in for beautiful, limpid, flowing prose. In any case he was white-white of skin and of hair, to a degree which struck me as gruesome.

Moore used to call frequently at Sylvia Beach's bookshop, and one day I entered to collect mail and Joyce soon appeared. Moore was already there. Sylvia was not sure whether Joyce and Moore wished to meet and did not introduce them. They recognized each other, however, and after Moore bolted Joyce asked why they hadn't been presented. Later there was an exchange of notes between the two, and a meeting was brought about, I believe. Whatever either thought of the other's work certainly was not expressed. They were both past masters at the art of *blague* and blarney and courteous formality in the old Irish manner, and this would have prevailed.

Mr. Moore bewailed the Paris of the past, and declared that his visit had not been a happy one. He was back within a month, however, but only, as he explained, because he had left a pair of pyjamas at his hotel. He was certainly not slow at accepting invitations to dinner parties, and for his age was lively, with ideas perhaps more romantic than actual about his way with the ladies. "There are those who kiss and tell," it was said of him, "but he tells when he hasn't kissed." This story of the old master may be unkind, but George Moore himself was never noted for kindness to younger writers, and although he was a greatly derived writer he was cruelly against many other writers who had in their work a more earthly and original strain. Literature would have become sterile under a Moore dictatorship. Hardy, Henry James, and Conrad, all more or less of his generation, were more open-minded, more sympathetic towards and receptive to the talents of writers unlike themselves, such as Stephen Crane, and others. There should be a rule in life that old age respect youth as well as youth respecting old age; particularly when receiving adulation and luxurious comforts, cannot old age afford to give youth that respect?

Frank Harris was in town at this period, newly arrived from America where he had been giving lectures and holding séances on Shakespeare, Wilde, and all his other old friends. Nina Hamnett, always glad to present a celebrity, escorted him about Paris. He was short and stocky, and looked to me as though his hair were dyed in black tea, as was that of an old professor of my childhood days. His drooping moustache was tobacco-stained, and he could have passed for a race-track bookie on his uppers, and his conversation did not eradicate that impression. Harris was deeply occupied writing of his life and loves, but little attention was paid to him, although he had written a short story or two and a biography that was possibly worth attention. His background was confusing, for he had definitely had a position and notable friends in the London literary world, and Shaw still appeared to like, admire, or respect him. Shaw will have to explain that himself.

Sisley Huddleston, then with the London *Times*, appeared fairly often, and was always ready to talk about the literary clock turning back to Romanticism and away from sordid naturalism. It might strike others that Romanticism was, like all other literary modes, still rampant, so that a writer could be what he wished and still be assured of being in some tradition. Harriet Monroe, of *Poetry* magazine, in Chicago, paid her first visit to France, and, while enjoying the café life, argued earnestly with her young poet discoveries that they must return to America and feel the urge of that rich soil. I mentioned that Mark Twain, Henry James, Stephen Crane, and a number of English writers, not to mention Turgenev, a Russian, lived much out of their native lands. As a matter of fact, we were seeing far too much of Americans of every type at that time. It wasn't a French Paris at all.

Miss Monroe was drinking fine old madeira out of a beautiful globelike glass when someone remarked that Ezra Pound was outside. With an eager cry, Miss Monroe arose. "Ezra, I must meet Ezra! Will he be the way I have imagined?" She went towards the door of the Stryx, and Ezra, hearing his name spoken, came forward to meet her. Miss Monroe returned, eager and happy, to have another fine old madeira. Then we moved to a table on the terrace, and Miss Monroe met Mina Loy, who was "too beautiful for description", and several others. It looked for a time as though Harriet Monroe, champion of an indigenous American literature, was going to surrender to Paris "exile" life, but she eventually returned to America. The heyday of *Poetry* was by then over, and it never again published verse much superior to that appearing in any brightly edited college magazine. One wonders if it was not H.D., Ezra Pound, Emanuel Carnevali; and Marjorie Allen Seiffert who were responsible as editors for the original open-mindedness of *Poetry*, when it first published Marianne Moore, Wallace Stevens, William Carlos Williams, T. S. Eliot, Ezra, and so on. Or perhaps

Margaret Anderson and Jane Heap, with their cerise tauntings in the *Little Review*, made Miss Monroe afraid *not* to be a pioneer.

Emma Goldman was also in the Quarter, having recently returned from Russia, disillusioned about that régime. It was interesting to observe her then in her broken-spirited moment, and to wonder at the impulses which directed her particular type of fanaticism. She seemed far too emotional and prejudiced a person to be reasonable or fair, and too complex a being without imagination to understand her own motives. In reading her memoirs some years later, I, although by no means believing the present social system anything but a dismal and tragic failure, would hesitate to follow the banners waved by such a type as Emma. She had undoubted magnetism, and she certainly believed in the honest and authentic value of her preachings. Well, Aimée McPherson and Texas Guinan had magnetism too, but they were businesswomen.

Emma shortly went to London, where she received a fair amount of attention after people ceased being afraid of her as a rampant "Red Queen" and troublemaker. Rebecca West and several other English writers helped her make a living, and she gave a few lectures, but in London she did not appear at all to be the fire-eating Red Queen of American legend. She seemed a tired, gentle, motherly type of woman.

The Heyworth Millses had a château in the country near Rambouillet, and within a ten-mile radius were several charming villages. One could take walks, sip a bit of refreshing wine, return for lunch, and work in the afternoon. On Sundays, and often on weekdays for tea, Brancusi, Léger, Picabia, and Blaise Cendrars visited the Millses. Brancusi came to plan the placing in the park of a huge "Golden Bird" which he was to execute. A French family had their château down the road, and one of the girls sang nicely and recited French poems, favouring Cocteau's at the time. Another sister played the music of Satie and "Les Six". There were two peaceful months of work, long walks, and a variety of companionship. The forests of the valley of the Chevreuse abound with deer, and a few kilometres from the village was the huge château of the Duchesse d'Uzès, its walls covered with the heads and horns of deer killed in hunts throughout the last seventy years. The château was used only as a show place, and for quartering the hounds, huge, slobbery-mouthed, dull-eyed, stupid-looking brutes. On the altar of the village church was a Virgin and Child, which the aged

Duchess had sculptured. She wrote plays, still rode to hounds at eighty, and, having been a leading feminist for years, was the head of innumerable charity and uplift organizations. She came to tea at the Millses' now and then, and I was a bit scared of the doughty and forceful old woman. Moreover, my French wasn't much, and perhaps she held it against me that I thought her hounds foul-looking brutes.

In any case, Gioella Loy, Mina's elder daughter, was spending a month with the Millses. She was then a bit gangly with adolescence, but very lovely, with sleepy blue eyes, long pale eyelashes, and slender, childish arms which made Mariette Mills wish to sculpture her, and abstract painters talk of doing her portrait. Gioella had a proper youthful scorn for me and used to ask when I was going to pull myself together, and why I acted like a cynical old uncle to her. We took long walks in the wood; deer crossed our path from time to time, and Gioella lectured on life and the bohemian world, saying she didn't think for a second that any of us were getting satisfaction out of being "intellectual". Only occasionally would she cease being patronizing and confess wonder and confusion. But generally she preferred scolding me mildly. Gioella, however, did stop lecturing me when I introduced her to the boy she married. He, Julien Levy, was going to open an art gallery.

There was a moving picture of one of Selma Lagerlöf's novels, *The Old Manor House*, that Man Ray and I went to see together. In one sequence a herd of ten thousand reindeer are seen crossing the snow, grey undulating waves against the white horizon. For pure beauty of scenic and dramatic effect, I have seen nothing to equal it, and it made me want to see snow again. The so-called summer-in-winter climate of the south is a snare, because inside one is always cold. I spent the early autumn months in Holland, writing short stories of the Middle West and doing short walking trips. As wintry weather came on, I went to Copenhagen, which I knew from previous years when Robert Hillyer and Foster Damon were there on scholarships, Damon writing a book on the mysticism of Blake. Ivan Opffer, caricaturist, whom I had known in New York, was there working for the *Politiken*, and with him I went to music halls, the theatre, and met various writers, among them one heavy-witted man who believed himself the modern of moderns because he had filled five pages of his last novel with x's, line after line of xxxxxxxxxxxxxxx, as a symbol of dead soldiers and their graves.

Lapland for snow, reindeer, snowshoeing, and the observation of Lapp life was my goal. Naturally it was via Stockholm, and Ludvig Nordstrom knew of my arrival. He met me with a reporter from one of the dailies, proud to think that in Sweden they were as quick on the uptake as in American journalistic circles. There was little one could say about one's impressions of Sweden after but a few hours' stay, but Nordstrom, the reporter, and I drank schnapps and got into a deep discussion. I commented that society's duty is to the individual and the citizen rather than the individual's duty being that of service to the state. The state must merely see that privileged classes and individuals do not impose on or enslave others. From this comment, the reporter created a two-column interview, indicating that Americans are highly individualistic, independent, and free-thinkers. Indeed?

Two years before this, William Butler Yeats had been in Stockholm, receiving the Nobel Prize for literature. He was staying in the same hotel as I, and as he was a friend of Ezra's, and I had been told he knew my work, I telephoned his room. It was morning, and he was leaving the next day and would be very busy. But "Come up at once, and have coffee," he suggested. So I had gone to Yeats's room, where he was with his wife. Yes, he did look "aesthetic" and somewhat deliberately vague, with his head in the clouds. Of course, some of his poetry is "beautiful", but I found it too Irish twilighty and sweetly mystic. It is impossible to recall much of the conversation beyond courteous and hospitable greetings. He mentioned truth and beauty and art, and I gathered that he was going to enlarge upon the point that "beauty or art is the eternal search"—you finish. It was some comment on Joyce or Pound or other poet which had started Yeats on this theme. "The eternal search for—" I pleaded another engagement and bolted. Mr. Yeats was entirely likeable, amiable, and sympathetic. If he had been nearer my own age I would have stopped his sermon on beauty. As it was, I knew it was hopeless. He was hardened into the poetizing mould, and just when he was receiving world honour as a Nobel Prize winner was no time for an unknown young man to question his noble clichés on the search for truth and beauty.

Nordström said that the Lapps would be inaccessible at this season, at least a three-day snowshoe run into the mountains. So I gave up the idea of visiting Lapland and lingered on in Stockholm. That year, 1925, I wrote a portrait of Miss Stein with no intention of publishing it. Knowing that it would please Pound, however, I sent him a copy. A year later Pound wrote me that he had sent the portrait to Eliot, at the *Criterion*, anonymously. He enclosed a letter from Eliot saying that the piece was the best criticism of Gertrude Stein that he had seen.[1] Here is the portrait which finally appeared in 1938 in Ezra Pound's *Exile*.

PORTRAIT

Gertrude Stein being a Sumerian monument at five o'clock tea on Fleurus Street among Picassos, Braques, and some Cézannes; slowly the slow blush monumentally mounting as in dismay pontificating Miss Stein loses herself in the labyrinthine undergrowths of her jungle-muddy forestial mind naïvely intellectualizing.

Early 1925, speaking of herself, Miss Stein said, "No, nobody has done anything to develop the English language since Shakespeare, except myself, and Henry James perhaps a little."

"Yes, the Jews have produced only three originative geniuses: Christ, Spinoza, and myself."

Miss Stein has been disconcerted by her thick intuitions having slowly suspected that her oracular proclamations are being adjudged rather than accepted as mediumistic deliverances of nature's slow-aged, giving-taking, uninterruptable continuance.

Slowly the slow blush mounts and her tone is of naïve plaint; embarrassment struggling suspiciously to exasperation. "But my manner could not remind you of anything Sumerian. I have never gone in for Babylonian writings."

Being, biblical, being obsessed with being, biblical, repetitively being, biblical, massively being, the slow slime breathes to being, slowly the biblical slime evolves to being. The aged elephant mastadonically heaves to being, breathing in the

---

[1] The letter from T. S. Eliot to Ezra Pound, dated April 1, 1926, reads in part: "Yours of the 21st acknowledged. I like the enclosure which is the best criticism of Gertrude Stein that I have seen. Cannot yet decide whether possible to use it. Until decision made I do not inquire name of author, but should like to know later whether it would have to be published anonymously." At bottom of the letter, Ezra Pound typed: "Dear R: So that's that. These things move with majestic slowness; so different from our own febrile tempo." And, below Ezra Pound's signature, these words appear, also typed: "Nooz of gt. metroPOLIS always pleasant in rural abodes."

slow slime with aged hope, breathing to be slowly. Slowly burdened with a slowly massive clinging slime, agedly the slow elephant ponderously moves in the ancient slime, slowly breathing to move heaving the idea, being; disconcertedly the slow blush mounts and the infant elephant idea panics at being adjudged rather than consulted as an oracle; the ancient mastodonic slow idea with slow suspicion moves agedly suspectful, resting to pause in the ancient slime, effortfully feeling slow being, going on being, to be evolving towards the slowly massive idea elephant, while slowly the elephantine idea evolves to the idea slow aged elephant, suspiciously being, heaving from the slime.

"She is shy, very unsure of herself," the mind warns a listener. "Don't frighten her or she won't talk and when she talks one can, if keen, select an idea which may be heavy but which may also be unique. The elephant's sensibility is not that of the humming bird's."

Shyly pleased by "Of course, you are not touched by time, so you need not think of your generation. Even the youngsters have not the sense of modernity which you had before the war," Miss Stein is monumentally deaf to the tones of flattery or irony. She confesses confidingly, naïvely being naïve.

"I sometimes wonder how anybody can read my work when I look it over after a time. It seems quite meaningless to me at times. Of course, when I write it it seems luminous and fine and living, and as you say it has a tremendous pulsation."

The slow earth moves agedly, massively the mastodon stirs in the mind, and slimed with mud is mud, pulsating with and in mud, but ponderously this mud slowly evolves to the identity, slowly to ponderously identify itself as an idea, slowly evolved, slowly dredged through the snow clinging mud, slowly to capture the slow slimed identity of the aged slow idea, elephant.

Leo Stein has said, from 1917 on: "Gertrude does not know what words mean. She hasn't much intuition but thickly she has sensations, and of course her mania, herself. Her idea of herself as a genius."

Leo Stein has said often: "Gertrude write a thesis against pragmatism which would win William James' admiration? She couldn't. Gertrude can't think consecutively for ten seconds. It was only after I discovered Picassos and had them in the studio for two years that Gertrude began to think she senses a quality."

Gertrude, in speaking of her work. "No, oh no, no, no, no, that isn't possible. You would not find a painter destroying any of his sketches. A writer's writing is too much of the writer's being; his flesh child. No, no, I never destroy a sentence or a word of what I write. You may, but of course, writing is not your métier, Doctor."

The Doctor-writer: "But Doctor Stein, you are sure that writing is your métier? I solve the economies of life through the profession of doctoring, but from the first my will was towards writing. I hope it pleases you, but things that children write have seemed to me so Gertrude Steinish in their repetitions. Your quality is that of being slowly and innocently first recognizing sensations and experience."

"I could not see him after that," Miss Stein said later. "I told the maid I was not in if he came again. There is too much bombast in him."

Slowly moving towards a slow idea the slow child repeating the idea being, slowly the child entangles itself in slow bewilderment of the forest of slow ideas; slowly the shy slow blush slowly mounts in suspicion slowly tormented by the harassing distrust, an idea, slowly but finally lost, slowly rediscovered, slowly emerging, slowly escaping, slowly confusion gathers, the dark blush mounts, while slow panic reveals that surely Miss Stein has slowly entangled herself and has slowly allowed the slow idea she was slowly expounding to slowly escape and slowly lost in slow confusion of slow panic shyly slowly Miss Stein wishes these people who listen adjudgingly rather than as to an oracle were away, slowly she is ill at ease, and slowly she realizes suddenly that she wishes these people quickly away, and quickly they go, slowly controlling themselves to quickly realize laughter upon relentlessly realizing being, surely, being outside, away from Miss Stein.

Back in Paris there was a period which was very Einstein or relativist. J. W. N. Sullivan arrived from London and lingered about the Quarter. He was interested in music, as befits a higher mathematician, and he was still passionate about Dostoevsky, who had been the inspiration for Einstein's discoveries. One day he and I called on Ezra, and somehow whenever Sullivan was about there was profound discussion, whether he was with Eliot, Pound, Wyndham Lewis, or myself. Ezra assured Sullivan that he highly overrated Dostoevsky, for Ezra was inclined to grant "them Rooshians" very short shrift indeed. Sullivan and I must have had the same bright suspicion at the same moment, because simultaneously we insisted that Ezra say which book of Dostoevsky's and of what Russian writers he was speaking. Ezra backed down gracefully, for his knowledge of Russian literature from the actual reading of it was very slight. Years before he had made the statement in print that one need not have read a book or an author to have a fairly clear idea about a book's quality, so neither Sullivan nor I pressed our victory.

Today I wonder if time will prove Einstein to have made such valuable discoveries as everybody so aggressively claimed in those days? Reading Munthe's *San Michele* and his account of the hypnotist converts, one may wonder what a later generation will think of psychoanalysts and Einstein. I found, however, that I like these higher mathematicians. They have an innocence and a limpid quality of sweet expectancy and gentleness which is appealing. Evidently, from Gertrude Stein's account, Whitehead had these qualities of tender concern about human destiny also. Possibly higher mathematics is the final romanticism after all.

Throughout a two-year period Bryher and I had an apartment in London, but I was generally away, in Paris, because of the publishing business, or in the forests of Rambouillet writing on a long book, *Family Panorama*, the scene of which started in the 1880s, and is resting now until I look it over at a later date and bring it up to the 1940s. Either it's good enough to lay aside and to belong to a later generation's acclaim, or it isn't good enough to risk the disapproval of a staunch old lady, my mother. She will not have it that I might use the venerable Mr. or Mrs. So-and-so, her friends, and former parishioners, as material for books. As she can always best me in any discussion, and I still recall her disciplinary methods of an earlier day, I am not too courageous when facing her ire. As the youngest of ten children I say that, knowing that I am not alone in my attitude. She out-thinks us all.

Quite simply I drifted into thinking of London as something to which I would resign myself for short periods. The English people I liked were mainly those who also preferred the Continent. Eva Le Gallienne stopped in London for a time, resting from a nervous breakdown after too long a period playing in *Liliom*. She intended going later to Budapest in search of new plays, but for a time was eager to rest and play. She amused herself by shooting craps, and gave the impression that she was on the stage playing the role of an actress shooting craps. Later she played in Mercedes de Acosta's *Jeanne d'Arc*, in Paris, the stage sets done by Norman Bel Geddes, and the criticisms of it written by Frenchmen to a large extent. They at least "came off". So, for that matter, did the play, very shortly.

In the early autumn I did a siege of Dublin, merely to escape London. Visually it was a great disappointment. There were still the remnants of the revolution of a few years back, but apart from this Dublin seemed grey and dull and meanly ingrown, with hardly a spark of gaiety and certainly no night life. It was too much a man's city, and Nora Joyce's comment, "Hasn't he the dirty mind", certainly applies to the usual attitude of the Dublin male towards women, notably towards "whores". A Frenchman lets them be *poules*, or *cocottes*, or "little friends". The Irish temperament is a strange combination. It produces an ugly thuglike foulness of mind, and brutality, and it also breeds that fairy-whimsy, twilighty and mystical rot. Both extremes are bad, the former being a heritage from Jesuitism and the tyranny of the Church.

In London I had been seeing various sons of Augustus John, two of whom I'd known in Paris. They disliked London and squirmed at being known as the great man's sons. In their teens they were precocious and apparently balanced and worldly young men, but later they became despairing and bewildered. One of them, Henry John, who was studying to be a priest, had written briefly, and his work appeared in Ernest Walsh's *This Quarter*, under the name of Ultramontane, and in Wyndham Lewis' magazine, the *Enemy*. Henry John's literary efforts, like his letters to me, were one long wail about carnal desire, and with it long expositions on morals and ethics and the metaphysics taught by Jesuit priests. (That quality is in Joyce, too, particularly in *A Portrait*.) We all have our adolescent torments about.sex, but the Jesuits appear to believe in magnifying that agony with something they call the spirit. Possibly the Protestant religion is as bad. I cannot say. Being a minister's son, and seeing the right and righteous and horrible specimens of my father's congregations, I felt that I didn't belong and didn't have to do much thinking one way or the other about the matter.

In Paris, Joyce had introduced me to Patrick Tuohy, a portrait

painter with a withered arm. Tuohy had done portraits of Joyce and
of Joyce's father, and he was now conducting an art class in Dublin.
While I was there he took me to see Mr. Joyce, Sr., and an amazing
old man he was. He sat up in his bed and looked Tuohy and me
over with fiery eyes, and complained of his weakness. The fact was
he didn't like to exert himself too much, but he rang the bell, and
his landlady brought barley water, and the three of us sat ourselves
down to a bottle of Dublin whisky which we had brought. He
assured me that he was fond of his son James but the boy was mad
entirely; but he couldn't help admiring the lad for the way he'd
written of Dublin as it was, and many a chuckle it gave him. I have
never seen a more intense face than that of old man Joyce.

The old man was staying in a typical boarding house of the type
I had known in New York in other years. The landlady was a none
too cleanly good-natured and rather shiftless Irishwoman, who
complained about the trouble and work the old man caused her. But
she appeared to like his presence in the house, and boasted of her
own self-sacrificing nature. Before I left, Mr. Joyce had become for
me the street-corner politician and aged man about town as
revealed in *Ulysses*. And I reflected that when I meet the Irish I'm
glad I have Scots blood, and when I meet the Scots, oh, bring back
the Irish to me.

Tuohy took me to meet other friends of his, people named
Hamilton, I believe. They had been intimates of Katherine Mansfield and D. H. Lawrence, and the innumerable legends about
these two writers were not so widely spread as now. Katherine
Mansfield was dead, and Middleton Murry and a few others in
London had begun their ghoul-like picking at the literary remains of
the "great artist". Miss Mansfield's memoirs, her letters, her notebooks were all to appear, and her name was to be played up as one
of the greatest of English writers of all time. It's too bad that the
Mansfields and the Lawrences couldn't have had some of that
attention before they died.

Various of the literary lights of Dublin talked to me brightly of
American writing. Did I know Ernest Boyd? I did not. And the
American Mercury and Mencken? I had little to say. We had at least
one fine woman writer, Fannie Hurst, and there had been Poe, and
Mark Twain, but did I believe that Dreiser's work was important?
These Dublin men were generally back two generations as regards
both English and American writing, for the censors did not permit

many of the better books to appear in Ireland. They were very "small country" and ingrown, and smug about morals and dignity and ethics. A few of them wanted to write in the true Irish language. Others quoted AE[2] and Yeats.

Judge Reddin had the year before won a prize for a short play written for the Abbey Theatre. He invited me to drive to his villa at Howth, and from there is a view as beautiful as any in Greece. He was entirely likeable and informed, and longed for a vacation on the Continent. We talked for hours about various countries, and about every writer of renown for the past two hundred years. The name Ernest Boyd would keep coming into all conversations, however, as well as the mention of the *American Mercury*. Irish literary circles did know of Padraic and Mary Colum, but didn't appear much interested in them. In fact the taste of the Irish did not strike me as distinguished. O'Casey did not impress them at that time, nor did O'Flaherty or Sean O'Faolain. AE generally had Sunday gatherings of the Dublin literati, and I was to attend one of them. Previously, however, I had met AE in the office of his paper, the *Irish Statesman*. He looked like a rugged and bearded sea captain, and told various anecdotes about Joyce and Yeats. He had written a rather favourable and certainly intelligent review of Gertrude Stein's *The Making of Americans*. To me he revealed none of his seerlike and mystical aspects, but he surprised me by knowing characters and plots of stories which I had written. Possibly he concluded I was not mystically mediumistic.

Tuohy, tiring of near starvation in Dublin, went to New York to make his way as a portrait painter. Things did not go well for him there, and a few years later he committed suicide. I can well understand that too much Dublin would leave a sour taste in the mouth of an Irishman with a liberal attitude towards living. Ernest Boyd went back at one point, intending, it was said, to remain, but a visit of a few weeks cured him of that idea and he returned to America. Do the Irish who have gone away and remained away awhile ever return to live contented in their homeland?

[2] AE was George William Russell, a famous author and painter.

Kay Boyle

1928

In 1927, in his publication the *Enemy*, Wyndham Lewis had launched an attack on *transition* (as well as on Communism, surrealism, Joyce, Stein, Negroes, Sherwood Anderson, D. H. Lawrence and Indians). And in the December issue of *transition* of that year the editors answered Wyndham Lewis in an essay entitled "First Aid to the Enemy". Mr. Lewis' proposal was to defend the West against "the dark powers of the East", the editors pointed out; "to defend the classical ideal against the spirit of disorder, or the romantic conception." But they admitted that they were not at all certain what Mr. Lewis meant by these terms. The two editors of *transition*, Eugene Jolas and Elliot Paul, and Robert Sage, an associate editor (who also had a book-review column in the Paris edition of the Chicago *Tribune*) replied to Lewis' condemnation of all English-speaking writers who had made their home in Paris with the statement that they did not wish to be good Europeans but good universalists. They were interested in the West as a means for new artistic expressions, they said, and they wished to see a new humanism born of the synthesis of intercontinental concepts. (I had to admit that I was not at all certain what they meant by that.) "We believe that only the dream really matters," they wrote. "We believe that there is a universal eternal line binding the nations and which has nothing whatever to do with the limitations of a Western psychology or an Eastern psychology. The dream has no racial characteristics."

These statements were of importance to me, just as later I would consider important the declaration (proclaimed by *transition*) concerning the revolution of the word. They at least approached a definition of the nature of my own undefined revolt. Eugene Jolas— of Lorraine stock, with a strong regionalistic feeling—spoke three languages with equal insight, imagination, and distinction; and he had, in the pages of *transition*, declared himself so forcefully on the subject of "the word" that even before going to Paris I had begun to understand my own impatience with at least nine tenths of contemporary American writing. Jolas was born an American, and he had been for some years a newspaper reporter both in America and on assignments in foreign countries; but he had been educated in Germany and France. He was thus well read in German and French poetry and psychology, and his awareness of "the dream", "the ancestral myth", had never been a part of my precognition, nor that of any other American I knew. At that time, only Sherwood Anderson among American writers wrote with an instinctive and never wholly acknowledged recognition of the presence of what Jolas called "the waking-sleeping hallucination".[1] Faulkner, as purveyor of both dream and myth, was still to come, and McAlmon, in his almost pathological mistrust of the subconscious, denounced Sherwood Anderson's and, even more vehemently, Faulkner's hallucinatory prose.

It is not strange, then, that the two isolated dreamers of American writing at that time (Anderson and Faulkner) should have had a language in common both in the context of their surroundings and the context of their dreams. After Anderson's death, Faulkner wrote[2] that once when they sat together on a park bench in New Orleans Anderson had told him of a dream he had had of walking for miles along country roads, "leading a horse which he was trying to swap for a night's sleep—not for a simple bed for the night, but for the sleep itself". Anderson had built the dream into a work of art "with the same tedious . . . almost excruciating patience and humility with which he did all his writing," Faulkner said, "me

[1] In the tenth anniversary number of *transition*, Anderson replied to Jolas' "Inquiry into the Spirit and Language of Night" in part as follows: "It seems to me that my nights and days come together, the night almost invariably carrying on the thoughts of the day. . . . There is often a phantasy—faces of people, old and young, appearing one at a time, sometimes slowly, sometimes rapidly. They seem to me to be accusing, and I have thought of them as people hungering to have their stories told."

[2] "Sherwood Anderson, an Appreciation," *Atlantic Monthly*, June 1953.

listening and believing no word of it: that is, that it had been any dream dreamed in sleep. . . . He didn't know why he had been compelled, or anyway needed, to claim it had been a dream, why there had to be that connection with dream and sleep, but I did. It was because he had written his whole biography into an anecdote or perhaps a parable: the horse . . . representing the vast rich strong docile sweep of the Mississippi Valley, his own America, which he in his bright blue racetrack shirt and vermilion-mottled Bohemian Windsor tie, was offering with humour and patience and humility, but mostly with patience and humility, to swap for his own dream of purity and integrity and hard and unremitting work and accomplishment, of which *Winesburg, Ohio,* and *The Triumph of the Egg* had been symptoms and symbols."

It was not difficult to be humorous about Jolas' graphing of the night-mind and his concept of it as a marvellously unexplored territory. It was even easier to ridicule *transition*'s wild celebration of not only liberated words but poems, and essays, and non-stories, that had been dredged up from the unconscious and heralded as if they were long-awaited travellers from a distant and mysterious land. (McAlmon and his Canadian protégés, Buffy and Graeme, were particularly adept at this kind of ridicule, I found when I got to Paris, and were frequently very funny. But their attitude was not very different from that of the doctor in Bryn Mawr in my childhood who was so convulsed over Gertrude Stein's *Tender Buttons* that he had to be taken upstairs to bed. McAlmon, unable to explain Gurdjieff by pragmatic argument, had burlesqued him, and the surrealists, Jolas, and *transition* were all to be dismissed in sardonic jest.) In their reply to Wyndham Lewis, Jolas and his co-editors wrote: "It is the artist's search for magic in this strange world about us that *transition* desires to encourage," and they added that the real trouble with Lewis was that he was constitutionally unable "to capture the magic of life".

On one point only did the editors of *transition* concede Wyndham Lewis was right, and that was that the surrealists were Communists. But in making clear that they themselves were no more Communist than they were Fascist, they emphasized that they in no way washed their hands of the surrealists. "If we have a warm feeling for both them [the surrealists] and the Communists," they declared, "it is because the movements which they represent are aimed at the destruction of a thoroughly rotten structure, just as were the

American and French revolutions." But their patience was totally exhausted by Mr. Lewis' confusion of Joyce with Stein, and Stein with Dada. "Anyone who has intelligently *read* one or two numbers of *transition*," they pointed out, "would have discerned the obvious facts that Mr. Joyce and Miss Stein are at opposite poles of thought and expression, and that neither of them has anything in common with the Dada or surrealist movements." They derided Mr. Lewis' definition of *transition* as a political organ, a "convulsive, politico-artistic form of radical propaganda", and thus one more menace to the safety of the Western world. Mr. Lewis' hysterical defence of the West they saw as a bourgeois impulse, and an inherent part of "the Anglo-Saxon superiority mania which in America has glorified the ignorant and the philistine into the belief of his racial superiority".

In Stoke-on-Trent I had read and pondered every number of *transition*, dissatisfied with my own work that appeared in it, but reading aloud to Germaine the poetry of Eluard and Rilke, and others, so many others, and parts of Jolas' "Revolt Against the Philistine". In this essay he cried out, in terms that, again, I was not certain I understood, that "the artist is the born enemy of the philistine in whom he sees incorporated all the qualities which his metaphysical orientation rejects". Germaine and I studied the reproductions of the paintings by Tanguy and Arp; and the work of the surrealist writer, Robert Desnos, moved us by his romantic visions and his passionate love for women. It was there, like a pulse, in every line he wrote. Desnos was an iconoclast of the imagination, according to *transition*, a poet who "juggles fates in a vast panorama of magic, and appears to be one of the hopes of French literature". This was language, I reflected then, that must have brought McAlmon to the point of apoplexy.

And then suddenly one evening in early May I was walking with Archie Craig up a flight of stairs in an apartment house in Paris. I had on a brilliant orange dress my sister had given me in London, and a black velvet cloak of the Dayang Muda's; and Archie, climbing slowly, slowly, because of his delicate health, wore a mauve whipcord jacket with a gardenia in his lapel, trousers of pastel blue, his sandals custom-made to fit his narrow feet, and carried a silver-headed cane. I remember every detail of that evening as if it had taken place no longer ago than the night before last: we climbed three flights of stairs because, as used often to be the case in Paris, the elevator was not functioning, and always a flight below us was a young man in a tweed jacket and grey slacks who also climbed slowly, not for any reasons of health, but apparently out of shyness. Every now and then he glanced up to estimate our progress, lingering over the pretence of tying first one shoe and then the other so that he would not reach the door of the Jolases' apartment at the same moment we did. He was Archibald MacLeish.

Archie and I had had tea with Maria and Gene and the two other editors of *transition* a few days before. Maria, statuesque and handsome in a long hostess gown, had poured tea (from what I erroneously took for her own Kentucky heirloom silver, but which belonged to the apartment they were occupying) and put me at ease with her laughter and her talk of children. Gene, then in his early thirties, broad-shouldered, heavy-set, had the fine head of a Roman senator and the wild gaze of a poet, and there were moments when he almost stuttered in his eagerness to say all he believed. During that first meeting he did not talk to us the way he wrote. He did not say that *transition* had "entered this moiling world with the avowed purpose of combining the various tendencies in art and literature into a single channel," a channel which he called "magic realism"; nor did he assert that "by retaining an anti-realistic, anti-photographic bias in favour of the metamorphosis of reality" one could embark on voyages of discovery. He did not announce that they "stressed work with a fantastic, dreamlike, apocalyptic trend", and that they intended to abolish the term 'short story' in favour of the term 'paramyth'," believing as they did that narrative should be given "a mythological prolongation". His thoughts were very simply and almost tentatively expressed; yet even in this atmosphere of family prosperity and ease his commitment to a mystical concept of literature was hauntingly and haltingly there.

Through our work, and through the letters Jolas and I had written to each other during the past year, the way had been prepared for us to like each other instantly; but it was not until almost a year later that Maria and I became close friends. Our first meeting had been in the setting of a more-or-less formal tea party, but tonight the ambiance would be quite different, although also without intimacy. At the end of the week Maria and Gene would be leaving with their baby daughter Betsy for Colombey-les-Deux-Églises, where they had rented the year before the house General de Gaulle would later buy. This was to be a farewell party with the friends of and contributors to *transition*, whom Maria, at least, would not be seeing as regularly as before. The Joyces, the Stuart Gilberts, Molly and Padraic Colum were often with the Jolases, and Maria's warm and unfailing hospitality, and her musical gifts, created an atmosphere that was uniquely and exuberantly her own. (Maria had lived for a year in Berlin, and five years in Paris, studying for an operatic career, a career which was interrupted by her marriage. But her singing—in German and French, as well as New Orleans patois, and American Negro songs learned, as she said, sitting as a child under the ironing board—was enough to set Joyce and everyone else off on their own repertoires. All this, however, I learned at a later time.)[3]

On Archie's and my arrival, there were perhaps twenty or thirty people in the music room and salon that overlooked the Place des Invalides. Almost at once Jolas took me to a sofa where Nora and James Joyce were sitting, he with a black patch over one eye and his long hands folded on his cane. Gene told them I had arrived from England the week before, and Nora said surely my dress could not be English, and she asked me with embarrassing deference what Paris collection it had come from. Joyce, thinking I was travelling from country to country during the summer months, "like our friend McAlmon," he said, inquired most courteously if I would like him to give me the names of *pensions* and restaurants in Switzerland of reasonable price, yet where the wines were good. Joyce himself was partial to a white wine grown on the slopes above Vevey. I told him I was visiting for a while in Paris with the Princess of Sarawak, and this immediately held his interest, for he knew the unique history of the British crown colony in north-west Borneo, and of the ship-wrecked ancestor of the present white Rajah who had been found by the natives on a beach of the China Sea, and who had, after he had fought and expelled Malay and Dyak pirates from the area, been made the ruler there.

Nora Joyce had a complexion of indescribable youthfulness and

[3] Of her meeting with Gene, Maria wrote in *A James Joyce Miscellany* published by the James Joyce Society in 1957, "At that time (1925) he (Gene) was writing a weekly literary column for the Paris edition of the Chicago *Tribune*, and I followed his articles with keen interest even before meeting him. Here, I felt, was that rare bird (they were perhaps rarer then than now), an American journalist for whom literature was the great adventure and who, in addition to his knowledge of English and American writers, was familiar with the new currents in Europe. When we met through his brother, the pianist, Jacques Jolas, I felt that I knew him already."

radiance, and a sociable, relaxed, and chatty way, and she smelled of tea roses when she moved. (Again, it was only later, much later, in another year in Feldkirch, Austria, that I was to hear Nora make the consummate relaxed and chatty remark to Maria Jolas. "To tell ye th' thruth, m' dear," she said, "I was never very much inthrested in me husband's work.") Then, that evening in Paris, there was a sudden pause in the talk and the movement of guests in the two crowded rooms. It was as if heralding bugles had sounded, and it was not unlike a parade advancing as the abruptly silenced guests fell back, holding their champagne glasses in their hands. A passage was now cleared for the personages to proceed in single file towards two armchairs from which the occupants, as if touched by an unseen finger, quickly arose. Maria Jolas graciously led the way, and behind her came the unmistakable figure of Gertrude Stein in a severe and nunlike dress of purple silk, followed by Alice B. Toklas in a tight little jacket with the winged shoulders of the turn of the century, and a long skirt in which a bustle would have been at ease. Pursuing them, on more hesitant feet, came Archie Craig and a handful of other young men who either knew or were eager to meet Miss Stein, and who presently squatted in a half-circle before her chair.

Nora and James Joyce had given no sign that they had seen the ceremonial cortege pass, but Sylvia Beach, who had been chatting with Soupault and Elliot Paul and Adrienne Monnier near one of the wide windows that opened on the mild spring night, turned and crossed the room, making her way through the guests who had now begun to talk and drink and laugh again, and drew up a footstool, and sat down in her grey, mannish suit before the Joyces. "Isn't she the thrue picture of an Irish colleen, with her dark hair and her misty blue eyes?" Nora said to Sylvia as she introduced us, and nothing else but this introduction might have been taking place anywhere in the room. In spite of the two glasses of champagne I had drunk, and the kindness of the Joyces, I was nearly paralysed with shyness, even when the talk had been of our daughters—theirs, Lucia, and mine, Sharon, "the Rose of Sharon", Joyce said. And now that Nora Joyce had commented on my eyes and hair, I said abruptly, with embarrassment and champagne hot in my face: "What about my broken nose?"

Joyce wanted to hear how this had happened to me, and even Sylvia Beach seemed enthralled as I sat there telling them like an idiot about the blizzard that had begun on the third of March one spring in the Poconos, and Joyce wanted to know where that would be. It was a three-day blizzard, I said, and on the day after it ended I was coasting lickety-split on my Flexible Flyer down a road into the village that had been ploughed out just wide enough for a sleigh to pass. And as I came down, up the hill had come two horses abreast, drawing a sleigh behind them, and it was a choice of either going under their hoofs, head on, or hitting whatever lay on the other side of the snowbank my sled would have to jump. So I pulled the sled sideways with all my might, and it jumped the snowbank at an angle, and the telegraph pole was waiting for me there. "I swallowed one of my front teeth at the same time," I told them, and Joyce shook his head in commiseration. "When I hear her talk," Nora said, "I can't help thinking, Jim, that our own lives haven't been very eventful." "It's true," Joyce said, "but the Americans are that way. Look at McAlmon fighting bulls in Spain and thinking nothing of it. But, on the other hand, Bach for one led a very uneventful life," he said.

I did not meet Gertrude Stein or Alice Toklas that night. Indeed, it would have seemed almost a disloyalty to have crossed the room and genuflected before Miss Stein. But it was strange to know then, and even stranger to reflect now, that it was neither Joyce's partial blindness nor the movement of other guests between them that made it difficult for Gertrude Stein and James Joyce to see each other seated there. It was, deep and impassable, their opposed concepts of a new syntax and a new vocabulary: a barrier as imponderable, and yet as concrete, as the *manner* of the revolution of the word.

When the evening came to an end, and Archie was bringing from the hall for me the Dayang Muda's velvet cloak and his own silver-headed cane, first Philippe Soupault and then Archibald MacLeish asked if they could see me home. But I went with my little Scots brother, with the gardenia in his buttonhole, the petals of which were now beginning to fade. He, too, was happy over the things that had happened that night. Gertrude Stein had asked him to drop in for tea some afternoon. But McAlmon was not anywhere around.

Robert McAlmon
1925-1927

Hemingway had become much of a bullfight enthusiast since his 1924 trip to Spain. In one of his earlier short stories one character says, "It's no fun if you can't skee any more," and the other character responds, "No, it's no fun if you can't skee any more." He now carried this manner of dialogue and the intonation of the American voice over to bullfighting stories. It was all muscular and athletic prose, but for this period in the spirit of "It's no fun if you can't see bullfights any more."

He talked a great deal about bullfights as the greatest art, the beautiful dance involving death, and one summer quite a number of people decided to do the fiesta week in Pampeluna, Spain. Having made a quick trip to Egypt, and back via Athens and Constantinople, I also hied myself to Pampeluna, and there before me were Donald Ogden Stewart, Dos Passos, William and Sally Bird, young George O'Neill, Hadley and Ernest Hemingway, and an English captain from Sandhurst who had known Hemingway in Milan after the war. This Captain and Hemingway had met at a club and agreed that after the war years it would be very difficult for our generation to adjust to the prosaic and dull routines of peace, war-shocked and disillusioned as we were.

The days and nights were hot with heat that sweated through one's flesh and bones. However, the fiesta spirit was rampant, and everybody was willing to drink plenty of pernod and forget the heat. The town during the first two days before the bullfights came on was quiet till noon, when the café terraces were crowded. After lunch the streets were empty again, but at six o'clock the fiesta gaieties began. Throngs of peasants from the mountains roamed through the city, their necks encircled with necklaces of garlic, and various-shaped goatskin bags of wine thrown over their shoulders. Some of these bags were made in the form of ships, and some in the shape of dolls or animals. To drink, one held the goatskin high with one hand and squeezed it with the other, and a small stream of goaty-tasting wine spurted into one's open mouth. This took some learning, but the natives were adept. Little crowds of natives continually came and went, blowing whistles or playing more or less primitive instruments. Groups formed and danced solos in circles. Donald Ogden Stewart proved himself a born comedian with an inherent clowning instinct, and after his first solo dance he was the friend of the peasants from all the surrounding countryside. He knew how to utilize his Yankee professor's appearance. With the Americans, he had the advantage of having his "crazy fool" cracks and witticisms understood, but he managed to troupe his comedy across to the Spaniards without a common language.

The first two nights, all of the American-English gathered there proceeded to lose one another. But each one eventually tagged onto or got picked up by some wandering group of musicians or boys from the mountains, and the dancing and drinking continued till early morning. The town slept till well past noon, and then we all went to inspect the bulls that were to be used in the corridas.

The third morning, the day of the first bullfight, everyone was up by six o'clock, and out in the boarded street down which the bulls for the day were to be driven. Hundreds of boys and young men stood along the sides of the street and ran ahead of the bulls that were being driven to the bull ring. A few got butted or knocked against the walls by an excited and bewildered bull, but no one was badly injured or killed, as is sometimes the case. Later, when the fierce bulls had been driven into their corrals to wait for the afternoon corridas, the amateur fun began. A heifer, light-bodied steer, or yearling bull—but seldom—would be released into the ring. Hundreds of aspiring bullfighters were in the ring, and the panic-stricken heifer, steer, or young bull would dash here and there, sometimes charging, but as often merely looking for a means of escape.

Hemingway had been talking a great deal about courage, and how a man needs to test himself to prove to himself that he can take it. I dunno. But Hemingway was persuaded that he must prove himself. With his coat he tried to attract the charge and the repeated charge of a steer, but the two-hundred-odd others in the ring were also trying to capture that mystified animal's attention. Finally Hemingway took a charge straight on face, and then, catching the steer's horns, attempted to throw it. He did break its strength, and got cheered by the crowd, but when the steer was released it ran away bellowing a bewildered moo, its tail wagging pathetically, and an expression on its face indicating that it was having no fun at all.

Bill Bird and Dos Passos were either the bravest or just plain quitters. Anyway, they didn't get into the ring to play with them calves. George O'Neill, then about seventeen, Don Stewart, Hemingway, the British captain from Sandhurst, and I were all there. The first day only Hemingway proved himself. My idea was to avoid getting butted, and the others also ran out of the path of a charge. Later, however, Hemingway talked more about bravery to Don Stewart. Stewart confessed to me that he thought one should probably save one's courage to put to use if an actual crisis should occur—if it is there to use. But the next day Don Stewart was all set "to take it" and he did take it. A young steer charged him, and from quite a distance. It floored him, but others drew it away almost immediately. Stewart said he wasn't hurt, and he went to the bullfights that day, but that night he left for Paris. A few days later there was a letter from him, informing us that one of his ribs had been broken by the charge of that steer.

I was drinking altogether too much pernod and goatskin-tasting wine, and eating heavy Spanish food. The idea of having a calf, steer, or young bull charge into my breadbasket did not appeal to me. I did nothing but dodge out of the way of those cattle, and if they appeared to be pursuing me I jumped the fence. Our Sandhurst captain, however, was a man of different calibre. He and I walked one night to Fortress Hill, and he admitted that during the war he had had plenty of chances to prove his bravery, but that no man is sure of his own courage. The next day we were in the ring, and he stood in the middle of it, waiting to see which animal would be released. Presently, out came a sizeable yearling bull, its tail lashing, its nostrils dilated with temper. Our doughty Britisher said that he was in for it, and he stood, and I knew he would take the charge of the animal, head on. I ran out, taking care to stay behind him, and shouted, "Run, you damn fool. That bull will break your back!" We both cleared the barriers, and that particular animal was soon taken out of the ring. By this time Bill and Sally Bird were making so many jokes about us intrepid bullfighters that neither the captain nor I felt called upon to prove our bullfighting courage again.

All members of the party liked aspects of the bullfights by the skilled matadors, but no one of us ever became the fervid enthusiast which Hemingway elected to become. Bullfights that are truly great are too rare, and one must see many in order to see a few fine ones. For the rest, nothing is more vulgar and disgusting than a bad bullfight, and clumsy killings of the bulls are more horrible than the horse part of the fight. The lost, babycalf look of wondering stupidity on a bull's face is heartbreaking, particularly when it is a brave bull but does not want to fight or to charge horses. It is complete nonsense that all bulls are naturally attacking and fighting animals. Even goaded by torture, some of them remain brave, and fight only to be let alone.

The fiesta over at Pampeluna, Bill and Sally and I boarded a bus and went to Burguette, a Spanish town near the French border. It was tiny and quiet, with one bare peasant inn, and but a few cottages. Herds of sheep and goats flocked in the surrounding hills, and muleteers drove their donkeys down the road, bearing cordwood or wine bags. Some miles up in the mountains was an old mine shaft and a stream where trout fishing was good. After a few days Hemingway and Hadley joined us, and we took walks to the fishing falls, and it was here that Hemingway fished one day while thinking out his story "Great Two-Hearted River". He was so intent thinking about what it was that a man who was fishing would be thinking about, and what Bird and I would be thinking about, that he didn't catch many trout, but he jotted down notes for the story. Some declare it is a great story. I find it is a stunt and very artificial, and I do not believe his mind works that way at all. I think he's a very good businessman, a publicity seeker, who looks ahead and calculates, and uses rather than wonders about people.

Walking one night in Roncesvalles, the scene of medieval romance and legend, Chanson de Roland Hemingway was most unhappy because he feared he was to become a father. He told Hadley it would be no fun at all any more if they had too many children at his age. She wouldn't be a good playmate any more either. He was tragic about it, and Hadley, too, became upset. Finally Sally Bird, who was walking ahead with Bill and me, turned back and said to Hemingway, "Stop acting like a damn fool and a crybaby. You're responsible too. Either you do something about not having it, or you have it."

For a few days things were restful and pastoral at Burguette, and the country was beautiful, with innumerable walks to be taken. Later our British captain, Dos Passos, and George O'Neill arrived, and the next day these three and I started off on a walk in the Pyrénées, intending to spend about a fortnight walking, with the little republic of Andorra as our goal. Hemingway accompanied us for about five kilometres and then dutifully returned to his wife. We made thirty-five kilometres that first day and were well into the mountains. In the beginning we had agreed to take it leisurely rather than make a race or a competition of the jaunt.

However, young George O'Neill was full of vim and vigour and, moreover, he carried a cane. Apart from striding along at a great pace, he took swings at passing stones with his cane. Our army man had the maps, and while swearing that he wouldn't try to show up the rest of us, he noted that Dos Passos and George both set a pace hard to follow. The next day we did forty kilometres, and another day, when we had been lost twice in the mountains, we did well over sixty kilometres. Eleven o'clock at night found us faltering, footsore, and leg-weary, on an endless rocky road, which led eventually into a rather sizeable town. That night we had to sleep in a haystack, but we slept all right.

At one little village, hardly more than a shack and a pigpen, George O'Neill noticed a letter stuck up on a fence post. The letter was for him. He had seen the name of the village on a map and given it as his address. For weeks he had been expecting money from his father, and this letter contained that money. It was pure luck to have found it, and pure luck that it had reached this village, for the mailman came seldom to these little so-called towns, and he came on foot from miles away.

Life in these places was going on much as it had hundreds of years ago. The local dress was skirted trousers and leggings of bright colours. The mountaineers had that air of nobility which simple and primitive people possess. Once, crossing a field, we inquired our way of a bearded patriarch, and he offered us a drink of wine from his goat sack and told us that we need not fear. They knew our kind here, he said, and many of their own were like us. Dos Passos translated, and we were naturally delighted that he had taken us for smugglers.

What food there was to eat had no variety whatever. There was goat cheese, black bread, and continual tortillas, a heavy egg concoction filled with potatoes and sometimes onions. There was coffee, again with goat's milk, and I never did get to like the goatskin-tasting wine. Dos Passos, however, loved it all, the cheese, the wine, the bread, the walking. There aren't many men in the world with more gusto and enthusiasm and zeal than Dos Passos. He and George O'Neill had exuberance and vivacity for all events. But I had started the walking trip unprepared. My *alpargatas* (canvas slippers) were not suitable for mountain paths; my Achilles' tendon began to ache.

Rheumatism, gout, and blisters on my soles had begun to assail me on the second day. They did not ease, either, and climbing up mountainsides was hard work, and going down the steep mountains, I went slipping and sailing and flying too fast. It had become a race, and I discovered that if I kept ahead there were more chances of longer rests. On the sixth day we struck a fairly large town which had a bus that ran towards the French border, and here I decided that Andorra could wait for a later visit. These long walking trips are very fine, but the distances between towns and the lack of places to sleep in many of the villages did not permit us any leisure. And en route we drank a good deal of *agua gigante*, a powerful and effervescent drink of the absinthe family. It tastes like ethereal nectar, and however tired we arrived in a village, after a drink or so of this we felt wings on our feet. The others continued on to Andorra, and it is to be regretted that no one kept notes of the trip.

Back in Paris I found Joyce feeling alone and deserted. Nora had taken Lucia and Giorgio to London and they were later to visit Dublin for the first time in many years. In the meantime there was political trouble in Dublin, and Joyce fretted constantly. He sent them wires and letters, and he sent me wires and notes to come and talk to him. "And do you think they're safe, then, really? You don't understand, McAlmon, how this is affecting me. I am worried all of the day, and it does my eye no good. Ah, well." Joyce would heave a sigh, and my heart sympathized, but my humour told me that friend James has a way of enjoying the martyrdom of his trials and tribulations. Joyce's worry proved justified, however, for Nora, Lucia, and Giorgio left Ireland on a train that was constantly bombarded, and they travelled lying flat on the floor of the coach. It struck me as useless to worry with and for Joyce about them, and my ruthless consciousness would recall the closing passage of *Portrait of the Artist*, in which Stephen (Joyce) forswears home, family friends, and native land and goes forth alone into the world to search for beauty, art, and freedom—and he intends to have the world understand that he meant "alone forever".

How fate tricked him. Joyce is lonely, desolate, and an anxious husband, parent, brother, and son, if home and family and a degree of loving or admiring friends are not about. He is not his kind of Irish for nothing. Now he has a grandson, he beams to think that the child recognizes him as "Nono". During these days he missed Nora and his children so much that he generally drank little, and it is doubtful if he did much work. At least he did not talk of it, and when he is working he likes to talk of what he has recently done, and to read it to a listener. Nora and the children returned after a time, however, and Joyce was no longer a lost spirit in the wilderness of Paris.

The late summer and early autumn of 1926 I spent in London, and it was not bad for London. Quite a number of Americans from New York or Paris were about, and for the first time in several years I was contented just being quiet in a city, and I read quantities of books, mainly travel, historic, biographic, and documentary. During that period I managed to complete a sort of poem, "North America, continent of conjecture," which I still like and which some reviewer spoke of as "very intelligent". By this time I damn well knew that when those reviewing boys want to kill all possible interest in you they call you "intelligent" and say no more.

During the General Strike, when various college boys volunteered as stevedores, porters at railway stations, and girls and ladies joyously rushed to service to do their bit, it was interesting to watch the English citizenry in a governmental crisis. As Dorothy Richardson monologued one night in our apartment, England muddles through, "lacking in imagination though we admit ourselves to be." There was a party in our rooms that night, and Otto Theis had delighted Bryher by suggesting that she sell the *Outlook* on the streets during the General Strike. It was only one sheet, as the printers were striking too, as well as the newsboys, and Bryher was pleased, although she was far too scornful of Englishmen and the idea of soliciting sales to do the actual work.

When Dorothy Richardson and Alan Odle came in, Bryher asked

them how they had managed to get there. "Friends had us to dine at the Café Royal," Dorothy began her monologue. "They brought us in their car. I am thrilled, positively, at the way we are handling this strike situation. It may be said of England that she is finished, but we have been finished in every generation, and still we muddle through."

Bryher indicated interest and spoke of how she loved those British ladies who sit around waiting for a strike or a crisis so that they may have an opportunity for being unconventional. "They'd die if one suggested to them what they really want when they solicit strange males to buy poppies."

Miss Richardson smiled benignly as she settled herself, preparatory to becoming a seer holding a seance. Her manner was detached and vague, but her warm low voice carried, patronizingly informative and protective. "We English deal with our dramatic situations quietly, and it is your old ladies, Bryher," Dorothy smiled comfortingly, "who are the backbone of our country, and whatever you may say of our public schools, at times like this they prove their worth. They turn out young men to a pattern, yes, but the pattern wears. I had no doubt that I would get here tonight. I have no doubt that every public school man who can be out is doing his bit, even if it is hard, manual labour. Alan was dubious, but I said, 'Alan we are English. We owe it to ourselves, to our class and to England, to go out, not only to see what is happening but to prove that even in a General Strike we have no doubt that England will carry on.' You Americans, with your aeroplane minds and their shining, dynamic velocity," Miss Richardson addressed me now, "find us stodgy and stolid, but generations of experience have taught us not to become easily upset, and all of our classes have born in them the tradition of non-interference. I would have no fear of venturing into any quarter of London tonight."

Otto Theis looked as if he needed a whisky, and I knew I wanted one. Miss Richardson had overlooked the books and plays and moving pictures suppressed in England. She overlooked the fact that Epstein's works had frequently been mutilated in London. A while later, friends telephoned to ask if I was game for a drive to the Poplar district and Chinatown, where there was rioting. I was ready, and some boys from Oxford soon arrived with two cars and a couple of other Americans. Miss Richardson completely understood it was a joke when I invited her to join us and venture into some of London's rougher quarters. She might safely have come. The whole jaunt was a washout, and there wasn't a pub open where we might get a drink. It was some time before the General Strike ended, but one must grant this: it was well managed, and there was less hysteria than there would have been in most countries.

While it had not been passionately the fashion to be an artist or a genius in 1920, certainly it was by 1929. Both on the Continent and in America, every second college boy, radical, or aspiring writer wished to start a magazine, and some of them did. The *Hound and Horn* in America modelled itself rather too much on the London *Criterion*, was sedate, pompous, "humanistic", and proper. *Pagany* was to take more chances and now and then published lively stories—Mary Butts, William Carlos Williams, and others. A variety of other sheets went in for their own versions of communism or aesthetics.

On the continent there was first the *Transatlantic Review*, with Ford Madox Ford as editor, though at various times Hemingway and Ivan Beede appeared to do most of the work. Ernest Walsh, an Irish-American poet who was an invalid, due to an aviation accident in the army, started in 1925 a quarterly magazine for the kind of writing which commercial magazines were not apt to consider. With him was associated Ethel Moorhead, a Scotswoman who had studied painting in Paris under Whistler, and who had been an impassioned suffragette in pre-war days. She had done her days in prison for the cause, hunger strike, etc. *This Quarter* published good work by a variety of authors, and praised or condemned any quantity of people in a lively way. For instance, the first issue of the magazine was dedicated to Ezra Pound, and contained a letter from Joyce and contributions from several writers who have now become known. Later, Ethel Moorhead withdrew that dedication. The publication was erratic as to appearance as well as editorial approach. At one moment they would be adulatory towards a writer, and in a later issue they would attack the same idol as violently as they had previously praised him.

Throughout Ernest Walsh's and Ethel Moorhead's editorship, they published Hemingway, Pound, John Herrmann, Kay Boyle, Djuna Barnes, Morley Callaghan, and a host of others. Shortly after Ernest Walsh's death there appeared in *This Quarter* some very fine poems of his, done in pseudo old English. He had perhaps started them in a spirit of burlesque, but they had a fresh, healthy quality which earns them a place in the poetry of the time. Walsh's critical articles were full of violent opinions, and at times his praise could be embarrassing to those whom he praised. Miss Moorhead also had a critical instinct which was keen, but she let personal likes and dislikes influence her critical sense too greatly. A year or so after Walsh had died, *This Quarter* passed into the hands of a Paris bookseller, Edward Titus. It changed its character entirely, and then it, too, ceased to be. The pompous and trite editorials which Titus wrote in his endeavour to be a parental editor, indicating the way the young should go, killed interest in the venture.

I would judge that it was *transition*, under the editorship of Eugene Jolas, Elliot Paul, and Robert Sage, which exerted the most influence on writers whom they considered worthy of the name. It was a constant example of how not to write. By the time these three boys had chased the hallucinatory word over the sleepwalking realms of a mythos, any balanced writer was apt to decide that either he or they were having delirium tremens, and to yearn for the normality of a simple and direct style in which words "meant" something. Jolas, from Lorraine, who reads and writes English, French, and German, flayed, tantalized, flagellated, and dreamed words all around the various bars of Paris. He had a "soul", and he was bewildered, and he sought a religion and an "answer" in such a way as to make Margaret Anderson appear a cold and practical woman.

Elliot Paul, a journalist of no exceptional talent, who had written various staid and dull novels in a conventional style, became very Dadaist-surrealist, or Joycean-Steinian. He would call on Joyce and Stein (more on Miss Stein) and after a seance with her could hie himself to a typewriter and explain her works. He discovered that his past-generation outlook, muse, and talents were so affected that he began to write prose which indicated that he also was aware of chaos, the subconscious, and the modern manner.

Joyce, I suspect, was not taken in by the various adulatory kneelings of the *transition* group, but evidently Miss Stein believed completely that at last she was being understood and appreciated. It was heaven on earth for her to have a group of yes-men about her, and they not only listened to her word as holy but they devoted whole sections of *transition*—and many of them—to explaining her as she explained herself. In the meanwhile, the only intelligent reviews

I saw of Gertrude Stein's work were by Katherine Anne Porter, Ethel Moorhead, and myself. All unbeknownst to one another at the times of writing our various reviews, we insisted upon her child-repetitive and biblical or Hebraic-mother-inarticulate quality.

Nevertheless, *transition* had its place. Bright people learned what some had thought years back, that Joyce, great genius that he was, was the end of a method and of an epoch rather than the beginning. He had carried words *as words* as far as they could be carried, to a literary end. Younger writers were now released to explore new materials and newer phases of social and psychological and circumstantial qualities. Far from having said all about life, Joyce's genius was a provincial and limited one intellectually, as well as regarding types and phases of life. Because of this, it had tremendous intensity but was often too introspective. His father, Dedalus, Buck Mulligan, Molly Bloom, and the newspaper and library scenes in *Ulysses* saved that book from excessive introversion, at least in these passages; but his later *Work in Progress* went beyond the beyond. It was nice to hear him read it in that soothing "Irish tenor", but to read pages of that punning, sentimental-remembering, meandering-wondering about life-death-birth, naughty jokings and flippant obscenities, was quite beyond my capacity. Pound gave up on Joyce's new work completely. Bill Bird and I, among others, would glance at any new extract and chuckle at an allusion or a pun or witticism here and there, but the interest did not carry on through several pages of the book.

At all events, various writers began to simplify their styles and to return to subject matter. Among the French, there is Joseph Delteil, Drieu de la Rochelle, Louis Aragon (although he has gone French Communist), René Crevel, and a few others. Indeed it is quite possible that not much of contemporary importance in French literature came from either the Dadaists or the surrealists, and their passionate intergroup battles had long since ceased to be taken seriously. In America, Faulkner and others were returning to plot and drama, and also to being more sordid, in the name of realism, than Zola had ever dreamed of being. Faulkner does not allow his characters "delicacy" and "sensibility" at times, and Kay Boyle is overcome by the swooning moonlight of his precious moments to such an extent that she, often a fine writer in a sound sense, goes too, too fine for the ordinary mortal. Such writing strangely affects one as pretentious, and therefore vulgar or cheap.

transition, however, took them all in, good, bad, and indifferent. They published a few things of mine, Elliot Paul selecting one extract from an early novel in order to show what a lousy writer I was in relationship to the masterpieces in that issue of the magazine. After Paul and Jolas had separated, Jolas got unduly excited about two authentically simple and rather "sweet" tales of child life of mine, which he got through Kay Boyle, a staunch backer of my work. Aware of Elliot Paul's statement that he wanted to "show me up," I had not been keen to send *transition* any more of my work, and I did not think any of the editors good editors, or writers, or possessed of discrimination. Later Jolas was excited by my article on Joyce's *Work in Progress* and kept muttering, "Sensitive, very sensitive." Having been urged to write the article by Sylvia Beach and Joyce, I read it to Joyce to see if he would mind it. The wily Mr. Joyce saw that all the "he hopes he has done this or that" or "he endeavours to" phrases were legpulling.

Unlike as Stein and Joyce are as regards personality, mind, outlook, and writing, people *will* bracket them. They are as unlike as the North Pole is from the equator. Joyce knows words, their rhythms, colours, assonances, capacity to evoke, their histories, and their emotional significations. Stein fumbles and mauls them. Stein's wit is almost too quick and, around a limited range of experience, variable. He is not afraid of being unmasked, for he is sure of himself, and I have never known him to boast without immediately withdrawing the boast in a "what do we all know about it?" manner. That cannot be said about poor Gertrude. She boasts, and is hurt if her listener does not boost her boast. I have implied before that I do not think she actually believes deeply in her work.

Joyce, on the other hand, quite healthily admits his doubts. "Do you think I may be on the wrong track with my *Work in Progress?* Miss Weaver says she finds me a madman. Tell me frankly, McAlmon. No man can say for himself." When the Quinn collection of manuscripts was sold, *Ulysses* brought a surprisingly low price, but Joyce said resignedly, "Probably they are right. Who can say what the next generation will think of me? What do we think of the great men of the past generation?"

Now he declares he is tired of hearing about *Ulysses*. There has been too much said about the book. When I suggest that perhaps in *Dubliners* there is writing of his much more apt to last, he does not disagree but wonders also if he should not have developed that style of writing rather than going into words too entirely. It was his eyesight, his inability to keep on reading freely, his inability to drink much without paying too great a price, as regards his health; it was his poverty, and the war, that decided many things which relate to his style and approach to writing. Nevertheless his infatuation with words was born in him. For those who say that Joyce has put it all down about life and its various types, let it be said that several Americans and at least one Irish person stopped him completely. He could not understand the florid, noisy, and altogether baby-exuberant Flossie Martin. He had difficulty believing that such a person really existed, at least while he was sober. He came mildly to accept Miss Martin as something belonging to the theatre, and believed that she had not a bad heart. As long as he could connect her with stage comics, it was all right. But Joyce's manner towards women is that of an older day. He is formal, staid, dignified, and has never been known to call a woman by her first name. She is always Miss or Mrs. There is no easy familiarity of approach with Joyce, but as there is also no pomposity, and as he has a real sense of humour, his manner is fine for him. However staid, sedate, or earnest he may be, his humour operates because his reflexes are very quick.

I had known Hilaire Hiler since 1920, in those days when life was young and blood flowed warmly, and none of us ever thought of taking a whisky or brandy other than dry or in one gulp. Hiler is beautiful in his way, but you have to get used to that way, and people do, very quickly. I have never known anyone with his ability to learn languages, argot, and to get intimately friendly at once with people of all classes and types. He looks rather like a handsome frog: dark and sorrowful, with brooding eyes, a big mouth, wearing often a lugubrious expression which instantly suggests comedy and clowning. He knows his routines as well as any show trouper. He sings and plays the piano: blues, jazz, Trinidad Negro, cowboy, and French songs. He knows Yiddish recitations, and his burlesques of every type of dance would ensure him a success as a clowning comedian on the stage in any country. When he enters a bar room or a cabaret where he is utterly unknown, within a few minutes he will be getting laughs from all present. But I must soft-pedal all this because Hiler is not only a serious painter but a good one, and apart from that he at one time had as valuable a library on the history of costumes as any in the world. After writing a scholarly book on the history of raiment, he disposed of the library and was soon doing research for a book on the medium of paint.

By this time (around 1926–27) Hiler had decorated the Jockey and the Jungle, and was doing the College Inn, all of them at one time or another very popular night clubs. On one occasion, when we were doing the town together, I found myself dancing with a lady done up in purple draperies, and she murmured to me that she had read my novel, *Village,* and thought it wonderful. She felt I had really reported American life amongst the young and lively. Would I write her autobiography for her? Sure I would, and without even asking who she was. When we got outside Hiler informed me it was Isadora Duncan. This was my first close-up of Isadora, and I did not know that she was asking everybody anywhere she found herself to write her autobiography. Who finally did it, I don't know. (Isadora was not the only person to speak of her love for my work who, the more she talked, the more I knew she hadn't read it.)

I never felt myself an expatriate or anything but an American, although not through excess of patriotism. My country is much too polyglot of race, type, and variety of faith, political and otherwise, for me to discover exactly to which qualities one would have to remain loyal in order to be a hundred per cent American. I had left America because of events and had never been, and am not now, romantic about Europe.

Nevertheless in Sweden several of my short stories had been translated and published in journals there; likewise in Italy and France. Carlo Linati, the Italian critic and author, translated some of my stories himself and spoke of my work as the most American of American writing. Antoine Goldet, a French woman attorney, had translated four of my books simply because they interested her, and other French commentators found me most American when writing of our land.

I decided to have a look at that land and boarded a Royal Mail boat going to Los Angeles. Incidentally, it was my suggestion that I felt my marriage was not a go. It represented to me more things that I did *not* want in life than I could cope with.

Kay Boyle

1928

During the May and June I wrote the memoirs of the Dayang Muda of Sarawak. The writing itself went rapidly enough once the bare facts of her life had been drawn, sentence by hesitant sentence, from this tall, blonde, passive, and strangely inarticulate Princess whose mind appeared to function in a state of shock. And this was quite possibly the case, for she who was armoured with shyness, and stubbornly generous with everything she owned, once told me with no sign of emotion that her hair had turned white overnight when her husband took her six children from her and made them wards of court. Exactly when this had taken place it was difficult to know, for her valiant attempts to relive the memories of all she had been, or had not been, served no purpose except to stun her into silence. Her childhood had been a fabulously rich one, with a thousand dolls, and sheepdogs and collie dogs, and ponies and horses. ("*Had* there been ponies?" I would ask; and after a long silence she would say: "Yes, surely there *must* have been ponies, don't you think?") Her girlhood had reached its zenith in her presentation at Court. Like the faces and titles and nationalities of her endless admirers, everything was dimmed and blurred, and the meaning of life itself somehow effaced, by the charm and grace and beauty of her mother, who had married Mr. Palmer of biscuit company fame. This union had obviously been beneath her mother's station, for, whatever the compensations, she had married into trade.

But how could the Dayang Muda be expected to recall the details of a life that had actually never been hers? Whatever she had been was so overshadowed by her mother's attributes that only the outsized albums of photographs remained, like the pieces of a jigsaw puzzle, to give the past a coherency. Lord Kitchener, George Meredith, and half a dozen other famous men had, it was more or less clear, at one time or another paid homage (if not court) to Mrs. Palmer before she chose the biscuit king. This the Princess was almost certain of; and also that Mr. Palmer had named a tea biscuit after George Meredith; and that Lord Kitchener had sent her mother a special message by British Intelligence before the Battle of Jutland; and that Oscar Wilde was a constant visitor at the house. But the events (not to mention the emotions) of the Princess' own life had been reduced to names and dates, their significance lost, obliterated, in some year and by some occurrence that she could not at the moment recall. It was therefore necessary to invent the story as one went along, and she herself was as entranced as it unfolded as Archie and I were. For all her desperate striving, she could not tell us what had happened in their stupendous home in Reading, or at Ascot Heath, or in the palace of Sarawak, or in her heart, so it was Archie and I who reconstructed for her what had perhaps never taken place.

Of her munificence, and of her speechless longing for love, there can be no question. But although I lived in close and tender intimacy with this aphonic and lonely woman, who smoked cigarette after cigarette in a long holder as she stubbornly and hopelessly racked her brains for memories, there is no one in the world whom I ever knew less about. Frantically, tragically behind that impregnable British (and only incidentally royal) armour, she was asking anyone who came and went in the room, or came and went in her life, to give her a description, however inadequate, of her own reality. It was this need (and Archie's urgings) that had made a Catholic of her some months before, and she and Archie had even had an audience with the Pope; and it was this that would, in the months ahead, when the literary life in Paris had somehow failed, make her a convert to Mohammedanism.

My room was across the hall from hers in the luxurious Rue Louis David apartment. Every morning before breakfast my bath was drawn for me by the English maid, Bentley, and scented with my choice of bath salts. On the silver tray the French maid, Louise,[1]

---

[1] It was only after one French maid had been replaced by another, and then by another, in the course of time, that I realized the name "Louise" never changed.

brought to my bed at nine o'clock was a crystal goblet of orange
juice, a half grapefruit on Wedgwood china, a tall silver coffee-pot
engraved with the coat of arms and the crown of Sarawak, black
caviar, imported marmalade, and melba toast, laid out on cut-glass
dishes fine as a spider's web. On the white linen napkin, as on the
towels, pillowcases, and sheets, the crown of Sarawak was magnificently embroidered, forever emitting rays like those of the setting
sun. At least one morning in the week (before I would begin
typing out the notes on the Princess' life, extracted from her with
difficulty the previous day), she would go through her wardrobe of
haute couture outfits and delete from it those she no longer wished to
wear. Then the modest dressmaker around the corner (with whom
Sharon was boarding) would be summoned to pin to my size and
alter the dresses and suits, the coats and fur-lined cloaks, from the
collections of Lanvin, and Paul Poiret, and Molyneux.

Archie had his bachelor's quarters on another floor, and there he
wrote his poetry and received his friends. He had written a group of
poems to Michael, which Ethel Moorhead published in the third
number of *This Quarter*, and in answer to them I had written a group
of poems "To Archibald Craig", which Jolas now accepted for the
September number of *transition*. Archie had been with me through
the weeks of Michael's dying, and he knew of the vow of fidelity to
his memory that I had taken, and now when we walked in the Bois
de Boulogne on these May and June afternoons, pushing Sharon in
her baby carriage, we talked of Michael and of Carnevali, and
Archie spoke lines of their poetry as we walked. Soon it would be
two years since Michael had died, and perhaps Carnevali would
soon have to die, and we wanted to go to Italy, to Bazzano, and
talk with him while he was still alive. When we made plans for the
future like this, Archie would take the handle of the baby coach
from me, and he would push Sharon firmly through the rose gardens
of the Bagatelle, past the lambent fountains, adjusting the hood so
that neither the blowing spray nor the sun would touch her face. It
was as if he had seized the future possessively, and he, so delicate
in his pastel outfits, with chain bracelets on his narrow wrists,
would ask me if I thought the passers-by would take him for the
father of the child. He called her "The Kidney", and he could not
bear to touch her, but it was through his forethought and at his

---

This made it easier for the Princess, Bentley said, for what did it matter to anyone
what the real names of these Frenchwomen were?

instigation that she and I were there. Everything for Sharon and me was taken care of through his arranging and through the Dayang Muda's generosity.

We printed handsome announcements for our poetry yearbook, and Archie put them up in the cafés of the Quarter, and in the bookshops of the Right Bank, and in Sylvia Beach's, where, having met her, he found an excuse to drop in every day. He felt certain that, once I had finished the memoirs and the book was actually in the hands of an English publisher, he could persuade the Princess to bring out our yearbook with a French printer—perhaps with McAlmon's printer, I said. But Archie always fell silent when I mentioned this man he had never clapped eye on. He resented McAlmon's book, *Distinguished Air*,[2] which Bob had subtitled *Grim Fairy Tales*, and which Bill Bird had brought out in a limited edition. We agreed that we would devote a section of the yearbook to Carnevali's poetry, and although I intended to have a selection of McAlmon's poems, too, I waited to speak of this. One of Archie's rules concerning the anthology was that he didn't want to print anyone he was afraid of; he said no editor should be afraid of his contributors; and I answered that all publishers, all editors, are afraid of the good artists they publish, and I still believe this is true.

Archie, this little Scotsman whom I called my brother, was the one who gave a direction to the Dayang Muda's existence; but his own existence from the point of view both of health and of moral conviction, was precarious. He could not decide whether he should become a priest and withdraw from the material world completely, or whether he should emulate the career of Jean Cocteau. In the meantime his suave manipulation of his cousin out of the sphere of the biscuit company, and the sphere of royalty, into the aura of artistic celebrities was a masterly performance. Following the evening at the Jolases', he had lost no time in calling on Gertrude Stein, and he had invited her and Alice Toklas to the Rue Louis David to tea. He reported that Gertrude Stein had expressed herself as delighted to have the opportunity of meeting the Princess of Sarawak, and I read aloud portions of *The Making of Americans* to the Princess so that she would have some preparation for the great day. Before their arrival the Princess was lost in speculation as to whether or not American

[2] McAlmon wrote of it: "At any rate the stories did deal with variant types with complete objectivity, not intent on their 'souls' and not distressed by their 'morals'. "

writers as a class could be counted on to come out of "the top drawer". Robert Sage, who had appeared in time for lunch one day, seemed to qualify, but Whit Burnett, Eugene Jolas, and Elliot Paul, who had dropped in on separate occasions, were relegated to the second, or even the third drawer. The Princess' mother's literary friends had, of course, all come out of the top drawer; but then, she added, they had been English. When I asked her how many drawers there were, she did not answer; and when I said the top drawer was always for handkerchiefs and gloves, she looked straight ahead into a vista that I could never manage to see. One afternoon late in May we watched from the fifth-floor balcony as the famous Stein Ford chugged up the incline of the Passy street and stopped below in the shadow of the marquee.

Except for Alice Toklas and Archie, we were stricken with shyness as we sat awkwardly down in the salon. Our faces were fixed in the various grimaces of it, our hands twisted into strange shapes by it, our feet monstrously out of place, and Gertrude Stein was perhaps the most uneasy of us all. She nervously touched the short hair at her temples and forehead, shyly, shyly, seeking the means to guide this anomalous company into some familiar channel. Alice Toklas and Archie maintained a civilized chatter of amenities, but with every word that was spoken or not spoken Gertrude Stein's authority slipped further and further away until it seemed beyond reprieve. The Princess clung like the drowning to the length of the cigarette holder gripped in her jaws, and once I had mentioned the graciousness of the weather to Gertrude Stein, and she had quickly agreed, with a fleeting, nervous smile, I could think of nothing more to say. I could have asked how her Ford was running, and told her I had had one like it in Cincinnati, only perhaps not exactly the same model, and said that once it had happened that, going around a corner fast, my father, sitting beside me in the front seat, had gone flying out. Or I could have mentioned the doctor in Bryn Mawr who had to be taken upstairs to bed. But all this would be bringing the conversation back to myself, I thought, to *me*. I could have asked her what she meant on page nine of her "An Elucidation" which *transition* had published in April as a supplement, because of the many mistakes the printer had made in its original appearance, but my tongue was dry in my mouth, and I could not speak. Bentley came in with the tea wagon, and she stooped to place a fine satin cushion under Gertrude Stein's gondola-shaped shoes, and Miss

Stein obligingly swung her feet up high, and smiled even more nervously as she brought them down.

What in the world am I doing here, she must have sat asking herself in increasing outrage with the situation; what in the world? She glanced from my face to the Dayang Muda's and back again to mine, smiling, smiling like the shyest of children, but surely within her she was racked by hideous questions as she fumbled and fiddled with the monogrammed silver and the serviette burdened with the Sarawak crown. Had she come across town for the mere sake of the title, I asked myself in awful despair of ever being able to speak aloud again; or because she believed that a coterie of Archies would form a half-circle at her feet (while she formed the other half), asking nothing of life but to hear her say: "I can explain visiting. I can explain how it happened accidentally. I can explain that fortunately no explanation was necessary?" She must have been asking herself, in her own shrewd, sly version of truth and consequences, what in the name of literature she was doing here, as she nervously, nervously ate first a chocolate éclair and then a baba au rhum. Why she had put herself at this disadvantage, no one could possibly say.

Then the doorbell rang, and the miracle happened. Once Bentley had answered its summons, she returned to the salon followed by a barelegged, grey-haired man in a white, woven tunic. "Monsieur Raymond Duncan," she murmured in the direction of the Dayang Muda, and Archie jumped quickly to his feet.

"When I met you last week, you said I should stop in for tea one day," Raymond Duncan said to Archie; and he added so openly, with such disarming frankness: "I love all kinds of pastry—and as I happened to be passing by, here I am!"

He was a man of fifty or so, lean and muscular, neat and scrupulously well kept, with his long hair pinned in silky grey braids in a crown around his small, eagle-like head. One end of his elegant tunic was flung across his left shoulder, and his bare feet, in the simplest of thonged sandals, were immaculately clean. (I was later to learn that this tunic was his special tunic for social occasions, and therefore it was doubtful if he had been accidentally passing by the Princess' door.) He was of the same flesh and bone as Carl Sandburg, I thought at once, and thin as a lath. His palm was like rock to the touch when one shook hands with him, and the hands themselves were spread square from the kind of work he had perhaps always done. He spoke with the flat twang of a Midwestern farmer, and his corded, lean neck was that of a man who has worked in the fields or on the sea. As he sat down in a fine armchair near the Dayang Muda, he had some of the dignity of a Roman emperor, and no matter what drawer he had come out of, she seemed quite interested to see him there.

As for Gertrude Stein, she was a transformed woman. His entrance had jerked her back in time to the town where they had grown up together, and she was chuckling so with laughter that even Alice Toklas looked at her in mild surprise. "You weren't much when you were up at bat, Raymond!" Gertrude Stein chortled. And "You weren't too good yourself at home runs," Raymond said not quite so pleasantly. How many years ago it had all taken place they did not want to remember, and they could not decide when it was that they had come to Europe on the same steamer. "You were such a fop, such a dandy, Raymond!" Gertrude Stein said, almost choking with laughter. "The crease in his trousers—it had to be *just so!*" she cried out in real joy. "Oh, Raymond, Raymond, who would think it to look at you now!" she said, with all of her shyness dropped away.

It ill befitted a Roman emperor to give ear to this kind of recognition, and Raymond sought to introduce more agreeable subjects, such as his colony in Neuilly. But Gertrude Stein was far too diverted by this unexpected visitant from the long-dead past to relinquish a moment of her delight. Raymond spoke of the goats that were herded, their bells ringing, through the alleys and by-ways of Paris early every morning, telling the Princess that the children in his colony would go out with their wooden bowls to drink the fresh milk that the goatherd would draw for them from the udders of his flock. "Oh, Raymond, Raymond!" Gertrude Stein said with another chuckle, her whole body shaking with laughter. "I remember when you used to drink sherry! I remember when you didn't mind at all having a glass of wine!" Goat's milk, my eye! she might have been saying as she sat with the gondolas of her shoes stamping her gusto out on the satin cushion under her feet. Now that she had the upper hand, she wasn't going to let him go. She remembered too that, before he was Greek, he used to wear carnations in his buttonhole and smoke long cigars. "You have an excellent memory, Gertrude," Raymond said, smiling grimly at her; "probably due to the fact that you keep repeating things over and over." At this moment Alice Toklas glanced at her watch, exclaimed at the lateness of the hour, and reminded Gertrude Stein of a dinner engagement they had in Fontainebleau.

I had become such a lady, such a bloomin', perfect lady, with my grand cast off clothing from royalty, and my caviar for breakfast, and the proletariat was somehow eking out an existence without me being anywhere around. I'd ask the four corners of the room at night what had happened to the world of Lola being trampled under the hoofs of a policeman's horse; and Mother, a little girl in the humblest of homes on the Kansas prairies, carrying the hot glass chimney of an oil lamp across the room, and not setting it down; and the world of a man in prison saying that as long as there was a lower class he was of it. One morning there was a small poem from Carnevali in the mail, a very foolish poem, he said, but the words of it were to me accompaniment to all I could not say.

> I bring you simple daisies and buttercups,
> But that is very little,

went the pure untroubled lines of Carnevali's poem;

> For there is nothing simpler than your ways.
> I bring you love but that is very little,
> Because I have squandered so much love in my life.
> I can bring you nothing big, nothing great. I'm a poor
>   bereaved poet,
> I have only words to offer,
> And to call you a dear is a very little thing,
> You who are dearest of all.

What had happened to my simplicity, I asked myself, I who was now writing not about the things I believed in but about the head-hunters of Sarawąk, who placed the severed heads of their victims, some grinning, some with the corners of their mouths drawn down, as architectural decoration along the cornices of their homes?

July and August 1928, I cannot bear to remember you now. It was then that the ego took over like a madman, like a rabid fox, a runaway horse dragging its fallen rider by one foot twisted in the stirrup; the well-bred ego that had been kept in hand for a quarter of a century now took the bit in its teeth, kicked over the traces, set love at naught, wet its whistle, and liked it so well that it spliced the main brace, blew loud as the wind, and finally fell on evil days. But before this is mentioned, two or three things of value must be set down. The first is my friendship with Jolas, which no words can adequately define. Camus has written that the artist's life is a search for the way back to the few great simple truths he knew at the beginning. That is the search Gene was on, and after we met he took me with him—as friend, never anything less or more than friend—from the time we met until his death in 1951.

In May, when Gene would come up from Colombey to collect manuscripts at the office of *transition*, to discuss contributions with the other editors, and to confer with Joyce, we would meet for at least one meal a day. We might have lunch in a brasserie, or at Ferrari's in the Avenue Rapp, for Gene had all the gusto of the European for an excellent lunch as well as a fine dinner. Nora and James Joyce joined us twice for lunch at Ferrari's; and once when lunching there with Gene, who had Laura Riding and Robert Graves as his guests, I took exception to their intellectual stance and finished my lunch alone at another table. I was ashamed of this for a long time afterwards. (Once the Italian *patron* of Ferrari's asked me what my blind friend with the cane did for a living; and once at lunch this blind friend, who was Joyce, spoke of McAlmon's story, "Miss Knight", one of the stories in *Distinguished Air*, saying he thought very highly of it, and that it had been at his suggestion that it was translated into French and published here.) But more often Gene and I met for the apéritif before dinner at the Place de l'Alma on the Right Bank, after my work on the Princess' memoirs was finished for the day. We would dine with whomever Gene felt like seeing, sometimes in the Quarter, sometimes at Lipp's on the Boulevard St. Germain; sometimes with Soupault, or Desnos, or Marcel Noll, or Tristan Tzara, or Robert Sage, or Derain, or Aragon, and sometimes with none of them, for Gene had his dark moments of impatience with the greater part of humanity. Like Carnevali, he was haunted by the memories of poverty in America, where he first made his living as a grocery boy in Brooklyn; and haunted too by his memories of police brutality during the Palmer raids of 1920, when he was a reporter in Waterbury, Connecticut. At times a look of childlike terror and total incomprehension would come across his face as he spoke haltingly, almost stuttering, of the breaking down of doors and the rounding up of men as they assembled peaceably. Such were the stories he had covered in 1920, and he still could not bear the thought of what had taken place.[3]

Gene was modest, genial, gregarious, and loquacious in three languages, and he was as well one of the best listeners I have ever known. All his gifts were of unique proportions, but the ability to listen intelligently was a tremendous, an outsized gift. He would give an ear with reverence (as did I) to Soupault speaking of Rimbaud, and Baudelaire, and Lautréamont as the three men who had started the undermining of the throne on which French literature sat so pompously. Lautréamont had been published in translation in *Broom*, and I knew a little of his quality. But it was Soupault who made me see the actual vision of him "shrieking, howling in the desert" because he was afraid that literature, LITERATURE, would get him and finally smother him. For the public, the critics, always have their own way of dealing with great men, Soupault went on saying: Baudelaire was looked on as ailing, spiritually sick; and Rimbaud as a destroyer whom it was not safe to have around; and Lautréamont—for Lautréamont the public, the critics, reserved the best dismissal of all. They ignored him completely. But still these three men had brought about an upheaval, a furious tempest, in French letters, Soupault said, such as had never been seen before or since. "And there are even some," he added bitterly, "who insist to this day that the tempest never took place!"

There were evenings when Pascin would sit down for a moment with us, always elegant, vital, restless, inevitably on his way to somewhere else, speaking of the look of the evening beyond the *terrasse* as if speaking of a desirable woman's flesh. All that Pascin said of painting would stir Gene to genial argument, and he would say:

[3] In *A James Joyce Miscellany*, published by the James Joyce Society in 1957, Maria Jolas writes of Gene: "Eugene Jolas was the eldest of eight children of poor, devoutly Catholic parents who lived in a little town on the Franco-German frontier. Although he was actually born in the United States, his parents' return to Europe when he was two years old made him linguistically and intellectually a European, as he only returned to America when he was fifteen. German, then French, then English—this was the order of his linguistic evolution, to which Greek and Latin had been added quite early for, like Joyce, he was the object of especial attention on the part of the Catholic pedagogues, and he actually did spend two years in the Seminary in Metz. Being himself convinced that he did not have the vocation to become a priest, he was taken out of the seminary at the age of fourteen and before he was sixteen, he left for America. There the direst, most sordid poverty and loneliness, plus a sense of violent revolt against both the Church and society drove him to the need for alcoholic oblivion, that he and Joyce shared till the end."

"Even you, Pascin, even you as an artist will have to arrive at a complete denial of the surface of what appears to be reality or else you will have to cease to paint." Although it was summer, Pascin usually wore a handsome black felt hat, with a snap brim, and at times very good leather gloves, buttoned at the wrists, and pleated shirts, even his way of dressing the most exquisite refinement of depravity. The charm of his manner had nothing to do with the restless grief in his eyes; his urgent hospitality, so his worldliness and wit kept insisting, had no possible connection with what solitude might eventually have the power to do. "*Jamais de la vie, mon cher Gene,*" he would say, his eye turned sharp for the beauty of any woman passing. "The moment of ejaculation cannot be abstracted," he said one evening. Then he smiled, and stood up, and he set his hat at a better angle, and scrupulously paid for his drink before he left. But when I think of him now it is not this Pascin that I see but the one hanging dead in his studio with the words "*Pardon,* Lucie", written in his own blood on the wall.

Desnos, whom Jolas called "an iconoclast of the imagination" and "one of the hopes of French literature", was another who came to sit and talk with Gene and the others at our table. Desnos was one of the original surrealist group, and it was from his novel, *La Liberté ou l'amour,* published in Paris the year before, that my first tentative understanding of surrealism had come. Parts of this book appeared in *transition,* translated by Gene, and there are paragraphs of Desnos's surreal vision that I have carried with me and cannot forget. Chapter One begins:

Robert Desnos

Born in Paris, July 4, 1900
Died in Paris, December 13, 1924
the day he wrote these lines.[4]

---

[4] Noble Desnos, this was a *blague,* this recording of your death. For years I knew your eyes like those of a great brown moth, and your brown suit, as transparent from wear as a moth's threadbare wing. You were twenty-eight then, and you lived to become a metaphor for a totally unconceived France, and to die in agony for that France on your way back from German concentration camps. You were not permitted to fulfil the promise as "one of the hopes of French literature", but there was one more eternal moment written in the history of that literature when the great and the humble of Paris kneeled in the streets outside St. Germain des Prés (kneeling in homage even on the terrace of the Deux Magots) the day of your funeral, of the burying of the handful of bones that were left, in 1945, of all you were.

. . . I assure you that this was an astonishing period of my life, one during which each nocturnal minute marked the carpet of my room with a new imprint: a strange mark which sometimes made me shiver. How many times, in stormy weather or by moonlight, I arose to contemplate by the gleam of a wood fire, or the light of a match or that of a glowworm, these memories of women who had come to my bed, wholly nude save for their stockings and high-heeled shoes, retained through regard for my desire, and more unsettled than a parasol found by a steamboat in the middle of the Pacific. . . . My door, then, was wide open to mystery, but the latter entered, closing it behind her, and henceforth I heard, without a word being spoken, an immense tramping, that of a crowd of nude women assailing the keyhole. . . . The multitude of their Louis XV heels made a noise comparable to a wood fire in the chimney, to fields of ripe wheat, to clocks at night in deserted rooms, to a strange breathing next to one's face on the same pillow.

Meanwhile, I turned into the Rue des Pyramides. Wind wafted the leaves torn from the trees of the Tuileries, and these leaves fell with a soft noise. They were gloves, gloves of all kinds, kid gloves, suède gloves, long lisle gloves. . . . From time to time, heavier than a meteor at the end of its course, a boxing glove fell. The crowd trampled these souvenirs of kisses and embraces without giving them the deferent attention they merited. I alone avoided bruising them. Sometimes I even picked up one of them. It thanked me with a soft embrace. I felt it tremble in the pocket of my trousers. . . .

There were late afternoons when Gene and I would drive through the Bois in a victoria, with Sharon sitting on my lap, and then he would recite in German the poetry of Rilke, and in French the poetry of Apollinaire. One evening we drove by moonlight in the Bois, and Gene intoned Heine's "Dichterliebe", and the "Winterreise", which Mother had often sung to me. But our sentimentality, our romanticism, was without gesture or glance, belonging as it did to those who—through death or temporary absence—were grievously not there. Gene revealed a quite new time and place to me, another climate, very different from that of William Carlos Williams or of Ernest Walsh, and one that was in total opposition to McAlmon's universe and conjecturings. It was a time and place, and a climate, in which I was far from at ease. The determined exploration of the subconscious on which Jolas insisted did not seem to me one of the essential actions of creative life. I did not want to write with a definite sense of procedure. Perhaps I was afraid to question where my—or any—writing was coming from and where it was going in the end. I just wanted it to be. I was not at all sure, listening to Gene talk, that the "dual reality of dream and life" could alone liberate the static forms of literature. But I did believe with him in Freud's concept of continuous creativity as a tradition that runs always parallel to the materialistic, bourgeois tradition; and I knew then, as I know now, that if Western civilization is not finally to crumble into corporeal dust, it must be the tradition of the artist, the creator, that outweighs the other and prevails.

Gene had been pulled in three quite different ways in his life by three different languages, three ethoses, and three national memories. If Valéry and Blake, Baudelaire and Poe had all had a part in shaping his awareness, still Schiller and Fichte had moulded him as well, and, for that matter, all the philosophers of the Storm and Stress and Romantic movement had touched him deeply, men whose minds were as strange to me as an unfamiliar music score. In the long years of our friendship I dedicated two books to Gene, in one dedication quoting his words (which had seemed at times like an admonition to me): "Follow the voice that booms in the deepest dream, deeper go, always deeper. . . ."

Gene's response to women was Latin in its eloquence, and his sense of camaraderie with men, his need for the stimulus of their talk, his earnest curiosity about their minds and hearts, was almost German, but not quite. His passion for justice was democratic and entirely without nationality; his humour was at times disturbingly American (which may be explanation for his publishing the senseless doggerel about exiles in *transition* that year). Genial he was, but if wounded or outraged by an irresponsible statement about poetry, or politics, or love, he would rush from the café or restaurant and leap into a taxi, abandoning the subject he had had enough of and the faces he no longer wished to see. His deepest commitment, the commitment of his blood, was to the culture and ratiocination of France; for Lorraine was French in spirit, its underground language was French, and Gene's grandmother had been jailed after 1870 for the crime of speaking that illicit tongue. Yet he was deeply influenced by Goethe (who has said, incidentally, in a hundred

different ways that the living roots of man are in the unconscious) ;
but how German was Goethe, anyway, Gene would ask me,
insisting that I answer; but I could not.

Archie made a great business of letting me know that McAlmon
was in Paris. Sylvia Beach had told him, and wasn't it really
strange, he said, that such a good and devoted friend of mine had not
taken the trouble to find out where I was? Whatever I had thought
before coming to Paris, it was clear to me now that McAlmon
frequented other bars and restaurants than did Jolas and the
surrealists, probably with intention, and apparently met with quite
other friends. He was not at the Bal Nègre when Jolas took me
there one midnight to meet two new acquaintances of his, Caresse
and Harry Crosby; and he was not in the shooting galleries of the
fête on the Champs de Mars, or in the crazy bumping cars there the
night Gene and Noll and Kisling and I rode in them; nor was he at
the Russian fortune-teller's—a dark-eyed lady of royal lineage,
wearing a pearl-embroidered headdress, who told one's fortune
across a tray of fire—when Gene and André Breton took me there
one day. But one night McAlmon walked into Lipp's, searching
from face to face across the crowded tables, and if his cold eye gave a
sign of recognition when he saw me, or even if he saw me, I could
not tell. He did not turn his head again in our direction, and I got
up and left the others and went to where he stood alone at the bar,
beginning to drink a beer. "Bob," I said, unable for the moment to
think of anything more to say. He scarcely turned his head, but he
put the francs for the unfinished beer down on the counter. "Come
on," he said. "Let's go up to Le Grand Ecart. There may be some
lively people there."

Robert McAlmon

1928-1929

Lady Brett of *The Sun Also Rises* had acquired an American boy friend, much younger than she, and they discovered a huge bare studio on the Rue Broca. They couldn't afford to pay what the French call the *reprise*, or to buy the few bits of furniture left by the former occupant, so I took it on a year's lease, installed my books and excess baggage, and went off on a motor trip to Spain with Bill and Sally Bird. I was to go on to the south of France for the summer, and then upon my return was to have the studio, while they would pay me rent for the months they occupied it. I didn't entertain any false hopes, however, and the rent of the studio was very little.

Of the various "ladies" who were on the loose in Paris, Lady Brett was the most imitated, the least witty or amusing, and she could switch to acting "her Ladyship" at most dangerous moments. Once in an apache dive in the Rue de Lappe, in company with her boy friend, she decided she was insulted when asked to dance by one of that quarter's toughs. A taxi driver kept the boy friend from getting a knife in the back. Lady Brett was also much given to that "one of us" and "people of our class" and "we don't let each other down" palaver which many English make use of while in the process of letting everybody down. Poor Lady Brett was entirely a product of London and England and she had nothing to do with the spirit of Montparnasse.

Jimmie, the barman of the Dingo, began writing his memoirs, and chose as title *This Must Be the Place*.[1] This is how it came about. A

---
[1] *This Must Be the Place*, by James Charters.

dignified lady drove up in her car and stopped before a Montparnasse bar. As she and her lady friend were alighting, Flossie Martin came out of the bar exuberantly shouting the kind of language she loved to use, because, as she declared, being a virgin she simply had to have some outlet. The lady driver turned to her friend and said, "This must be the place."

An unidentified letter writer to the Paris edition of the Chicago *Tribune*, who signed himself simply R.A., wrote of Flossie that after an hour's conversation with her he would feel "absolutely happy and sublimated".

> If I happened to be in a blue funk [he wrote], instead of going to the Folies-Bergères, I would make a special trip from my luxurious Etoile quarters to the Dôme, where I was sure to find Florence as gay and exuberant as ever. . . . I always compared her to a sea breeze or a fireworks display or anything else that struck me as being refreshing and enlivening. I loved to observe the rubicundity of her cheeks heighten with each new compliment I paid her. Each cheek was a rose, and each rose a rapture, as one of her many admirers was wont to say of her. . . . I recall the memorable occasion when I first had the pleasure of meeting her. . . . I was with Sinclair Lewis, and Florence was on her best behaviour, as effervescent as I ever found her later. After the usual, so to speak, exchange of formalities. she began telling us how glad she was to have discarded her Ziegfeld spangles and to be in Paris. "XYZ. . . . . !!! . . . . ." she said. ". . . . . ???!!! PQR. . . . . ?!?!?!? . . . . . !!!!!! . . . . . ARTHARODEST. . . . . !!!!!!" Such conversational prowness I am sure neither Lewis nor myself had previously experienced. ". . . . . !! . . . . . ODIN. . . . . THR. . . . ." Florence continued. "!!!!!! . . . . . ??? . . . . . HMRF WKN . . . . . !?!?!?." I have often thought of that remarkable assertion, and I believed then, as I do now, that no one who had not the liberal-mindedness and freedom of spirit of Florence Martin could have ventilated such an original idea in the circumstances. Lewis agreed with me about that some three or four days later, after he had weighed the matter and decided to put her in a book.

In Nice were two Canadian boys from Montreal whom I had

known in Paris when they spent a year in the Quarter. They had discovered an Italian tea room *pension*, and the compact little apartment above it the proprietor let the three of us have, charging for it and the meals very low *pension* rates. The rooms faced the sea, and the beach was not a minute's walk away. We settled in, Buffy Glasco and Graeme Taylor and I, and each of us was writing: Graeme a family novel, I a thing called "The Politics of Existence", which is still going on, and Buffy some memoirs. He was then eighteen, and much the oldest, most ironic and disillusioned of the three of us. Graeme, who was a bit older and had been his chum since childhood, was a close second. The doorway between their room and mine was left open, and I could hear the clatter of their typewriters, which helped me to work and concentrate, as it had in the old reporting and advertising copy writing days.

When I eventually got back to Paris it took more than gentle suggestions to get Lady Brett and her boy friend out of my studio, and once they were out I found it needed new plumbing, and a cleaning such as it had never needed in its earlier phases, I am sure. Down the hall lived Gwen Le Gallienne, a half sister of Eva, and Yvette Ledoux; and across the street Hilaire Hiler had his studio. Not far away was a brewery with a huge beer hall and a good restaurant attached. Mornings, Gwen and Yvette often tapped at my door to know to what degree I was alive, and on occasion went out and got lamb chops, eggs, bread, vegetables, and wine or beer, and prepared a breakfast-lunch for us.

By 1928 Kay Boyle was in Paris, and like most others, not too well supplied with money, and had an infant daughter to look after. She stayed for some time with the Dayang Muda of Sarawak, who called herself "Princess". She was the sister-in-law of Sir Charles Brooks, white Rajah of the kingdom of Sarawak, which is in the northern part of the Malay island of Borneo; and she was mother of the heir apparent. Ford Madox Ford insisted, when she appeared at his parties, that she be called Mrs. Brooks, and doubtless he knew the protocol about titles better than we did. Later this Princess had herself baptized a Mohammedan in a special ceremony, flying from London to Paris. She believed religion to be too spiritual and ethereal a matter for anything so mundane as entering the faith on the ground. Before that, she had visited the Pope in Rome and had been made a Catholic. She talked of writing her memoirs, and a volume of memoirs supposedly written by her eventually did appear, but we won't be indiscreet about who wrote them. We'll just say that two very bright-witted Canadian lads, and one American authoress, and myself did a great deal of chuckling together as we invented witty remarks which great men of the 1890s, or thereabouts, had made. It might be added that Oscar Wilde, George Meredith, and others who had been friends of the Dayang Muda—but particularly Wilde—did need a few new epigrams given them. The old ones were too dated and well known.

Kay managed to have a home in her capacity of secretary to the Princess, but naturally she was restless. For a time she was saleswoman for the Raymond Duncan shops in the Rue St. Honoré and the Boulevard St. Germain, and she managed to sell quantities of his hand-woven rugs, tunics, draperies, etc. She didn't get a percentage, however; only a small salary, but then Raymond Duncan was never a practical man. What could money mean to him when it was Kay who needed it? But Kay was also writing short stories, and Caresse and Harry Crosby published a book of them. They were by no means as good as some she has done since, but they helped her to get recognition from more commercial publishers, and certainly in those days events for Kay were too hectic for the soundest writing.

Raymond Duncan had always liked good-looking and bright young people, and art and poetry, but, unlike Isadora, Raymond does not approve of drink. He thought people in the Quarter drank altogether too much, and through Kay he invited us to his colony in Neuilly for an evening. We were to get drunk on joy, primitive Greek dishes, and a punch which Raymond prepared. He put spices and fruit into this concoction to make us believe that it contained alcohol. But the word spread like wildfire through the Quarter that Raymond was giving a party, and without liquor. The French knew it, the Russians and Poles and Serbs knew it, and the Americans and English knew it. About forty people turned up at the party and several of them brought bottles of gin and brandy, which they concealed beneath the hall table. Raymond was very happy. We were all drunk, and apparently on his punch.

Raymond Duncan talked with Robert Desnos, the French surrealist poet, but poor Raymond was not contemporary in his knowledge of Paris writing groups. He mentioned his love for Cocteau's poetry.

"If Cocteau were here I would kill him in a second," Desnos said being true to type as the passionate poet of his group. Raymond was taken aback. "Now, now, Monsieur Desnos," Bill Bird said dryly. "You wouldn't really kill poor Cocteau just like that! Think of his poor mother." Raymond's guests decided that he was not a bad old thing, and that his long hair done in coils about his head and his draperies were all exhibitionism done in self-defence. He didn't want to be just Isadora's brother.

A party which Hilaire Hiler gave soon after was much more of a success. In a great empty hall, not far from the Lion de Belfort, Hiler and his father installed a long wooden table, tubs full of bottled beer on ice, and jugs full of a potent punch, and let the party rip wide open, although many particular invitations were given. Hiler *père* asked old-time vaudeville performers, and various people of the stage, and most of the French-English-American bohemian art world. Constance Bennett, not at the time a moving picture star, showed herself for a time, but except for a romantic collegiate noting the fact with an infatuated air, no one else knew.

The Swedish and Russian Ballets had been appearing in Paris about this time, and everybody felt called upon to become ballet dancers. In the huge vacant spaces of that hall, Florianne, our French beauty queen, executed various solo dances, Eastern, Chinese, or merely fluttery. Kiki was surrounded by a constant, but changing mob, as she sang vulgar French songs in her buxom Burgundian manner. Pascin and Kisling, Desnos, Nancy Cunard, Mary Reynolds, Marcel Duchamp, Brancusi, Kay Boyle, the Heyworth Millses, and whoever, sampled the drinks and the pastimes of various groups. An orchestra played steadily, but few people bothered dancing anything but solo, interpreting their own moods and the spirit of the beer or punch.

I was fancying myself as Nijinsky, demonstrating what long, flying jumps I could take, when suddenly I was accosted by an apparition who accused me of being just who I was. "You don't think your work significant, McAlmon," he said, "but it has no fearformulize moanings and wriggles no pretensifications."

Now this was not a costume ball, but I thought the man was in masquerade. He was long-faced and slightly Joycean in aspect, a distorted caricature of Joyce. One of his eyes looked this way and the other looked that, and I looked still another way, wondering if d.t.s had come upon me. Then the figure spoke again. "I am Lincoln Gillespie, and find you the only form packing, symbol-realisticator, tuckfunctioning moderncompactly." He had come upon me too suddenly for me to recover immediately. I had heard of him but certainly was not at the moment prepared to compete with him in using large words and adding several syllables to each of his self-formulations. I suggested a drink. Gillespie didn't mind that either and assured me, or so I understood, that he knew I was taken aback and didn't like him; but he also knew I was not a snootintellectualizer except for escaping dumbdoddered smudgeflattering cashaskers.

Later Lincoln Gillespie's tale was told me. At one time he had been a teacher of mathematics in a high school, but a truck had assailed him, knocking him momentarily unconscious and one of his eyes permanently agley. Someone had remarked that he had a head shaped slightly like Joyce's, and so Lincoln had grown a goatee and come to Paris. He took to writing, and sent his works to Eugene Jolas, who at once discovered Lincoln as a great new word inventor and stylist. Lincoln had always been interested in music, abstract discussion, and companionship. At one time, it is said, he gave a lecture at the American Women's Club in Paris, and explained the works of Joyce and Stein. He also described his encounter with the truck. Then, sagelike, he paused for a moment before proceeding with his explanation of the great writers. "And mind you," he confessed to the gaping audience of ladies, "I did not understand their work myself until after my accident."

Bill Bird came to see me one evening not looking so well, and soon explained. He had been out the night before with Mr. Joyce, and his story rang too true to experiences that I have had with Mr. Joyce. Joyce had had Bird and Sally to dinner with some others. Now Bird is knowledgeable about wines, having written a book on them and tested them for years. Mr. Joyce's preference, however, is for a horrible, sour concoction called "natural champagne". As usual at dinner, Mr. Joyce had said, "And you'll try this with me", to his guests. They submitted to the natural champagne. After the fourth bottle two of the ladies (according to Bird) could be seen pouring their wine into flowerpots, and later the ladies left, Sally among them. Bird and Mrs. Joyce remained, and Joyce insisted upon going on with the evening. But Nora by this time was putting up an argument. "Jim, do you hear me? You've had enough," she'd say. "Jim, I'm telling you, this has been going on for twenty years and I'll have no more of it. It's me that has to tend you when your eyes are giving you trouble and raising a nuisance for all of us. Jim, I'm telling you, I'll take the children and go back to Ireland. Mr. Bird, you see how it is. His eyes will be bothering him. Come on, Jim, be sensible for once in your life."

But Joyce would have more drink, and then insist on going to Fouquet's. Nora appealed to Bird, but Bird's persuasive powers did not affect Joyce's decision. It had been going on for twenty years or more, and for twenty years Nora had been threatening to leave him, but she didn't and I don't think ever would. At about five in the morning Bird managed to get Joyce into a taxi and they drove to Joyce's apartment. The apartment was five flights up and the elevator was not working. When helped out of the taxi, Joyce flopped. (I know that one too.) Bird, who is by no means a hefty individual, and who was a bit of a wreck from work and worry, carried him up the five flights and felt weak and trembling at the top. Once there, however, Joyce could stand up. He could even unlock the door of his apartment and enter. Once inside, he went into the bathroom, locked the door, and sulkily refused to come out.

Just before closing the bathroom door, however, he turned to Bird and said, "You see how it is, Bird. I have brought them through the war and now they threaten to leave me." At that moment Joyce was the martyr of the ages; the man who, as Jane Heap wrote, "had been crucified upon his sensibilities as no other." Nora pled; Bird argued and cajoled, but it was a quarter of an hour before Joyce would come out of the bathroom. "Mr. Bird, what are you to do with such a man?" said Nora. "And to think I have put up with him like this for all these years. What a damn fool his admirers would think me if they knew it all! He may be a genius to them, but look at him, what is he to me?"

In his early Paris days Mr. Joyce was very self-righteous about not drinking spirits, whisky, gin or beer, that "slimy drink". He was rather impatient that I could stand beer. However, as an Italian friend from Trieste had written of him, Joyce changed from a provincial into a man of the world during his Paris years—to an extent. At any rate now when he had gatherings at his house he served not only good wine but whisky and gin and all the elements necessary for a cocktail. His son Giorgio may have been partly responsible, but by now Joyce had come to conceive of other tastes in the world besides his own.

At one tea gathering he gave a reading of his *Anna Livia Plurabelle*. And here I must protest that although I drink, and have certainly mentioned drinking often enough in these pages, it isn't necessary that I be offered a drink on sight. In Los Angeles in 1927, visiting my mother, and in small towns away from the nervously upsetting and also stimulating contact of many people, I have gone for from a month to six weeks without a drink, not even beer. However, when I arrived at this gathering Joyce took me quietly aside and slipped me a glass, and indicated the whereabouts of a bottle of whisky. Perhaps he was right, and knew that one was about to be put to a severe test.

Mary and Padraic Colum, Hemingway, Bill and Sally Bird, Sylvia Beach, Stuart Gilbert—in all, some twenty people—were seated in the room, all of them as grave as owls. I didn't know the Colums, while the others I did know, or at least by sight. Joyce began reading, and the passage was deeply effective, read in that Irish tenor voice of his. In this passage, he had told me, was the word "peace" in twenty-nine languages, the names of hundreds of rivers on earth and a few in heaven and hell, and the passage was, moreover, melopoetic, to suggest night and the flowing of the river, the Liffy. (At the time Joyce told me he was studying a new foreign language, Lapland, or Eskimo, to develop his style and contribute to his word genius. I recalled a remark of Anatole France's when a man commented on his wonderful erudition. France smiled, saying, "Yes, *Le Petit Larousse.*" Joyce, too, smiled, liking the story and the insinuation. Would, one wonders, T. S. Eliot have done likewise? Joyce remarked that Huysmans also had his little methods for appearing to be startlingly erudite. But Joyce does actually possess a tremendous erudition and has besides a marvellous memory.)

The fact that Joyce had learned the word "peace" in so many languages didn't impress me any more than does the fact that the pattern of Joyce's *Ulysses* was taken from Homer's *Odyssey*. It is the emotional and sensitive rather than the erudite tour-de-force aspects which give Joyce's writing the greatness it possesses. It would be dull, inanimate, and pretentious if it were not that Joyce is full of sentiment, sentimentality, Irish wit and Irish twilight, even when he is most cruelly ironic. And now he read this passage of his work in progress in a way that gave it its full emotional value. It was night, night, night, life haunting me with wonder and despair, and the mystery of birth and life and death and twilight and the dark river ever flowing and Joyce-Hamlet delving into the mystic and eternal chaos questing-Stephen Dedalus a little less precious, a little less the aesthete, intent upon the incarnate spirit— But I, listening, saw only those grimly determined faces which *would* look intense and intent. Mary Colum now and then forced herself to acknowledge a comic touch with a smile, but her position as an intellectual also forced her to "understand". The others looked at space or at Joyce, and nodded their heads as Joyce's melodious voice continued. Sometimes his lovely tenor broke as he chuckled, a real live chuckle, at his own wit in the script. Then strained smiles broke on the faces of the assembled listeners. But they had set their faces into what they believed the proper expression for listening, and it was cruel to ask them to crack the wax or break the mask with a natural grin. Holy, holy, holy—and not one of them got more out of that reading than I did, and I had read the passage—indeed, Joyce had once read it to me himself. Hemingway commented afterwards that the passage did actually give one the feeling of night and of the flowing river, and I thought of how the old Polish actress, Modjeska, once said that she could recite the alphabet so that an audience would weep, and proceeded to prove it. Joyce has that kind of voice, but aside from the quality of his voice, the passage is moving, and does evoke thoughts of night and the deep, dark, flowing river. I would never read it in bed when a night crisis of despair about the value of life assailed me.

Not long after this Adrienne Monnier, Sylvia Beach's close friend, was to give a reading in her bookshop of a French translation of that same passage. I had no intention of going, but Bill Bird turned up at the Coupole accompanied by a doctor recently returned from South America, where he had been on an exploring expedition. The doctor was a very likeable individual and had had interesting experiences. We had a drink, and then Bird departed, after asking me to show the doctor around Paris. Bird had assured the doctor that I would take him to the Joyce-Monnier reading, and I did, but I was in a far more hilarious than reverential frame of mind.

It is indeed a ghastly thing to observe the ghouls, the frustrated old maids of various sexes, the dandruffy young men, and the badly dressed women who clutter up literary gatherings. They are too pathetic to be tragic, and they are too dumbly worshipful to know what is actually going on. There must have been two hundred people crowded into the back rooms of Adrienne Monnier's shop. I remember seeing Mina Loy and her younger daughter, the lovely twelve-year-old Fabie, with a sense of relief. For the rest, at least in the back room where I sat, there were only elderly Frenchmen and women, and dowds. Adrienne, after what seemed a long time, started to read, in French and quickly. She read very well indeed. Her articulation was clear, decisive, rhythmic, marked, and her reading very intelligent, but it was not emotional. It by no means rendered the passage as Joyce rendered it. And many of the Americans and English present certainly could not have understood that complicated passage even in English if read as quickly as Adrienne was reading it in French.

Nevertheless, the whole crew sat about with expressions painted on their faces that made one feel one was in Madame Tussaud's wax-works museum. Adrienne read in the other room, and despite her clear enunciation, she could not be heard well in our room. The doctor stirred restlessly. We were packed in. It was not possible to escape. Seeing the worshipful, mask-like faces, I lifted my hands for a second in a gesture of prayer. The doctor smiled, but an old man rushed across the room and slapped me in the face. I was naturally disconcerted, but decided that if the old man felt that holy about the session it was his right. Finally the reading ended, and Sylvia and Adrienne had a few of us up to their apartment. Mary Colum, Mina Loy, Lucia Joyce were among the livelier ones there.

It was not until the next day that I learned who the old man was who had slapped my face. It was Monsieur Dujardin, an aged French author who is supposed to have originated the interior monologue in literature. But it was not because of my lack of reverence for the reading that he had slapped me. It appears that his wife has very thick ankles, and the old man is touchy about that matter. He thought I had looked down at her feet and put up my hands in mock horror. When this was told me, I explained to both Joyce and Sylvia Beach what my gesture had meant. Later Monsieur Dujardin asked Joyce for my address and asked if he dropped me a note would I call upon him so that he could apologize; but I was not at the time in Paris.

After Adrienne's party I took the doctor to Bricktop's to recover from the humiliation of that slap. Bricktop's mother is Irish-Negro, and she is no negligible character herself. This mother of hers was, some years back, a policewoman in Chicago in the Negro district, and was a friend of Jane Addams of Hull House. The old lady had remarkable stories to tell of her experiences, and yet remained naïve and simple, as little hardened by the world as any kindly grandmother. Bricktop has much of this same quality.

At this time Brick's night club was having a good deal of success, and while she sang and danced now and then, she generally sat at her cashier's desk keeping accounts, while at the same time observing every action that went on in the cabaret. If ever a person possessed perfect co-ordination of faculties and reflexes, Brick is that person. She is large and firm-fleshed, and although she "lays down the law" while singing her songs, she thinks more of her dancing than her singing. It's a great show to watch her skipping about the floor while rendering "Bon-Bon-Buddie, the Chocolate Drop", or to listen to her singing a recent blues, torch song, or Cole Porter's latest witty song. She has singing feet, and she puts across her songs with intelligence and wit.

When the doctor and I arrived there the place was crowded. One drunken Frenchman wanted to get away without paying his bill. At another table a French actress in her cups was giving her boy friend hell and throwing champagne into his face. In the back room several Negroes were having an argument. Brick sat at the cashier's desk keeping things in order. With a wisecrack she halted the actress in her temper, cajolingly made the Frenchman pay his bill, and all the while she was adding up accounts, calling out to the orchestra to play this or that requested number, indicating to the waiters that this or that table needed service; and, when asked, she began to sing "Love for Sale", while still adding up accounts. Half-way through the song there was a commotion in the back room where the argument was taking place, which meant that the coloured boys had now come to blows. Brick skipped down from her stool, glided across the room, still singing. She jerked aside the curtain and stopped singing long enough to say, "Hey, you guys, get out in the street if you want to fight. This ain't that kind of a joint!" Then she continued the song, having missed but two phrases, and was back at her desk again adding accounts.

The quarrelsome lads quieted down, for Brick's admonition had been altogether understanding. She herself liked to drink, and liked an argument, and those of her race understood this. Her reproof had been good-natured, and it somehow suggested the possibility of jokes later, when most of the cash customers would be gone. The doctor and I lingered on, and seven o'clock in the morning found him and me standing at the bar where all the Negroes drop in for cheap drinks. As Brick suggested, why pay her cabaret prices when we could get the same gin at that bistro for one tenth the price, and in this case Bricktop herself set up the drinks. She told me that night that I was too human, and she gave an uproarious description of how I looked the day she got Jimmie the barman and me out of jail.

After two nights of my showing him Paris, the doctor disappeared, and I have forgotten his name, but he swore that was the medicine he needed after the wilds of South America.

Kay Boyle
1928-1929

That was in the middle of June, and the ego was still comparatively
docile. It had not yet started flinging itself around the place and
convoluting into another shape entirely the perfect lady that I was,
so charming and modest and diffident, decked out in the Princess'
cast-off finery. When we made our exit from Lipp's that night
McAlmon at once began joking wryly about Jolas and the other
editors of *transition*, grinning over their published defence of Antheil
(even Bill Williams' defence of him[1]), and the description some
writer had given of Antheil in the March issue as "a mirror held up
to America". In the taxi driving to Montmartre, McAlmon had said
that it certainly wasn't his America that Antheil was mirroring, not

[1] In *transition*, 13, 1928, in an article entitled "George Antheil and the Cantilene
Critics", Williams wrote:

I myself have but one bit of observation worth anything to present: Here
is Carnegie Hall. You have heard something of the great Beethoven and it has
been charming, masterful in its power over the mind. We have been alleviated,
strengthened against life—the enemy—by it. We go out of Carnegie into the
subway and we can for a moment withstand the assault of that noise, failingly!
as the strength of the music dies. . . . But as we came from Antheil's Ballet
Mécanique a woman of our party, herself a musician, made this remark:
"The subway seems sweet after that." "Good," I replied and went on to
consider what evidences there were in myself in explanation of her remark.
And this is what I noted. I felt that the noise, the unrelated noise of life such
as this in the subway, had not been battened out as would have been the case
with Beethoven still warm in the mind but it had actually been mastered,
subjugated. Antheil had taken this hated thing, life, and rigged himself into
power over it by his music. The offence had not been held, cooled, varnished
over, but annihilated and life itself made thereby triumphant. This is an
important difference.

to mention blaring into a ballet of discord. "My America has to do with jack rabbit drives, I suppose, and hobo jungles, and potato picking, and—oh hell," McAlmon said; and now, sitting at the bar of Le Grand Écart, he ordered gin fizzes for both of us and laughed his hard dry laugh. "How can you sit for hours listening to the talking about the 'revaluation of the spirit in its intercontinental relations', and the 'destruction of mechanical positivism'? Maybe it's time you stopped putting things between yourself and reality," he said. After the first gin fizz, and fifteen minutes of listening to him talk about what I was and what I wasn't, I tried to make a joke of it, and I said my reality was doing very well.

The dimmed lights and the muted music made a dreamy, shadowy place of the night club, but McAlmon didn't ask me to dance. It was the son-in-law of the *patron* (the *patron* being the famous Moÿses of the Boeuf sur le Toit, Bob was to tell me later, who was so renowned that he frequently received mail from tourists in distant countries addressed merely to Moÿses, Le Boeuf sur le Toit,[2] The Universe). He was tall, and as broad-shouldered and heavy as a prize fighter, this son-in-law who came in his dinner jacket and black tie to the bar and bowed to McAlmon and me. "Go ahead," Bob said, and because I was disturbed by his disparagement of Jolas, I danced with this man I did not know. "You've used some pretty fancy language yourself in your critical pieces," I was thinking of saying to McAlmon after the dance with the Frenchman would be done. "What about that piece of yours in the *Little Review* about 'the voluptuous impulse'?" I was going to ask him. But I did not say it, and if I had, Bob would have fixed me with his icy stare and asked me: "Well, what about it?" And I would have had no answer, and it would have ended there.

[2] In his *This Must Be the Place*, James Charters explains how the Boeuf sur le Toit acquired its name. He says it came "from a ballet of that title produced by Cocteau . . . derived from the familiar tale of the man who lived in the attic of an apartment building in Paris. Here he kept a whole menagerie of birds. . . . Eventually his neighbours started to complain about the stench that drifted down from the attic, but he refused to get rid of his fowl. Finally the neighbours banded together and brought suit against him. Just at this time the attic dweller added a bull calf to his zoo. The trial went along with the usual legal delays and one fine day the neighbours found themselves victorious: the court ordered the owner of the fowl and the bull calf to dispose of them so that there might be no further annoyance to his neighbours. But, alas, when the police came to enforce this order, they found that the trial had taken so long that the bull calf had grown into a full-size bull and that it would be impossible to get it out of the building without tearing down all the doors and passageways. Hence it remained . . . the bull on the roof."

A very small, highly polished square of the darkened nightclub floor had been set aside for dancing, and couples were packed on it, clasped in each other's hotly clinging arms. Beyond the dance floor and the tables was the figure of McAlmon, sitting hunched into himself at the bar. Moÿses' son-in-law wanted to know everything about him. All he knew was his name, and that told him nothing. Was he an American newspaperman? No, he wasn't that, I said. (In the taxi McAlmon had had a word or two of dismissal as well for the two newspapermen, William Shirer and Jay Allen, who had been with us at Lipp's that night.) A novelist? Yes, a novelist, but I loved him as a poet, I said. "Where are the pieces, quivering and staring and muttering?" I remembered, and I tried to put the words into French for Moÿses' son-in-law, but he wasn't interested. "What's he looking for, wandering around night after night alone?" he asked me, and I was a bit outraged by the question. That night, and every night that summer when I was with McAlmon, I made the mistake of believing he had actually put the pieces of himself together and that he was seated in high and mighty and inaccessible security somewhere.

After a while the music took a turn for the better, and the couples began to extricate themselves from the turmoil of dancers, and when the floor was nearly empty a cone-shaped beam of light sought out Moÿses' son-in-law and me as we danced in the half-dark. It was not strange that it should have selected us, for the others who moved in close embrace to the glimmering of the glowworms and the wailing of the violins were squat and very graceless people. They had no music in their veins and no elegance in their limbs, and the women's heels were as savage as the hoofs of the policeman's horse under which Lola had fallen, their eyes as ruthless as the eyes of the British who had watched MacSwiney die. With their own hands they would have pulled the switch which turned the tongues and the hearts of Sacco and Vanzetti to lava, and they would have driven Ernest Walsh from every café terrace where he stopped to rest, and drawn back in fear of Carnevali's illness as he went shivering and shuddering past.

When I had gone back to the bar to sit with McAlmon again, what happened then was in a sense a parable acted out for exactly what this man was. He had switched from gin to scotch, and we were sitting there silenced and saddened and embittered by the ugliness and the opulence of the middle-aged people, French and American and English, who danced, and ate, and drank, and threw their money away in handfuls instead of giving it to the poets and beggars of the world. And then, between the silk draperies that completely concealed a window that stood open on the summer night (they were green, those curtains; I can see them clearly, stirring, wavering a little in the night air), suddenly a miserable hand reached in from the deserted street, a black-nailed, dirty, defeated hand, with a foul bit of coat sleeve showing at the wrist. Without a word McAlmon placed his fine, tall glass of whisky and soda into the fingers of the stranger's hand, and the fingers closed quickly on it and drew it back through the draperies into the lonely dark.

From there we went on to Bricktop's, and she sat down and had a drink with us; and here was a woman to be cherished. I liked her tinted brick-coloured hair, her cocoa flesh, her lively and almost impossibly beautiful legs, her dogwood-white teeth, her clear-eyed poise in the dancing, drinking, worldly turmoil of the place. Her ability to be the heart of, and yet remain detached from, the activity around her, gave them—the others—the look of ants in panic, and she, doe-eyed, was the warm, sweet mammal, with daisies in her ears and a cud as sweet as honey in her mouth. (A decade later it was said that she was entering a California convent, and this seemed to me quite plausible, for there was a spiritual efficiency, as limpid as spring water, in her eyes, in her smile, and in her quickly and softly spoken words, that would have been as pleasing to God and His ordained representatives as it was to man.) The decisions she took in the hour we spent with her that night were made as quietly as the turning of the pages of a book, taken, there could be no doubt out of some unshakable recognition of right and wrong, some individual and untroubled concept of natural law.

The good days of the Quarter were finished, Bob kept telling me; I had come too late. But still we would go back to the Left Bank, and to the Coupole, where I had never been. Nina Hamnett had moved to London and was holding court at the Fitzroy Pub, Bob said, and Flossie Martin's beauty and exuberance were on the wane. But Flossie was there as we walked through the door of the Coupole bar, her voice clamorous as an excited child's, her milk-white arms and throat, her bosomy flesh, packed with care into a baby's flawless, silken skin. A green straw hat with an enormous brim was over one eye, and there were orange tendrils of hair curling around the sea shells of her ears; and the sea that came and went was her voice calling out McAlmon's name. She seized him in her arms and placed lipstick kisses like little footprints on his brow.

To Florence Martin's official dossier should be added the following small and seemingly insignificant things, but which are to me the most significant I ever knew of her. In a book picked up in a secondhand bookstore in Los Angeles in the 1960s were found a handful of post cards that had been mailed in the years 1923 to 1925. They were all in different handwritings, written by different men from different countries, and they were addressed either to Miss Flossie Martin, Café du Dôme, Paris, France, or to Mme. La Marquise de Montparnasse, née Florence Martin, Paris, or to Miss Florence Martin, Somewhere near the Dôme or Dingo, France, or to La Belle Martin, Reine du Quartier Montparnasse, Royaume de France. Between the pages of this book, scrawled on the back of a nearly illegible pencilled note from an English admirer who was seeking to find Florence Martin to invite her out for an evening on the town, was my name and address, done in unmistakably my own if rather inebriated and uncertain hand. A letter dated August 13, 1925, had likewise been preserved, its words as fresh as if written yesterday, in spite of the forty years that have elapsed. It was written half in French, half in English, by a French sailor on furlough near Toulon, who began it "*Ma petite Flossie*" and went on to say that he was working "very much in the landscape" and was black from the sun. The letter is signed "your very small friend, J E A N, who loves you always and kisses you very much". Below his signature are affixed those of a naval electrician from the battleship *Edgar Quinet*, a Toulon lawyer, a second lieutenant from the cruiser *Yser*, and a British sailor, all of whom, Jean says, are eager to go to Paris to meet Flossie at the Dôme.

Among the post cards, the snapshots, the scribbled pencil notes, the visiting cards and newspaper clippings gone yellow, and the contract cracked through at the seams, worn thin as gauze, offering Miss Florence Martin a role in a French film, was a typed letter dated February 5, 1924, which seemed to hold itself aloof from all the rest. It had been dictated by the American consul general, one A. M. Thackara, at 1, Rue des Italiens, in Paris, and the message it bore is as sad as the yearning cry the hippies of a later time cannot shake from their ears as they walk barefoot the city asphalt, sadder even than the lament that shudders on the strings of their guitars as they crouch in doorways, wrapped in their Indian blankets, encased in their serapes. It was the same message that these modern exiles from all that is familiar seek to cancel out as they write LOVE, in some kind of hopeless denial of it, in letters as tall as a man on a city's crumbling walls. The American consul general's communication says this:

> Madam:
> I have to inform you that I am in receipt of a telegram from M. Martin, 362 Commonwealth Avenue, Boston, Mass. requesting me to report relative to your welfare.
> Will you please call at this Consulate-General to see me at your earliest convenience.
>> I am,
>>> Very respectfully yours

M. Martin, father or mother, uncle or aunt, brother or sister, must have been there at the bar with her that night in 1928, unseen and perhaps unanswered, and every time she gave a thought to M. Martin, she ordered another drink, and whooped aloud, and talked about getting up early tomorrow or maybe the day after that, and going on with her operatic career. "Is there something wrong with Otto Kahn," she sang, "or something wrong with me?" "Wiz Otto Kahn, definitely," said Kiki from the far end of the bar. That night I met Kiki too for the first time, as well as an American painter friend of Bob's, Hilaire Hiler. But Bob said that Flossie and Kiki and Hiler were no more than three survivors of another and far gayer company and of a wilder, more adventurous time. The lines that people spoke now were flat as stale beer, he said, and the props, the scenery, no longer had any meaning. So as to change the look of things, there was nothing to do except have one more drink, although he complained about the taste of it, and then one more, and then another after that. "If only Djuna Barnes or Mina Loy turned up, the evening might be saved," he said, looking at the door.

Hiler was ponderously tall, with a long black oily mane of hair and a loose red mouth that was like a gaping wound in his face. His enormous eyes were strangely glazed, either from drink or from some excruciating mental pain, and his ears stood out from his great, heavy head as the ears of an elephant fan out when it trumpets its rage. (In the many years I was to know him after this first night, I learned it was neither wholly drink nor wholly anguish of the psyche that had drawn a glaucous veil across his eyes but rather a desperate alliance of the two. It was there in his eyes when we would walk into night clubs together, and he would go straight to where the piano player played, and take his place, and bang out the current jazz and blues with such brilliant melancholy that girls would leave their escorts to come sit at Hiler's feet, and the whole night club would shout for more when he was done. It was there, this transparent silking of his sight, in 1931, the day after he ran down a cyclist on the Promenade des Anglais in Nice, struck him and killed him in the rain and dark. "I didn't even know I'd hit anything," he said, the glaze of anguish blinding him now to what had taken place. "I swear to God I didn't know until after I'd gone a kilometre 'or more and his feet started hitting the windshield," he said. It was there in 1961, when I last saw him: the monstrously grotesque mask of pain, worn as if for a carnival, but the carnival was every night and every day.)

At the Coupole bar Hiler had listened for a while to McAlmon lamenting a time that was past and the people who had lived in that time, and then he began speaking of his own bereavement. It was for a particular woman that he mourned, and as an opera singer will divulge confidentially to the audience the confused proceedings of the opera's plot, Hiler told the dozen or so people still left in the bar that she lay buried in a cemetery outside Paris, and McAlmon began singing high and mock poignantly: "With the wild goose grasses growing over me!" Or else she had gone off with another man, Hiler went on with it, talking over the rim of his glass to the strangers in the place, and paying no attention to McAlmon warbling in mock tenderness. It was all unclear; it might even have been that she was neither dead nor faithless, but that she was dying, dying, in the public ward of a hospital the name of which he could not for a moment recall. He talked so loudly of the condition of the grievous state of his soul that Kiki, at the far end of the bar, shouted hoarsely at him: "*Cache tes oreilles, imbécile!* She was in here with you last night, giving you a piece of her mind!"

Man Ray had designed Kiki's face for her, and painted it on with his own hand. He would begin by shaving her eyebrows off, she told me, and then putting other eyebrows back, in any colour he might have selected for her mask that day, sometimes as fine as a thread and sometimes as thick as your finger, and at any angle he chose. Her heavy eyelids might be done in copper one day and in royal blue another, or else in silver or jade, she said. Tonight they were opaline. She was heavy-featured and voluptuous, her voice as hoarse as that of a vegetable hawker, her hair smooth as a crow's glistening wing. She made me think of Germaine Garrigou, and I loved her for this likeness, but however different they may have been, this much I know: when you knocked at Kiki's white stone flesh for entry, she too opened wide her heart and moved the furniture aside so that you could come in.

McAlmon decided that we should cross the Boulevard Montparnasse and see if there might be at the Sélect some people he knew. (It was only some time later, perhaps a year or so, when I came to know Djuna Barnes, and Mary Reynolds, and Nancy Cunard, that I learned that whomever he was with, Bob was always seeking another name, and another face, in quite another place. I wrote a short story called "I Can't Get Drunk"[3] about his endless search, saying:

> Whatever you said to him was drawn with labour word by word from the bog of his interest in something else. Up and down and around was he looking for something that might catch his curiosity. If I stay up all night was he thinking perhaps something will happen after all.

Nancy Cunard once said to me, her laughter quick, bright, and minuscule as a hummingbird, her eyes like jewels in her lovely head: "Ah, me, my dearest, the nights Bob and I spent looking for you all over Paris, in and out of everywhere before I so much as knew your name!" It was like that the nights we spent looking for her, when we *had* to find her, or else for Bob it seemed the night would die.

There at the Sélect that night was Harold Stearns, the Peter Pickem of the Paris edition of the Chicago *Tribune*, Bob told me, who picked the winners at the racecourse at Maisons-Laffitte (or else failed to pick them). He was standing drinking at the bar, with a brown felt hat set, in a shabby parody of respectability, quite high on his head. McAlmon ordered drinks for the three of us, and I knew it must be nearly dawn, but my will was gone, sapped utterly by

[3] *The First Lover and Other Stories*, Harrison Smith and Robert Haas, Inc., New York, 1933.

alcohol and the need for sleep. The collar of Harold's black and white striped shirt was frayed, and the ear that was turned towards me was dirty, and the side of his face was in need of a shave. But under the brim of his disreputable felt hat it could be seen that his eyelashes were jet black and as luxuriant as an underbrush of fern. This was the single mark of beauty Harold had; but beauty did not matter, for once he began to talk you forgot the stubble-covered jowls packed hard from drink, and the stains of food on his jacket lapels, and the black rimmed fingers holding his glass. As soon as he began to speak that night, and on through all the nights and years that we talked (or that I listened) in the Sélect together, I never questioned the truth of every word he said. I knew if the things he described had not happened in this lifetime they had happened sometime, somewhere else, or else they should have happened; and if they had not happened to him, he believed by this time that they had, and one had no right by any word, or look, or gesture to take this desperately accumulated fortune of belief away. (I wrote a book about this man, and it is to me the most satisfying book I ever wrote.[4])

That first night he talked of the horse that had fallen in a steeple-chase and broken its leg (a low break, he said, somewhere around the pastern), and he had persuaded them not to destroy it but to let him take it home. He'd borrowed the money to get a horse van to haul it into Paris, and he was taking care of it in the overgrown courtyard that his apartment opened on. The leg had been set, it was going to mend, he said, but the horse was eating him into the poor-house: oats, bran, alfalfa, not to mention the rye straw for its bedding. He talked quickly, looking straight ahead. And then there was the veterinary's fee; the vet had had to visit the horse every day. "Stearns, I admire you," Bob said, and he jerked his mirthless laughter out; and Harold stubbornly, earnestly went on saying: "So several times in the evening I have to take up a collection for him. I have no choice." He went out now into the terrace of the café, where the crowd was beginning to thin out at the end of the night. American tourists were usually touched by this modern myth, saving Jolas' presence, Bob said, and he went on laughing; they usually gave very liberally. Harold came back looking modest, and grave, and pious, both pockets of his jacket carelessly stuffed with all that had been given him for the horse whose pastern bone was going to

[4] *Monday Night*, Harcourt, Brace and Company, New York, 1938. Reprinted by New Directions, New York, 1947.

mend. "I'd like you to come and see him sometime," he said to McAlmon and me, and he ordered drinks for everyone, and paid for them across the bar. "Better not tempt fate too far," McAlmon said. "We might take you up on that, and then where would you be?"

McAlmon had begun to sing again. "Me and My Shadow," he was singing, and although it wasn't a cowboy song, still it was sung so high and clear and plaintively that it made me remember Monte Carlo when he had come there, and it made me yearn for the baby asleep in somebody else's house now, and to think of things even sadder, sadder than Joyce's rain falling on Rahoon. "Next time I'll tell you about another horse," Harold Stearns was saying to me, looking straight ahead across his glass. "I'll tell you about an American horse who happened to be travelling with us on a freighter flat as an ark that was passing through the French Sudan, and when the natives laid eyes on him they dispersed like leaves before the customary storm. The fact was they'd never seen a horse before, never seen so much as the picture of a horse, they'd never put money on a horse, never exchanged views on bangtails or feminines of the turf. They'd never attended a cinder classic, if you can believe it," he said, and Bob was singing that he and his shadow were strolling down the avenue. "Those natives," Harold said, looking at me now with dark, fern-fringed eyes, "they were untouched by civilization. They'd never heard ponies thundering into the stretch. . . ." On the other side of me, Bob sang that he didn't have a soul to tell his troubles to, and it seemed to me then, not knowing the entire story, that he'd had his heart broken in pieces sometime in another year, but that he'd put it together again without much tragedy.

When Bob stopped singing I looked quickly around and he was no longer there.

By the time I had finished the Dayang Muda's memoirs my social conscience was in such a bad way that I decided to join Raymond Duncan's colony. Ever since his first visit to the Rue Louis David he had been coming to dinner at the Princess' every week, and he had urged me gently and understandingly to join his followers and bring my baby with me, and learn to milk goats when the herd passed in the early morning, and to weave tunics on his looms, and to wrest sandals out of the raw hide. I would also be in charge of one or the other of his two shops, Raymond said, either the one on the Right

Bank, in the Rue du Faubourg St. Honoré, or the one on the Left Bank, on the Boulevard St. Germain. One day a week, as was required of every member of the colony, I would prepare the vegetarian lunch and dinner for the seven or eight adults and the equal number of children in the colony. On that day Ayah, Raymond's companion since his wife's death in Greece, would take my place as saleslady in the shop. Sharon, he said, would be in the healthiest of atmospheres all day in the large back garden of the colony's villa, and, besides our board and lodging, I would be paid three hundred francs a month to cover my of-the-world expenses, such as subway fare to and from work, necessary bits of clothing, and my lunches (which it was understood would be of goat cheese, yogurt, and fresh fruit), to be eaten in the back room of the shop so that it would remain open without interruption throughout the day.

The Princess was happy that I was going to the colony, for she and Archie would be leaving Paris for the summer, and she wanted to keep a tie of friendship with Raymond. Why this was I learned as she and I sat one June evening in the Bois, with Sharon asleep in her baby carriage beside us. Isadora Duncan had lost her children too, the Princess said hesitantly as we sat together in the twilight. "She lost five of them," she said, enabled to speak these words of emotion only because I could not see her face in the dusk. "I lost six. But the number isn't of any importance. They're gone. Perhaps through Raymond I'll be able to meet Isadora one day, and then . . ." And then I thought in sorrow for her, but with impatience too, then you'll sit absolutely silent, drawing the smoke in through your cigarette holder, sitting paralysed as you are sitting now, and the names of the children, hers or yours, will not be mentioned, and you will look steadily away from the memory of their thin brown legs, and their silky eyebrows, and their shining hair. However fervently you make the additions and the subtractions beforehand, it will all mount up to zero in the end.

It took some time to discover that the three Duncans, Isadora, Elizabeth, and Raymond, were separate and even violently opposed individuals, with no commitment through blood or conviction to one another, and, for the most part, not an instant of family or professional loyalty. In the six months I spent in Raymond Duncan's colony I learned the origin of the two bathtubs that stood in the back garden, bathtubs that Raymond and his followers used for the preparation of batiks and the dyeing of scarves. Some years earlier, when Isadora was absent from her flamboyantly furnished Neuilly villa, Raymond, with the help of a plumber's saw, had severed these bathtubs from their pipes and, in settlement of some bitter financial dispute, had taken them for his own. And if Elizabeth (whom I came to love) and Raymond were on speaking terms it was only, I learned in my deep involvement with them both, because of the attractive financial possibilities in their separate enterprises. The Paris School of Duncan Dance, which Elizabeth opened that October, was a place where Raymond, who was constantly in evidence, adjusting lights, shifting scenes, manipulating curtains, might recruit colonists from among the dancers and customers from the audience for his two shops. On the other hand, it was at the Neuilly colony that the tunics required by Elizabeth for the dance students were fashioned (and sold for an exorbitant price which Elizabeth and Raymond split between them), and in the artistic setting of Raymond's spacious shop on the Boulevard St. Germain Elizabeth could receive and interview the prospective students for her classes. It was good business, Elizabeth and Raymond had each decided, to appear to the public to be working together in cultural harmony.

(I have written a novel about Sharon's and my stay in the colony,[5] and because the story of that sojourn is only obliquely concerned with McAlmon, I shall not enlarge upon it here. It need only be noted that the soles and thongs of the sandals that were on sale in Raymond's shops had not been carved out of raw leather by his or any other colonist's hand, but were purchased in a little shop off the Boulevard St. Germain and stitched together by workers in the colony. The tunics and rugs we sold, moreover, had not been woven on hand-looms in Neuilly, as Raymond declared, but had been woven a decade before in Greece, in the time when Raymond's beautiful and efficient and persevering wife had been alive. The most elaborate of them he permitted me to wear on the occasions that he and I appeared together in society.)

One of McAlmon's two Canadian disciples (who had crossed on a freighter with little baggage to speak of save their two typewriters and a copy of *Ulysses*) had been hired by the Dayang Muda to help me with the final typing of her book. Archie had fixed the price, and he kept careful watch on how many pages Buffy, then nineteen, turned out a day. During the hours of work Buffy and I (at times incorporating suggestions made by McAlmon) inserted in the

[5] *My Next Bride*, Harcourt, Brace and Company, New York, 1934.

mouths of the long-dead great additional flights of repartee and far more brilliant *bons mots* than I had managed to invent alone. (On one occasion we had Oscar Wilde scandalizing the Princess' mother's dinner guests with the time-worn limerick that goes: "There was an old lady of Sheen/Whose hearing was not very keen./She said, 'It is odd/But I cannot tell God/Save the Weasel from Pop Goes the Queen.' ")

When Buffy left the Rue Louis David at the end of each day he would come into the salon to bid good night to the Princess and Archie, hoping to receive his daily wage before he left. But as is frequently the case in the households of the rich, there was likely to be a shortage of actual cash on hand, and often Buffy was paid only a portion of what was due to him, and at other times Archie asked him in a discreetly lowered voice if he would mind waiting until the next day for his money, or for two days, or until the end of the week. Through these constant postponements, confusion would arise as to how much Buffy was actually owed, and after he had been under-paid on a number of occasions, he took action of his own. It puzzled me when, on entering the salon, he took to bowing stiffly from the waist both to the Princesss and to Archie, and that now he stood at a distance from them, near the grand piano, nervously refusing to sit down as he had done before. I concluded this must be a belated awareness of the deference a Canadian owes to British royalty, and I felt I must respect this and not discuss it with him. It was only long, long after that Buffy told me he had begun slipping gramophone records from the Princess' collection inside his jacket every day, and he had to move with caution to avoid breaking them. The records compensated for what he had not been paid, and the sale of them in the Quarter was usually enough to buy his supper that night.

Once in the last days of the pre-R. D. era, as Archie called it, while I was still living in the Rue Louis David, he took me to tea at Gertrude Stein's. Alice Toklas and I immediately started to talk of cooking, and to exchange recipes, and it was on that afternoon I heard for the first time Miss Toklas' engaging comments on the tracking down of recipes for Spanish iced soup, called, I believe, *gazpacho*. The search for these recipes had become for her, during a trip to Spain, far more important than cathedrals, museums, and the paintings of El Greco, or the drama of the bull ring. But Archie told me later, toying uncomfortably with his silver-headed cane, that Gertrude Stein had asked him not to bring me back again, as she found me as incurably middle-class as Ernest Hemingway.[6]

Once McAlmon and I had dinner with the Joyces at the Trianon, and the talk that night was almost entirely about Lucia's eyes, and whether or not there should be an operation to lengthen the muscle that caused her left eye to turn inward, thus marring the beauty of her face. "It's twice as noticeable when she's nervous," Nora Joyce said, and Joyce himself shook his head and asked if she wasn't continuously too nervous, too shy. He wondered if her interest in her art work and her bookbinding might not give her the confidence she needed. McAlmon suggested that perhaps her dancing would be a better release for her tensions, and once she was well launched in that career, the eye might straighten of itself. "Do you think so, McAlmon?" Joyce asked, seizing eagerly on this. "Have you ever heard of a case that such a thing took place?" Yes, yes, she was born to dance, he repeated in some relief, and he explained to me that she was going to Salzburg to study with Elizabeth Duncan, as the more famous sister, Isadora, was not holding classes now. "She's not even holding her liquor," McAlmon said, and, "Ah, the poor soul," said Nora Joyce; but Joyce himself was too concerned with the vision of the dancing future that might be the salvation of Lucia to hear anything else that was being said.

Joyce drank a great deal of white wine that night, but not that year or any of the years I knew him did I ever see him prostrated by drink, as both Jolas and McAlmon have described their nights with him. When he had enough of the faces around him, or the talk, Joyce would be likely to slip quietly under the table, the stories went, and then he would have to be carried inanimate, to a taxi, and up several flights to bed. There were to be times in the thirties when he sang for an entire evening, with Giorgio and Laurence Vail, French and Italian ribald drinking songs, and one "naughty" Cockney number that went: "I've a little pink petty from Tommy,

---

[6] It will be understandable that I was pleased with Jolas' story about Gertrude Stein which Maria Jolas repeated to me some time later, and which was published in *A James Joyce Miscellany*, by The James Joyce Society, 1957. It goes as follows:

MISS STEIN: Jolas, why do you continue to lay such emphasis in *transition* on the work of that fifth-rate politician, James Joyce? Haven't you understood yet that the leading English-language writer today is myself, Gertrude Stein?

EUGENE JOLAS: Miss Stein, you will excuse me, but I do not agree with you. (*Jolas rises, walks to the door, picks up his hat.*) Miss Stein, I bid you good-morning. (*Exit Jolas.*)

and a little blue petty from John, but the point that I'm at is that underneath *that*, I haven't got anything on!" On those evenings Giorgio, whose voice was a deep bass, and whose accent a mixture of musical Italian and an Irish brogue, would look across the table at his father and shake his head. "For ten years he *would* have me a tenor," he said. "Baritone, bass, the voice teachers would tell him, and so he'd cart me off to somebody else. Tenor he *would* have me, and if you want to know the truth, that I couldn't comply was what drove him to drink and broke his heart!" The last meal I had with Nora and James Joyce was in Zürich in 1938; they took Laurence Vail and me to the health food restaurant where they were now lunching every day. It was a depressing place: cold oatmeal was moulded into the shape of pork chops, and then sprinkled with bread crumbs and fried; and beefsteaks were fashioned out of some other substance, and tinted red. Cranberry juice was served in wine glasses, but no alcohol could be purchased there.

McAlmon took me one day to Brancusi's studio in the Impasse Ronsin off the Rue de Vaugirard. And the next week I went back alone and had lunch of *saucisson*, and cheese, and figs, and red wine, with Brancusi under the trees, and helped him plant beans and lettuce along the side of his studio wall. We talked of Michael, and he gave me the design he had made for the stone that sealed Michael's grave in Monaco. It had been drawn up to the specifications Ethel had sent him, but whether or not she had had it executed he did not know. Once, when he went away for two days, Brancusi gave me his snow-white Samoyed to keep for him. He said Michael had played with the dog all one evening, and had made lumps of sugar come magically out of its ears. In the Princess' apartment, I slept two nights on the floor with the Samoyed, my arms around its neck, and this was perhaps the first sign and signal of the orgy of self-pity that was to come.

In the week before I moved to Raymond Duncan's colony McAlmon took me for a weekend to Clairefontaine, near Rambouillet, to Mariette and Heyworth Mills's château. Bob and I walked all that first afternoon in the woods together, and after a while he began talking as he had the day we drove to La Turbie from Monte Carlo, saying he wanted to find a place in the country, that he didn't care if he never saw a city again, or a city bar. He said he would like it to be in the south of France, and maybe raise blue rabbits. He said there were places in the south of France, back in the hills, that you could buy for next to nothing, abandoned vineyards that could be restored. They'd been left like that for fifty years or more, when some kind of blight of the vines had come along, and you could buy young vines and start all over again there, and make a good enough living out of it, he said. Even the houses, fallen partially into ruin, but made of stone, could be built up again. From their windows you could see the Mediterranean, a long way away, but seemingly close because of the intensity of its blue. And after a little I was talking and talking to him as I had never been able to before. The plans for the yearbook of poetry were being postponed until the autumn, for Archie's lungs were giving him increasing trouble. All summer he would be in the mountains, but I would go on collecting manuscripts, I told McAlmon, and that evening he gave me a great many of his poems to read. I wanted to show them to Jolas, I said, for I thought they should do a group of them in *transition*. "Never again," Bob said. "They published a piece of prose of mine in the same number with the surrealists just to show how bad my writing was. They've probably told you. Although that was probably less Jolas than Elliot Paul."

I hadn't heard the story. But if there's any truth in it, I said, then let them read your poetry signed by another name, and see how they react to it. So Bob took the name Guy Urquhart—Urquhart being his mother's maiden name—and when I got back to Paris on Monday evening I had dinner with Gene at Lipp's and I gave him McAlmon's poems. I said they were written by a young man living in the Middle West, who had never been published in his life, and who had sent these poems for Archie's and my anthology. In the summer issue of *transition*, "The American Number," McAlmon's poem "The Silver Bull" appeared, on pages 131 and 132, under the name of Guy Urquhart. "Above the blue-flowered alfalfa/a wave of yellow butterflies" hovered on these pages, and "At nightfall the silver bull came lowing home/to meet the cows returning to their stanchions." After the bull's day of stampeding violence, during which the boy of the poem is tossed into the water trough, he is able to lead the bull "without persuasions to his stall", and there to scratch the expanse of brow between his horns, and feed him salt, "liking the silver glisten of his massive neck,/the thwarted, dumb nobility of his ruthless sharp-horned head".

On pages 86 and 87 of that same number of *transition* appeared, ironically enough, some limping and would-be waggish doggerel, the blunt barbs of which were directed against American exiles, doggerel which a group of New York literary men had apparently spent an uproarious night composing in a room at the Chelsea Hotel. Two of these jingles concerned McAlmon, which is doubtless fame of a sort. One, labelled a parody of Heine, went: "I dreamt that I was Pound himself,/Whom heavenly joy immerses,/And ten McAlmons sat about/And praised my verses." The other, which achieved a certain amount of notoriety: "I'd rather live in Oregon and pack Salmon,/Than live in Nice and write like Robert Mc-Almon." Well, that kind of thing was easy to do, and it seemed to me that summer, just as it seems to me now, that had my tastes been formed by academic standards, or had I felt compelled to give allegiance to any group or state of mind, rather than allegiance to individual women and men—or to give consideration to the requirements of American publishers and editors—I could not have loved both McAlmon and Jolas so deeply and wholly without question as I did. I was grateful then, and I am still grateful now, that I lacked the intellectual effrontery, and subsequent embitterment, that might have diminished my acknowledgment of all these two men stood for and all that they had done.

I had hoped that Jolas would publish McAlmon's "Romances", because of their satirical, "stinkweary", fatalistic tone, the strident voice of which could lower without warning to the tender lullabying of such lines as "If I recall you now/not for beauty or mind/you linger,/but for a posture/as you sat one day/high upon a cliff above the sea/looking no way/but captured by bewilderment . . ."; or for the "gull-odorous cries" sounding from his pages, "lost and dismayed./The octopus slime upon the beach . . ." I wanted Jolas to publish Urquhart's "The Wild Boar" and "The White Wolf"[7] and an early draft of his "Neurotic Correspondence". But once I had told Gene who Guy Urquhart actually was, he struck the café table in fury with his fist and quite rightly said that he would have no more of that kind of subterfuge. What point I had made by tricking the editors of *transition*, I do not know. I had perhaps merely reassured myself that McAlmon was the poet I believed him to be.

A few months later Jolas did publish more of McAlmon's prose, under his own name, including his "Mr. Joyce Directs an Irish

[7] Two poems later published in *Not Alone Lost*, poems by Robert McAlmon, New Directions, Norfolk, Conn., 1937.

Ballet," In this valuable piece (which McAlmon himself dismisses so lightly) he wrote in this way of the "Jean qui rit" and "Jean qui pleure" passage of Joyce's *Work in Progress*:

> Here Joyce cannot forget childhood, parenthood, mother affection and anxiety, but most of all he cannot forget Dublin (Lublin), the memory of a Dublin folksong punned on and joked with, the lucky load to Lublin, the wage-earning father, and Ireland, poor brittle little magic nation, dim of mind. Ireland little Jean qui pleure, with Joyce crooning an Irish tenor twilight refrain to comfort the weeping child who wakes in fright from having had a nightmare. . . . The refrain of mother to child is all comforting, as Joyce sees it, but after a time he also sees that he has given it other implications. "Gothgored father" is perhaps a priest who is praying as the mother tells of the no bad faathern, dear one, who goes the lucky load to Lublin for to make the family groceries, while every silvery (elvery) stream winds sailing (seling) on to keep the barrel of bounty rolling.[8]

Had I known that Bob's "Neurotic Correspondence" was addressed to Nancy Cunard I would have studied her with even greater interest than I did on the night of Hiler's enormous party near the Lion de Belfort. Nancy was the heroine of Michael Arlen's *Green Hat*, and that first night I met her she wore broad ivory bracelets from wrist to shoulder of her slender arms. I did not immediately recognize her in McAlmon's lines of poetry:

> He recalls your strawpale hair,
> your brittle voice machine-conversing,
> allotted speeches, no neglect,
> a social sense of order,
> a sharp dry voice
> speaking through smoke and wine,
> a voice of litheness;
>   a hard, a cold, a stern white body.
>
> Someday your ankles, thin, so trim,
> must break with walking,
> as your brittle voice now—almost—
> breaks with talking.

[8] *transition*, 15, February 1929.

There's much distinction in your pallor
and your houndish rigid leanness.
If you wear silver,
things that glisten,
then your blue-mist face, your blue steel eyes,
have even more abstraction,
one that glitters.

That night Kiki sat on a grand piano that had been placed under the green branches of the trees and hoarsely sang or spoke her famous bawdy songs while Hiler played. Papa Hiler, the theatrical agent, wearing large, dazzling diamond rings, stood with two barmen behind the long table and the bottles of drink, and mixed the punch, and measured out the whiskies and the gins. McAlmon was Nijinsky that night, leaping to incredible heights over the lighted paper lanterns; and Harold Stearns, still wearing his brown felt hat, appeared and reappeared, taking up a collection for the steeplechase racer that did not exist, either bedded down in rye straw in his courtyard or anywhere. Link Gillespie, and Buffy and Graeme (the two Canadians) and I did a wild ring-around-a-rosy dance hour after hour, while Desnos glided and stamped in an apache tango, flinging an imaginary partner to the other end of the leafy, illuminated square, and dragging her furiously back again. At the end of the evening Hiler began to weep for the girl who had left him for another man, or else lay buried deeply, deeply, in French soil, and Nancy put the ivory coat of mail of her lean arms about him, and comforted him, her eyes like sapphires, but bluer than any sapphires, even her warm laughter saying nobody is ever betrayed, darling, nobody ever dies.

Robert McAlmon

1928-1930

A sad thing happened in Paris. From Japan about a year before had arrived an artist from the interior provinces. He belonged to the ancient tradition of Japanese painting and it was said that his fishes and his flower-women pictures were comparable to those of Hokusai, Utamaro, Hiroshige, and other outstanding artists. He spoke, it was also said, very little else but the dialect of his region and he was not seen about much with any of the other Japanese artists, who were generally French derivative. He might be standing in the same bistro or bar where Foujita was, but he, Toda, would not seem to be aware of it. Foujita, with his bobbed hair, earrings, kimono shirts, and altogether arty get-up, is certainly not in the ancient tradition of Japanese artists.

Toda had a wild, primitive quality. His magnificently shaped head and indeed his entire appearance made one think of the legends of the Samurai knights in the days before upstarts from the Western world invaded Japan. He drank recklessly, and generally in the company of Japanese of a type not known in the Quarter. During his year in Paris he became known to other artists too, and was conceded admiration, both for his talent and his great personal beauty, and also for his savagely ribald humour. After a while he was not seen around the bars or cafés, but no one gave much thought to his absence from the scene. Then he was discovered dead of starvation. Possibly his friends had not known that he was without money. Because of the old Japanese tradition of honour, he had told no one of his troubles. Certainly there were people who would have helped him had they known, myself among them, but his pride kept him silent.

There seems to me no reason for sentimentality about suicide, and generally the suicides of people I have known do no more to me than make me wonder a little more about life. But Toda's death, and the suicide of the little French girl, Rita, did depress me. Both were needless. Rita killed herself when she was wild with drink, and Toda died because he was too proud to ask for momentary financial help or food. As for Isadora Duncan, it was too strange a death to have been planned beforehand, but many people insist that it was suicide. Her last dance programme at the Théâtre des Champs-Elysées was not without its depressing moments. Although she must have known that her dancing days were over, she tried to do one leap, and it was grotesque and sad, and she was aware of it. But long before this I had seen a constantly despairing and rather shamed look in her eyes.

There had also been much wailing and weeping over the suicide of Pascin. That case was a tragedy, for Pascin had genius, a market for his paintings, friends, and appeared to enjoy life, although in a strangely morbid and exotic way. He made the decision, however, and it was his to make. Such is our human destiny in this world, and it was human destiny also that Contact Editions ceased publishing. During the summers of 1925 and 1926 Bill Bird went to Spitzbergen to report the Byrd polar expedition, and I was mainly out of Paris. Paris bookshops had not shown much interest in limited editions, and such books as we published and tried to send to England and America were held up at the customs, and in most cases we were not notified. In America the books were seldom commented on and, if mentioned, they were referred to as Paris and expatriate productions even if their authors were living, and had been living, in America. William Rose Benét apparently felt it his duty to be merciless on such books because, although they were printed in English, they had come from France. Meanwhile he was praising inferior works that had been published in America. It did not help matters to realize that MacLeish was the great new name in America among the poets. But one had only to recall that Picasso, Gertrude Stein, Joyce, Pound, etc., have all often bemoaned the fact that those who are derived get attention before those who originate. Those who are derived remain traditional, conventional, academic, and contrive not to startle anybody with clarity or their harsh brutality of observation.

Possibly Contact Editions might more than have paid its expenses had we concentrated on the commercial aspect, that is, on collecting the monies that were due us on the books delivered to bookshops. As it was, with great portions of each confiscated at the docks, the venture merely lost money, and as long as the simple facts that books were printed abroad caused them to be censored, we let the whole matter drop. I wish now I had a few copies of the books we published, if for no other reason than that booksellers in America can get ten to twenty times what we charged for copies of most of these editions. The works of Ezra Pound, Mary Butts, Robert Coates, Gertrude Stein, Hemingway (his first two books appear), John Herrmann, Gertrude Beasley, Hilda Doolittle, Ford Madox Ford, Mina Loy, William Carlos Williams were all on the list of Contact Editions.

Paris was by now, as it probably always has been to "old-timers", completely finished, with all of the old crowd gone and the Quarter impossible. I had dinner one night with Nora and James Joyce, and went afterwards to their apartment to drink, and gin this time. Joyce had finally learned that people do drink whisky and gin and that many do not care for inferior white wine or natural champagne. Later Joyce sang a few Irish "come-all-ye's", and told of the night in Dublin, before 1904, when he and John McCormack sang on the same programme. The critics had then predicted a great singing career for Joyce and had not been so favourable to Mr. McCormack.

Nora started the phonograph because she had a record by a great Spanish baritone which she liked very much. Joyce was fidgety, waiting for the record to finish so that he could play a record of John McCormack's. "There is no voice like a fine tenor, do you think, McAlmon?" he said earnestly. "You are a glutton for flattery, aren't you, Joyce?" I answered. Joyce brightened up and said, "And why are you saying that? Now tell me seriously."

"Ah, sure, he knows you, Jim," Nora Joyce said brusquely. "You want to hear McCormack's voice because it's like your own entirely. Was there ever such a vain man! But you don't fool all of us. Come on now, and we'll have a rich good baritone for once in a way, and if you must have that tenor sweetness, you can sing us some of your favourites yourself. But mind you, Jim, what I said. You'll not be drinking too much this night. I'd better put the bottle away." Nora proceeded to put the bottle away, but Joyce later saw that my glass was empty, and Nora must not neglect a guest. The bottle came back, and Joyce, Nora, and I each had more, but as he was in his own apartment Nora was not worrying so much about how much he drank. No one would have to carry him upstairs.

Joyce always liked to celebrate birthdays and fête days, and when St. Patrick's day came around Sylvia Beach and Adrienne Monnier arranged a dinner party at the Trianon. The prospect did not excite me as I knew that Joyce's adulators, imitators, editors, translators, and explainers would be there in force, and perhaps too serious withal. I arrived late and had a few drinks in me. At the far end of the table I found a seat near Bill Bird and Lucia Joyce. At the other end were Nora and James Joyce, Herbert Gorman, and then came Mary and Padraic Colum, Stuart Gilbert, Sylvia Beach, Adrienne Monnier, Maria and Eugene Jolas, Giorgio Joyce, and Helen Fleischman. Lucia confided in me that she did not think too much of these parties that had been thrown together without rhyme or reason.

It is impossible to say what the others drank, but surely most of them ate and only sipped at the wine. I did not eat, but drank armagnac, and planned to plead a rendezvous and skip. However, the dinner ended, and Joyce had had a great deal of white wine, and now he began to feel that something must be done to liven up affairs. The fatal and awful words were spoken about someone making an after-dinner speech. Who made the suggestion I do not know. If it was Sylvia Beach, she knew better, for she was surely aware that after-dinner speeches are a trial to all concerned and not a convention in France. The suggestion had been made, however.

There sat Stuart Gilbert, who had been translating *Ulysses* and explaining it for several years. There were Mary and Padraic Colum, both Irish, who understood the "Irishness" of *Ulysses* and Joyce; and there was Herbert Gorman, who had written of Joyce's first forty years. and who was at the time working daily with Joyce with the intention of writing a biography. There was no reason whatever for me to make a speech. I had the worst seat at the table, dislike after-dinner speeches, and had not been a prime mover in getting the party together. Added to which, I cannot make an after-dinner speech. But Lucia and Bill Bird said, go ahead, and so I did. "This is the day that St. Patrick drove a lot of snakes out of Ireland, but one gathers there are many things left on that island that he might better have driven out," I said, and sat down. What the speech meant I do not know, and I doubt if any of the others did.

But somehow gaiety now broke loose in the party. Joyce sang

songs, Bill Bird came through with an effort, and he has no pretensions as a singer, and I broke loose with my "Chinese Opera".
Joyce wanted me to sing it, and I did. It is the corncrake and
calliope wail of a Chinese virgin in a snowstorm, not understanding
where she got her newborn babe, and the neighbour's son claims it is
not his inasmuch as he never saw her before. This is a performance
that has had me thrown out of several bars and most respectable
households and the police of various stations know it well. If they
have any comedy in them it prevents them from putting me in for
the night.

Later, when we left, Joyce wanted to climb up the lamp-post. He
fancied himself various kinds of dancers, tap, Russian, and belly.
Nora was there, however, and protest as Mr. Joyce might, she got
him into a taxi, and, despite his bitter wailings and protestations,
drove home with him. Gorman, it developed later, had become
discouraged about writing the Joyce biography, and it is easy to
understand why. Mr. Joyce had a way of answering questions by
saying, "Well, my father could tell you more of that. He's in Dublin.
You'd better go over and see him." Or, "That is for my brother to
say. He's in Trieste." There were friends and authorities in Zürich,
London, and elsewhere, and had Gorman done all the travelling
Joyce suggested he'd be travelling still.

Jimmie the barman was then working at the Trois et As bar near
the Hotel Foyot, and for a time that bar had quite a following. One
evening there was an amusing gathering to watch, although the
leading actors may have been uncomfortable. Lady Brett was there
with her new man; the first Mrs. Hemingway arrived, and soon in
came Hemingway with his second wife. Shortly after appeared
Boonie Goosens with Dan Reagan, whom she later married, after he
and Caroline Dudley were divorced. Dan Reagan had been about
with Hemingway who, having turned Catholic, was then endeavouring to convince his first wife that their marriage had not been a
marriage at all as it had not been performed by a priest. Hadley
Hemingway had answered, "All right, then the child is altogether
mine."

Such a collection of ex-wives and ex-loves would have been
difficult to find anywhere except in a Keystone comedy. Hadley
Hemingway, it should be recorded, was poised and dignified, and
her wit and discretion were to be admired. After greeting all the
others, she came to sit with Louise Bryant, William Bullitt, and me,

and she too saw the high comedy in the situation. None of us had known, until she informed us, that Hemingway was now a Catholic. With the Bullitts one night I met the novelist Owen Johnson. They went home to dinner, and Johnson did not want to be deserted. In spite of the fact that he was hard on the younger generation, and cruel about its pretences, we got on. Finally he began telling his own story. He had no patience with the theory that it was Scott Fitzgerald who first put the flapper and the jazz age into literature. He, Owen Johnson, had done this in several books long before, particularly in *The Salamanders*. He didn't have to argue with me about the beginning of the jazz and the flapper age. It began actively for me when I was fourteen. As a child I had noted it without curiosity in my elders. That means the jazz age proper and the flappers were going strong before 1910, some years before Scott Fitzgerald was beyond his own childhood. It was in its heyday when Irene and Vernon Castle were famous as ballroom dancers, and none of us as children considered ourselves grown up unless we could bonton, pigeon-trot, barn-dance, Spanish tango, or turkey-walk our two hundred miles a week of so-called dancing. In those days the hobble skirt and the sheath gown were creating a sensation, and I remember seeing the smart young ladies from the university doing a step or two on street corners as they waited for the streetcar to come along.

Because of all this I was able to solace Mr. Johnson a bit, and I assured him that he was at least as good as, if not a better writer than, Scott Fitzgerald. At the time I am writing this, it would be difficult to say which dates the most. Unlike Gertrude Stein, I agree with Scott himself in thinking that most of his books will not be interesting to later generations, except to intellectuals who will perhaps "revive" him in order to show their own extreme sensibilities.

Caresse and Harry Crosby, who had begun publishing works in de luxe editions, were planning to do a book of Kay Boyle's short stories, Joyce's *Tales Told of Shem and Shaun*, poems of Hart Crane's, Archibald MacLeish, and Jolas' *Secession in Astropolis*. Kay wanted me to meet them, and although I did on several occasions, I never knew them well. Caresse was an attractive, smartly dressed woman, and Harry, pale and with an elongated face, talked much of sun-worship rites, having recently returned from Egypt. The few times he and I talked I found it difficult to make any kind of contact. He was too full of hero-worship (Rimbaud, Verlaine, Villon) and of ecstasies and ideas about experimenting with life in order to harvest all the sensations it has to offer. Others who knew Harry Crosby much better than I did (Kay among them) found that he had not only a great deal of charm but also generosity and an impulsive readiness to help other people. With Kay and others I spent the New Year weekend at the Crosby country place, known as The Mill, and there Harry gave me a mixture which he later boasted was calculated to make me delirious and send me to the hospital. It did no such thing.

What Paris had once offered was no longer there so far as I was concerned, and I decided that Hiler's idea about a voyage was a bright one, and I went back to New York en route to Mexico. Rumours about a vital art movement and group in Mexico City had been drifting about for several years, and I had friends in Mexico City. Why not go and see?

Kay Boyle
1928-1930

The first week after I moved into the colony, Raymond suggested that he give a garden party for all of my friends. "Let them come by the dozens," he said, and even at that early date the unworthy suspicion crossed my mind that he might be thinking of them as potential customers for his wares. It would be a non-alcoholic party, naturally, as total abstinence was one of the rules of this Greek colony. He would make the punch himself, he said, and in it would be not alcohol but fresh fruit juices and it would prove that people could talk and sing, and dance and rejoice, without any need of stimulants. Raymond was a man of tremendous efficiency and energy, and he hung the trees in the back garden with Japanese lanterns and set bowls of fruit out on the long wooden tables. As I baked the cakes and put the icing on them, Raymond stocked the ancient icebox with milk, cow's milk, brought in two covered cans from the *épicerie*. Some of the guests might wish to drink milk as the evening wore on, he said. (Only once in the six months I was there did I see the herd of goats of which Raymond had spoken. It went past the front gate early one morning, and did not stop, and the children of the colony did not look up in recognition or even in curiosity when they heard the goatherd's musical piping in the street and the quick ringing of the passing bells.)

When the guests began to arrive on that summer evening, forewarned by Bob, they carried bottles under their jackets and hid them behind the severed bathtubs against the former greenhouse wall. Little by little, surreptitiously, they added whisky and gin and brandy to Raymond's punch bowl that stood, wreathed guilelessly with flowers, in the front hall. Within an hour the party was tremendously gay, and within two hours almost riotous, and Raymond maintained later that, although some of the poets had been drinking before they came, it was evident they enjoyed his punch as much as if it had been stronger stuff. On his narrow lips, in his grey, anxious eyes, hovered his habitual half-smile (a smile I came to know well, even to knowing, eventually, the exact measure of shrewd calculation or displeasure that it masked). There can be no doubt that Raymond knew on that evening, as always, precisely what was taking place.

My sister was in Paris for a day or two, and she came to the party with Ed Lanham, whose *Sailors Don't Care* Bob was to publish in 1929, and whom my sister was to marry that same year. McAlmon had brought Bill Bird along, and it was there, in Raymond's back garden, that I met for the first time this loyal and gentle man. (Look at his photograph: the necktie askew, the eyes forthright and shy, the high brow dedicated to depths of sacrifice and understanding that few men or women have any vision of. If he could efface his own likeness from the page, he would do so, for he existed to serve, to commemorate, with the same modesty and simplicity that Bill Williams did.) After several glasses of the strongly spiked punch it seemed only logical—there being by this time no bench or chair available—for me to sit on Bill Bird's knee under the lighted paper lanterns, and to talk to everyone from that secure and tranquil place.

(We were in Paris together in 1945, Bill Bird and I, both of us in American uniform with war correspondent patches on our sleeves, during the last bitter winter of the war, and he spoke of my sitting quite impersonally that summer night on his right knee, nearly twenty years before. "You did it so sensibly, wearing a golden tunic, and leaning forward to talk with Desnos, and Hiler, and Man Ray," he said; and he remembered the things that we had talked about. "With Desnos about that boy who used to be called 'the youngest poet in France,' Jacques Baron," Bill said as we sat in the Press Club in Paris, talking between the singing of French Resistance songs with David Schoenbrun and others who had rightly taken on the French revolt and triumph as their own; "and I told you McAlmon was the third corner in every triangle. I remember that. He deserved better, much better, and I wanted you to do something about him then, but I didn't know how to tell you what I meant."

(And in 1947, when Bill Bird and I, as journalists, covered together the inauguration of a French president at Versailles, he talked about that night again. "All I could tell you was," he said, "that McAlmon had been exploited, betrayed, neglected, deceived, and imitated beyond recognition, but anyway preyed on by the vultures of the writing world, and I wanted you to take it up from there. Was it really 1928? Was it that long ago? I remember the gold tunic you wore, and the different things you said sitting on my knee, and I didn't know what more to say to make you understand. Mention the name of almost any American writer of the twenties, and some English writers too, and I'll tell you the exact story of how every one of them did him in. Stein driving out to the printer's in a taxi and absconding with what amounted to the better part of the whole edition of *Americans*, and Hem making Bob the goat of that trip we took to Spain. All the bills were paid by Bob, of course, but when a choice of seats came up at a bullfight, Hem would throw his stalwart honour to the wind and have to have the one good seat left, down by the ring, because he was 'studying the art of it', while Bob and I, not knowing anything, I suppose, about art in any shape or form, could just as well sit in the bleachers as long as Hem would explain it all to us anyway after the dust had cleared. But it wasn't just that: Hem had to have his bottles of Johnnie Walker, or whatever the brand was, even in Spain, and at Bob's expense. The price of them was enough to ruin a millionaire, and Bob was never that, and then Hem settling accounts with him in Paris by socking him in the jaw."[1])

Once I experienced the full measure of Raymond's solicitude, and that was at the end of the party when I sprained my ankle jumping from the front seat of Hiler's moving car. He and my sister and Ed Lanham had decided to drive straight from Neuilly to Chartres, to see the cathedral in the light of dawn, and Hiler was shouting to the stars in sorrow that he was going to redecorate the place. Raymond was pleased that I had refused to be borne away, and he carried me back to the villa, and bathed, massaged, and bound up the torn and painful ligaments. He told me of the stricken he had nursed during a cholera epidemic years before, in a country from which even the

[1] Hiler once told me the story of Hemingway knocking Bob down in front of Jimmy Charters' little bar, but whether it was the Falstaff or the Dingo he couldn't recall. At that time Hemingway weighed over two hundred pounds, Hiler said, and Bob about a hundred and fifteen soaking wet.

doctors had fled. As he talked, the familiar half-smile played on his lips, and his expert fingers sought the knots of pain and smoothed them gently, gently away. But even in his tenderness he could not refrain from speculating on the time it would take my ankle to heal. "Rest tomorrow, Sunday," he said, "and soak it frequently, and then you'll be fine and dandy on Monday morning to get down to the store."

By the tenth of July the Dayang Muda and Archie had left Paris for the mountains; Jolas had gone back to Colombey, and was then going on to Lorraine, and wouldn't be back until September; Brancusi was in Switzerland; and in the next few days McAlmon too would go. I went to bed early every evening in the cool of Neuilly, contented that Sharon was nearby. Six days a week I opened one of the two shops by nine in the morning (while Ayah opened the other), washed the sidewalk clean with a long-handled scrubbing brush and buckets of water, and then sat down and wrote short stories and poems on the backs of envelopes, on odds and ends of paper I found in the back room of the shop, and even at times on the other side of the sheets of poetry that had been submitted for Archie's and my yearbook. (Oh, dead poets, forgive me this!) When customers came through the door, I would slip my writing under a cushion on the Grecian bench. Many of them—among the Americans, at least—entered tentatively, almost in guilt, because of the contrast the shop seemed to present to their own materialistic way of life. Little did they know.

Once Lucia Joyce came to see me at the Rue du Faubourg St. Honoré to talk of Elizabeth Duncan's School of Dance in the *Schloss* on the outskirts of Salzburg. Whether it had been suggested to her that she come, or whether she had come of her own accord, I did not know. But as she sat in the sunlight that came hot through the plate-glass window, I felt her tragically reaching, seeking for what could probably never be found, and for a fearful moment I believed I was looking at my own reflection in a glass. She was like the high, perishable, wishful tendril of a vine moving blindly up a wall, and the vine from which she sought escape was rooted in a territory that had for her no recognizable name. I thought of Joyce's poem to his blue-veined daughter, and there in her delicate wrists I could see the veins, so vulnerable under the silky, transparent skin. She was (as perhaps I too was then, and as perhaps all daughters are until they cease being merely daughters) precariously only half a person, and the other half she sought for in panic first in one direction and then in another, not knowing in whose mind or flesh or in what alien country it might lie. She was uneasy about going to Salzburg alone for the summer session, and she wondered if I might not be able to go too. There was nothing I could say except that I had a job and a child, and that we could plan to dance together in October when Elizabeth would be opening her Paris school.

Once Joyce stopped in at the other shop on the Boulevard St. Germain, a figure of gentlemanly distinction coming through the door, a British diplomat, you might have decided if you didn't know otherwise, in his well-cut grey suit and his felt hat imported from Italy. It was always information he was interested in, exact and detailed information, his mind and his ear sharp for whatever you would say. He wanted to know about the weaving of the tunics and rugs, and where the looms were. McAlmon had told him this and told him that about the colony, but still he wasn't quite sure that he understood. He walked from table to table, his long, strong, well-kept hands (with a jewelled ring on one finger of the left hand) touching the materials which his eyes could not adequately see. It was on the tip of my tongue to tell him that the only weaving I'd seen in my time in the colony was my own art of weaving in and out and back and forth the worn-out collars and cuffs of the shirts Harold Stearns and George Davis brought me to repair for them, they both being on the threshold of the poorhouse, great men of life that they were. But I felt too shy of Joyce to mention this. The information he asked for so quietly and listened for so intently I could not give him, but this one time at least it was not of great importance, for there was something in the back of his mind that was troubling him more. After a long moment of silence he asked me hesitantly if I thought it might be harmful for a young girl to go off alone to a foreign country. "Lucia and you are maybe within a year or two of each other, but maybe not," he said. "But surely close enough for you to know what her tribulations and misgivings could be." Ah, well, he sighed at the end, who in the world can decide for another? It would be asking too much to think that one young woman could take the responsibility of entering into another young woman's hopes and fears. "As far as my children are concerned, I am always asking the impossible. A father feels at a loss," he said. In a short time, he said he and his wife would be leaving Paris too.

These isolated moments of my own balance and sanity have remained with me, ineffaceable in their clarity. Harry Crosby, his pallor, his leanness, his self-deprecating humour, the poems he brought to the Rue du Fauborg St. Honoré, are not remembered by an effort of the will. They have simply never ceased to be. George Davis came to read me chapters of the novel he was writing, and share goat cheese, and yogurt, and dried figs with me at noon; and Harold Stearns came to talk about the book he was working on, the definitive biography of Rabelais. Germaine Garrigou came and went; and as each of them left me I knew it was not a door they were going through out into the street, it was never an actual door they were closing. It was their lives that were being withdrawn from me, their complete, articulate lives that they were taking away with them every time they left, leaving me speechless and afraid. I could not write letters any more. That kind of definition had failed me. I could not even write to Carnevali, for the fatuous ego was on the point of taking over entirely.

The night before McAlmon left for the south of France, or for Greece, or Mallorca or Mexico, or whatever it was, Richard arrived unexpectedly from England on a business trip. He came to the shop on the Boulevard St. Germain, and we went to Montparnasse for dinner, and I introduced him to McAlmon at the Coupole bar. Everyone was there: Kiki, and Hiler, and Flossie Martin, and Buffy and Graeme, and Kisling, and Desnos, and Pascin, for a brief moment, and perhaps a dozen others. But it was a sad evening, an evening of goodbyes being said for the summer, and suddenly McAlmon got down from the bar stool he was sitting on, and walked to the end of the counter and leaned across it and jerked the handsomely printed announcement of Archie's and my yearbook of poetry from the wall. He looked me straight in the eye with his glacial blue stare as he tore the announcement into two, and then into four, and flung it on the floor. "That's what I think of your crazy, senseless undertakings! That's what I think of your taste in poetry!" he said. At our feet lay the scattered uproarious words: "the best . . . ever published . . . most sought-after . . . renowned . . . LIVING POETRY . . ." screamed the poor hysterical words with their throats cut now, writhing their last on the bar room floor. I had been drinking from a tall glass stein of beer, and before Richard could stop me, or before I myself knew what I was about to do, I threw the stein after McAlmon, who had started back to his seat again. But it missed him, and hit the edge of the counter, and the great splash of beer smacked into Buffy's face. The laughter of everyone—including Bob's grim laughter—was a terrible thing to hear, and in the moment before I rushed out onto the Boulevard Montparnasse I saw Buffy put his head down on the bar and cry.

Sometime in the middle of July, Ayah told me cheerfully one day that they would all be going off to a house they had in Nice for the summer, the entire colony. Other years she had had to stay behind to keep the shops open so that revenue would be coming in, but this year they would close one shop entirely, and I would keep the other going. They would be gone six or even seven weeks, and she knew the time would pass quickly for me because of all the friends I had. So off they all went one night, packed into two third-class compartments of the train, taking Sharon with them, and off into the deep I went without any trouble at all. In and out of every bar in Montparnasse I tripped and reeled and stumbled in my fine blue cape. (That cape which Bill Shirer was later to write became my symbol and signature. Symbol for what? For a total disintegration of whatever I was or was not, the shroud of a symbolic suicide, it might be said, a signature scrawled without grandeur on the riverbank or stuffed with its strident, illegible message into a bottle that was not washed up on any shore.) I consorted with this one and that one, love having nothing to do with it (love, indeed, the most uproarious joke of the century), probity scattered to the north, east, west, and south (if such directions should still be recognized), and perhaps the most side-splitting chapter of the sage was Mama and Papa Hiler taking me (wall-eyed, scarcely able to stand) to lunch at the American Women's Club (because I dressed so nicely and was such a lady) to ask me gently but directly if it was my intention to marry Hiler. "Dear young Kay, it would be a fine and respectable thing for the two of you," Papa Hiler wrote me after (Papa Hiler from the Broadway theatrical world, with diamonds on his plump little fingers, Papa Hiler whom I liked far better than his son). I tore the letter into pieces and threw it down the privy in the courtyard behind the shop on the Right Bank, but I can still see the words written out in his sloping hand, as regular as if the ruled lines of the high school copybook were forever there. How could I answer that I was committed to the dead?

Off the deep end I had indeed gone, and week in week out my

grief for myself was a pretty thing to see. If there was any compensation offered, it was that from now on I could look with passionate compassion on any fallen sisters, and could even stoop to give them a hand up from the gutter, French or English, Swiss or American, or whatever they might be. The puritanical conscience is the coldest and cruellest of all the self-flagellating consciences to bear, for it stamps the sweet abandon out of life entirely. It was not sufficient that I go on the loose, but it must be with those I could not consort with in tenderness. The puritanical conscience, with its little grey bonnet tied under its chin, kept me from taking with gusto all these fine experiences I was having at nightfall, and I went around trying to cleanse myself of the shame of them come the brutal light of day. But I could not turn to the high pure shape of any church, or to any man decked out in holy trappings, no matter how humble he might be; for had not all good men in holy trappings laid aside their garments and braved the waters of George Moore's lake, and swum to final clarity? The resolve like the redemption must come from somewhere within me; this terrible and hopeless portion of the truth I knew. About this time I wrote a story called "Vacation Time".[2] It begins:

> I was walking around like a nut in the streets after the train had gone off, and the black was running down my face from my eyes. I was going like a crazy woman from one place to another thinking that tonight I must get into something deeper, the eyes full, the mouth full, to be sunk in it, to wallow like a sow. What good would it do to drink if to go home to that place empty of any sound. A good deal of your violence is not I thought. The trouble with you is.

> I went into one place where there was a man I knew at the bar drinking and I sat talking for a long time to this man I knew. I was listening to him talking with my eyes rocking in my head and when I had had a lot to drink I said I just sent my little girl off to the south I said . . . That's too bad he said. Yes, I could believe very much in something I said I could believe in something but what it is I cannot explain. I am seeing that to be a believer you are to be blinded to your own satisfaction.

---

[2] *Wedding Day and Other Stories*, by Kay Boyle, published by Jonathan Cape and Harrison Smith, Inc., New York, 1930.

You cannot believe and see clear at the same time. What about your religion I said. I've tucked it away he said and am taking something to drink in the place of it.

... I am not able to stay home in intellectual quiet I am beginning to get tired of what is sensitive unable to acclimatize I am for the gay the biddy a great thing it is to roll home in the furnace of anybody's mouth blasting rust like wine all night and no sleep but the brain too going hot as a black bottom.

but then morning gentlemen oh the morning with the long sad face the black eyes crooked in the mirror the rouge standing up like an army oh beauty not lovely enough or strong enough some day I'll give you a piece of my mind and it'll be a great gift to you.

... How flat the clouds lie on mornings like these when I remember other mornings other clouds riding the wind of the last breath of do you see the light in the window the dawn has come over Monte-Carlo isn't it too lovely lovely and he answered me I can't hear you the cocaine is ringing too loud in my ears

were those his last words to you

no there were more

and which my lovely strained-eyed lady pull your gaze out of the mirror for five minutes and answer the district gendarmerie. His last words to me were harsh ones I cannot bring myself to repeat them here before all these unmelting hearts have melted. He said I cannot hear you the cocaine

Did he amplify that statement

Yes he said that the cocaine was ringing like. She hung her head and said she did not remember. We must have the scene arrange itself clear with dawning yawning over Monte-Carlo and the Sister of Mercy drawing her wet thumb along her head-dress pleats and the bags of oxygen deflated in the corner. What were his last words Mrs. Stick-in-the-Mud

He did not draw himself up to his full height as a poet he
sagged in the middle there was a bright fan of red velvet fluttering
from his mouth and he was saying speak louder for Christ's
sake the cocaine is ringing like hell in my head

I looked into the bottom of my glass of and I murmured to the
soft blue clouds of gin I too I too should have spat my way
to heaven with him.

Sometimes when I couldn't stand any more the shabby scenery of
their rooms, or the smell of their breaths, I'd let myself into the
darkened shop on the Boulevard St. Germain late at night, and
stagger from Grecian pillar to post, and sleep on the floor. Once
George Davis, unable to pay the rent of his hotel room, and his
book not finished, wrapped himself up in a tunic and slept with me
there. But finally the moment came when I found there would be
trouble to face nine months ahead, and who the happy and proud
progenitor might be I was unable to determine. All I knew was that
it could not, must not be born, and I denied it its life with the cold
calculation of an executioner. What would its face be like? was my
excuse. I cried this out to Caresse, who came to the shop one
afternoon to see me: whose features would it bear? The answer I
should have given to that was: *my own*; but I was ruthlessly determined on annihilation. Caresse helped me find the place and time,
and Harry (who had had no part in it) paid the enormous bill. And
then they too left Paris, and I began again trying by writing to
transform the image of what I knew I had become, but so flagrant
the failure that I did not have the will to put a stamp on it, and send
it off for those I believed in to hold up to the light.

Far back in the innocent days of Le Havre, I had lied and I had
stolen. It was merely a cat that I stole, any rational person would
have argued, but for myself it was the simple circumstance that I had
learned the way to steal; and now I had learned the way of depriving
of its promised life a creature without defences, perhaps sucking its
thumb already and dreaming gentle dreams of milk and stars. These
things I had done were all the flowering of the tenderest care and
cultivation, the results of a privileged upbringing, of a youth in
which the spirit had been gently nurtured. I had never for a moment
doubted that the integrity of that spirit would be extended without
effort, without the necessity of conscious thought, to integrity of

conduct. I could not have been more mistaken. Not until Le Havre had I questioned the inevitability of the transfer from thought to act. And now I was faced with the knowledge that if I, with the love of a gently bred family to shape me, had become what I was then the whole moral fabric of our society was in jeopardy. It was in terms as dramatic and outsized as these that I viewed my own collapse.

I reflected on Gertrude Stein's dismissal of me as being too bourgeois for consideration even as a visitor at teatime, and I asked the distressed face in every mirror that I passed if it was only because there was no longer any necessity to buy shrewdly in the markets, or to save snail shells once the snails were eaten, boiling them clean of their garlic and butter and using them over and over again, that I was adrift now without moorings on a wildly tormented sea? Was it only because there was no longer any need for me to polish a floor (for who would walk across it?), or draw the threads from the inner seams of a man's jacket so as to weave his trousers or his coat like new—was it because I was deprived of these humble, daily acts that I could no longer give order and dignity to my nights and days?

I might never have survived to tell the tale at the pace I was going had not some kindly hand (perhaps that of the privy in the courtyard behind the shop, the doctors at the hospital suggested) intervened and presented me with meningitis one late August day. There I was riding in style in a shining, wailing ambulance, with each bar of sunlight that struck across the windows of the sumptuous vehicle striking like blazing iron across my eyes, my skull. The pain was such that they tied me down to keep me from beating my brains out against the white cage of the bed. Not even Carnevali's "Sick Men's Hymn"[3] had prepared me for what was taking place. "The hospital waits:/" he wrote, "I today, you tomorrow;/ five days, ten days, a month,/ six months, a year, ten years . . ." I hadn't believed a word of it, except poetically, and the American Hospital in Neuilly, and the medical profession in general, weren't doing much about poetry that year. My mother was inexplicably there, moving down the narrow, low-ceilinged corridors of pain with me, but always a little way behind me or a little way ahead. When I took my cranium in both hands and turned it forcibly so as to find her, turned it like a bowling-alley ball, with my thumbs hooked into the sockets of my eyes for stability, the voice that I heard screaming at the sight of light I knew was not my own.

[3] *This Quarter*, Vol. 1, No. 1 (Paris, 1925).

But I could not quite manage to see my mother's face until the morning they did the spinal puncture. Suddenly, in the agony of that, there she was, sitting quite close and fragrant, exactly as when she used to put the kisses in my palms at night in Pocono, and I would not open my clenched fists all night in fear they would get away. She had come over from England, and eventually there was my sister too (with Ed Lanham), paying the six-week hospital bills. At the beginning of September Jolas came back and pushed me in a wheel chair onto the sun porch of the hospital, and I closed my eyes when he did this and pretended it was the boardwalk at Atlantic City, and that I was eleven years old, and that it was Charlie Sheeler pushing me in a rolling chair. McAlmon wrote me from the south of France that he was having Laurence Vail send me some of his (Vail's) poetry for Archie's and my anthology, and that he himself was working on the "Politics of Existence", and on some poetry he wanted me to see. I would lie in bed in absolute peace in the great white ward of the hospital, with letters and typescripts of poetry around me, reading at times, but mostly not reading, lying as if in a tranquil pool of sunlit water, breathing and eating and sleeping in singular happiness. I would wait for Mother to come through the door in the afternoon visiting hours, and I knew I was not going to be a failure any longer. I was going to repay everyone the sums of money I had cost them. I was going to live humbly and soberly.

Ayah had had to come back from Nice to open one of the shops after my collapse, but she did not come to see me. I could understand their irritation with me because of the summer's ruined plans. When I could go back to work it was already October, and I walked on two canes still. I would get off the bus, as I could not manage the subway steps now, and the block that stretched before me to Raymond Duncan's shop seemed to reach into eternity. Raymond reproached me on the score of loyalty, saying it was "mother-sickness" that had laid me low. I had the official document from the American Hospital to show him, with "cerebral meningitis" written large as life or death upon it, but he preferred to look at something else. With the nervous half-smile on his lips, he spoke of the Family, the Family as an Institution, saying that if only everyone could free himself of the chains and shackles of that prison of the spirit and will, what miracles would then take place. Substitute the Institution of the Family by a community of brotherly understanding, he said, and there would be an end to all psychological disorders and to individual as well as collective aggression. In the ideal community that he envisaged, peace and pulchritude would reign, he said, flinging the tail end of his tunic across his shoulder, in a world that had been rendered evil by parental possessiveness. The inference in all he said was that it would be very difficult for him to put his entire faith in me again (and how right he was).

Early in November, without any fanfare or pennants flying, two modest-looking American ladies walked into the shop on the Boulevard St. Germain and began looking at the things on display. Only after a half hour or so of tentative questions about the prices and the quantities, did they say rather diffidently that they had come with twenty-five thousand dollars (or was it fifty thousand?) to spend on a collection of Raymond Duncan's tunics and scarves and rugs and draperies. They had the intention of establishing a Raymond Duncan wing as a gift to a Kentucky museum devoted exclusively to American art. (These are the details as I recall them after forty years, but about the vast sum to be spent I cannot be in error, for the money was given to Raymond that year.) The realization for all the plans we had talked of now seemed possible: the hand-printing press which Raymond was going to set up, and on which I was going to print our poetry anthology; the kiln, the looms, constructed like those which Raymond's wife had used years ago in Greece; and the reorganization of the house so that the eight or nine children need not sleep on a pile of sheep hides on the floor; and some kind of outfits, Greek as he might want them, so that the children might be able to go outdoors in the cold Paris winters, which at present they could not do. But although Raymond did set up some makeshift looms at the colony, during the week that a professional photographer came to take pictures for the museum catalogue, none of the plans we had made in the months before were ever spoken of again. Instead, Raymond bought himself a rather fancy American car.

It was after the purchase of the car that I told Raymond I could not stay on at the colony, that the things I had come to work for there simply didn't exist, and that when he had found someone else to run the shop Sharon and I would go. I was not in the best of positions, actually, to take issue with Raymond's integrity, for Caresse and Harry Crosby had gone on a trip to America, and Harry had insisted on leaving me their limousine and chauffeur for the time they would be away. Every morning the long, black, elegant car would call for me at the colony, and the chauffeur would open the car door and place a sable lap robe across my knees; and on the days of Elizabeth Duncan's dance classes, she and I would ride in state to the hall she had rented, the cracked and broken toes of our ancient shoes emerging shamelessly from under the lap robe's sleek fur. Raymond, once I had spoken of going, took me in his lean Greek arms and whispered: "Bear with me. Everything will change," and I saw there were tears on his lashes. It was Ayah, her pink cheeks glowing, who danced like a partridge with rage when she knew. "*You* may go," she cried out, "but not the child, ah, never! You gave the child to the colony! We assumed all expenses for it, took it away on vacation for the summer! You abandoned it! We've had cases like this before, and we always won them in court. Go, get out! You are free to leave!" But she amended it: "As soon as I've made an inventory at the stores and see that everything is there. But the child remains!"

During November and December I worked steadily with Raymond on the enormous catalogue for the museum in Kentucky, for hundreds of pieces had been bought, and each one must have its own paragraph of history. At times we worked between customers in the shop on the Left Bank, at times in the main room of the colony in the evening, and it was as if my leaving had never been spoken of; but the Dayang Muda and I were making our covert plans. Archie had not returned to Paris but had gone to the sanatorium in the Haute Savoie, for his lungs were not improving. He was in a state of deep depression, his close friend, Jacques Convert d'Arnault, barely twenty, having died that summer of the same malady. (In *transition* 13 a moving poem of Archie's, dedicated to Jacques, was published.) The Princess and I were convinced there would be actual physical interference if I tried to walk out of the house with Sharon, for there were strong and determined men and women in the colony. We had begun to hear talk of things that had happened in the past, and Elizabeth Duncan confirmed that there had been lawsuits through the years over the guardianship of certain of the children. Sharon had been illegally registered in Nice, and I feared I might have trouble proving she was mine before the law. On the occasional nights when I was left alone with the children (the other members of the colony having gone to a movie, or an art exhibit, or to take part in a dance recital), the Dayang Muda and I would stagger up and down the cellar steps with boxes of my books and papers that Richard had sent on from England, and suitcases of my Paris clothes, and we would put them in Harry's limousine that waited outside the gate. By the time the others returned, the Princess, with the long cigarette holder clenched in her teeth, and Harry's chauffeur would already be unloading my possessions at the Rue Louis David, and putting them in the cellar there.

But it would not be wise for me simply to go to the Princess' with Sharon. That would be the first place Ayah and Raymond would go to look for me. Yet the choices were few, for I had only a few francs in the world, and no job prospect, and it never came into my head to repeat history and inflict myself on Richard as before. One evening just before Christmas I closed the shop on the Right Bank as usual about six o'clock, and I walked through the lightly falling snow to the Métro station at the Place de la Madeleine. I remember still the extraordinary happiness, almost exhilaration, that filled my heart. I stopped to buy a branch of holly and a small bouquet of mistletoe on the way, and I decided not to go back to the colony at once, but to go to Montparnasse for a little while. It was months since I had been to the Coupole, and I didn't want a drink, but I knew I could have milk and a sandwich with Gaston, the barman, there. Instead I met Clotilde Vail and her brother Laurence for the first time. They were sitting at a table in the Coupole bar with McAlmon, whom I had not seen since July. "Come and have a drink and supper with us! We've just ordered oysters and white wine!" Laurence called out, as he would have to any young woman he happened to see. Then he got up and took the mistletoe from me, and held it over my head, and kissed me on the nose, and the eyelids, and finally on the mouth. McAlmon leaned back laughing in his chair, and Clotilde put her small, nervous, white hand, the rings of it much too heavy for her delicate bones, and she pulled me down beside her on the banquette. "I'll sit between you and my brother," she said, "so he won't eat the mistletoe."

I drank buttermilk, which Laurence thought an amazing thing to do, and after he and Clotilde, he tall, she short, but both as blond as lions, had left, McAlmon and I moved to the bar and talked until very late. It was he who thought of the last step of the escape plan from the colony. He had heard the Crosbys would be back for Christmas, and this was true. Caresse's children, Polleen and Billy, would be out of boarding school for the vacation, and Caresse had written me that she and Harry would be at their place in the country with them, at Le Moulin, perhaps an hour's drive

from Paris. "That's the place to go," Bob said. "I wouldn't mind
getting out of Paris at all, so pick me up at the hotel when you've got
Sharon out of the colony, and we'll go." But it was the Dayang
Muda who manœuvred the actual getaway. Through Ayah, she
invited me and the nine children to lunch the last day of the year.
Bitter and grey it was, and preparing to snow again, and the
children's bare legs under their tunics, and their bare feet in their
sandals, were blue from the cold. The oldest girl (Ayah's and
Raymond's daughter, it was said) took four of the children in one
taxi, and I took Sharon and the four others in another. When we
reached the Rue Louis David everything went according to plan. All
the children went up in the elevator to the Dayang Muda's apartment, and I stayed in the taxi with Sharon and immediately drove
away. It was almost eleven o'clock, and, although I had arranged
the hour with Bob the day before, he was asleep still. While he
showered and shaved and dressed, Sharon and I went to sleep in
each other's arms on his bed for a little while. About noon he
ordered coffee and croissants in the room, and he woke us up,
saying: "You'd better wash her feet before we go."

There were too many people at Le Moulin that December afternoon,
and none of them—except for Caresse's two children, Polleen and
Billy, who were twelve and ten—were the kind of people McAlmon
liked. Whenever I looked at him across the chaos of the great, wide
room, where a fire burned in a raised fireplace vast enough to
barbecue a steer in, he had the look of a bolting horse in his eye. It
was almost always the case in Caresse's and Harry's gatherings: one
had to hold onto a clear knowledge of what they were seeking and
what they had relinquished, sacrificed even, in that search, in
order to by-pass the people who surrounded them. Somehow, even on
that disordered afternoon and evening, I was able to sit in a small
vacuum of quiet on the flagstones of the fireplace and talk to Harry.
I spoke about Bob's long poem, "North America, Continent of
Conjecture," which was then taking shape (and which Ethel Moorhead was to publish twenty-two pages of in *This Quarter* 4). I was
still not drinking, and so I could talk coherently about the different
portions of the poem: the "Race Riot Blues", and "The Wall Street
Chant", and the "Law Twisting Blues", and "Strut Your Stuff",
and the "Lumberjack Blues". "McAlmon is trying his hand at
something no American writer has yet done," I said, or something

like that. "Far, far ahead, there will be American writers caught up in it as well," I said to Harry, "but McAlmon just happens to be doing it twenty years earlier than anyone else." When I had said a few lines of McAlmon's "Wall Street Chant" to him, Harry cheered and wanted a copy to send to his father, the businessman, whom everyone knew as Steve.

But the struggle to keep close to Harry, and to isolate his fanatical purity of spirit in the welter that always pressed upon him, was not an easy thing, and sometimes one gave up in despair. (How was one to know that Harry would be dead before the next Christmas came around?) After his death, I spoke of all this in the homage I wrote to him,[4] saying that he was a man who had "no time nor inclination for cynicism or for slander", and continuing (in part):

> . . . there should be no confusion, no question, in judging the work of a young man who took his time and his contemporaries to heart. With all the nobility of his belief in them, and all the courage of his determination to make his life a testament of stern and uncompromising beauty, he wrote his poems and wrote his diary in words that never faltered in their pursuit of his own amenable soul.
>
> . . . His heart was open like a door, so open that there was a crowd getting into it. And with his mind it was the same way. His protection was not in closing himself up when he found he was invaded, but in retreat. Retreat from knowing too much, from too many books, from too much of life. . . . If he went into retreat, into his own soul, he would go trailing this clattering, jangling universe with him, this ermine-trimmed, this moth-eaten, this wine velvet, the crown jewels on his forehead, the crown of thorns in his hand, into retreat, but never into escape. . . .

In that same number of *transition*, which appeared six months after Harry's tragic death, among other tributes to him was Hart Crane's "To the Cloud Juggler", dedicated to Harry. The final lines of it go: "Wrap us and lift us; drop us then, returned/Like water, undestroyed, like mist, unburned/But do not claim a friend like him again,/Whose arrow must have pierced you beyond pain."

On that last evening of 1928 Harry concocted a particular drink

[4] *transition*, 19–20, 1930.

for McAlmon (and for any others who had the temerity to try it),
which was intended to send Bob into poetic delirium for the next
twenty-four hours. No one who had ever taken this preparation,
Harry said, had ever been quite the same. Bob maintained that it had
no effect on him of any kind, and that he had drunk far more
deadly mixtures with Jimmie the barman. But when I left the
riotous mill room just after the new year had come in, and was
crossing the cobbles of the courtyard in the starlight to the farm
building where Sharon and Polleen and Billy and the servants
slept, McAlmon was suddenly there beside me in the cold. "It's too
damned depressing," he said; "so depressing that I can't even get
drunk. They're wraiths, all of them. They aren't people. God knows
what they've done with their realities."

We walked for a minute or two around the courtyard, around and
around, not arm in arm, or holding hands, or anything like that, but
always keeping a little distance between us. I said maybe sometime
he ought to try reading pages of Harry's diary, and some of his
poems, sentimental as Rilke's, but humorous too, in order to know
what Harry was. I said maybe the Black Sun Press would do a
collection of his (McAlmon's) poetry, and if they did I thought the
book should begin with the poem I'd been saying aloud to myself
since 1923. "Which poem?" McAlmon asked. "You know—'Oh,
let me gather myself together,' " I said, and I found it difficult to go
on saying: " 'Where are the pieces quivering and staring and
muttering . . .' " McAlmon did not say anything until we were
near the farmhouse door again, and this time I opened it, and the
light from inside fell on his face. "For Christ's sake, six years saying
the same poem? When are you going to grow up, kid?" he said.
Then he began jerking out—not laughter this time but the words of
self-vituperation. "The God-damned, fucking, quivering pieces of
me! Good enough to be flushed like you know what down the drain!
Stinking enough to be tacked on the barn door in warning to the
young!" he shouted. "Fouled up enough for—what? You finish it!
I'm fed up with whatever it is I'm carrying around inside this skin,
rattling around inside these bones!" He struck his chest violently
with his fist, and his face was as hard as stone. "For Christ's sake,
don't care about me! Stop it, will you? Let the God-damned
pieces fall apart!"

Then he went back across the courtyard, and I went into the
hallway and closed the door. When I woke up in the morning and

carried Sharon across the courtyard to breakfast, the chauffeur said McAlmon had already taken a taxi back to Paris. The snow was just beginning to fall.

I had hoped the Black Sun Press would do a collection of Bob's poetry, but this never came about. In 1933 Caresse brought out a volume of his short stories, entitled *Indefinite Huntress*. Bob was not in France then, but we worked out the selection of stories by correspondence, and he let me choose the title. Ezra Pound wrote (in part) of it:

> For ten years criticism at that level below which one is uncertain as to the applicability of the term, has snarled and snapped and demurred about the work of McAlmon. . . . Mr. McAlmon does not do the American waste-land all dolled up with onyx and brass fittings; he does not give one half of an underdone damn for my early suggestions as to how American verse-slop could be expurgated. . . .
>
> McAlmon, like Professor Beebe, the oceanographer, descends to unexplored levels, at least to levels Henry James never dreamed of; but his descent is entirely and utterly different from that of the writers of "rough stuff". . . . His truck driver, let us say, has a soft spot or a curiosity which the 47 cliché truck drivers in the editorial reserve desk have not. . . . The value of McAlmon seems to me largely in that during ten years of American realism in its present phase he has refused to move towards the impoverishment of the subject matter, towards the simplification of types. . . . In short, show me an author in whose pages I or any other European can learn more about the nature of contemporary Americans, and I will endeavour to do him justice. In the present state of my acquaintance with current American prose I know no one who covered such an extent . . .[5]

And William Carlos Williams wrote (again in part):

> An American publisher for McAlmon's work remains yet to be discovered. . . . Get published? Not get published? Do it yourself? Somebody else do it? It's all one, but no man can go on alone in this way forever. . . .

[5] "McAlmon," *New English Weekly*, London, February 9, 1933.

If there is in writing a form without form, it is that of McAlmon. What he does is not realism. It has about it a strong moral tone. It is a return of the meaning, moral, to the word. . . . It is the word used with a conscience, and for its proper significance as a word, not just as the *mot juste* in the pattern. . . . To him it is moral to state the truth even at its most distasteful. . . . It is no matter what the scene is or who it is who is talked about, what kind of pattern portrayed, it must be portrayed above all else truthfully, with the words that belong to that portrayal and with the mind that sees it, and sees the word, simultaneously, alongside. This is the art of the word. . . . McAlmon is the first today in England or America who has in fiction this quality. . . . He has not chosen what he would and would not see. . . .[6]

In 1937, when McAlmon's collection of poetry was published by New Directions, William Rose Benét wrote (in part) of it:

It is direct. It is simple. It uses a sort of free-prose statement, and rhymes not very well. Yet its description is clear and forceful . . . His last poems are of fighting Spain, and express perfectly the loyalist spirit in that ravaged land. Mr. McAlmon *is* of this time . . . He writes in broken rhythms, he finds felicities almost by accident, as Whitman found them. He feels nostalgia for his American childhood, and recalls it not merely wistfully, but with the quick imagination of a child . . .[7]

Laurence Vail and I celebrated the Quatorze Juillet of 1929 with Hart Crane in Paris. Hart was going to come and visit us in our little house, with a vast studio for Laurence's painting, in a village called Ste. Aulde, on the river Marne. It was there that Laurence and I began our long life together, beginning it with two children, Sharon, and Laurence's son, Sindbad. Hart wanted to find a quiet, farmhouse room near us and work there, for he was in despair about the little amount of writing he had got done.

When the first week in August came and he did not arrive, we began telephoning his hotel in Paris. He had not been seen there for over a fortnight, they said; so we drove the two hours into Paris in search of him. From Maria Jolas we learned that Hart was in

[6] *The Transatlantic Review*, Vol. II, No. 2 (Paris, 1924).
[7] *Saturday Review of Literature*, June 5, 1937, New York.

prison, in the Santé, and had been there nearly three weeks. He had got into an argument with Madame Sélect late one night, apparently because of his refusal to pay for the drinks he had had. This, at least, was her interpretation of Hart's wild French and his antic gestures, and she had called the police. Four of them had dragged Hart down the Boulevard Montparnasse, Maria had been told, with his head banging against the cobbles of the street-car tracks. She had learned all this only a day or two before, and she had immediately notified the American Consulate and found a lawyer for him. Laurence said we would stay in Paris as long as necessary to help her get Hart out, and then we telephoned Caresse and Harry Crosby at Le Moulin. They too had been looking for Hart. They would drive in early the next morning to help in any way they could.

When Laurence went off to the lawyer's office that late afternoon, I set off for the Coupole bar to keep our rendezvous with Clotilde, and her French fiancé Alain Lemerdy, and Bill Bird. Paris is a ghost city in the month of August, and there are long stretches of total silence in almost every street—or there were then. I walked alone in the slow dying of the day's heat, filled with guilty contentment, knowing that, having found Laurence, I would never be alone again. Our first child was going to be born in December, and there would be more children; and we would write books, and translate the books of the French writers we liked; and we would paint pictures, and climb mountains, and cross glaciers, and travel with all our children, forever together. But all McAlmon had been to me, and had not been, all that he had said, or had not said, was never to be effaced. I was to see him only once more, in 1931 in the south of France when he came to dinner one night with us on the Col-de-Villefranche. There were a number of friends there that evening: Helen and Giorgio Joyce, and Emma Goldman over from St. Tropez, and Alexander Berkman, and Mary Reynolds and Marcel Duchamp. Afterwards, we all walked down the sandy, rocky, winding lane to the sea, Bob and I for the first time walking hand in hand in the dark blue, Mediterranean night, with the peacocks screaming at us from the trees beyond the garden walls. Victoria McAlmon was to say after his death that even as a little boy he had believed everyone was out "to get him", and that he had feared betrayal even before he had been so bitterly betrayed. She was to say that the word "love" was synonymous to "lie" for him because one woman had made it seem that way.

The Coupole bar was empty that August afternoon in Paris, and I sat on a high stool to talk with Gaston until Clotilde and Alain and Bill Bird would come. Gaston, the barman, was also part-owner of the Coupole, and without his handsome presence, his quiet generosity to artists, his beguiling smile, and his white-lipped fury for any kind of violence, the Coupole would have been a quite undistinguished place. When one came back to Paris, one came back to Gaston as well, to his eyes lighting up as one came through the door, and to his discreet talk about all that had taken place in this territory that we loved. After we had talked for a little while, Gaston remembered a note that McAlmon had left for me when he took off for America and Mexico over a month before. It was written in pencil, on ruled paper, and if the Germans had not occupied France some years later, I would have this letter still. It did not say very much; only that my typewriter had looked in pretty bad shape to him, and so he had left me his. "It's with the *patronne* of the Café du Métro at the corner of the Boulevard St. Germain and the Rue de l'Odéon," McAlmon had written. "It's a fairly new Remington portable, so it ought to last through several books. I'll pick up a more recent model in New York, so no thanks are due." On that typewriter, my part of the dialogue continued year after year, the words of it banged out in country villages, in mountain chalets, in unfamiliar cities, the testimony of my belief in him written from Italy, Switzerland, Austria, France, America, until he died.

It was in New York or in Mexico that summer of 1929 that Bob met Katherine Anne Porter. He wrote Bill Bird that he was outraged over the pitiful size of the edition of her book the publisher was bringing out. "They expected to sell no more than six hundred copies," he wrote, and he added that both Katherine Anne Porter and Kay Boyle were better writers than Katherine Mansfield, but because no legends had been manufactured for them, their reputations would probably remain scandalously small. Katherine Anne, Bob said, was in his judgement the sounder writer of the two, for she wrote with greater authenticity, while Kay, come hell or high water, had to romanticize every situation. This may very well be true.

Kay Boyle

Afterword

The pronoun "I" is an awkward one to deal with, and I do so with impatience; for I have come to believe that autobiography to fulfill a worthy purpose should be primarily a defense of those who have been unjustly dealt with in one's own time, and whose lives and work ask for vindication. If autobiography is to be more than an exercise in self-absolution, it must be above all the brief presented in exoneration of the inequitably judged, of those denied an unbiased hearing and summarily sentenced to oblivion. To this end, *Being Geniuses Together* was compiled to present as accurate a portrait of Robert McAlmon as memory and his published books, as well as the books of others that he published, could provide. This present book is his, and the bite of the title is his. Thirteen chapters of the twenty-five are McAlmon's. It was my beloved friend, that brilliant editor, Ken McCormick of Doubleday, who, during a visit to me one summer at the MacDowell Colony, suggested alternating McAlmon's chapters with those of my own. Mine were written ten years after McAlmon's death, and after my failure to find an American publisher for his book, which had been brought out in London by Secker and Warburg in 1938. And it may be of interest to note here that, following the publication of the Doubleday edition in 1968, a Milan publisher wanted to bring out a translation in Italian, but of McAlmon's chapters only, deleting mine.

In my account of the years 1920–1930, I attempted to record the times and the settings in my life that served to prepare the way

for a recognition of McAlmon and his work. Yet I did so aware of
the violent truth in the words the young French surrealist, René
Crevel, had written in his book *Babylone*. "Memory is the tattooing
by which the weak, the betrayed, the exiled, believe they have
armed themselves," he wrote. And perhaps out of his despair over
the ravages of psychoanalysis all about him in that time, he cried
out in defiance: "Memory is the ink which corrodes all flesh, all
splendor!" Crevel was among our comrades in arms in Paris in
the late Twenties, but he himself had little time left for memories.
He took his own life at the age of thirty-five.

In an angry and deeply moving lecture that Nelson Algren gave
in higher places of learning in the last decade or two of his life, he
stressed the tragedy of a number of our gifted male writers. "Thinking of Melville, thinking of Poe, thinking of Mark Twain and Vachel
Lindsay, thinking of Jack London and Thomas Wolfe, one begins
to feel there is almost no way of becoming a good writer in America
without being a loser," he wrote. Algren believed it was the ruthless
demands of the American writing scene, the pressure of publishers
for success after success, that ultimately broke the spirit of these
men, and with it their hearts. Look at Scott Fitzgerald's life, look
at what Hemingway turned into, Algren was saying to us; look at
Hart Crane's end. But I believe the collapse is brought about as
well by the terrible hunger of those who do not write to *know* the
writer, to encroach upon his privacy in order to maneuver the secret
from him, to violate the territory of his private life.

I doubt if Algren received much applause from creative writing
students or their teachers in the colleges and universities of our
country when he told them that "the struggle to write with deep
emotion and at the same time live like a millionaire so exhausted
Fitzgerald that he was at last brought to the point where he could
no longer be a good writer and a decent person." Or when he
quoted Fitzgerald's despairing words (from *The Crackup*): "So I
would cease to be a person, kind, just, and generous. I would be
one with the beady-eyed men who say 'business is business,' or 'you
should have thought of that before you got into all this trouble,'
or 'I'm sorry, but that just isn't my department.' " And in the end,
Algren said, "Fitzgerald became so submerged in the waters that
have no shore that he had at last in anguish and bewilderment to
cry out: 'Why was I identified with the very objects of my horror

and compassion?' '' Algren told the devotees of writers' conferences it was in his personal failure that Fitzgerald's art succeeded, "for he recorded life through his own heart and flesh and brain; until the flesh, like Wolfe's, failed under its emotional load."

And what of the story of Mark Twain, Algren asked, who, after one of his public lectures, turned to a life-long friend to say: "I am demeaning myself. I am becoming a mere buffoon. I cannot endure it any longer."

It was the bitter recognition of public demands made on the private self that outraged McAlmon. The mere sight of an American publisher transformed him into a scornful, scathing man. Yet he was the man of whom Ezra Pound wrote: "Others could go on from where he started. He opened up a whole new vein of writing. Tough realism. . . . Nobody's ever given him credit." And out of my belief in him and in his work, I have also written that it was McAlmon "who, in liberating himself from genteel language and genteel thought, spoke for his generation in a voice that echoed, unacknowledged, in the prose of Hemingway and that of others of his time."

Until the Twenties, we Americans as a people had shown little, if any, interest in revolutionizing the written word. The literary critics and the academic authorities of the time, as well as the majority of discerning readers across our land, seemed to be entirely satisfied with the language we had inherited from another country. But to the self-exiled in Paris, the invigorating of that language until it was completely transformed was where the responsibility of the writer must begin. We had been shocked into this realization by the work of Joyce, Gertrude Stein, Eugene Jolas, and by that of a mortally ill and obscure young poet named Lincoln Gillespie. (Earlier in the century, Djuna Barnes had demonstrated her awareness of this responsibility. In 1916, when she was twenty-one, Djuna began writing short stories and dramas which, despite her at times startling innovative treatment of phrase and metaphor, appeared regularly in New York City newspapers. But until these were collected for the first time in 1982,* Djuna was known for her later, less venturesome, more stylized work.)

Because our classical native writers had never so much as at-

* *Smoke and Other Early Stories,* by Djuna Barnes. Sun and Moon Press, College Park, Maryland.

tempted to free themselves of the English tradition, the Paris expatriates dismissed with intolerance almost the entirety of nine-
teenth- and twentieth-century American writing. We were going
to imbue the language of our forebears with a fresh spirit, to release
it from the shapes and forms in which it had solidified on the
printed page. It was a desperate undertaking, the revolt against
everything on the prevailing scene that "denied the urgent need
to use words of one's own fashioning (as our proclamation declared)
and to disregard existing grammatical and syntactical laws." Publishers in America had no interest in our work. Even Joyce and
Gertrude Stein had to rely on the small presses of Paris for their
revolutionary writing. It is not easy for a language to begin again,
for literary revolutions, like social revolutions, are not accomplished
by proclamation or decree. They occur when the spirit of the time
demands a change, whatever the cost of that change may be. The
cost in Paris in the Twenties was tragically high.

The revolt that *Being Geniuses Together* bears witness to was
against all literary pretentiousness, against weary, dreary rhetoric,
against all the outworn literary and academic conventions. "Down
with Henry James! Down with Edith Wharton! Down with the
sterility of 'The Wasteland'! " the self-exiled revolutionaries cried
out. They (and I among them) had Walt Whitman to turn to, but
the most highly respected American authors of the past century
were given no quarter. There was no grandly experimental, furiously disrespectful school of writing in America, and we were going
to create it. We were there, as were the thirteenth-century children
of the crusade that bears their name, who gathered on French soil
in the high hope that they might succeed where their parents had
failed. The children crusaders failed in the thirteenth century as did
most of us in the twentieth century reality of Paris. One contingent
of children was sold into slavery by the captains of the ships on
which they set sail, while others died of hunger and disease. There
was death from hunger and disease among the expatriates in Paris,
some dying of their hunger for recognition; and there were others
who were to sell their talent to the dealers in slavery of the publishing world. The lives of the very few who survived have now
become barely recognizable in the distortion of time and memory,
and constitute the fragile substance of myth.

In an essay on the background of American literature, the Spanish-American philosopher, George Santayana, spoke of our New England poets, historians, and essayists, as well as of our fiction writers, as "harvesters of dead leaves." He wrote:

> Sometimes they made attempts to rejuvenate their minds by broaching native subjects in an effort to prove how much matter for poetry the new world supplied, and they wrote 'Evangeline' and 'Rip Van Winkle'. . . . Their culture was half a pious survival, half an intentional acquirement; it was never for a moment the inevitable flowering of fresh experience.

That "inevitable flowering" was what we were seeking over half a century ago in a foreign country. We celebrated the work of Joyce, and the short stories of Sherwood Anderson—those stories that Anderson himself said were "a revolt against the cold, hard, and stony culture of New England, in which gentility and respectability became the passion of our writers." We hailed the true simplicity of the early work of Hemingway (although with certain misgivings as to what was to come), and we cherished the poetry and prose and the illuminated spirit of William Carlos Williams. We were sustained by the work of Marianne Moore, but rejected that of Emily Dickinson, who seemed to us attenuated by the English poetic tradition. Gertrude Stein (without whom there might not have been as articulate a Sherwood Anderson, and undoubtedly a less disciplined Hemingway) was difficult to celebrate. She had a monopoly on reverence for herself, and she frequently mentioned that no one since Shakespeare had done anything to revolutionize the English language—except Gertrude Stein. She was also given to announcing that the Jews had produced only three original geniuses: Christ, Spinoza, and herself.

Being Geniuses Together ends in 1930. In April 1931, Laurence Vail and I were married in the south of France, with our three daughters, Pegeen, Sharon, and Apple, our flower girls. McAlmon, while travelling from country to country, was still very much in our lives. In 1932, I wrote to him that we had had lunch with H. G. Wells "on Saturday and he and I were talking about modern people—out of a blue sky he said: 'Do you know the work of Robert McAlmon?' He went on to say how much he liked it, what an unusual and vigorous feeling for the language you had, and how good your stories were. He said he was not particularly sympathetic to your perverted types, but that your style interested him very much. I wanted to find out what book he had seen of yours, but Dorothy Dudley being social on his other hand got the conversation on to other things. . . . But the lady next me (sic) said she had just bought *Indefinite Huntress*, and would now rush home and read it after hearing Wells, and me, speaking so enthusiastically. . . . Laurence says why don't you come and spend a week or two with us if you're fed up with Barcelona? Perhaps Ethel Mannin and Jimmy Stern will come in this direction. It would be nice to see a few decent honest people. Wells is very good, by the way . . . I like him—being gay and bright and unpretentious the way great men seem usually to be. The great have a nice quality of easiness which is good for casual meetings. If only people (could) manage to get somewhere—either inside themselves or out—instead of this struggle, this climb, this hysterical reaching such as the Dudleys indulge in. WHAT could Carnevali have found in them except society (ladies) being nice to an outcast? ' "

In that same year, McAlmon had managed to procure from Ethel Moorhead the manuscript of Ernest Walsh's unpublished poems. These, with the poetry of his that had appeared in various magazines (*The New Masses, Poetry, This Quarter* among them), I wanted to see collected in a book to be published in America. Caresse Crosby succeeded in interesting Harcourt, Brace in the prospect of such a collection, and upon my agreeing to submit my next two books to this same publisher, a contract was signed with Ethel Moorhead. Any connection of mine with the publication was not to be mentioned to her.

"Her hate for you has now become an obsession," McAlmon had written me from Malaga in December 1933. Laurence and I and the children were temporarily stranded in a bitterly cold and economically shattered Vienna, where destitute, barefooted families, the mothers with half-starved babies wrapped in their shawls, stood with lowered heads, begging for coins or for bread, or for whatever one could give. "The moment she knows you're involved," McAlmon wrote, "she'll shoot herself or you before she'll sign anything. . . . She'd stop the publication and ruin anybody to get at you. Talks of suing you for libel for your book.* . . .

* *Year Before Last*, Harrison Smith, 1932.

The poetry is Walsh's, not hers, and her obstinacy, jealousy, and madness, have nothing to do with his right to a posthumous publication. . . . [She is] inherently a trained and privileged-class snob, and her little detour into bohemianism or art came from her desire for 'love.' It's cruel that there are so many lonely, sex-starved and thwarted old gals in the world, but it is cruel also that a war-worn, sick poet should be made the butt of any old lady's rancour and jealousy because he, as he was dying, wanted to clutch a younger life. . . . I will swear that Miss Moorhead sent me the Ms. to place, as she did, though she came to Cagnes and gave it to me. . . . The Ms. was as copied from This Q, (Quarter) or from his Ms., and she knows it, and has no right to edit it. . . . There's no use talking fairness because E. M. does not possess that quality intellectually or emotionally. . . . I've spent hours trying to explain that very few give a damn about poetry or art, and that W.'s name means very little—that many a better known poet (Ezra, for example, and many others) don't get published or paid (if they are published). . . . I'll back up things and swear that the Ms. was given to me with full rights to authorize its publication."

Due to McAlmon's tireless efforts, Ernest Walsh's poems were published in 1934. But the sensitive introduction to the volume, written by Archibald MacLeish at my request, was torn up in a rage by Ethel Moorhead because Archie (despite specific counselling) had mentioned in it the young woman Ernest Walsh had loved in the last year of his life. Harcourt, Brace had been pleased with the introduction, but were obliged to do with one Ethel Moorhead wrote. In it, she quoted from Ernest Walsh's article, "What Is Literature?", written some years before Eugene Jolas's heralding of the revolution of the word. "Words are only men at the door," Walsh wrote, "but a man at the door can make a big story about the man who lives inside. . . . A word must stand for something besides its sound in the ear of the listener, or the shape of it to the reader's eye. . . . A word must get its history each time anew from the thing behind it."

In the spring of 1936 I wrote McAlmon from England, telling him that Carnevali was in serious trouble. Ezra Pound and I had managed to get him transferred from Bazzano to the encephalitis wing of a hospital in Rome as a free patient. But the drug they gave him there had made him so violent that he had savagely attacked hospital nurses. The hospital director had then sent a telegram to the medical people in Bazzano, saying Carnevali was going to be committed to the "madhouse." "I've been arguing with Pound for weeks now," I wrote McAlmon in whatever far country he might be, but I was unsure of the address. "I sent a friend of mine who lives in Florence, a young man, the money to go to Rome as Ezra said he had washed his hands of the whole affair, and wouldn't telephone Rome. This boy speaks Italian, adored Carnevali, interviewed the professors and they said Carnevali might be cured if someone would pay thirty lire a day to keep him in a private place where they would continue the cure. . . . Laurence scraped enough money together to get Carnevali back to Bazzano —where he owes 5000 lire! . . . My friend is going to argue with the bistro people and try to get the debt reduced and agree to take him back. Now Ezra is stopping his monthly stipend—we can send so little from time to time that it could not possibly keep him alive so I feel desperately about him. He has written me many letters in his own hand so the new cure did do wonders for him and it is cruel he cannot keep it up. . . . "

In 1941, while Ezra Pound was broadcasting to American troops the propaganda of the Rome-Berlin Axis, Carnevali (the man of whom William Carlos Williams had written, "Jesus, Jesus, save Carnevali for me. . . . He is slipping into the afternoon at twenty-one. . . . I believe he will go crazy or quit rather than write in a small way. . . . ") died in Bazzano of what is known as "the silent death." Long after the war was over, we learned that, abandoned and alone, he had choked on a piece of bread caught in his windpipe.

But there are a few more things to add to this portrait of McAlmon. There is the fact that he had the satisfaction, grim though it was in part, of seeing at least three of his books brought out by publishing houses other than his own. And there is the fact that McAlmon's mother, until her death in 1943, his schoolteacher sisters (three remarkable women), and his brothers (all of them older than he), stood by him through every decade of his life. It was the active devotion of his family that saved him from internment in German-Occupied Paris in the spring of 1940, and who gave him financial support and rare understanding in the final years of his return.

In June 1941, McAlmon wrote to Hilaire Hiler from a hotel in

El Paso, saying that his brothers had bought a cotton ranch near Isleta.

. . . I'll build an adobe there, and settle in and try raising things, [he wrote] letting the Mexican leasee handle the cotton. . . . I'll try vegetables, turkeys, chickens, pigs. . . . That is, I hope I can stick it. . . . I still take the gas on my lung weekly, left lung completely collapsed, and to be kept so until I'm cured.

And he continued:

Don't myself take any stock—from my feelings—that TB peps one up, unless it is in a much longer run and at a higher temp. of fever hallucinations than I have yet endured. . . . People like to think that opium, or mysticism, or religion, some fever or madness, does the work of rational and concentrated work. . . . Joyce got drunk on his words more than he ever did on his alcohol, and a happier or more satisfactory drunkeness [sic], with some ecstacy [sic] in it.

He had seen Brancusi before leaving Paris, he wrote, and Brancusi had urged him to stay on, but he had no way of getting money either from England or America. But the plan to "settle in and try raising things" on the cotton ranch did not become a reality, and his brothers gave him a job as salesman in the Phoenix, Arizona, branch of their Southwestern Surgical Supply Company. In one of his later letters to me, typed on the stationery of that company, he wrote:

Went to Mexico City in September and there was Bricktop in all her glory, her own *bôite de nuit*, and tremendously popular, with a magnificent apartment in the swankiest part of the city; balcony, private bar, four bedrooms, beautiful outlook, furniture, silverware and dishes, and she's become devoutly Catholic without letting it cramp her style as regards drink. Reading the confessions, lives or letters, of the various saints. So far I have sent her *St. John of the Cross*, *Thérèse*, *Catherine of Sienna*, etc. Nightly I do Juarez for meals and tequilla, but Jesus, Kay, how nice it would be to have a few drinks and a pub crawl with you there. Doesn't perturb me, but you damn well know this ain't no center of art and cultuah.

In November 1951, I wrote to McAlmon from Germany that Brancusi was still alive when I was last in Paris, and so was Kiki, singing in various little nightclubs, and remembering nothing from one night to the next. It must have been that I did not want to tell him that Kiki was also selling safety pins and matches from table to table on the café terraces of Montparnasse.

Every time we had a drink together, [I wrote] she asked me about Mary (Reynolds), and I told her in detail every time what happened. . . . Finally, one evening, I took off a pair of white earrings which Mary had left me (among other little ornaments she knew I loved) and I put them on Kiki and told her I knew Mary would like her to have them. Then tears came into her eyes, and she looked so bewildered, and had to sing a couple of dirty songs to get back in the groove again.

But the saddest letter of all is the one McAlmon wrote to his agent in New York, Madeleine Boyd. It is dated June 16, 1952, and it goes in part:

I am sending you a collection of short stories and a long poem, to show Cap Pierce, or someone who also knows about my being now at re-work on an entirely new write-up of the material, and that of years before and after. . . . The short story collection are just a lot of short stories I have done in the past. . . . I call your attention to and want you to call the publisher's attention to *Miss Knight*. . . . James Joyce, Ezra, and several others—even Hemingway—thought it a great story. . . . With the others I think there is a volume of short stories that will stack up beside any collection published in many a year.

Four years later, with no recognition given this collection, or any other of his writings, Robert McAlmon (like Emanuel Carnevali, Mary Reynolds, Clotilde Vail, Robert Desnos, Jane Heap, Jules Pascin, Eugene Jolas, Lola Ridge, Harry Crosby, Archie Craig, Alexander Berkman, James Joyce, Raymond Radiguet, René

Crevel—and how many others whose lives had touched his) was dead.

"Why," Robert Knoll asks in the edition of McAlmon's stories he edited in 1962*, "was McAlmon incapable of making full use of his gifts in his own work?" It is perhaps William Carlos Williams who has best answered that question. "He cared for nothing so much as excellence in his craft as a writer," Williams wrote, "but he could not be a liar to obtain it. And he had an eye and a fierce tongue when he saw others among the writers about him—liars in one form or another—who were lying to make their reputations. Many of them were doing just that. Not he. But he suffered for it in the world's estimation." And to that Knoll adds: "Men of fierce integrity being rare, he does not deserve oblivion."

K. B.

1984

---

* *McAlmon and the Lost Generation, A Self-Portrait*, edited and with commentary by Robert E. Knoll, University of Nebraska Press, Lincoln.

Index

Index

348 INDEX

Bentley (English maid), 258, 261,
262
Berkman, Alexander, 331
Berlin, McAlmon in, 95–98
Better-Than-Thou, M. and Mme.,
147, 150, 155
Biddle, George, 34
Bien-Talonés, M. and Mme., 147–
148, 150, 155
Bird, Sally, 34, 89, 222, 270, 276;
at bullfights, 243, 246–47
Bird, William (Bill), 34, 89, 90, 91,
116, 161, 164, 253, 260, 271; and
bullfights, 244–47; and Contact
Editions, 304; and Desnos, 275;
and discussion group, 221; on
Hemingway-McAlmon quarrel,
183n; and Joyce, 376–77; Kay
Boyle and, 312–13, 332; on Mc-
Almon, 182, 312–13, 332; and
Three Mountain Press, 182;
Trianon party, 306
"Bird in Space", 19
Black-of-Ear-and-Eye, Farmer, 147,
148
Black Sun Press, 328–29
Blake, William, 40, 172, 226, 269
Bodenheim, Maxwell, 124
Boeuf sur le Toit, 93, 113, 115, 197,
284
Bogoraz (Russian anthropologist),
76
Boyle, Jesse Peyton (grandfather),
14, 18, 19, 21, 22
Boyle, Howard Peterson (father),
19, 22
Boyle, Katherine Evans (mother),
18, 40, 44, 47, 67, 85, 143–46, 192,
211–12; and daughter's illness,
321, 322; influence on daughter,
18–22
Boyle, Kay: (1922–23), 11–24, 39–
48, 63–70, 83–88, 103–9; (1923–
1924), 121–29, 139, 153–54;

(1926–28), 171–93; (1927–28),
209–19; (1928), 233–42, 255–70,
273–75; (1928–30), 283–301, 308,
311–32; and daughter, family
(see specific individuals); and
Dayang Muda of Sarawak (see
under Dayang Muda); describes
McAlmon, 22–27, 283–92; and
Duncan colony, 293–94, 297,
311–25; and Ernest Walsh, 173–
193, 209, 211, 214, 215, 217, 218,
251; and Hiler party, 275; and
husband Richard Brault (see
Brault, Richard); illness, 155,
321–22; and Laurance Vail, 322,
325–26, 330; and London, 153;
and McAlmon, 11, 22–24, 45,
86–88, 103–5, 107–9, 210ff.,
214, 242, 260, 270, 273–75,
283–301 passim, 308–32 passim;
McAlmon on, 254, 274; and
Paris (see under Paris); and
specific individuals (see by name);
works: "Book of Cincinnati",
123; First Lover and Other Stories,
290n; Gentlemen, I Address You
Privately, 149n, 150, 215; "Harbor
Song", 123; "I Can't Get Drunk",
290; Imponderables, 152; Monday
Night, 291n; My Next Bride, 294n;
Plagued by the Nightingale, 139n,
179, 215; "Vacation Time",
318–20; Wedding Day and Other
Stories, 318n; Year Before Last,
175n
Brancusi, Constantin, 8, 19, 21, 111,
112, 113, 116, 175, 225; at Hiler
party, 275; Kay Boyle and, 297;
of peon stock, 203; Satie and,
198; in Switzerland, 314
Braque, Georges, 27
Brasserie Lutetia, 32
Brault (Maman), 41–47 passim, 64,
65, 71